Passive Solar Commercial and Institutional Buildings

A Sourcebook of Examples and Design Insights

INTERNATIONAL ENERGY AGENCY, Paris, France

Principal Editor

S. R. Hastings
ETH Zürich
Swiss Federal Office of Energy

Participating countries of the
IEA Solar Heating & Cooling Task XI

Austria	Germany	Sweden
Belgium	Italy	Switzerland
Denmark	Norway	United Kingdom
EEC	Spain	United States
Finland		

JOHN WILEY & SONS
Chichester · New York · Brisbane · Toronto · Singapore

Other Wiley Editorial Offices

John Wiley & Sons, Inc., 605 Third Avenue,
New York, NY 10158-0012, USA

Jacaranda Wiley Ltd, 33 Park Road, Milton,
Queensland 4064, Australia

John Wiley & Sons (Canada) Ltd, 22 Worcester Road,
Rexdale, Ontario M9W 1L1, Canada

John Wiley & Sons (SEA) Pte Ltd, 37 Jalan Pemimpin #05-04,
Block B, Union Industrial Building, Singapore 2057

Library of Congress Cataloging-in-Publication Data

Passive solar commercial and institutional buildings : a sourcebook of
  examples and design insights / International Energy Agency, Paris,
France ; edited by S.R. Hastings.
        p.   cm.
   "International Energy Agency : Solar Heating & Cooling Programme,
IEA solar task XI."
   Includes bibliographical references and index.
   ISBN 0 471 93943 9
   1. Solar buildings.   2. Commercial buildings—Heating and
ventilation.   3. Solar energy—Passive systems.   4. Atriums.
I. Hastings, S. Robert.   II.   International Energy Agency.   Solar
Heating and Cooling Programme.
   TH7413.P367   1994
   725'.20472—dc20   93–5246
                                                                                            CIP

British Library Cataloguing in Publication Data

A catalogue record for this book is available from the British Library

Cover illustrations (Background) The Sun. (Top) Technical University – ELA, Norway.
(Middle) South Staffordshire Water Co. building, UK. (Bottom) The Jungfrau
Restaurant, Switzerland

ISBN 0 471 93943 9

Typeset by Lasertext Ltd, Stretford, Manchester
Printed and bound in Great Britain by Bookcraft (Bath) Ltd

Contents

Preface

The effective use of solar energy can drastically reduce the heating, cooling and lighting energy required to condition buildings. This sourcebook encourages the design of buildings which are adapted to and profit from the climate. The buildings presented as examples are designed for the future when non-renewable energy sources are scarce and expensive and solar energy is valued for its environmental benevolence, dependability, and long-term economy. While on any given day the amount of sun is an uncertainty, the finiteness of our fossil fuel supplies is a certainty.

The decision to build a solar-designed commercial building need not be based on the relative cost of conventional energy alone. A building which is adaptive to its climate may still be habitable if the mechanical services are interrupted, whereas a conventional structure such as a sealed glass office tower, fully dependent on air conditioning and electric lighting, may have to be vacated if the mechanical and electrical services are interrupted. Under such circumstances the presumed less expensive conventional building becomes very expensive indeed.

There is a growing body of experience in applying solar concepts to commercial buildings. This sourcebook examines recent work on solar building design and analysis in twelve countries to avoid re-inventing concepts and repeating mistakes.

Many but not all passive solar concepts which have proved effective in residences can also be applied to commercial buildings. Other concepts seldom applied in residential design, such as window air collectors, are particularly suited for commercial buildings. Daylighting design or atria can not only save energy but also lead to a light, airy architecture of great beauty.

We hope this document will encourage building clients to demand this kind of architecture, will offer architects a better conceptual understanding of solar design concepts, and will provide engineers and energy consultants with insights from both our positive and negative experiences.

S. R. Hastings

Coordination and Editing

The sourcebook represents the work of over thirty experts from twelve countries plus the European Economic Community. Individual contributors are identified in the respective parts of this document.

This book is dedicated to Lars Engstrom (Sweden) and Alan Hildon (United Kingdom) who always brought both fresh ideas as well as humor to our meetings.

Project Leader

S. R. Hastings
ETH Zürich
Swiss Federal Office of Energy

Group Leaders

Solar Usability:
P. Case
EN-SOLAR, Switzerland

Heating:
P. Kristensen
Esbensen Engineers, Denmark

Daylighting:
N. Hopkirk
EMPA, Switzerland

Cooling:
F. Butera
University of Palermo, Italy

André De Herde
Catholic University, Belgium

Atria:
A. G. Hestnes
Norwegian Institute of Technology

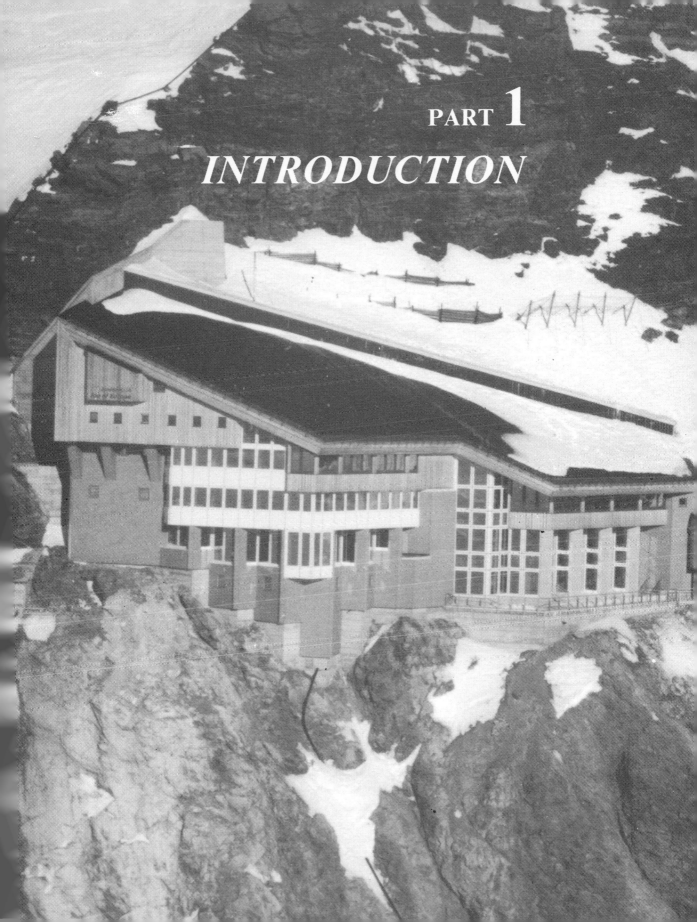

PART 1
INTRODUCTION

CONTRIBUTOR

Part 1
S. R. Hastings
Solar Architecture
ETH-Hönggerberg
CH-8093 Zürich
Switzerland

1 Background

This book presents the results of research on a diversity of passive solar buildings, both commercial and institutional. The work was carried out by solar experts from twelve countries during the years 1986 to 1991. Of forty-five building case studies, twenty-two were monitored and analyzed in detail as part of Task XI of the International Energy Agency (IEA) Solar Heating and Cooling Program. The buildings range from a large university complex with multiple atria in Norway to a sports hall employing a mass wall in Spain.

Insights gained from these projects have been expanded by conducting parametric studies using computer models, some of which were developed specifically for this IEA research. For example, a program was written to link the results of detailed daylighting models with detailed energy analysis models. Daylighting strategies are thereby assessed for their effectiveness in reducing electricity consumption for lighting as well as for heating and cooling.

2 Parts of the Book

2.1 SOLAR USABILITY

These chapters explore the often expressed and frequently exaggerated notion that heat gains from lighting, computers and other office equipment make solar gains superfluous in commercial buildings. Selective measurements in Switzerland and Austria suggest that lights and equipment are actually switched on during much less time than is assumed. Many new models of office equipment cut back to extremely low power levels during idle periods. Furthermore, electric consumption is drastically reduced when lighting is regulated by the availability of daylight. More efficient use of electricity gives renewed importance to using solar energy in the form of daylight, as well as a heat source for peripheral spaces.

2.2 SOLAR HEATING

The wide range of solar heating strategies for diverse building types is illustrated in Part 3, Solar Heating. Each chapter offers information on a specific passive solar heating strategy, including data from energy systems monitored in buildings. These systems have been proved to be effective even under extreme climate conditions. In one example, a restaurant on an exposed Swiss mountain peak is heated during the day entirely by internal and direct solar gains. In another example, an absorber wall which uses a heat pump is described as a passive or hybrid design.

2.3 DAYLIGHTING

The use of solar energy in the form of daylight is of obvious importance for commercial buildings which are occupied primarily during the day. These chapters of the book describe standard and advanced daylighting strategies with several examples. Results are given from parametric studies conducted by linking a daylighting model with an energy analysis computer simulation. The effectiveness of daylighting strategies is evaluated by measuring energy consumed for heating, cooling and lighting.

2.4 COOLING

Solar radiation control, heat avoidance, internal gains reduction, and natural cooling strategies are described in the part on cooling. The 1992 International Exposition facilities in Seville, Spain, are the main examples in these chapters. The extreme temperatures of Seville summers pose a major design challenge leading to several innovative cooling solutions. The organizers of the Exposition emphasized that the pavilions and outdoor spaces should be passively cooled as much as possible. Selected concepts were evaluated with computer simulations after a pilor pavilion and outdoor space were built and monitored. A building studied in Italy provides a further example of a night cooling technique.

2.5 ATRIA

Several chapters throughout the sourcebook describe objectives for providing heat, light and cooling. Atria can be a means to achieve all these objectives. Atria are exampled in Part 6, using case studies from the countries participating in Task XI. Extensive data are given from detailed monitoring of atria in Norway, Finland, Germany and Switzerland. The potential amenity and energy savings of atria are confirmed with these data.

3 Chapters

3.1 CHAPTER STRUCTURE

An introduction to each chapter presents basic concepts or principles, followed by a review of the advantages and disadvantages of the system. Techniques are then illustrated using building projects [1/1]. Detailed results and design insights are based largely on either monitoring results from buildings and systems [1/2] or from sensitivity studies conducted with computer models. The analysis section describes these tools and their appropriateness or capabilities.

The conclusions provide advice based on the examples, monitoring and simulation results. Finally, publications are listed in two ways: a short list of references at the end of chapters indicates where material is published in detail, and abstracts of select documents are included after each part of the sourcebook for the reader seeking additional information.

3.2 CONVENTIONS/UNITS OF MEASUREMENT

$$*\text{degree day} = \Sigma_{i=1}^{n} (20°C - T_{EXT})$$

T_{EXT} = daily average ambient temperature
dd   = degree day (Celsius)
n = period reported, e.g. 1 October to 30 April

The choice of measurement unit reflects the mix of engineers, architects and physicists as well as the geographical mix of countries represented in Solar Task XI. For example, heating degree days used throughout this report are simply 20° Celsius (C) minus the average daily ambient temperature for all days colder than 20°C.* This differs from the convention of middle European countries which use 20/12: the same base of 20°C is used, but only days with an average temperature of 12°C or colder are summed. The American convention differs in its use of a 54° Fahrenheit base. Degree days are reported here merely to provide the reader with a sense of the different climates.

Solar radiation values for both global horizontal surfaces and vertical south surfaces are reported. The latter values indicate the available solar energy in winter, particularly for northern latitudes.

4 Integration of Strategies

Integrating solar strategies into a building is the job of the designer. Clearly some strategies work more effectively in combination while others may conflict; the evaluation of solar strategies should consider all energy uses.

The importance of a comprehensive approach to energy utilization is illustrated by a parametric study conducted for the design of a new office building in Copenhagen [1/3], where the influence of the glazing area relative to the total facade area on primary energy consumption was modelled. Any increase in glass area facing east or west resulted in increased heating and cooling demands. The obvious conclusion based on this condition alone would be to minimize the glass area. Conversely, increasing the glass area to 45% of the facade area strongly decreases the lighting electricity demand.

When primary energy demand for heating, cooling and lighting are considered together, then increasing the glass area to 40% of the facade area results in increased total energy savings (Fig. 1.1). The savings in electricity from daylighting has a dominant influence because of the assumption that thermal energy is produced with an efficiency of 67% versus an efficiency of 27% for energy in the form of electricity.

Further examples of system interactions are presented in Solar Usability, Daylighting and Atria. It is, of course, impossible to report all possible interactions, which is why each design must be analyzed individually. The material here merely provides points of reference.

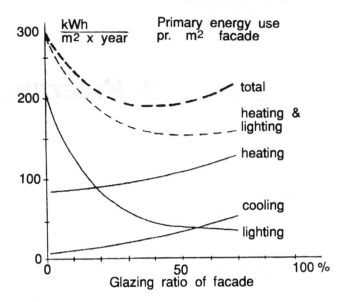

Fig. 1.1   Primary energy use per m² double glazed windows facing east or west in Copenhagen

5 References

1/1 Hildon, A. and Seager, A. (eds.), *Passive and Hybrid Solar Commercial Buildings: Basic Case Studies*, Energy Technology Support Unit, Harwell Laboratory, Oxfordshire OX11 0RA, UK, 1989.

1/2 Seager, A. (ed.), *Passive and Hybrid Solar Commercial Buildings: Proceedings of the Seminar Advanced Case Studies*, Energy Technology Support Unit, Harwell Laboratory, Oxfordshire OX11 0RA, UK, 1991.

1/3 Kristensen, P. E. and Esbensen, T., Passive solar energy and natural daylight in office buildings, *Proceedings of the ISES* 1991 *Solar World Congress*, ASES, 2400 Central Avenue, Boulder, CO 90301, USA, 1991.

SOLAR USABILITY

CONTRIBUTORS

Part 2   Editor
Peter Case
EN-SOLAR
Burgdorfstrasse 44
Postfach
CH3515 Oberdiessbach b. Bern
Switzerland

Chapters 7 and 9
Manfred Bruck
Kanzlei Dr Bruck
Garnisongasse 7
A-1090 Vienna
Austria

Chapters 7 and 8
Hanspeter Eicher
Martin Stalder
Dr Eicher & Partners AG
Oristalstrasse 85
CH-4410 Liestal
Switzerland

Chapter 7
Lars Engström
EHUB KTH
Royal Institute of Technology
S-1044 Stockholm
Sweden

Chapter 7
Anne Greta Hestnes
Norwegian Institute of Technology–Architecture
N-7034 Trondheim NTH
Norway

6 Introduction

The usefulness of passive solar energy clearly depends on the extent and timing of internal gains from lighting, electrical equipment, and people. Unfortunately, there is no way to avoid these internal heat sources, except by selecting equipment which uses little electricity or turning it off when not needed. Solar gains, on the other hand, may readily be controlled by appropriately sizing and orienting windows, and using shading devices. Thus from a design point of view, internal gains must be regarded as a primary heat source.

Design values for internal gains are usually derived from the total rated power of installed equipment integrated over time and reduced by a factor to reflect likely usage patterns. These data are used for dimensioning cooling equipment and hence, to be conservative, maximal likely internal gains are reported. This overestimation leads to an underestimation of the passive solar contribution in winter. To obtain a realistic assessment of the solar contribution to meet heating demands and to quantify the extent and time distribution of internal gains, three steps were taken.

1. The average power output of a sample of office equipment was monitored.
2. A small sample of commercial buildings was monitored, and the actual electric consumption of office equipment and lighting measured.
3. These results were entered into a computer model and detailed simulations carried out to determine the relative contributions of solar and internal sources to heating demand.

Recommended internal gains which can be assumed for office equipment and measured values for entire offices and buildings are listed in Chapter 7. Simulation results are summarized in Chapters 8 and 9, first assuming ideal heating systems and then based on actual heating systems.

The simulation results demonstrate that passive solar use in non-residential buildings is significantly more important than previously assumed. Standard design values overestimate the magnitude of the internal gains by a factor of up to four and thus underestimate the magnitude and cost-effectiveness of the passive solar contribution. This may lead to inappropriate design of buildings and to higher investment and operating costs for heating and cooling equipment.

There may in fact be much less need for mechanical cooling in summer time than is assumed. Simulation studies show that a medium-weight building shell in combination with an air heating system makes best use of solar and internal gains.

7 Internal Gains

The useful heat contribution of electrical equipment, lighting and persons, commonly referred to as usable internal gains, was determined using two approaches.

1. Electricity consumed by typical office appliances and lighting was measured over a period of time. Total consumption for an office building was obtained by summing these measurements for all equipment.
2. Total electricity consumption of an office building was measured directly over a period of time.

The estimated heat contribution of persons was added to the above to

Table 7.1 Recommended rate of heat gain from selected office equipment

Appliance	Maximum input	Ready state input	Typical energy demands	Recommended rates
	(W)	(W)	(W h)	(W)
Personal computer AT with or without coprocessor 40–200 MB hard disk Year 1990	80–100	80–100	—	80–100
13–14 in Color monitor Multisync Year 1990	50–60	50–60	—	50–60
Laser printer 4–8 pages/min Years 1988/90	500–600	30–40	0.7–1 per copy	70–90
Telefax Years 1988/90	60–80	10–20	—	30
Photocopier (small) 15–20 copies/min Years 1989/90	600	100–200	—	250–350
Photocopier (large) 60–70 copies/min Years 1989/90	1600–1800	150–170	0.5 per copy	270–300
Tape drives	80–300	80–300	—	80–300
Paper shredder (small)	300	50	—	70
Coffee maker (10 cups)	900–1000	70–80 (plate warming)	70–90 per cup	180
Automatic telephone answering machine	5	5	—	5

obtain total usable internal gains.

The first method of determining usable internal gains was used for an office building in Austria [2/2]. Table 7.1 gives measured values for maximum and average continuous (steady-state) energy consumption for a range of office equipment in the office building and recommends appropriate design values for internal gains.

As expected, the recommended rates for internal gains of a given appliance are below the maximum by as much as a factor of seven (for a laser printer).

Total usable internal gains of an office may be estimated by multiplying the number of appliances by the rate recommended and

Table 7.2 Measured coincidence factors in Swiss buildings

Building	Type	Inst. power (W/m²)	Office equipment (Winter/ summer)	Lighting (Winter/ summer)	Persons (Winter/ summer)	Total (Winter/ summer)
Civic	Office	84	0.14/0.12	0.19/0.39	1/0.07	0.21/0.24
Thali	Office	51	0.59/0.92	0.07/0.07	1/1	0.29/0.37
Nixdorf	Office	82	0.14/0.16	0.86/0.78	0.76/0.6	0.25/0.25
Amidro	Warehouse	12	—	0.43/0.88	1/1	0.57/0.87
Ikea	Warehouse	4	—	0.83/0.86	1/1	0.84/0.86
Grammar school	School	60	0/0	0.31/0.06	0.88/0.78	0.62/0.48

by the total number of hours in use and finally adding the heat contribution of persons.

The second method of determining usable internal gains was adopted for a few buildings in Switzerland [2/3], where electricity consumption of all equipment and lighting was measured. The coincidence factor, defined as peak measured power of equipment and persons divided by total rated power including the estimated heat contribution of persons, is shown in Table 7.2.

In Table 7.2, the first three buildings with power ratings between about 50 and 80 W/m² have coincidence factors in winter between about 0.2 and 0.3. The other building in the same power category, the grammar school, has a coincidence factor of 0.6. This much higher value results from the large heating contribution made by persons to heating demand, and the fact that the actual occupancy approximates the predicted occupancy. Buildings with low installed power between about 5 and 10 W/m² have coincidence factors from about 0.60 to 0.85. The coincidence factors for the first three buildings fall below the design value of 0.70 according to the Swiss Institute of Engineers and Architects [2/6]. Although the above sample of buildings is not statistically relevant, this result indicates that internal gains have previously been overestimated. If reliable values for internal gains are to be provided, statistical analysis for different building categories is required.

A summary of design and measured data for internal gains in offices and other buildings in three European countries is given in Table 7.3. For Sweden, the values were deduced on the basis of purchased energy, whereas for Switzerland, they were measured directly. For Norway, total internal gains according to Standard NS-3031 are shown. The Norwegian values for usable internal gains lie well below those of Sweden and Switzerland for comparable buildings, with the exception of hospitals. In the Standard, somwhat confusingly, the term usable describes the total internal gains for the commercial buildings listed in Table 7.3 [2/5].

Table 7.3 Internal gains in three European countries

Building type	(h/d)	(d/w)	Ti (°C)	Rated power (W/m²)	Lighting (W/m²)	Lighting (kWh/m²a)	Lighting + equipment (W/m²K)	Lighting + equipment (W h/m²a)	Lighting + equipment + persons (W/m²K)	Lighting + equipment + persons (W h/m²a)
SWEDEN (1)										
Banks, insurance							197			
Offices							109			
Sales							178			
Hospitals							89			
Schools							82			
Sports, baths							213			
hotels, restaurants							160			
SWITZERLAND (2)										
Office				84	11	98	18	250	23	310
Office				51	2	46	14	281	19	351
Office				82	8	134	19	509	22	545
Warehouse				12	7	87	7	87	10	139
Warehouse				4	4	78	4	78	4	79
School				60	6	58	6	58	37	349
NORWAY (3)										
Library	10	6	20		12	36	12	37	16	37
Shopping center										
w/ food	9	6	20		15	42	19	53	29	81
w/o food	9	6	20		15	42	16	45	26	72
Daycare center	9	5	20		12	28	12	29	18	43
Hotel	24	7	20		8	70	9	79	11	96
Sport center	14	7	18		13	57	13	58	23	103
Office	9	5	20		12	25	16	33	20	42
Museum	8	7	20		10	29	10	30	14	42
School	10	5	20		13	26	15	30	27	56
Hospital	24	7	22		8	70	10	88	13	114
Machine shop	9	5	10 – 20		8	17	11	23	13	26

1. [2/4].
2. Measured total gains for one representative room per building [2/3].
3. According to Norwegian Standard NS 3031 for total internal gains [2/5].

When comparing the values of measured internal gains for lighting and equipment in Sweden and Switzerland, there are large difference both between one country and another, and among different buildings within a particular country. Thus for offices, Swiss values exceed those for Sweden by factors of between 2.5 and 4.5. For schools, the Swedish value exceeds the Swiss value by a factor of 1.4. The Swiss values differ among themselves by a factor of up to two.

The Swiss values for internal gains from equipment, lighting and persons range from 80 kW h/m² a in a warehouse to 550 kWh/m² a in an office. Interestingly, the value for the school ($350 \, \mathrm{kWh/m^2 \, a}$) is precisely the same as that for one of the offices. There is no obvious correlation between rated power and total power (see column for lighting, equipment and persons). Rated power values exceed those for total power by a factor up to four. Swiss measurements of time-dependent internal gains [2/3] are given in Chapter 8.

8 Simulation Studies with an Ideal Heating System

Simulations were made for a small sample of non-residential Swiss buildings [2/3] to estimate the energy saving potential of passive solar gains and the need for air conditioning in summer. The main objective was to calculate the proportions of the total heating requirement covered by internal and solar gains in winter and to determine how these affect room temperature in summer. Another objective was to compare the passive solar contribution calculated on the basis of actual (measured) internal gains with the contribution which would occur

A self-contained optimized heating, ventilation and cooling plant. (Source: NASA, Washington DC, USA)

assuming standard design values. An ideal heating system was assumed, one that reacts instantaneously to room temperature changes.

A field study was conducted for six buildings. Of these, two office buildings, the school building and one of the warehouses were selected for detailed simulations. Single rooms were selected in each of the buildings to represent the whole building. The simulations were performed using climate data from Oslo, Rome, and Zürich to investigate the influence of climate on solar usability. See Fig. 8.1.

8.1 SIMULATION STRATEGY

Simulations were carried out using the program SUNCODE.

To calculate the relative contributions of auxiliary heating energy, internal gains, and solar gains, it was assumed that internal gains are a primary source of heat. Should these not be sufficient to cover heating demand, the deficit is first filled by available solar gains. Any remaining demand is supplied by the heating system.

To calculate the heating energy consumption, separate simulations were made for the following three configurations: heating system without internal and solar gains, heating system with internal gains, and heating system with internal and solar gains. The energy from the heating system was obtained by subtracting the used internal and solar gains from the total heat load.

The simulations are based on three different categories of internal gains: measured gains, standard gains, and minimum gains, as follows:

- *Measured gains* were obtained from average hourly electricity consumption for lighting, office, and computer equipment. The heat emitted by the occupants was not measured and was estimated. Variations of internal gains for typical days in summer and winter were obtained by averaging corresponding hourly values for workdays over the measurement period.
- *Standard gains* were calculated in accordance with Swiss SIA DOKU 70 [2/6] which is based on the total power installed multiplied by a coincidence factor of 0.7.
- *Minimum gains* were estimated on the assumption that future power consumption for computers and terminals can be reduced to the level used by current laptop computers. It was assumed that equipment is automatically turned off when not in use. The minimum value of installed power for lighting is taken to be $10\,\text{W/m}^2$, a value that may still be too high for the latest energy-saving lighting appliances.

In addition, the following assumptions were made.

- Minimum room temperatures are 20°C during working hours and 16°C otherwise. For the warehouse, the corresponding figures are

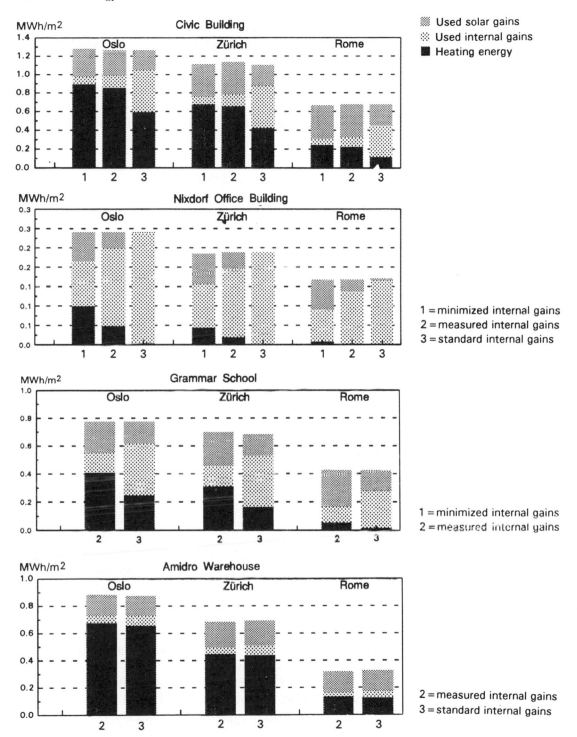

Fig. 8.1 Yearly energy demand for four Swiss buildings at three locations

17°C when occupied and 12°C when unoccupied.

- During the heating period, excess heat is vented if room temperatures exceed 24°C.
- Surplus heat in summer is vented by opening windows if the room temperatures exceed ambient temperature, but no cooling is applied.
- No window shading in winter, window transmission reduced to a constant 20% in summer.

All buildings were assumed to have their main window front facing south, although not all buildings actually do. Rooms adjoining the test room were thermally decoupled to ensure that no external heat transfer took place. Shading from protruding roofs and adjacent buildings was assumed negligible.

This program uses a combined coefficient for radiation and convection and thus the calculated air-to-wall heat transfer coefficient is approximated. Also, because no distinction is made between radiative and convective parts of internal gains, some inaccuracies in room temperature are expected. Since the program does not enable the shading devices to be operated in accordance with solar radiation levels, a constant transmission factor of 20% was assumed for daytime in summer. This procedure reduces calculated solar gains at the beginning and end of the heating season. In winter, no shading was applied.

8.2 BUILDING AND ROOM CHARACTERISTICS

The physical characteristics of the four buildings simulated are summarized in Table 7.3. The Nixdorf office building located near Zürich was selected for the presentation of detailed simulation results. This is a high-tech building with extensive office equipment and a building shell designed according to the latest Swiss building codes (Fig. 8.2).

8.3 RESULTS

Measured internal gains used in the simulation of the Nixdorf building are shown in Fig. 8.3. Also shown are the standard and minimum internal gains calculated as described above.

Simulation results for all four buildings under climatic conditions in Oslo, Zürich and Rome are summarized in Fig. 8.1.

The results for the Nixdorf building show that the *absolute* value of the solar contribution depends very little on climate. However, the *percentage* value of the solar contribution relative to the total heat load increases markedly from colder (Oslo) to warmer (Rome) climates, as

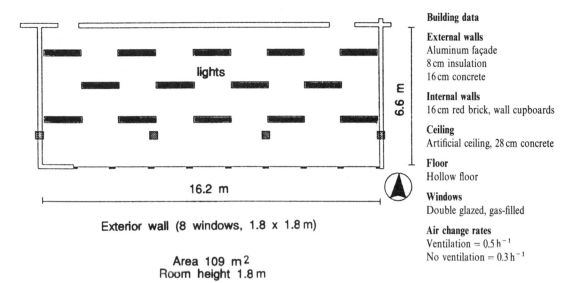

Exterior wall (8 windows, 1.8 x 1.8 m)

Area 109 m²
Room height 1.8 m

Fig. 8.2 Data describing the Nixdorf office building

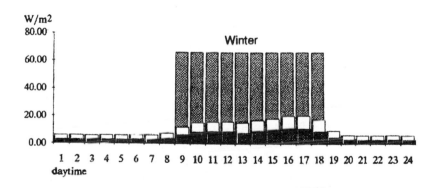

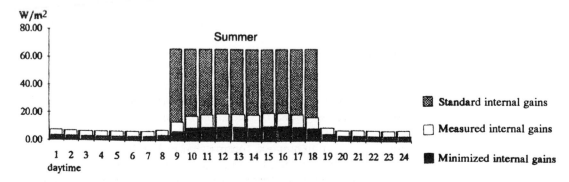

Fig. 8.3 Internal gains for the Nixdorf office building

expected. This result is essentially the same for the other buildings. The proportions of heating energy, internal and solar gains depend strongly on the assumption made for internal gains (minimum, measured and standard). Note that particularly in the case of modern, well-insulated buildings (such as the Nixdorf office), the contribution of internal gains to heating demand is greatly overestimated with standard internal gains.

In Fig. 8.4 monthly values of energy demand for the Nixdorf building in Oslo, Zürich and Rome are shown for the three categories of internal gains and unused solar gains.

The parts of Fig. 8.4 show that internal gains can provide a large fraction of the heating demand, especially when standard gains are assumed. For measured internal gains, however, solar gains cover between 6 and 32% of this demand (depending on location and time of year). For minimum internal gains, the corresponding figures are 6 and 55%.

Heating load coverages by internal gains are similar in Oslo and Rome. However, in Rome, the insolation is greater and the climate is milder so a smaller percentage of total solar gains are usable.

Table 8.1 compares the usable solar gains to the total available solar gains, given the assumptions of measured or minimized internal gains.

Two kinds of values are reported. Column B shows the maximum usable solar energy and the month in which it occurs. In Oslo, the maximum occurs in March while in Rome the maximum occurs in January. Column C reports this maximum value as a percentage of total available solar gains. Column D gives the month in which the greatest percentage of usable to solar gains occurs and the corresponding percentages. In all cases, this occurs in December or January but the highest percentages occur in Oslo.

Figure 8.5 illustrates the extent to which internal gains influence the need for air conditioning. The figure shows the frequency distribution of the number of hours the room is above a specified temperature (T_r) for the three categories of internal gains for the period of 1 June through 31 August. In Zürich, taking the curve for standard internal gains into consideration, room temperatures above 28°C occur during approximately 280 working hours, or six working weeks. This would be sufficient to justify installing a cooling plant. The maximum room temperature is 35°C.

For measured internal gains, however, the room temperature has a maximum of 30°C and thus lies 5°C lower than the maximum for standard internal gains. If the transmission factor of 20% for the windows with external blinds lowered (assumed in the simulations) could be achieved in practice, then mechanical cooling would no longer be required.

This illustrates that unrealistic assumptions about internal gains can lead to false conclusions about room temperature and to excessive or even totally unnecessary investment in mechanical cooling.

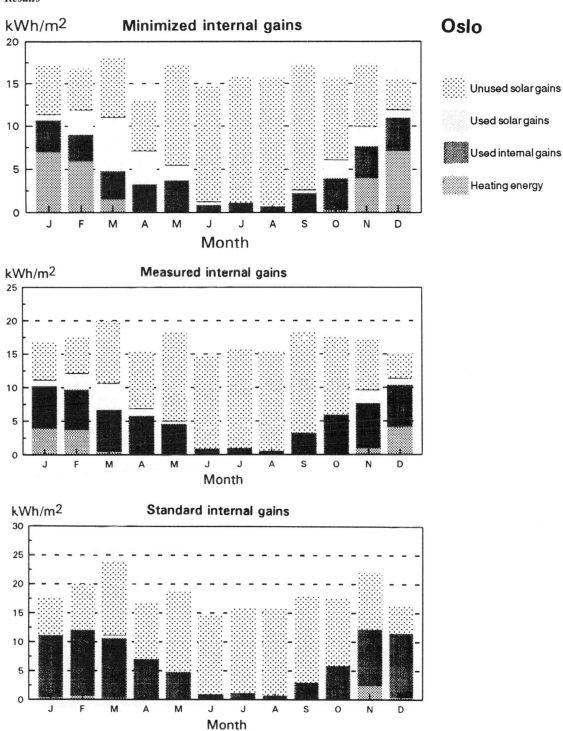

Fig. 8.4 Monthly energy demand for three categories of internal gains and unused solar gains for the Nixdorf office building in Oslo, Zürich and Rome

Zürich

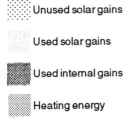

Unused solar gains

Used solar gains

Used internal gains

Heating energy

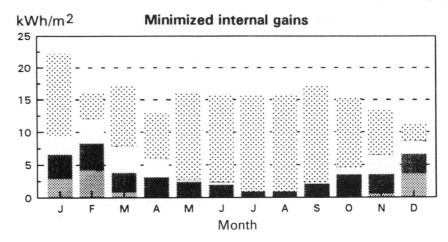

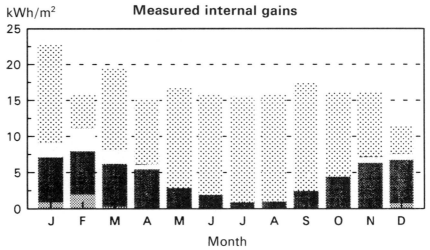

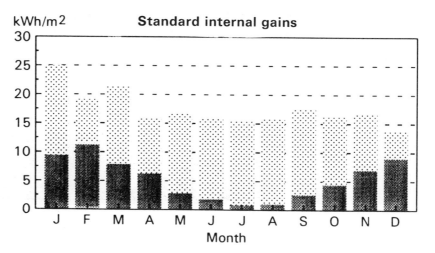

Fig. 8.4 *continued*

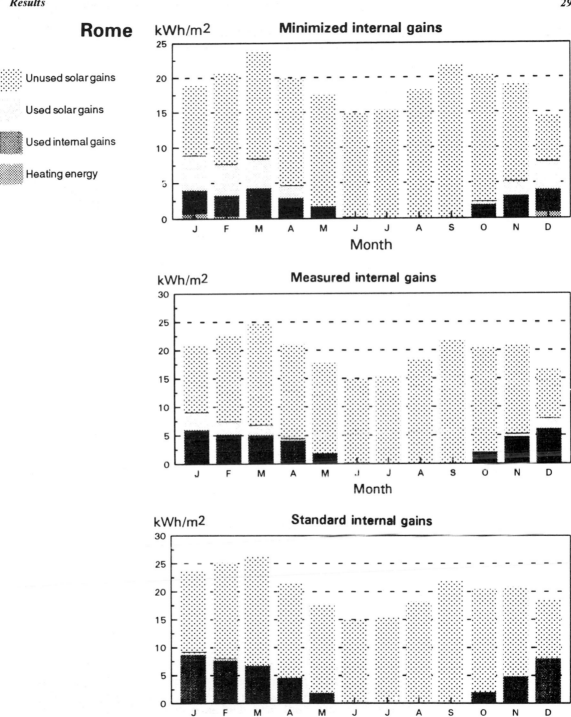

Fig. 8.4 *continued*

Table 8.1 Summary of used solar gains for the Nixdorf office building

A Location	Assumed internal gains	B Maximum usable solar gains (MWh)	C Usable to available solar gains (%)	D Highest percentage of usable to available solar gains (%)
Oslo	Measured	0.45 (March)	25	59 (January)
	Minimum	0.68 (March)	38	56 (January)
Zürich	Measured	0.36 (February)	42	44 (December)
	Minimum	0.45 (March)	31	50 (December)
Rome	Measured	0.33 (January)	20	17 (December)
	Minimum	0.54 (January)	33	38 (December)

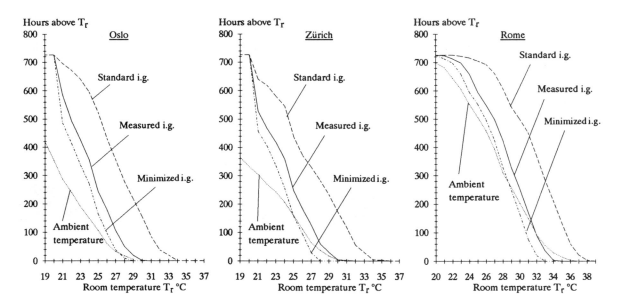

Fig. 8.5 Frequency distributions of room temperatures for the Nixdorf office building

For new buildings, approximate estimates of annual heat demand may be made on the basis of internal gains and coincidence factors quoted in Chapter 7. If detailed design optimization and cost-effectiveness analyses are necessary, more accurate data may be obtained by simulating the building using measured internal gains from an existing building of similar construction and use.

9 Simulation Studies with Actual Heating Systems

To determine the effects of structural mass, heating system and building location on solar usability, simulations were carried out in Austria using a single room in a commercial office building [2/1].

9.1 SIMULATION STRATEGY

Two computer models were used.

1. The program RAUM uses the Fourier method to provide a dynamic simulation of the thermal behavior of individual rooms or a group of rooms for a single day.
2. The program INTEMP uses a finite difference method (explicit) and performs longer-term simulations (e.g. winter, year, etc.) using a one-hour time step.

Both programs treat the radiative and convective heat transfer within the room separately. Surface heat transfer coefficients are calculated at each time increment for air and surface conditions. Shading devices are operated according to solar radiation levels. In addition, absorptance, emittance and reflection effects on the facades are taken into account.

Floor and air heating systems were studied, as were radiators.

The following assumptions were made.

- Room temperature is kept at 20°C with an allowed (measured) temperature variation of ± 2°C permitted during working hours (08:00–16:00).
- Night set-back is 17.5°C for heavy, 16°C for standard and 14°C for lightweight construction.
- For all heating systems, excess heat is vented if the room temperature exceeds the preset value, provided the ambient temperature is below room temperature. No cooling is applied.

9.2 BUILDING AND ROOM CHARACTERISTICS

The physical characteristics of the office simulated are summarized in Fig. 9.1. Simulations were performed for window fronts facing south and east. The remaining walls, ceiling and floor are internal to the building.

The office has a floor area of 92 m^2 and nine individual workplaces. It is equipped with the following electrical appliances: seven AT personal computers, two laser and three matrix printers, one telefax machine, two coffee percolators and various desk lamps.

Three classes of building structure were investigated: heavy, standard and lightweight, as detailed in Fig. 9.1.

To obtain the heavy structure, part of the existing insulation in the original standard building construction was redistributed in the calculations from the inside to the outside surface of the exterior wall. Thus the thermal storage effect was increased while the same heat transfer coefficient was retained. For the lightweight structure, extremely lightweight surrounding walls were adopted. In Austria, there are several examples of commercial buildings having a structure of this

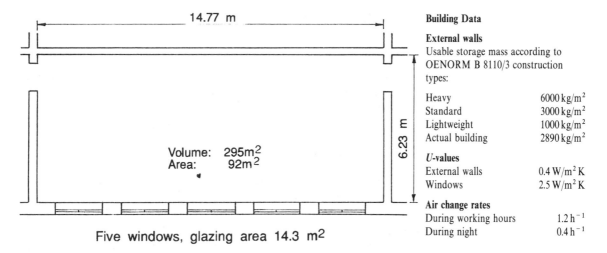

Fig. 9.1 Data describing commercial office building used in simulation

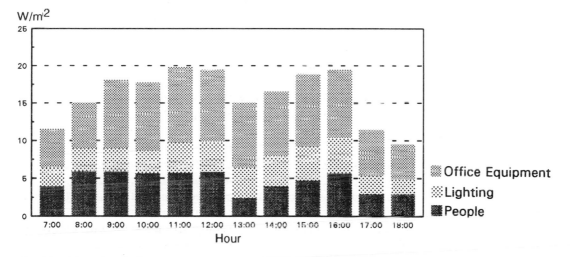

Fig. 9.2 Mean hourly internal gains in Vienna during winter

type. The *U*-value remained the same as for the heavy and standard structures.

9.3 RESULTS

Hourly heat production was measured over a period of four weeks (20 November through 5 December 1989 and 28 January through 12 February 1990). The mean hourly gains are shown in Fig. 9.2.

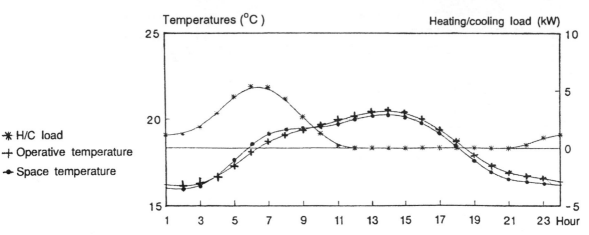

* H/C load
+ Operative temperature
● Space temperature

Fig. 9.3 Calculated temperature and heating load distributions for radiator heating system on a typical day

When the heating load is calculated according to Austrian standard OENORM M7500, the hourly heat gains are $54\,W/m^2$ (Fig. 9.3).

9.3.1 Results from the RAUM program

Floor, radiator and air heating systems were simulated for a cold and sunny winter day (typical day) using the program RAUM, Figs. 9.3 and 9.4.

Figure 9.3 shows the temperature and load distributions for the radiator system and standard construction. The room temperature rises from 16°C during the night (night set-back) to 20.3°C at 14:00 hours. The main heating load occurs between 03:00 and 09:00. Similar distributions were obtained for the remaining systems.

Table 9.1 shows that for heavy construction, the floor heating system makes approximately equal use of solar gains as radiator systems, better use of internal gains but requires about 30% more heating energy than radiators. The total heating load for the floor system also exceeds that for the radiator system by about 30%. Essentially the same outcome is observed for the lightweight and standard constructions.

The distributions of heating energy, used internal gains and used solar gains for the three heating systems are shown in Fig. 9.4.

The higher energy requirements of the floor heating system compared with the radiator system result mainly from the high thermal storage capacity of the floor. The floor system cannot react quickly enough to room temperature changes and excess heat must be vented.

Table 9.1 also shows that for the heavy construction, the air heating system makes better use than the radiator system of both solar gains

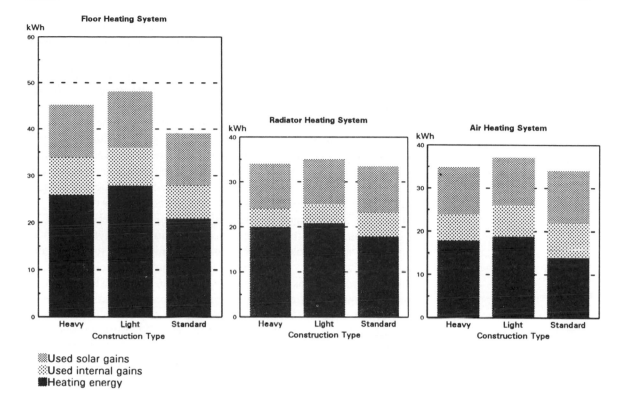

Fig. 9.4 Energy demand for three heating systems for heavy, light and standard constructions on a typical day

Table 9.1 Summary of heat loads for heavy construction from Fig. 9.4

	Floor heating (kWh)	Radiators (kWh)	Air system (kWh)
Solar	10.9	9.7	10.6
Internal gains	7.1	4.0	5.9
Auxiliary heat	26.3	19.7	15.9
Total	43.3	33.4	32.4

and internal gains. The heating energy for the air heating system is about 20% lower than for the radiator heating system. The total heating demands for the air and radiator systems are nearly equal. Once again, essentially the same behavior is displayed for the lightweight and standard constructions.

The better performance of the air heating system is explained by its extremely rapid response to temperature changes, thus making best use of solar and internal gains and avoiding overheating.

Comparing the effects of building mass on the performance of the radiator heating system, the standard structure makes better use of solar and internal gains and requires less heating energy than the other two structures. The lightweight structure proves to be slightly less efficient than the heavy construction. These results are essentially the same for the floor and air heating systems.

Under the conditions assumed in the calculations, a heavy building construction not only offers no advantage over a standard mid-European construction (already massive compared with North American construction), but may indeed make less use of solar and internal gains and require increased heating energy. The extent to which this occurs depends upon the responsiveness of the heating system and how it is operated.

This may be explained by the fact that solar and internal gains are effectively hidden in the heavy structure during the daytime without causing any appreciable temperature rise. At night, due to the thermal lag of the structure, the desired temperature set-back cannot be achieved, and the gains are effectively lost to the exterior. Furthermore, if the room temperature has to be kept within narrow limits, the heating effect of the structure cannot be reduced quickly enough when solar and internal gains are available and excess heat must be vented to the exterior. In summer, although a heavier structure would be advantageous to avoid overheating, this result can be achieved just as effectively using adjustable shading devices.

Note that these results are based on a typical day during the heating season, and change when considering longer time periods. They are also dependent on the assumed night set-back and temperature extremes, and may not be applicable under other conditions. Yearly simulations using INTEMP confirmed the above tendencies.

9.3.2   Results from the INTEMP program

The relative contributions of heating energy, internal and solar gains to the heating load in Copenhagen, Rome and Vienna were calculated using the program INTEMP and are shown in Fig. 9.5 for the complete heating season (1 October through 30 April). The results are given for an air heating system and heavy building structure.

Comparing the values for south-facing windows, the total heat load decreases from northern (Copenhagen) to southern (Rome) climates, internal gains remain approximately constant, and used solar gains increase by a factor of about two.

In Copenhagen and Rome, internal gains cover between 18 and 36%, auxiliary heating energy between 73 and 25%, and solar gains between 10 and 40% of the total heating loads.

The solar contribution for east-facing windows are similar. This result, although surprising, may be explained by the fact that solar

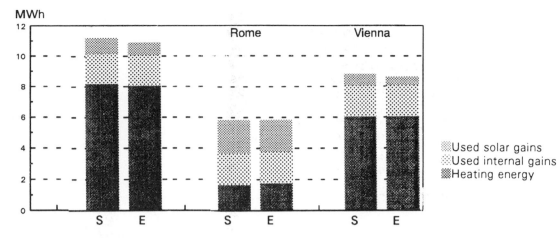

Fig. 9.5 Heat demand for three climates for windows facing south and east during heating season (using an air heating system and heavy construction, 1 October through 30 April). A summary of the results for windows facing south is given in Table 9.2

gains from east-facing windows, which occur earlier in the day than for south-facing windows, are more useful, and assist in heating up the building in the morning. Also, the gains are higher than might be expected due to the lower angle of incidence of the sun in the morning hours.

The values are generally comparable to those obtained for the civic building in Fig. 8.1 described previously, but for which a full year was simulated. The above results and other results from a large series of simulations [2/1] suggest that optimum use of internal and solar gains as a substitute for part of the heating energy requires that:

- The building shell is of medium weight (approximately 3000 kg/m²).
- The heating system reacts quickly to temperature changes (low thermal inertia).
- The control system is able to detect temperature rises from internal and solar gains (temperature sensors within the room are required).
- Movable external shading devices are adjusted to avoid overheating in summer, to avoid glare and to match solar radiation gains to heating requirements.
- The main window front is orientated between east and southwest in the northern hemisphere.

Table 9.2 Summary from Fig. 9.5 of heat demand for windows facing south

	Copenhagen (%)	Rome (%)
Solar	10	40
Internal Gains	18	35
Auxiliary Heat	72	25
Total	100	100

10 Conclusions

The results show the extent which passive solar energy can cover the heating need of a building. The primary factor in determining the degree of solar usability is the effective magnitude and time distribution of internal energy sources from lighting, equipment and persons. Under the conditions assumed in the simulations, a medium-weight building shell in combination with an air heating system makes best use of solar and internal gains.

Assumptions about the magnitude of internal gains vary widely in different countries. Measurements carried out in Switzerland and Austria have shown that values currently assumed are too high by a factor of up to five. This overestimation of internal gains leads to an underestimation of solar potential. In particular, in those cases where internal gains cover a large proportion of the heating load, small percentage changes in internal gains result in large percentage changes in solar usability. This has led to grave underestimation of solar potential.

Measurements and simulation results for this IEA Task show that coincidence factors, defined as maximum measured power divided by total rated power of internal sources and persons, are in the range of 0.2 to 0.3 in winter for office buildings with specific power ratings of between about 50 and 80 W/m^2.

The currently specified value of coincidence factor according to Swiss codes for cooling plants is 0.7. For schools, the measured value is about 0.6. Buildings such as warehouses with specific power ratings between about 5 and 10 W/m^2 have coincidence factors ranging from about 0.60 to 0.85 in winter.

Simulation studies show that for a particular climate, the lower the assumed internal gains, the higher both the values of heating energy and used solar gains. On the other hand, when comparing values for the same building at different locations, the combined percentages of solar and internal gains relative to total heating load are higher for warmer climates. The auxiliary heating load is reduced accordingly.

Furthermore, unrealistic assumptions about internal gains can lead to false conclusions about room temperature and comfort. Thus the need for mechanical cooling in central Europe, in particular for buildings with office equipment, may be overestimated.

An unexpected outcome from the simulations is the finding that extremely heavy office building construction may offer no advantage over standard mid-European construction, and indeed make less use of solar and internal gains and require additional heating energy. The extent to which this occurs depends on the type of heating system and whether it is set back or shut off at night, and on the level of building insulation and climate.

Results of the work carried out in the Task yield the following recommendations to maximize the usability of solar and internal gains:

- The magnitude of usable solar and internal gains should be carefully estimated. If detailed design optimization and cost-effectiveness analyses require more accurate estimates, simulation studies for the building based on internal gains from an existing similar building should be performed.
- The heating system should react quickly to temperature changes, thus making the best use of solar and internal gains without venting excess heat. An air heating system combined with a medium-weight building shell may be optimum to achieve these objectives.
- Adjustable external shading devices should be provided to avoid overheating in summer, to avoid glare, and to match solar radiation gains to heating requirements. The transmission factor of windows with the blinds closed should be less than about 20%, a value readily achievable with exterior blinds.

Further work is in progress to obtain statistically relevant data on internal gains for different building types that can serve as input for simulation programs.

11 References

2/1 Bruck, M., Wärmetechnische Optimierung von Büroräumen, Project 'Werk-Stadt'-Geiselbergstrasse, W. Kallinger & Co., Schlossgasse 13, A-1050 Vienna, Austria, 1991 (proprietary document).

2/2 Bruck, M., Panzhauser, E., Fail, A., *Bericht über die Entwicklung und über die wohnhygienische Beurteilung eines Niedertemperatur-Heiz-, Kühl- und Lüftungssystems*, Innovationsreferat des Wissenschaftsförderungsinstitutes der Handelskammer Niederösterreich, Vienna, Austria, Kanzlei Dr Bruck, Garnisongasse 7, A-1090 Vienna, Austria, 1991.

2/3 Eicher, Hp., Stalder, M., Interne Lasten und ihre Auswirkungen für die passive Sonnenenergienutzung-Schlussbericht (*Bundesamt für Energiewirtschaft*), Dr Eicher & Pauli AG, Oristalstrasse 85, CH-4410 Liestal, Switzerland, May 1990.

2/4 Engström, L., Private Communication, EHUB, KTH, Royal Institute of Technology, S-10044 Stockholm, Sweden.

2/5 Hestnes, Anne Grete, Private Communication, Norwegian Institute of Technology-Architecture, N-7034 Trondheim NTH, Norway.

2/6 *Schweizerischer Ingenieur- und Architekten-Verein* (SIA), Kühlleistungsbedarf von Gebäuden, Dokumentation-Nr. 70, SIA, PO Box, CH-8039, Zürich, Switzerland, 1984.

PART **3**

SOLAR HEATING

CONTRIBUTORS

**Part 3   Editor
and Chapter 13**
Poul E. Kristensen
Esbensen Consulting Engineers
FIDIC
41 Havnegade
DK-1058 Copenhagen
Denmark

Chapter 16
Philippe André
Fond. Univ. Luxembourgeoise
Avenue de Longwy 185
B-6700 Arlon
Belgium

Chapter 18
Manfred Bruck
Kanzlei Dr Bruck
Garnisongasse 7
A-1090 Vienna
Austria

Chapter 13
Alexander Casanovas
Dept. Thermodinamica
Universidad Valencia
E-46100 Burjassot, Valencia
Spain

Chapter 17
Hans Erhorn
Fraunhofer Institut für Bauphysik
PO Box 80 04 69
D-7000 Stuttgart 80
Germany

Chapter 15
**Charles Filleux and
Markus Hänni**
Basler & Hofmann
Forchstrasse 395
CH-8029 Zürich
Switzerland

Chapters 14 and 19
Simonetta Fumagalli
ENEA-FARE-CORLAB-DIM1
c/o CCR Building 1 4D
I-21020, Ispra
Italy

Chapter 13
S. Robert Hastings
Forschungsstelle Solararchitektur
ETH-Höggerberg
CH-8093 Zürich
Switzerland

Chapter 14
Matthias Schuler
ITW, University of Stuttgart
Pfaffenwaldring 6
D-7000 Stuttgart 80
Germany

Chapters 13 and 19
Rolf Stricker
Fraunhofer Institut für Bauphysik
PO Box 80 04 69
D-7000 Stuttgart 80
Germany

12 Introduction

Passive solar energy can reduce the auxiliary heating costs in commercial buildings, without compromising occupant comfort. Thermal storage, efficient solar control, and shading devices are important components in a building with good utilization of passive solar energy. Solar heating strategies for commercial buildings should always be considered with other energy saving measures, addressing lighting, ventilation and cooling.

In Part 2, Solar Usability, examples showed how internal heat gains in commercial buildings are much lower in practice than normally anticipated and that solar gains can reduce heating costs. Part 3

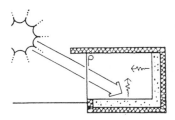

Direct gain system

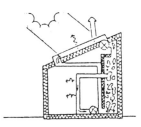

Air collector system with storage

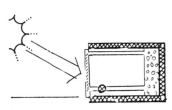

Air flow window system
connected to heat storage

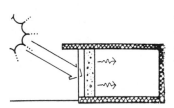

Mass wall system

presents strategies to realize this potential. Individual chapters each address a specific solar heating strategy.

In Chapter 13, Direct Gain Systems, the whole room is used as the solar collector. To control overheating and glare, shading systems are added to the window construction, which also serve to reflect solar energy onto an interior storage mass. A system of this type is illustrated with a school in Los Molinos, Spain.

In classical solar air collector systems, air is heated by the sun in a collector, then is transported directly to the building. When combined with a storage system, the energy can be used from one to two days after collection. Air Collector Systems are discussed in Chapter 14.

Solar shading devices sandwiched between two glass panes can be used to collect solar energy, which can either be utilized in other parts of the building or stored. This is the concept of an Air Flow Window system, addressed in Chapter 15.

If a solid and dark wall is covered by glazing, solar energy will be absorbed in the thermal mass of the wall and be transmitted to the room behind the wall. The thermal capacity of the wall enables solar energy to be released in the room hours after it was collected. This is often an advantage, because the heating load increases after the hours of solar collection. Mass Wall Systems are discussed in Chapter 16.

In temperate climates, heat loss through a mass wall during days with no sun can be significant. While insulation added in the mass wall reduces heat loss, passive solar gains may be less than the gains. New transparent insulation materials with good optical and improved thermal properties have been developed. Transparent Insulation Systems are discussed in a separate Chapter, 17.

Solar energy can also be transferred from the outer surface of an unglazed exterior wall via a hydronic system for use in other parts of the building. If a heat pump cools the absorber, glazing in front of the wall is unnecessary. Such a system is described in Chapter 18 as the Absorber Wall concept.

Storage of solar energy is important in commercial buildings to make the best use of passive solar gains and to reduce overheating. The practical application of various storage systems is described in Chapter 19, Storage Systems.

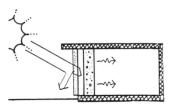

Transparent insulation of mass wall

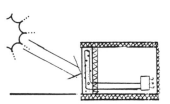

Absorber wall connected to heat pump

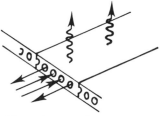

Thermal storage floor (hypocaust system)

13 Direct Gain Systems

Fig. 13.1 Jungfrau Restaurant

13.1 INTRODUCTION

The solar gains through windows can exceed the heat losses out of the windows if the design of the building is optimized. This simple approach is called direct gain solar heating.

Direct gain design for commercial buildings combins well with daylighting strategies described in Part 4 of this sourcebook.

There are several techniques which enhance the performance of direct gain systems. New glazing systems promise a net energy gain even for windows facing east or west. The use of insulating shutters to prevent

Improved glazing

Standard double glazing:
$3.0 \, \text{W/m}^2 \, \text{K}$

Low emissivity double glazing (1985):
$1.5 \, \text{W/m}^2 \, \text{K}$

Low emissivity triple glazing (1990):
$0.9 \, \text{W/m}^2 \, \text{K}$

Evacuated low emissivity double glazing (1995?):
$0.4 \, \text{W/m}^2 \, \text{K}$

heat loss during the night is another opportunity to improve the performance of direct gain solar energy. Systems with high efficiency windows and shutter systems are also effective. An innovative system is presented which combines an insulating shutter with a reflector to increase the gain of solar energy in a building.

13.1.1   Advantages

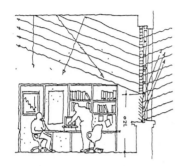

Glare control without rejecting passive solar energy and daylighting

A direct gain system can be very inexpensive: in its simplest form, it implies minimal extra building costs. Unlike several other passive solar concepts, a direct gain system allows direct visual contact through the collector to the exterior.

13.1.2   Disadvantages

Large window areas oriented towards the sun invariably require a control device to avoid glare and overheating a room. Glazing with a permanently high reflection or absorption of sunlight is not a solution. The reduced solar gains may be less than the heat losses. Conventional shading devices, like venetian blinds, are an accepted and standard solution to glare, but also prevent full use of solar energy to the extent that they reflect sunlight back out of a window. The blades should be adjustable to reflect sunlight onto the ceiling.

Rooms with a narrow comfort band generally do not allow good utilization of passive solar energy. Direct solar gains can be more efficiently used if the room temperature can rise during daytime so that the room mass is warmed and can cool down at night to release stored heat.

13.2   SYSTEM TYPES AND VARIATIONS

An ideal direct gain system would maximize the collection and use of solar heat gains while minimizing window heat loss. Key design parameters are: orientation of the windows, size of the window area relative to room volume, solar transmissivity of the glazing, heat loss coefficient of the window assembly, and thermal mass of the rooms. Also crucial to the good performance of a direct gain system are the control strategy for the heating system and occupancy profile of the building (time of occupancy and amount of internal heat gain).

The position and amount of thermal mass in a building is an important variable. The thermal mass may be sunlit directly, which is often preferable, or thermal mass may be indirectly air heated as is the case with a non-sunlit ceiling or walls away from windows.

The Blanco Wall system in the Los Molinos School in Fig. 13.2 shows a mirror panel reflecting solar energy onto the interior mass. When closed in summer, the panel reflects solar energy back to the exterior.

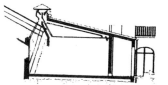

Fig. 13.2 Blanco Wall in Los Molinos, Alicante, Spain

13.2.1 Heat loss and heat gain control

Emphasis on utilization of direct passive solar energy means larger window areas. Controlling heat loss then becomes important so as to retain more useful energy than what is lost from the increased window area. Selection of highly insulative glazing and frame construction are the best means of reducing heat losses through windows. In Scandinavian countries, triple glazing or low emissivity double glazing is becoming standard in new building codes. In Norway, for example, the maximum allowed U-value in a new building is $2.0\,\mathrm{W/m^2\,K}$.

Fig. 13.3 Manual shutters at the Haas office building in Jona, Switzerland

Industrial mass production of triple glazed and double glazed, gas-filled windows with selective coating has reduced previously high costs of these solutions, making them cost-effective in northern and central European climates. Development of super glazing with U-values between 0.5 and $1.0\,\mathrm{W/m^2\,K}$ is underway and the first commercial applications of some of these glazing types already exist. Widespread applications can be expected before the year 2000.

Shutters are another efficient means to reduce heat losses. They can cut the heat loss coefficient from $2.8\,\mathrm{W/m^2\,K}$ for double glazing to 0.4–$0.8\,\mathrm{W/m^2\,K}$ when closed at night. However, in commercial buildings one cannot normally rely upon manual operation of the shutters, and automation is complicated and expensive.

Exterior or interior blinds used to control glare have some positive (although minimal) effect on the U-value of the window.

13.2.2 Thermal mass

Thermal mass offers two important advantages. Mass stores heat when there is an excess of passive solar energy and/or internal gains in a building and releases the stored heat as the building starts to cool down. Mass also reduces the temperature swing in a room from passive gains. Therefore, thermal mass is often required in a passive solar building to bring the temperature variations within acceptable limits and/or to reduce the cooling load peaks.

Thermal mass is not a substitute for solar shading. The best solution to maximize utilization of direct solar energy with good comfort is the combination of thermal mass with solar shading.

13.3   EXAMPLES

In this chapter, two different examples of direct gains are described. The first is the Jungfrau Restaurant at a 3500 m altitude in Switzerland, and the second is the Los Molinos School in Alicante, Spain.

13.3.1   The Jungfrau Restaurant

Location
Interlaken, Switzerland
Latitude: 46°N
Elevation: 3500 m

Description

The Jungfrau Restaurant was built in 1987 with requirements for good thermal and visual comfort and minimum heating energy. Situated near Interlaken, Switzerland, it is exposed to severe climate conditions: the average annual temperature is −8°C, compared to Zürich with +8°C. Strong winds are frequent and have reached a velocity of 250 km/h. Solar radiation is intense, occasionally exceeding the solar constant of 1367 W/m^2, as a result of the high reflectivity of the glacier. The number of hours of sunshine is 1770 hours/year.

The restaurant is used only during the day, when the occupancy ranges from 1800 to 2100 visitors. This produces high internal heat gains and humidity. Air from ventilation with heat and moisture recovery is provided at 40 m^3/hour per person.

Design details

Walls are insulated with 180 mm of insulation. The roof has a cross-beam construction to reduce thermal bridges, with a total of 300 mm of insulation material.

Windows contain four layers of gas-filled glass with selective coatings to reduce heat loss, and a solar shading coating to reduce glare. The mean U-value of the glazing including the perimeter is $0.7\,\mathrm{W/m^2\,K}$. Aluminum window frames have a thermal break, bringing the U-value of the frame down to $1.4\,\mathrm{W/m^2\,K}$.

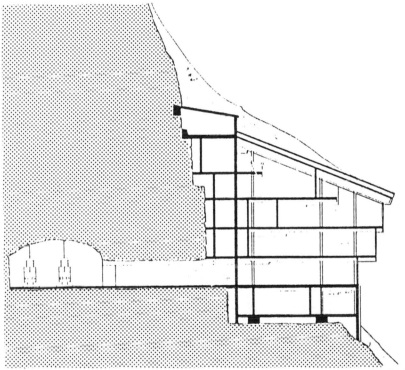

Fig. 13.4   Section through the Jungfrau Restaurant

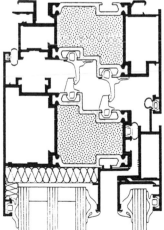

Good insulation and air tightness of the windows eliminates the need for radiators below the windows so that visitors in the restaurant can comfortably sit next to them. Auxiliary heating, used primarily at night, is provided by the ventilation system. During the night, the ventilation system runs with 100% air recirculation. The high insulation standards of the building limits heating plant requirements to 150 kW, corresponding to less than $50\,\mathrm{W/m^2}$ of heated floor area.

To increase the usability of the solar gains, the room temperature may swing from 18°C in the early morning to 24°C in the afternoon on a sunny day. This allows the massive floor to function as thermal storage.

Fig. 13.5   Section through the window frame. Window U-value: $0.7\,\mathrm{W/m^2\,K}$

Table 13.1 Estimated energy balance in one year 1987/88

	MWh/year
Passive solar gains	140
Internal gains	120
Gains from motors	120
Heating	340
Total	720

Table 13.2 Calculated energy balance on a sunny day with 10°C ambient temperature

	9:00–17:00 (kWh)	17:00–9:00 (kWh)
Heat losses		
Transmission losses	320	710
Infiltration	305	440
Ventilation	550	0
Total	1175	1150
Heat gains		
Internal gains	720	330
Passive solar gains	380	0
Heating	75	820
Total	1175	1150

Design highlights
- Glazing U-value 0.7 W/m^2 K
- Storage of solar energy in massive building components
- Ventilation with heat and moisture recuperation

Conclusions

The annual auxiliary energy needed for heating, ventilation and fans is 140 kWh/m^2, which is low for a building under such extreme conditions. This low energy consumption is the result of a successful combination of a highly insulated building shell, an appropriate control strategy and good utilization of passive solary energy.

References

13/1 Wyss, Andreas, Das Berghaus Jungfraujoch, *Energie Solaire*, January 1990 (CH).

13/2 Wyss, A., Huber, R., Weber, H., Die Neubauten auf dem Jungfraujoch: Bauphysik und Haustechnik, *Schweizerische Bauzeitung*, 30-31/87. Schweizer Ingenieur und Architekt, Rüdigerstrasse 11, Postfach 630, CH 8021, Zürich.

13.3.2 Los Molinos School

Description

The mild winter climate of Crevillente in Alicante, Spain and intense solar radiation values enable the passive solar heating systems in the Los Molinos School to meet all of the building heating requirements. The designers, however, had to avoid overheating the building.

The Blanco Wall is the main heating system used in the classrooms and laboratories of the building. This passive system is based on heating the inside of a thermal mass wall by solar irradiation. Solar energy enters the building through slanted windows and is directed to the wall using reflective interior window shutters (Fig. 13.7).

Location
Crevillente, Alicante, Spain
Annual degree days (base 20):

1421 dd

Global solar irradiation:

1800 kWh/m² year

Latitude: 38°N

Altitude: 300 m

20 km from the Mediterranean

Cost (1984)
Pta 25 000 000
ECU 179 000

Fig. 13.6   Los Molinos School

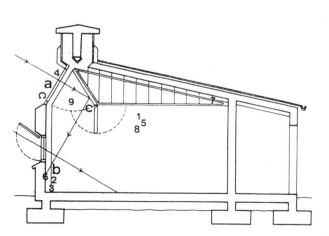

Gross heat load:	6950 kWh
Solar irradiation on the tilted plane (60°):	1920 kWh/m²
Internal gains:	1740 kWh
Net heat load:	5420 kWh
Solar energy received by Blanco Wall windows:	36 100 kWh
Thermal capacity (kWh/k)	
Primary heat storage:	16.4
Secondary heat storage:	22.2

Fig. 13.7   Section of Blanco Wall: (a) slanting windows; (b) concrete or water thermal mass in the wall; (c) slanting reflecting mirrors/night insulation

Floor area (m^2)

Gross:	579
With passive solar system:	330
South classroom area:	112

South classroom values

Thermal transmittance:	W/m^2 K
Floor:	1.4
Roof:	0.62
Window single:	5.7
Window single with shutters:	0.75
External wall:	0.61
Blanco wall:	0.57
Global heat loss coefficient:	549 W/K

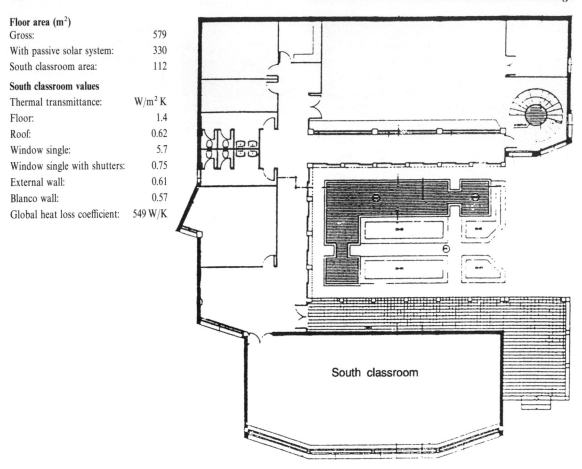

South classroom

Fig. 13.8   Plan of Los Molinos classroom building

Passive solar features

The Blanco Wall is the main passive solar strategy in the building. It permits the white, Mediterranean appearance of Los Molinos architecture. Construction is traditional: brick walls with fiberglass insulation together with a tiled pitched roof. Glazing is placed in the south facade.

Overhead windows slant to enable maximum direct solar radiation on the thermal mass wall via the reflective shutters. Normal, vertical windows also occur in the wall. The concept is simple and reduces many of the drawbacks of classical direct gain systems.

The Los Molinos School has two ways to avoid overheating, which a monitoring program proved are completely adequate. The first is merely to tilt the shutters to an appropriate degree to control the amount of sun that enters the rooms; the second is to open the conventional windows for cross-ventilation.

Monitoring program

From March 1987 through February 1988 the building's heating system was monitored and computer modeled in detail. The purpose was to assess the energy savings of the Blanco Wall, to establish its optimum design and to evaluate comfort (using Fanger's Predicted Mean Vote (PMV) comfort index). One classroom with a concrete Blanco Wall and one room with a Blanco Wall with water tank were monitored. Among the monitored parameters were external and internal temperature and humidity, room temperatures, and temperatures of the thermal mass and of internal surfaces. The thermal fluxes through walls and ceilings were also monitored. Global radiation (horizontal and on the plane of the tilted glazing) was monitored as were wind velocity and direction.

During the winter the amount of solar energy collected exceeds the net heat load. It is therefore possible for the passive solar features to supply all the building's heating needs. In summer, solar energy must be rejected and heat gains vented.

The occupants use cross ventilation extensively. Monitoring confirms, however, the need for this to avoid overheating in the classrooms with Blanco Walls.

The south classroom is almost isolated from the rest of the building. This $112\,m^2$ room was chosen as a convenient environment to test and simulate the performance of the Blanco Wall. As a control, the ARMA dynamic monitoring system was operated in the south classroom for ten days when it was unoccupied. A heat loss coefficient of this room of $595\,W/K$ was obtained with a simple ARMA fit. This is acceptable with the calculated value of $549\,W/K$.

The excess solar radiation and minimal heating demand in Crevillente result in the Blanco Wall being relatively insensitive to design changes in the environment. Static monitoring, therefore, gives little information about the best design of a Blanco Wall. An objective of parametric studies on the wall therefore was to analyze the building's heating needs and comfort in climates colder than Crevillente.

Monitoring parameters

25 parameters measured

Full sampling every 2 minutes

Averaging and recording every 30 minutes

Parametric studies

Temperatures in a classroom with the Blanco Wall (simulated with a water tank) are compared with those of a similar classroom where the $112\,m^2$ slanted window is altered to a vertical window without reflector and night insulation. White curtains are drawn in front of the windows to avoid glare whenever the vertical solar radiation outside the window exceeds $350\,W/m^2$. The overall heat loss coefficient of the room is the same in the two cases.

SUNCODE was chosen as an appropriate simulation tool for the Los Molinos Blanco Wall. The performance of the $112\,m^2$ Blanco Wall classroom has been modeled in different climates: Rome, Zürich, Brussels and Copenhagen. The building's properties and occupancy

Internal loads

3.5 m²/pupil in the classroom (32 pupils) and 1 staff, 80 W each

Lighting:

17.45 W/m²

Occupancy schedule

Rome: 08:00 to 12:00 and
        14:00 to 15:45 Monday to Friday

Brussels, Zürich:
                        08:00 to 12:00 and
        13:00 to 17:00 Monday to Friday

Copenhagen: 08:00 to 11:00 and
        12:00 to 15:00 Monday to Friday

schedule were adapted to the different climates, and the user schedule was adapted to the country (Table 13.3).

Table 13.3 South classroom building parameters

Climate	Ceiling	Walls	Floor	Glazing
		U-value (W/m² K)		
Rome	0.33	0.44	0.44	2.84
Copenhagen	0.13	0.28	0.28	1.60
Brussels & Zürich	0.20	0.23	0.14	1.60

The required room temperature is 20°C in all climates. The room is cross-ventilated if the temperature exceeds 24°C. The set-back temperature during night is 16°C.

Simulation results

The version of SUNCODE used allows the distribution of solar energy on the internal surfaces in patterns to be specified. In Fig. 13.9, the results of this variation are illustrated for Rome. If 100% of the incident solar energy is anticipated to reach the Blanco Wall, then the performance is obviously the best. If only 40% of incident solar energy is anticipated to reach the Blanco Wall, the auxiliary energy load increases from only 3.3 to 3.9 kW/m² year. In that case, the remaining 60% of the solar radiation will be absorbed in the indoor air.

This result is important because in practice it is impossible to control the Blanco Wall mirror so that 100% of the solar energy reaches the mass wall. The remaining simulations assume that 44% of solar energy reaches the mass wall.

Performance improves by increasing thermal mass, but stabilizes for water tank thickness greater than 0.4 m; a thickness of 0.2 m may be sufficient. The original design of Blanco Wall includes splitting the south facade in three slightly different azimuths. The benefit of such a design may be a better use of incoming solar radiation throughout the day. Simulations, however, showed no distinct advantage.

Figure 13.10 shows the performance of the Blanco Wall classroom compared to a conventional classroom for different climates. The Blanco Wall performs considerably better than the conventional design in all climates. The Blanco Wall system allows direct solar radiation into the room, whereas conventionally direct radiation above a given level is shaded off to avoid glare. This feature accounts for the superiority of the Blanco Wall system. The best absolute results are achieved for Rome and Copenhagen.

The result of tilting the Blanco Wall window is shown in Figs. 13.11 and 13.12. The optimum tilt of the Blanco Wall window in Rome is

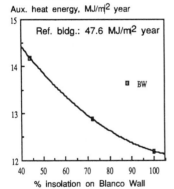

Fig. 13.9 Variation in the percentage of insolation coupled to the Blanco Wall, Rome

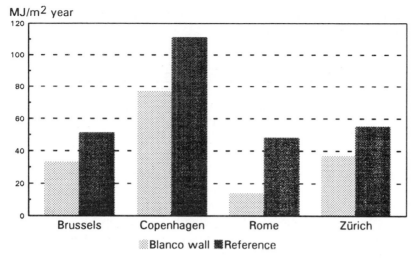

Fig. 13.10   Auxiliary heating energy for four European climates

Effect of the tilt of BW windows
Rome climate

Auxiliary heat, energy, MJ/m² year

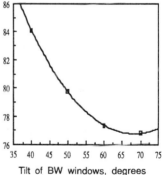

Fig. 13.11   Auxiliary heating versus tilt of the Blanco Wall windows, Rome

59° from horizontal, whereas the value for Copenhagen is 69°. These values are equivalent to the latitutde plus approximately 15°.

The Blanco Wall advanced case study [13/5] includes additional results from the parametric variations. There it is shown that the performance of the Blanco Wall system improves with increasing area of the Blanco Wall window; the maximum occurs when window area equals wall areas. The use of a water tank having equal thermal mass to the concrete wall improves the performance slightly in the Rome case because of the improves heat transfer in water versus concrete.

Conclusions

The Blanco Wall displays distinct improvement over the traditional direct gain system for the conditions of the classroom studied. The Blanco Wall window transmits passive solar energy to the building without glare, a common problem in traditional classrooms. In an actual design, special considerations should be given to problems with glare when the mirror is inappropriately adjusted. The concept prevents visible contact with the surroundings, and therefore, might find good use in stairways and corridors.

Effect of the tilt of BW windows
Copenhagen climate

Auxiliary heat, energy, MJ/m² year

Fig. 13.12   Auxiliary heating versus tilt of Blanco Wall windows, Copenhagen

References

13/3 Casanovas, A. J., and Martinez-Lozano, J. A., Los Molinos, Crevillente, Spain, *Project Monitor, Issue 24*, Directorate General XII of the Commission of the European Communities, July 1988. Available through J. Oven Lewis, School of Architecture, University College Dublin, Richview, Clonskeagh, Dublin 14.

13/4 Casanovas, A. J., and Martinez-Lozano, J. A., Los Molinos School, *IEA Solar Heating and Cooling Task XI: Passive and*

Hybrid Solar Commercial Buildings, Basic Case Studies, BCS no. 25, 1989.

13/5 Los Molinos School IEA Task XI, *Advanced Case Studies Seminar*, April 24, 1991, Oxford, Great Britain. Proceedings available from REPD, ETSU Harwell Laboratory, Oxfordshire, OX11 0RA (60).

13.4 DETAILED RESULTS

This section is devoted to a detailed discussion of the design and performance of direct gain passive solar strategies.

The results of parametric studies on the Haas office building in Jona, Switzerland are described here and in more detail in Chapter 15, Air Flow Windows. Although the building has a window air collector, it has also been monitored and modeled as a direct gain building. Data from modeling work for the Haas office building in both direct gain mode and airflow window mode are discussed in more detail in [13/6].

A parametric study of the ENTE building in Stuttgart, Germany is also presented here. A $17\,m^2$ office room has been monitored, and analyzed for variations in the main parameters. the ENTE building is described in more detail in [13/7].

13.4.1 Haas office building

This $225\,m^2$ office building is partly earth-sheltered to minimize heat losses, and has windows facing south to maximize passive use of solar energy. The building is constructed of concrete with external insulation.

Heating consumption 1 October 1987 through 30 April 1988

Measured: $11.7\,kWh/m^2$
Calculated: $12.0\,kWh/m^2$

The performance of the building while operating in direct gain mode was monitored from 1 October 1987 to 30 April 1988. This performance was compared with predictions made by the SERIRES/SUNCODE computer model and results are shown in Fig. 13.13.

On an annual basis, the measured performance compares well with predicted performance where the difference is only 3%. Although the difference between predicted and measured performance on a monthly basis is greater than the yearly figures, this can be explained by the fact that the contribution from electricity and people could only be estimated. Furthermore, the control of auxiliary heating was partly manual, affecting the measured heating load, and automatic control was assumed for the simulations.

The SERIRES computer model was then used to investigate changes in the following parameters:

1. Influence of night shutters;
2. Influence of required room temperature;
3. Influence of climate.

The fixed parameters are shown in Table 13.4.

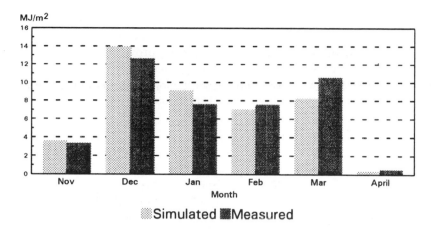

Simulated **Measured**

Fig. 13.13 Predicted and measured heating consumption 1987/1988

Table 13.4 Fixed parameters

	Internal gains (kW)	Heating set point (°C)	Air change rate (h⁻¹)
Working day 07:00–17:00	2.2	20	0.3
Non-working time and weekends	0.2	(no heating)	0.15

Window U-value:

Daytime: $1.60\,W/m^2\,K$

Night-time with shutters: $0.35\,W/m^2\,K$

Night insulation

At night, heat loss is reduced with manually operated insulating shutters, which reduce the U-value of the four-pane window construction from $1.5\,W/m^2\,K$ to $0.36\,W/m^2\,K$. Figure 13.14 shows the influence of insulation on night heat loss and on the monthly auxiliary energy load (heating and electricity). Insulating shutters used at night have a significant influence on auxiliary energy load from November through March. On an annual basis, the heat required is reduced from $35\,kWh/m^2$ to $28\,kWh/m^2$, corresponding to a 20% energy saving.

Low emissivity triple glazed windows with a U-value of around $0.9\,W/m^2\,K$ are now available. Such glazing represents a good alternative to shutters and has an added advantage of not requiring any mechanical operation.

Room temperature

The room temperature was kept at a minimum of 20°C during working hours 07:00–17:00; however, the influence of variations of temperature set point on the heating load is substantial, as illustrated in Fig. 13.15.

Note that if 22°C were required instead of 20°C, the auxiliary heating demand would increase by approximately 25%, which is unusually large. A rule of thumb frequently adopted is that the auxiliary heating

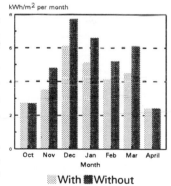

With **Without**

Fig. 13.14 Auxiliary energy load with and without night insulation

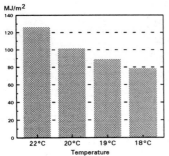

Fig. 13.15 Auxiliary heating demand for variations in heating temperature set point

consumption is increased by 5% for each degree Celsius increase in room temperature. The large sensitivity in this case is explained by the large percentage of the gross heating load provided by solar and internal gains to maintain room temperature near 20°C. Only a small auxiliary heat input is needed to reach this set point. If the set point is raised to 22°C, the additional heat input required is almost entirely from the auxiliary heat.

Climate

The performance of the building was simulated for the various climates shown in Table 13.5. The thermal properties of the roof, wall and floor have been changed according to the climate, as indicated in Table 13.6. The window construction remain unchanged; three-pane glazing was used in all cases.

Table 13.5 Mean ambient temperature and horizontal solar radiation (October–April inclusive)

Site	°C	kWh/m^2
Jona	+4.8	330
Davos	−0.5	530
Lugano	+8.0	390
Oslo	−1.3	240
Copenhagen	+3.3	290
Rome	+10.8	640
Dallas	+12.5	790

Table 13.6 Insulation values for different climates

Site	Roof U-value (W/m^2 K)	Wall U-value (W/m^2 K)	Floor U-value (W/m^2 K)
Jona, Davos, Lugano	0.20	0.23	0.14
Oslo	0.09	0.14	0.14
Copenhagen	0.13	0.28	0.28
Rome	0.33	0.44	0.44
Dallas	0.33	0.44	0.44

Figure 13.16 shows that auxiliary heating consumption is negligible in Dallas and Rome and small in the case of Lugano. Increased insulation assumed for both Copenhagen and Oslo compensates for their lower winter temperatures and less sunshine than the warmer climates.

The effect of increased insolation at the high altitude of Davos is pronounced compared to Jona, despite the higher gross heating load from the low ambient temperature. Also, solar energy is as great a component of the heating supply in Copenhagen and Oslo as in Jona resulting from the longer heating periods in northern climates.

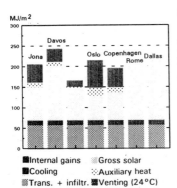

Fig. 13.16 Gross energy balance depending on climate, October–April inclusive

13.4.2 Office module

The influences of internal gains, window area, orientation, thermal mass and climate on the performance of an office module from October through April were simulated using SUNCODE. Solar shading was not considered, so that solar energy entered uninterrupted.

The 16.8 m^2 office module has a 12.1 m^2 facade area oriented toward the south. The module is presumed to be situated in the middle of a building with heat loss transmitted only through the facade and by air infiltration. The base case values as well as variations after simulations

Table 13.7 Parameter variations

	Base case	Variations
Windows		
Glazing area	3.75 m²	6.82 m²
Window area	5.74 m²	10.50 m²
Glazing type U-value	3.0 W/m² K	1.5 W/m² K
		0.9 W/m² K
Transmission factor	80%	64%
		50%
Wall, ceiling, floor	concrete	plaster
Internal gains	15 W/m²	30 and 60 W/m²
Weather data	Würzburg	Oslo, Brussels, Zürich, Rome, Copenhagen

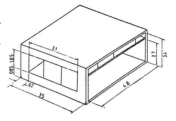

Fig. 13.17 Dimensions of the office module

are shown in Table 13.7.

Internal gains were set at 15 W/m² which is considered average for a modern office, provided that electric lighting is controlled in accordance with available natural daylight. The value of 15 W/m² corresponded to 250 W per office. If, however, the general office lighting is uncontrolled or is less energy efficient, 20 W/m² might be the installed value, or 335 W per office module. If lighting is assumed to be on most of the time, then a mean value of 325 W for the general office lighting is used.

When the room temperature exceeds 24°C, users are expected to open the windows and vent the room at a 5 h⁻¹ air change rate. The energy lost by venting a room with internal gains of 15 W/m² is limited. When the temperature exceeds 28°C, cooling starts. Most of the energy lost by venting or by cooling is useless passive solar energy which enters the room.

Effects of building mass
The importance of mass is illustrated in Fig. 13.18. Here, the reference case has concrete walls, floor and ceiling, compared with a low mass case, using light materials like plaster and wood. The need for ventilation rises with the low-mass case to reduce overheating from solar gains during the winter.

Variation of glazing type
Figure 13.19 compares energy balances for various glazing types. An improved U-value gives the expected results of decreased heat loss through the windows, but this reduction is offset to some extent by the reduction in solar energy transmitted. The net auxiliary heating load is reduced from 68 kWh/m² with normal double glazing to 53 kWh/m² (12%) with low emissivity glazing (1.5 W/m² K). Using 'super E' glazing (0.9 W/m² K), the load is reduced further to 49 W/m² (8%).

Table 13.8 Internal gains for the office module

Office item	Gain (W)
One person, 100 W, present 75% of the time	75
One PC, total 100 W, on 50% of the time	50
One desk lamp 100 W, on 50% of the time	50
General office lighting 15 W/m², on 30% of the time (i.e. lighting control)	75
Total gains during working hours	250

Air exchange rate
0.8 h⁻¹ during working hours

Required temperature
21°C 08:00–17:00
17°C 17:00–08:00

Venting
room temperature > 24°C

Cooling
room temperature > 28°C

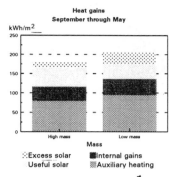

Fig. 13.18 Effect of building mass on heat gains

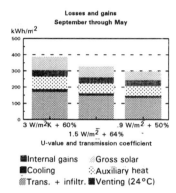

Fig. 13.19 Variation of glazing type

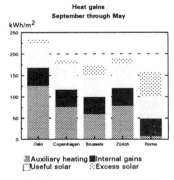

Fig. 13.20 Influence of climate on heat gains

Less solar energy transmitted with super-glazing results in a smaller amount of useful solar energy. If low emissivity glazing has a poor solar transmission coefficient, the savings on purchased heat will be less than the lower U-value suggests, due to the lesser solar contribution. Furthermore, the daylighting provided by the windows will also be decreased.

Climate

The influence of climate on solar loss and gain is illustrated in Fig. 13.20.

The gross heat loss, and hence the gross energy needed, varies with climate. In the cases of Rome and Denver a considerable portion of the solar energy transmitted through the window is then lost again through venting and cooling, and solar shading must be used to prevent overheating or reduce cooling loads even in the winter.

Among European climates studied, the largest absolute amount of useful solar energy occurs in Oslo. In Rome and Denver, useful solar gains almost meet the heating demand of these mild climates, reducing auxiliary energy to nearly zero, but the heating season is short so the total amount of usable solar gain is less than in Oslo.

13.5 CONCLUSIONS

The projects reviewed in this chapter show that there are many opportunities to use direct gain solar energy in several commercial building types.

The percentage heating load covered by solar energy varies from 29% for an office building (Haas) with windows facing south simulated in Oslo, to 100% in the case of the Los Molinos School in Alicante, Spain.

In the cold but sunny climate of the Jungfraujoch in Switzerland, passive solar energy covers 19% of the annual heating load of a restaurant at 3500 m altitude. Internal gains from people in the restaurant cover another 17% of the annual heating load. This good result is achieved with a combination of large high-performance windows and heat storage in the heavy construction and the acceptance of room temperature variations from 18–25°C.

Optimum effective utilization of solar energy from direct gains requires effective solar control devices to avoid glare and overheating. They can also enhance the usefulness of solar gains by directing the sunlight on to thermally massive walls on the ceiling.

In the case of the Los Molinos School, avoiding overheating has been as significant a design criteria as passive solar heating. Solar control is provided with a reflecting panel inside the slanted roof windows. This reflecting panel also serve the purpose of reflecting direct solar energy on to the interior thermal storage wall. The Haas building uses venetian blinds integrated into the window construction. On one side, these blinds are reflective to reject unwanted solar gains in summer, while on the other side they are dark-colored so that in winter they provide glare protection while retaining solar heat.

Thermally massive construction improves the use of passive solar energy, because surplus heat is stored from daytime to be used at night. This has been illustrated by modeling thermal properties of an office building in central Europe. The building modeled with high thermal mass could better use passive solar gains. The useful solar contribution was $55\,kWh/m^2$ versus $30\,kWh/m^2$ for lightweight construction, or an increase of 85%.

13.6 REFERENCES

13/6 Haas & Partners Office Building, IEA Task XI *Advanced Case Studies Seminar*, April 24, 1991, Oxford, Great Britain. Proceedings available from REPD, ETSU, Harwell Laboratory, Oxfordshire OX11 0RA (GB).

13/7 ENTE Building, IEA Task XI *Advanced Case Studies Seminar*, April 24, 1991, Oxford, Great Britain. Proceedings available from REPD, ETSU, Harwell Laboratory, Oxfordshire, OX11 ORA (GB).

14 Air Collector Systems

Fig. 14.1

14.1 INTRODUCTION

Using air to collect and transport heat offers many advantages over liquid-cooled collectors. Such systems are rare in Europe, as are air heating systems of any type. Large buildings, such as office buildings and schools, are more and more being constructed with mechanical ventilation systems. Further, given the increasingly well-insulated residential construction, the potential for greatest energy savings lies with mechanical ventilation with heat recovery from exhaust air. As more and more buildings are planned with mechanical ventilation systems, the possibility of integrating a solar air collector into the system becomes increasingly important.

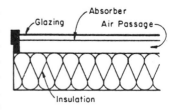

Fig. 14.2 Air collector design

14.1.1 Design

In an air collector, air is blown by natural or force convection over or through a sun-warmed 'absorber'. The resulting warm air can be used directly for ventilation (an open loop between the collector and room) or in a closed loop that may include thermal storage (Fig. 14.3). Heat storage, for example, a rock bed, increases the usability of solar gains of the air collector, in most situations. Chapter 19 provides additional information about thermal storage.

14.1.2 Air collector

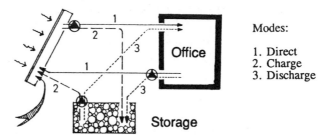

Modes:

1. Direct
2. Charge
3. Discharge

Fig. 14.3   Three modes of an air collector system

Fig. 14.4 Wall integrated collector

Advantages
Compared to conventional heating systems, air collector systems have several advantages: they can respond quickly in a direct air heating mode; they provide weather protection and can easily be integrated in a roof or facade; and they work as a warm envelope around a building in periods of low radiation.

Compared to water-cooled collectors, air systems can easily be integrated into ventilation and air heating systems, they present no frost or corrosion problems, and leaks are not catastrophic.

Disadvantages
The disadvantages of air collector systems are:

- Air collector systems may compete with window area.
- Careful detailing is required to minimize noise from fans and air movement.
- Fans require electricity.
- Air collector systems are difficult to combine with hydronic heating systems.
- Air ducts take up more space.
- Dust filters are required in open-loop systems.

Fig. 14.5 High volume flows require large ducts

14.2 SYSTEM VARIATIONS

14.2.1 Preheating ventilation air in a direct system (open loop)

Outside fresh air is warmed in a solar collector, and delivered to the room, from which it escapes by exfiltration, or via the mechanical system.

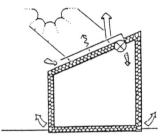

Advantages:
- simplicity
- ease of control

Disadvantages:
- only active when the building is ventilated

14.2.2 Room heating with direct heating system (open loop)

The room air is heated in an air collector, distributed within the house and returned to the collector.

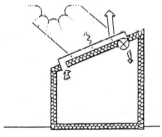

Advantages:
- simplicity
- ease of control
- quick reaction

Disadvantages:
- air movement in the room

14.2.3 Indirect heating system

Air circulates in a closed loop between the collector and channels in walls on floors which then radiate the heat into the room.

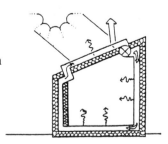

Advantages:
- no air movements

Disadvantages:
- high volume flow necessary
- slow reaction

Example: Meteolabor, following.

Fig. 14.6 System types

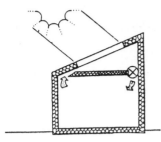

14.2.4   Positioning of collectors on a wall or roof

The glazed roof space is used as a collector.

Advantages: •   simple collector construction
Disadvantages: •   space required
Example: Kägie-Warehouse, following

14.2.5   Wall integrated solar chimney

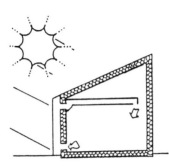

The difference in density of warm and cold air provides natural circulation through the collector.

Advantages: •   simplicity
                   •   self-activating
                   •   no auxiliary energy needed
Disadvantages: •   low collector efficiency due to low air flows
Example: Solar chimney, Ispra, following.

14.2.6   Closed loop system with storage and active discharge (see also Chapter 19, Storage Systems)

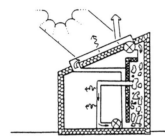

Fig. 14.6   System types

A room is heated by a radiant wall or floor area, which is connected directly to the collector. Surplus heat is used to charge the storage. At night or on overcast days, heat can be extracted by fan from the storage.

Advantages: •   high storage temperatures possible
                   •   controlled discharge (less room overheating)
Disadvantages: •   additional discharging system
                   •   more complex control system
Example: Schopfloch Kindergarten, Germany, following.

14.3   EXAMPLES

14.3.1   Schopfloch Kindergarten, Germany

The Schopfloch Kindergarten includes group rooms and a gymnastic hall. It is a single-storey, flat roof building with a shed in an east–west direction over the entire roof. The north side of the shed is glazed, daylighting the rooms. Large glazing walls on the west, south and east surfaces offer full views of the green surroundings.

     On the southern slop an air collector is fitted for space heating. 38 m^2 of air collectors are coupled to 20 m^3 of rock bed storage. Heat is discharged to the rooms through radiant floors and walls, similar to the hypocaust floors of ancient Roman structures.

Location:	Leonberg-Ezach, Germany
Latitude:	47° 50′
Gross volume:	805 m³
Surface areas	m²
Ground floor:	270
Envelope:	638
Walls:	200
Windows:	157

Window data

Orientation	Glazing distribution
East	70
West	52
South	61
North	31

Fig. 14.7 South-east view of the kindergarten

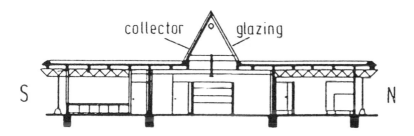

Fig. 14.8 North–south cross section of the building

Building services

The hot air floor and wall heating system has the advantage of low heating temperatures without the disadvantage of a direct air heating system, such as dry air or air movements.

Direct air heating without storage is also possible. If the solar collector output is lower than the heat demand, a gas-driven auxiliary heater supplies heat to a water–air heat exchanger. Solar gains which are not needed for heating are fed into a rock bed storage consisting of Serpentinit rocks 50 mm in diameter. An additional water–air heat exchanger allows wall surfaces to be overheated to heat rooms quickly in the morning. Flaps in the charging and discharging ducts of the storage prevent an uncontrolled discharge to the collectors or the heating system. Ventilation is provided by opening the windows.

Air collector	
Gross area	38 m²
Absorber area	28 m²
Storage	
Volume	20 m³
Thermal mass	15 kWh/K
Installed capacity	
Auxiliary heater	100 W/m²
Hypocaust fan	
Low	0.5 kW
High	2.5 kW
Collector fan	0.25 kW
Design room temperature	
	19.5°C

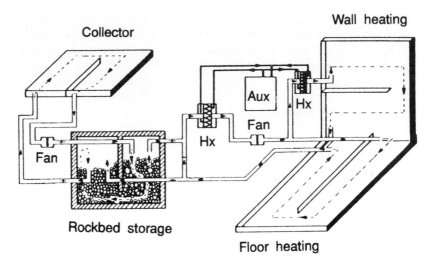

Fig. 14.9   The heating system

Control system

The solar and heating systems are regulated by a programmable control device. Heat from the air collectors or from the storage is given preference over heat from the auxiliary system. The hot air is heated further if the actual inlet temperature deviates from the required set point, which is influenced by the ambient temperature. The additional heater for the wall inlet air is activated if the room temperature falls below 19.5°C.

A sensor measures the temperature of the outlet air from the floor heat system, and the controller opens a bypass flap if this temperature exceeds the maximum storage temperature. Manually controlled ventilation flaps in the northern slope of the shed-roof allow individual conditioning in summer based on the users' requirements.

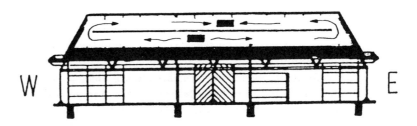

Fig. 14.10   Air flow through the collector

Air collector

The site-built air collector also serves as a roof covering. The absorber is black foil, with a solar absorption factor of $\alpha = 0.97$. Double polytetrafluoroethylene (PTFE) films are stretched over an aluminum grid structure below which is a gap of 150 mm through which air circulates. The transmission coefficient of the Hostaflon films (thickness 150 and 50 μm) is approximately $\tau = 0.9$ for solar radiation. For thermal radiation with a temperature range of up to 50°C, the transmission coefficient is $\tau = 0.02$, which is nearly opaque. These figures are valid only using new manufactured material. The aging process may degrade these values significantly. The underside of the collector is insulated with 100 mm glass wool. Since the aluminum grid supporting the covering films is the only thermally effective mass of the collector, it heats up quickly as radiation increases, so that short periods of sunshine can be utilized efficiently.

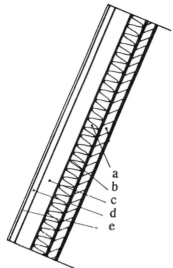

a: insulation (100 mm fiberglass)
b: absorber
c: air gap for circulation (150 mm)
d: aluminum grid
e: covers (2 Hostaflon films)

Fig. 14.11 Roof with integrated air collector

Collector measurements The coefficient of solar energy which is transferred through the covering and absorbed ($\tau\alpha$), can be calculated as 0.75, based on new material values and a measured decrease in transmission of 5% from dust and aging of the cover.

Figure 14.12 shows measured values for solar collector efficiency versus temperature difference between input air and ambient air. The collector efficiency curve shown was obtained using a linear regression. The intercept with the y-axis is defined as $F_R (\tau\alpha)$, with a value of 0.61. Consequently, the collector efficiency factor, F_R, can be calculated as $0.61/0.75 = 0.80$. This is a rather poor efficiency factor, due to the poor heat transfer between absorber and flowing air. The linear regression leads to an $F_R k_{eff}$-value of 5.4 W/m² K, resulting in a heat loss factor $k_{eff} = 6.8$ W/m² K. This is also a poor value for a double covering. Investigation showed that, after 12 months, the stretched films came to rest on each other in large areas, so that the double coverings were actually working a single glazing. Double films are not suitable for outside unless measures are taken to ensure that these covers are kept separated.

The thermal behavior of the system

Measured results of the air collector system show a strong inverse correlation between daily aailable global radiation and daily auxiliary heat consumption. This substantiates the fast response of the building with its low inferior thermal capacity. The total heat losses of the envelope, including transmission and infiltration, were measured in the range of 600 W/K, a high value, explained by the large glazing areas.

The direct connection between the collectors and the heating system works well, but there are some problems with storage. Flaps in the ducts to the collector were installed to prevent discharge of the heat

Definitions

η: efficiency of collector

F_R: collector efficiency factor

k_{eff}:   heat loss factor

t_i: collector inlet temperature (°C)

t_a: ambient temperature (°C)

E: global radiation on collector surface (W/m²)

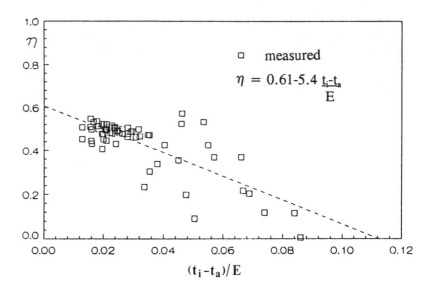

Fig. 14.12   Collector efficiency curve for a volume flow of 35 m³/h m²

Annual load	kWh
Heating season 88/99	
Auxiliary gas	20 500
Collector fan	190
Distribution fan	4 320
Lighting	670
Data acquisition control	1 560

from storage during the night through the collector. However, because they were not absolutely airtight, discharge from storage heat through the heating system created a vacuum in the storage. Cold air was then drawn from the collector to the storage, disturbing its temperature stratification.

Consequently, the following results show the behavior of the system with a nonfunctioning storage. Simulations predicted a solar fraction of 25% with storage and a fraction of 12% without storage for the active system. The latter value was verified by the measurements. Figure 14.13 shows energy consumption for space heating split into auxiliary energy and solar energy. The solar portion is calculated as the difference between the total calculated losses and the measured auxiliary energy consumption. Starting in January, the active solar portion was measured separately.

Solar energy provides a considerable part of the heat required through the winter. However, in late spring and possibly autumn, active and passive solar compete, making one of the systems redundant.

Reference

14/1   Schuler, M., The Schopfloch Kindergarten, *Advanced Case Study Report*, Task XI, REPD, ETSU, Harwell Laboratory, Oxfordshire OX11 0RA (GB).

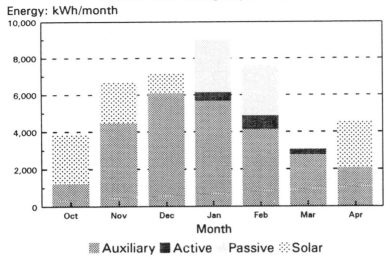

October 1988 through April 1989

Energy: kWh/month

Heat balance October 1988 through April 1989 (inclusive)
Auxiliary energy:
$$Q_{aux} = 27\,240\,\text{kWh}$$
Active (Q_{act}) plus passive (Q_{pas}) solar energy:
$$Q_{sol} = 15\,300\,\text{kWh}$$

Fig. 14.13 Energy consumption from different sources

14.3.2 Meteolabor, Switzerland

Location: Wetzikon, CH
Latitude: 47° 20'N

The multipurpose addition to the facilities of the firm Meteolabor AG, Zürich, Switzerland, incorporates solar air collectors and a greenhouse. Heat storage is provided by the building structure. A near-constant storage temperature of 20°C is achieved from October through April.

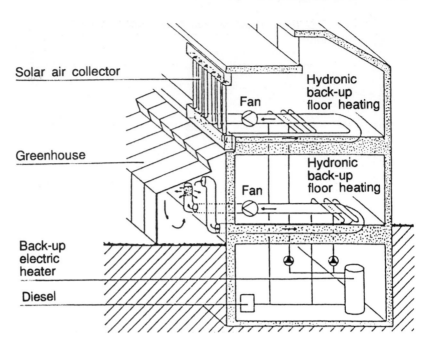

Fig. 14.14 Cross section showing the energy system

Greenhouse

Volume	126 m³
Floor area	50 m²
Glazing area	110 m²
Roof inclination	30%

Collector windows

Absorber volume	1.5 m³
Glazing area	27 m²

Storage

Volume	317 m³
Thermal mass	209 kWh/K

U-values — W/m² K

Walls	0.28
Roof	0.21
Windows	1.98

Building heat loss

320 W/K

Solar features

Solar heated air is provided from a greenhouse at ground level and by black metal tubes behind wooden-framed, double glazed panels on the upper level. In summer, the collectors are shaded by reflecting roller blinds. Small windows that open manually or mechanically reduce overheating in the greenhouse, which has no solar protection. The rooms are cooled by natural ventilation. The glazing is minimal, but the rooms still receive sufficient daylight. In the upper rooms, clerestory windows underneath the lean-to roof provide more light.

System control

All control functions (solar and auxiliary) are integrated in a sophisticated system that uses meterological data. Air flow rates for the air collectors and the greenhouse are regulated after temperature changes in the collectors and the storage. Auxiliary heating is controlled by an algorithm, which forecasts outside and inside air temperatures for the next two days according to the building's present conditions and the weather pattern of the past days. The blinds are automatically lowered over the air collectors and the fans stop if temperatures in the concrete floor rise above 25°C. Alarms prevent overheating the collector or the greenhouse; and the system prevents low temperatures in the greenhouse to protect the plants.

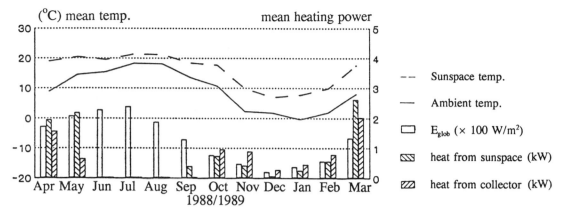

Fig. 14.15 Energy input and mean temperatures

Monthly performance

Figure 14.15 shows monthly mean values comparing greenhouse and air collector performance over a year. The vertical air collectors contribute more energy to the building from October to February when sun incidence angles are low. The collectors deliver a total of 5500 kWh and work with a mean seasonal efficiency of 55%. The greenhouse delivers the most heat to the building in spring (March through May) when energy demand still occurs and the sun angle is higher, improving the collection efficiency of the shallow 30° greenhouse roof slope. In winter, the poor insolation is usually just enough to heat the greenhouse; little excess heat can be transferred to the building. The heating efficiency of the greenhouse during the heating season is only 16%. This still amounts to 6500 kWh of heat delivered to the building.

Conclusions

Solar energy (active and passive) offers 60% of the total energy needs of this office building. Excellent insulation allows the remaining annual heating demand to be met by only 33 kWh/m² of auxiliary and process heat. The air collectors work satisfactorily; however, possible improvements might include:

- Multilayer Plexiglas, instead of insulating glass, would cost less and scatter light better. The absorbing tubes would then be more evenly irradiated.
- The use of aluminum tubes instead of steel tubes would provide more even heat distribution and better heat transfer.

The greenhouse can be considered as a good solution but it delivers little active energy to the building during the coldest winter months. Its ventilation capacity of 5800 m³/h (or 24 air changes per hour), however, proved to add value to the greenhouse as a solar air system.

This simple and comprehensive energy system requires the user to adjust to the seasons. For successful results, room temperatures should be in the range between 18°C and 24°C. Temperature differences from day to day and from one room to the other do not exceed 1°C.

Reference
14/2 *Advanced Case Study Report*, Office Building METEOLABOR AG, Greenhouse and Collector Solar Air Heating System IEA-TASK XI, ETH-Höggenberg, CH-8093, Zürich.

14.3.3 Kägi warehouse, Switzerland

Location:	Wintherthur, Switzerland
Floor area:	3250 m²
Volume:	32 000 m³

Fig. 14.16 The Kägi warehouse with roof collectors

The Kägi warehouse is a typical industrial hall, unheated, without insulation, and used for storing metal pipes and profiles. Half of the ground floor is elevated to make room for a basement with a 0.45 m thick concrete ceiling.

Gross collector area:	108 m²
Collector volume:	130 m³
Flow rate:	9400 m³/h
Storage capacity:	930 kWh/K

Natural air stratification made the cellar cold in winter and spring, leading to:

- condensation on and corrosion of the steel surfaces and
- frequent illness of workers due to the large temperature difference between hall and cellar.

These problems were solved by heating the cellar with solar warmed

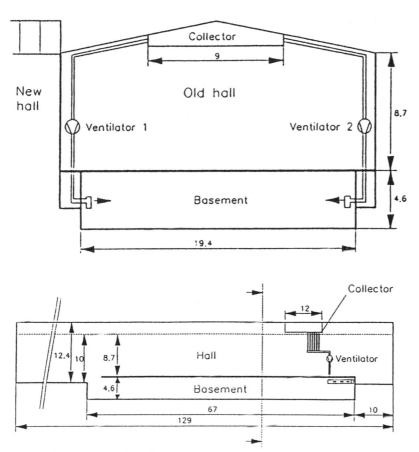

Fig. 14.17 Cross-section through the warehouse

air from a specially constructed attic under the hall roof. The attic is divided from the hall by a suspended lightweight ceiling, open at both ends, see Fig. 14.18.

Measurements of the building during the first heating period showed that the fans were rarely used, indicating a problem with the control system. Calculations and comparisons to the measurements showed that the control function of relative humidity was incorrect. Accordingly, the whole control system was changed. As of April 1989, the system has been controlled by calculating the actual dewpoint temperature of the collector air compared with the cellar temperature. Condensation is possible only if the cellar temperature, which is nearly that of the steel surface, is lower than the dewpoint temperature of air coming from the collector.

Conclusions and recommendations
It would be more cost effective to simply extract the air from under the roof without an additional ceiling. Generally, temperature

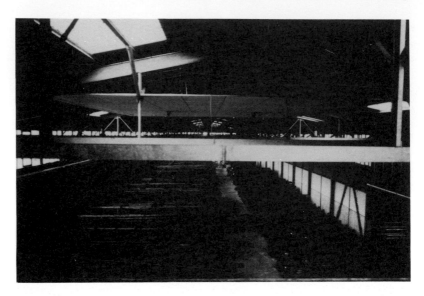

Fig. 14.18   The collector viewed from above

stratification is as good as with an insulated collector construction. However, a lightweight ceiling under the *whole* roof area with only small air inlets at either end of the hall would have many additional benefits.

- With a white painted ceiling, the light intensity and distribution in the hall would be improved.
- By fabricating the ceiling in the form of a rock-wool sandwich, it would thermally decouple the hall from the roof, thus avoiding extreme temperatures and improving the level of comfort.
- By separating the south-west and the north-east part of the roof by a lightweight partition, energy output could be increased, especially in winter.

In the present case, or when the hot air is collected directly under the roof, ventilation capacity is insufficient and should ideally be increased. Assuming, however, that collector construction were optimized as suggested above, the present ventilation capacity should prove sufficient for buildings of similar weight and volume. This would also have some useful side-effects on hall climate and is therefore preferred.

The time constant of the concrete storage mass (basement, ceiling and foundation) is calculated by extrapolation to be about one month.

The control system of the fans should ideally be based on measured dewpoint to prevent condensation, although dewpoint control is expensive. The project showed that if the system is working correctly and is controlled only by temperature difference and relative humidity, it is possible to keep the temperature level above the dewpoint at almost all times. This would make dewpoint control superfluous. Although this system is attractive in terms of cost, it represents a compromise between number of hours below dewpoint, amount of energy transferred and season of operation.

In general, the project showed that the concept of using solar heated air to raise basement temperature and reduce relative humidity was satisfactory. There is a considerable potential for such systems to heat basements used for storing a variety of industrial goods.

Reference
14/3 IEA TASK XI, Steel Warehouse Kägi, *Advanced Case Study Report*, Solararchitektur, ETH Höggenberg, CH-8093, Zürich.

14.3.4 Nautilus building, Ispra, Italy

Location:	Ispra, Italy
Latitude:	45° 48′ N
Areas (Block B)	m^2
Surfaces	6710
Windows	105
Roof shed glazing	200
U-values	W/m^{2}K
Walls	0.35
Windows	3.7

Fig. 14.19 South facade of the Nautilus building

This new office building of the Italian Agency of Nuclear and Renewable Sources of Energy (ENEA) incorporates a mixture of innovative solar technologies. The design objective was to achieve low energy consumption while testing the efficiency and reliability of different solar energy distribution and storage systems.

The south facade of the building was designed as an integrated solar chimney and window facade using prefabricated fiberglass-reinforced concrete components. The absorber is positioned 36 mm from the single glazing and 67 mm from the insulation, to increase heat extraction by doubling the heat exchange area. However, the overall collector

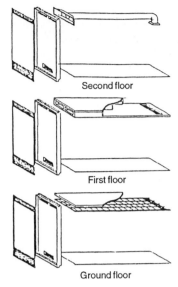

Second floor

First floor

Ground floor

Fig. 14.20 Solar chimney and heat distribution systems at different floors

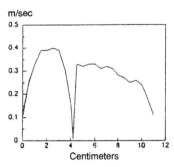

Fig. 14.21 Air velocity measured normal to the absorber plate at half height on the left side (15 March at 11:00)

performance is reduced from increased heat loss through the single glazing. The height of the solar chimneys is 2.62 m on the ground and first floor, and 5 m on the second floor where the laboratories are located.

Three different distribution and storage systems were installed. At the ground floor, hot air passes through an uninsulated false metal ceiling. A large flow area results. At the first floor, four ducts have been built into the concrete ceiling, one for each solar chimney.

Metal pipes suspended near the ceiling are used at the second floor. Warm air from the collectors passes through the rooms facing north. Air from openings in the lower parts of the doors returns to the solar chimneys. To avoid reverse circulation, mechanical dampers regulated by sensors are used. The same approach controls operational changes from winter to summer; in summer, ambient air is circulated through the solar chimneys to avoid overheating.

Performance of the solar chimneys
The distribution of air velocity on either side of the absorber plate is influenced by the plate's geometry and surface temperatures, as shown in Fig. 14.21. The ratio between the two air flows also changes according to the solar radiation values. When examining the air velocity profile for a high level of solar radiation ($700 \, \text{W/m}^2$) the profile is relatively flat for both channels, indicating the presence of turbulent air flow.

Efficiency
Figure 14.22 shows the efficiency values for the solar collectors with short and long channels. The performance of the solar strategy (i.e. collector and distribution system) is highly dependent on the hydraulic resistance of the circuit.

Metal pipes for air distribution
As mentioned previously, warm air from the chimneys flows through metal ducts to heat second floor spaces. The reason for this choice is that the rooms on this floor have a high ceiling. Convective heating would result in stratification of warm air high in the rooms. Radiant heating from the surface of the metal ducts was therefore considered a better strategy. The reduction of the air temperature in the ducts easily exceeds 10°C. However, this proved to be ineffective because the warm air tended to flow in the upper part of the tubes heating the ceilings rather than the space below where people work. One way to improve the performance of the system is to insulate the upper part of the tubes. Another solution is to add a vertical connection to the outlet with a small fan to send the warm air closer to the floor. Smoke tests have shown that the air at the outlet of the ducts flows down for only 0.2 m and then turns upwards.

Conclusions
- The natural effect of convection in the systems leads to air velocities measured in the air gap of up to 0.4 m/s. Recalculations of the thermosyphon effect lead to an optimal value of 0.9 m/s when only the chimney is measured.
- Measurements in the chimney duct system show a mass flow of 37 kg/h m² for the short channels.
- In the long channels, the mass flow drops due to the higher flow resistance. This decreases their efficiency by up to 50% as shown in Fig. 14.22.

Reference
14/4 Fumagalli, S. *The Solar Chimneys of the ENEA Bioclimatic Building at Ispra, Italy.*

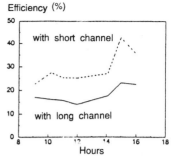

Fig. 14.22 Daily profile of the chimney efficiency

14.4 DETAILED RESULTS

A parametric study was done for the system installed in the Schopfloch Kindergarten, a closed loop system with pebble bed storage. The SIMUL program was used to simulate this solar-assisted HVAC system.

Table 14.1 System configurations

System-name	Collector field opened	Collector field closed	Mass flow* control	Storage type water	Storage type rock	Sys: air/water†
SYS01	x	—	x	—	—	—
SYS02	x	—	—	—	—	—
SYS03	—	x	x	—	—	—
SYS04	—	x	x	—	—	x
SYS05	—	x	x	—	x	—
SYS06	—	x	x	—	x	x
SYS07	—	x	x	x	—	x
SYS08	—	x	—	—	x	x

*Variable air flow depending on temperature and load.
†Additional hot water supply, air/water heat exchange.

The parameters that varied are: collector area, collector storage volume, storage characteristics and orientation of the collector. Various system configurations are studied, as shown in Table 14.1. Systems SY01 through SY04 are systems without storage, the first two being open loop systems and the other two closed loop systems. The data for the reference system is shown in Table 14.2.

Figure 14.23 shows that without a storage system the solar fraction of an air collector system for this building cannot exceed 10% of the heating demand in the Stuttgart climate. With a particular storage

Table 14.2 Reference system for parametric variations

Collector area:	38 m²
Storage volume:	20 m³
Storage capacity:	11 kWh/K
Collector/storage ratio:	1.4
Collector slope:	60°
Collector orientation:	south ($\phi = 0$)
Volume flow through the collector:	44 kg/h m² = 35 m³/h m²
Collector construction:	one pass, double glazed
Aspect ratio (l_K/b_K):	9.5
Duct length (non-insulated):	10 m
Heated area:	250 m²
Weather data:	Stuttgart

$$f_{GH} = \frac{Q_{sol,act}}{Q_{load}}$$

system, the solar fraction increases with the collector area. Compared to water, a rock bed is better suited for thermal storage in conjunction with solar air systems.

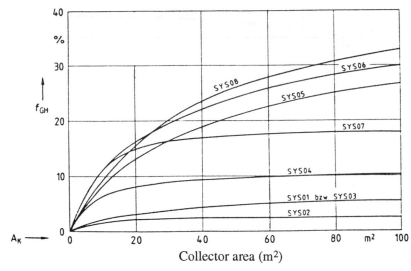

Fig. 14.23 Effect of the air system configuration on the solar fraction (f_{GH}) according to Table 14.1

type 4

type 3

type 2

type 1

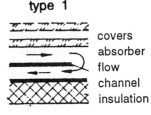

covers
absorber
flow
channel
insulation

Fig. 14.24 Collectors typed by air flow patterns

14.4.1 Collector design

In Fig. 14.25 the effect of variation in the collector design is shown. Types 1 and 2 are single-pass designs with air passing in front of or behind the absorber. Types 3 and 4 are two-pass designs. Type 3 has a parallel air flow in front of and behind the absorber. Type 4 uses preheating near the cover and a final heating in the absorber.

The ratio between the length l_K of the collector and the width b_K is an important parameter for air collectors. Also, double glazing ($n = 2$) is necessary for air collectors because, with the exception of type 3, the hot air is in direct contact with the inner cover. The type 2 collector results in the highest solar fraction (27%), followed by type 1 (24%). Type 4 is only advantageous for very short collectors.

14.4.2 Collector area/storage volume

Figure 14.26 shows the effect on the solar fraction when the capacity of a pebble-bed heat storage area is varied up to 17 kWh/K. This corresponds to a storage volume of aproximately 48 m³ with a rock density of $\rho_{St} = 2600$ kg/m³, heat capacity $c_{St} = 0.232$ Wh/kg K and ratio of rock volume to storage volume of $\chi_{Sp} = 0.43$.

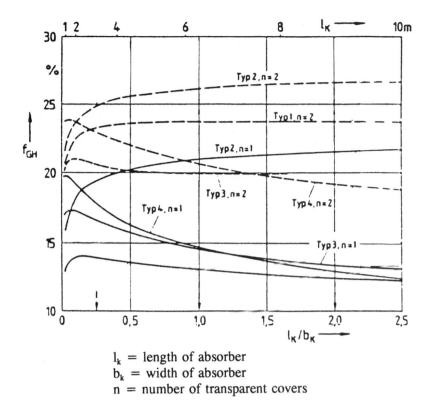

l_k = length of absorber
b_k = width of absorber
n = number of transparent covers

Fig. 14.25 Effect of the collector design number of covers and collector geometry (l_K/b_K) on the solar fraction (f_{GH})

For these analyses, the storage was designed as a cube. For a given collector area, the solar fraction at first increases with the storage capacity and then remains approximately constant with $C_{Sp,St}$ in the region analyzed here. An equation for the dimension of a pebble-bed storage are given based on empirical analysis of the results presented in Fig. 14.26.

storage capacity $C_{Sp,St}$ = collector area $A_K \times C_2$

where $C_2 \approx 0.066{-}0.078 \, kWh/K \, m^2$.

14.4.3 Collector orientation

The optimum orientation of the collector is facing south with an inclination close to the value of the geographical latitude. Steeper slopes of 60° are optimal for the winter period, when heat demand reaches its maximum (Fig. 14.27).

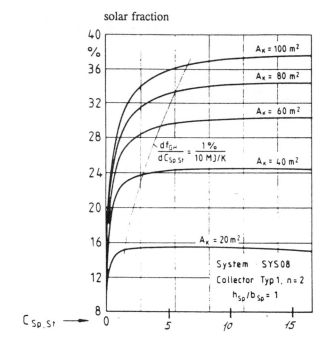

$$\frac{\mathrm{d}f_{\mathrm{GH}}}{\mathrm{d}C_{Sp,St}} = \text{optimum storage volume}$$

Fig. 14.26   Effect of rock-bed storage, capacity on solar fraction

14.4.4   Collector air speed

In Fig. 14.28, the influence on solar fraction of aspect ratio l_K/b_K is shown for varying collector area and mass flow rate. Longer collector fields (larger l_K/b_K) result in larger solar fractions. Furthermore, when the area increases, and when the length to width ratio (l_K/b_K) increases, a smaller mass flow rate can be chosen. For an area of $40\,\mathrm{m}^2$ and an aspect ratio of 0.05, corresponding to $l_K = 1.4\,\mathrm{m}$ and $b_K = 28\,\mathrm{m}$, an optimum air flow rate is $35\,\mathrm{kg/h\,m}^2$. For the same collector area and an aspect ratio of 2.5 ($l_K = 10\,\mathrm{m}$, $b_K = 4\,\mathrm{m}$) an air flow rate of only $25\,\mathrm{kg/h\,m}^2$ is preferable. Since the maxima are flat, this effect is relatively unimportant.

14.4.5   Duct length and insulation

Figure 14.29 shows that the heat capacity of ducts is of minor importance compared to the thermal insulation of the ducts. The influence of the thermal insulation rises proportionally to duct length. However, increasing the thickness of the insulation results in only a

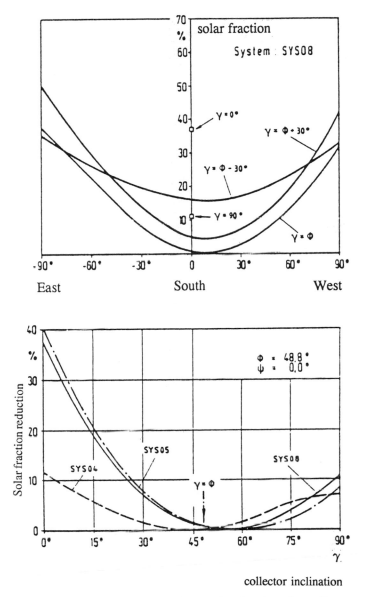

Fig. 14.27 The relative decrease of the solar fraction depending on the collector slope (γ) and the orientation (ϕ) of the collector field in Stuttgart

small increase of the solar fraction; e.g. for $l_P = 20\,\text{m}$ and $C_P = 1.11\,\text{Wh/K}\,\text{m}$, the solar fraction increases from 16.5% for the non-insulated duct to 22% for a layer thickness of 25 mm; a doubling of the thermal insulation layer to 50 mm results merely in an increase only from 22 to 23 in the solar fraction.

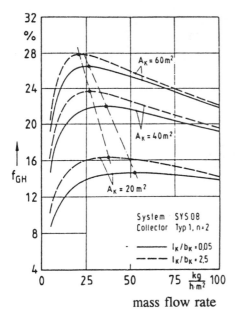

Fig. 14.28 Solar fraction versus mass flow rate for different collector areas (A_K)

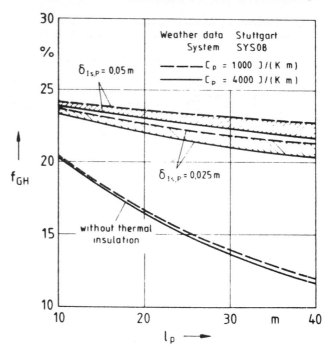

Fig. 14.29 Solar fraction as a function of the duct length (l_P), different thermal insulation thickness ($\delta_{Is,P}$) and heat capacity (C_P) of the air duct

14.4.6   Effect of climate

Figure 14.30 shows minimal effect on the solar-assisted system's contribution for different climates. The largest solar fraction occurs in Rome with its small heating load. In more northern climates with longer heating seasons the absolute solar contributions are greater. The total height of the columns is the total heating load covered by auxiliary and solar energy.

14.5   ANALYSIS TOOLS

14.5.1   SIMUL

Available for public use
Language and operating system: Fortran IV, IBM-compatible

Capabilities
Simulation of solar-assisted HVAC-systems, heating load of the building can be linked by an available data base or by given average UA values of the building.

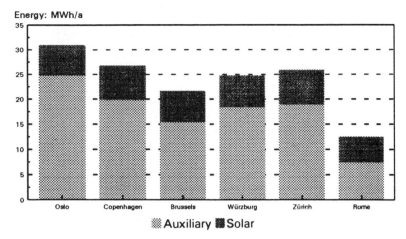

Fig. 14.30 Influence of the climate on the heating load and the solar input of the air-heated kindergarten

Brief description
Based on measured meteorological data, fixed building parameters and component parameters, the solar fraction is determined with the computer program SIMUL. This program is capable of considering four different air collector constructions and eight different system configurations. Hourly weather data parametric studies can be performed.

For more information, contact:

Dr M. N. Fisch
Institut für Thermodynamik und Wärmetchnik
Universität Stuttgart
D-7000 Stuttgart 80, Germany

14.5.2 TRNSYS

Available for public use
Language and operating system: Fortran 77, IBM-compatible

Capabilities
TRNSYS is a modular simulation program. It recognizes a system description language in which the user specifies the components that constitute the system and the manner in which they are connected. The TRNSYS library includes many of the components commonly found in the thermal (particularly solar) energy systems, as well as component routines to handle input of weather data or other time-dependent

forcing functions and output of simulation results. TRNSYS has been configured to facilitate users adding their own components to the library.

Brief description
It is not easy to create the input file for a simulation, but the hourly simulation time steps and the possibility to describe each component exactly yield results well corroborated with measured data.

For more information, contact:

  Solar Energy Laboratory
  University of Wisconsin, Madison
  1500 Johnson Drive
  Madison, Wisconsin 53706, USA

Cost: US $600

14.5.3   F-CHART

Available for public use
Language and operating system: Fortran 77, IBM-compatible

Capabilities
F-CHART is a versatile interactive computer program for the analysis and design of active, passive solar and heat pump heating systems. The self-explanatory program allows the user to describe a system easily and provides straightforward tables of performance results. Utilizing methods developed at the University of Wisconsin to estimate long-term average system performance, F-CHART features life-cycle analysis, system optimization and weather data handling capabilities.

Brief description
Based on monthly average weather data, the program calculates the monthly solar fraction, loads and auxiliary heating.

For more information, contact:

  Solar Energy Laboratory
  University of Wisconsin, Madison
  1500 Johnson Drive
  Madison, Wisconsin 53706, USA

Cost: US $600

14.6 CONCLUSIONS (CHECKLIST)

The following checklist, compiled from the examples, is useful when designing air collector systems.

- If possible, air collector systems should be integrated into HVAC systems.
- When combined with passive solar features, the air collectors should be connected to a heating system that responds quickly to temperature changes. Heavy structures connected directly to the heat emitting system, such as floor heating, decrease useful solar gains.
- To increase useful solar gains in air collector systems beyond 10–20%, a heat storage system is needed.
- In an air-collector loop providing 1 kWh heat, 0.04 kWh electricity is necessary to drive the fan.
- Collector ducts should be insulated.
- Airtight dampers must be used.
- In open-loop systems, the dewpoint of the air must be determined to anticipate condensation problems.
- In solar chimneys (vertically mounted air collectors) natural convection leads to air volume flows of up to $40 \, \mathrm{m^3/h}$ per $\mathrm{m^2}$ collector area.
- A two-path airflow around the absorber results in a higher collector efficiency.
- Material and construction (absorber and its fastenings) of the collector must withstand temperatures of up to $100^\circ \mathrm{C}$ in the collector.
- Plastic films without tension regulators are unsuitable for the bottom covering of collectors.
- If a roof space is used as an air collector, thermal decoupling of the occupied space is important to avoid overheating in summer.
- Effective use of excess heat from a sunspace requires a high air volume rate, which may be unsuitable to its occupancy.

14.6.1 System design

The following two equations are standards for the sizing of collector area and storage volume in a solar-assisted air heating system with a solar fraction of about 25%.

14.6.2 Collector area

$$\text{Collector area} = \frac{Q_{\text{load}}}{E_{\text{glob},h}} \times C_1$$

where:

Q_{load} = annual heat demand of the building (kWh/a)
$E_{glob,h}$ = annual global radiation on the horizontal (kWh/m^2 a)
C_1 = 2.0–2.5

14.6.3   Storage volume

Storage volume = collector area × C_2

where:

$C_2 = 0.30\,\text{m}^3/\text{m}^2$ collector area.

14.7   REFERENCES

14/5 *IEA Conference Paper on Air Collectors*, Utrecht 1988.

Contact: Novem BV: PO Box 8242
3505-Utrecht, Netherlands.

This is a collection of research done by IEA members in the field of air collectors, systems and storage. It provides an overview of the latest components and realized systems among international research organizations.

14/6 Gillett, W. G., *Solar Collectors, Test Methods and Design Guidelines*, Reidel, ISBN 90-277-2052-5.
This book is helpful for guidelines offered for the design of solar air and water collectors. The test methods are more interesting from a scientific point of view, but there are also good explanations of the different test methods used to evaluate collector data.

14/7 Garg, H. P., *Advances in Solar Energy Technology*, Vol. 1, *Collection and Storage Systems*, Reidel, ISBN 90-277-2430-X.
This reference book gives an overview of the advances in solar energy technologies during the last ten years. New collector types are described and judged for different applications. This book is a must for anyone working in the field of solar energy, collection and storage systems.

14/8 Fisch, N. M., *Systemuntersuchungen zur Nutzung der Sonnenergie bei der Beheizung von Wohngebäuden mit Luft als Wärmeträger*, ISBN 3-922-429-10-6, 1984.

Contact: Institut für Thermodynamik und Wärmetechnik, Universität Stuttgart Pfaffenwaldring 6,
7000-Stuttgart 80, Germany.

This dissertation is a thorough study of simulation work and validation by measurements in the field of air collectors and their application to room heating. The influences of numerous factors on collector construction, system parameters and loads are analyzed and the conclusions provide good guidelines. One result of this study is the simulation program SIMUL which is available for purchase.

14/9 Kublin, W., Krüger, E., Schuh K., *Handbuch der passiven Sonnenenergienutzung*, Schriftenreihe 04, *Bau- und Wohnungsforschung*, Heft Nr. 04.097, Munich, 1984.

Contact: Bundesministerium für Raumordnung,
         Bauwesen und Städtebau,
         Bad Godesberg Deichmanns Aue,
         D-5300 Bonn 2, Germany.

This handbook shows the spectrum of the passive use of solar energy. One chapter is about air collectors and explains the fundamental concept and several variations. Diagrams illustrate the influence of a number of collector and system parameters on the solar fraction for room heating.

15 Air Flow Windows

Fig. 15.1

Air flow windows have been known for more than a decade, originally used in Scandinavian countries. Successful applications are widespread, including most of the non-residential building types, such as hospitals. The primary goal in using air flow windows is to increase the energy efficiency of the window. Also important are comfort and the possibility of supplying fresh air. More recently, air flow windows have been used with thermal storage in residential buildings.

This chapter briefly describes different air flow window concepts and explores the possibility of using the windows as air collectors connected to a storage in non-residential buildings, such as office buildings and schools. The results are indeed promising.

15.1   INTRODUCTION

Air flow windows collect solar heat, transmit daylight, provide dynamic insulation and control overheating and glare. Applications exist in commercial buildings and schools as well as in residential buildings.

15.1.1   Design

An air flow window consist of a pair of spaced glazings: an exterior glazing (usually double glazing for better insulation) and an interior glazing separated by an air gap from the exterior glazing. For better thermal comfort, double glazing is also often used on the interior side. A solar absorber is located in the air gap. This absorber could be a venetian blind or solar absorbing roller blind. Depending on the design and mode of operation, air is circulated from the heated space, from the cold end of a storage unit or from outdoors through the air space between the glazing.

The solar absorber, heated by the sun, warms air passing it. The warm air is then returned through the ducts to the central HVAC system for redistribution or returned to a thermal storage or exhausted from the building. These variations are described in Section 15.2.

The heating efficiency of air flow windows is enhanced when the temperature of air supplied to the collector is low. If air is recirculated to the collector from the heated space or if it is supplied from the return end of a stratified rock bed storage unit, the air temperature is approximately 20°C. If fresh (outdoor) air is supplied, its temperature is often lower, so the collector efficiency is higher.

Air flow windows can also impede overheating, particularly when the absorber is cooled by outside air, which is then exhausted back to the ambient.

Figure 15.2 illustrates the influence of different positions of the absorber blind on the interior temperature distribution with variations in outside temperature and solar conditions. For an interesting comparison, the interior temperature is shown for a conventional window. The air flow window provides a more even temperature distribution, which deviates less from 20°C than the conventional window. The data shown

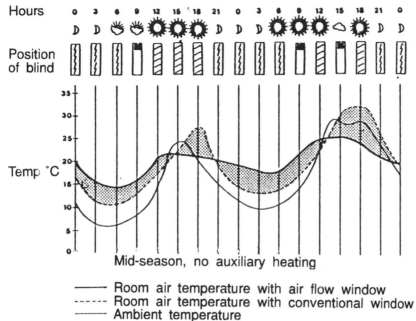

Mid-season, no auxiliary heating

——— Room air temperature with air flow window
------- Room air temperature with conventional window
——— Ambient temperature

Fig. 15.2 Interior temperatures in a low-mass room with air flow and normal windows

Fig. 15.3 Controlling daylight transmittance

Fig. 15.4 Open vent for cooling in summer

Fig. 15.5 Bulky air channels

are for a low-mass test cabin during the transition season (mid-season) temperatures without auxiliary heating.

15.1.2 Advantages

Air flow windows allow solar heat at its strongest to be collected and redistributed, or stored at times when conventional windows would require that sunlight be rejected. Storage allows the system to provide heat at least part of the time on overcast days. The blinds also provide privacy and control glare.

While solar conversion efficiencies in air systems are a few percent lower than in liquid systems, the advantages of warm air systems, compared with liquid systems, are freedom from freezing and corrosion hazards and a reduced possibility of damage resulting from leakage.

15.1.3 Disadvantages

The disadvantages of using warm air systems are that they are bulky, particularly with heat storage in rock beds and large conduits for air circulation. Electricity is necessary to drive a fan or ventilation system and careful design is required to minimize electricity consumption to run the system.

In central European climates, orientation of air flow windows is restricted to south (see Section 15.4) because overheating is a problem for east and west orientations during summer months.

15.2 SYSTEM TYPES

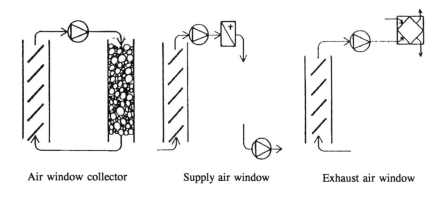

Air window collector   Supply air window   Exhaust air window

Three variations of air flow windows are defined, according to where air comes from and where solar heated air flows to:

- from collector to a storage is an air window collector,
- from outdoor directly to the room is a supply air window,
- from the rooms to the central HVAC system is an exhaust air window.

15.2.1 Air window collectors

This type of air flow window was built in a test cabin and then in several Swiss houses. It was investigated extensively by a group of Swiss engineers, architects and scientists beginning in 1979. The system is also used in commercial buildings; see the example of the Haas office building (Section 15.3.1).

The absorber is a venetian blind with a dark color on the outside, but not necessarily black. The inner surface may be bare/IR reflecting. The inner and outer glazing are preferably doubled to reduce heat losses to the ambient and to prevent higher inner surface temperatures.

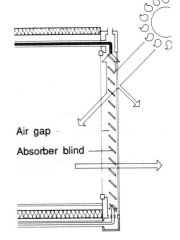

Air gap

Absorber blind

Fig. 15.6 Construction details of an air window collector

Four modes of operation are possible, according to the blind and damper positions.

Active collection
With the blind lowered and the fan in operation, most of the collected heat will be transported by the moving air to the storage. Only a small amount of direct radiation together with some heat from the warm inner glazed surface enters the room directly.

Direct gain
When the radiation does not reach a certain level, i.e. when direct sunlight to the heated space is acceptable, the blind is raised and the fan stops.

Night mode
The blind is lowered to reduce heat loss through the window and electrically operated dampers are closed to prevent reverse flow from the storage through the collector.

Summer mode
The blind is lowered with its reflecting side facing the outside. Outdoor air cools the blind preferably by thermosyphon to reduce electricity consumption.

15.2.2 Supply air windows

The use of air flow windows is reported both from France (fenêtre ventilée, ASOLBA) and Finland, where they have been studied since the 1940s. More recently, supply air windows are also known as fresh air daytime heaters in the Netherlands. Numerous apartment blocks equipped with mechanical exhaust ventilation systems use these systems. The most common modes of operation are described below

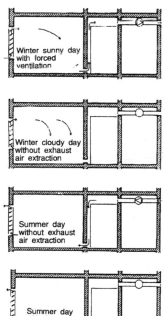

- On sunny winter days, the window preheats ventilation air. Forced ventilation extracts air from rooms facing south and fresh air is introduced by the supply air window. Intake air temperature is regulated by a fan.
- On cloudy winter days, the fresh air supply is stopped and room air is recirculated.
- In summer, the air circuit is inverted and exhaust air passes through the supply air window to the outside using cold air from the north zone of the building.
- During summer days with less sunshine, exhaust air extraction is stopped.

For all modes, the absorber blind remains closed, but its angle of inclination may change.

Fig. 15.7 Different modes of operation of a supply air window

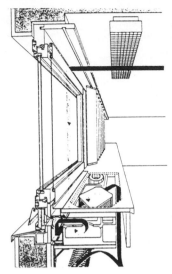

Fig. 15.8 ISAL exhaust air window

15.2.3 Exhaust air windows

Exhaust air windows were developed in the early 1970s by EKONO in Finland. The special construction of the exhaust air window makes it possible to use maximum solar radiation falling on the window. A downward ventilated window with the heat recovery unit placed below the window panes is known in Switzerland as the ISAL system.

In contrast to several modes of operation of the supply air window, exhaust air windows always run in a single operation mode: air is distributed with a ventilation system throughout the building and exits each room through a narrow slot at the bottom edge of the inner window pane. The room air is drawn up between the panes of the exhaust air window and is collected into the air recirculation ducts. The air, which is warmed both from the sun and from the heat losses of the room, is then transferred to a heat recovery unit or extracted from the building in summer.

Because the movable blind between the glass panes is operated manually, heat collection is subjected to the influence of the users.

Exhaust air windows are found in external walls of all orientations, especially in northern countries. Winter solar energy is scarce in these countries, which demonstrates that these windows provide comfort even at low outdoor temperatures.

15.3 EXAMPLES

15.3.1 Haas office building, Jona, Switzerland

Site and building description
Most air window collector applications in Switzerland are in private homes, but one exception is the Haas office building. All windows are oriented south to utilize passive solar energy. During the night, heat loss through the windows is reduced via manually operated insulating shutters. The Haas Office building is also described in Chapter 13, Direct Gain.

Solar strategy

Glazed collector area:	41 m^2
Specific air flow rates:	
	18 or 43 m^2/h m$^2_{coll}$
Fan power:	6.5 or 15.4 W/m$^2_{coll}$
Storage volume:	60 m^3

The building is equipped with a relative large collector area of 41 m^2 which faces south. The collector is connected through ducts to an under floor rock-bed with a volume of 60 m^3.

The air window collector is composed of two double glazings with a venetian blind in between. A two-speed fan circulates air through the collector at high or low speed, depending on the absorber temperature. During the night, interior insulation shutters are manually lowered over the windows.

Location:	Jona, Switzerland
Latitude:	47° 15 N
Altitude:	500 m
Heating degree days:	3370 dd
Heated floor area:	213 m²

Fig. 15.9 Haas office building

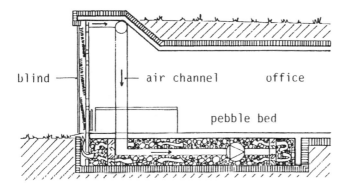

Fig. 15.10 Cross-section through solar system in Haas office building

Summary of results
The system has been monitored, with the following results:

- The average collector efficiency is 39% for the entire heating season (Table 15.1).
- Temperatures are comfortable, despite the rather large collector area (see Fig. 15.11).
- The annual auxiliary heat requirement of the building is extremely low: less than 14 kWh/m² of floor area. This is about one-tenth the value of a conventional multi-storey office building in Switzerland with moderate ventilation load.

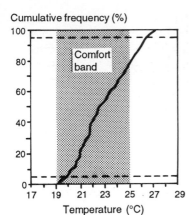

Cumulative frequency (%)

Fig. 15.11 Cumulative frequency of room air temperatures during active collection mode (September through April)

- Electricity consumption for artificial lighting is increased by approximately 15% compared to direct gain windows.
- The storage volume proved to be too large by a factor of two or three, and consequently the storage temperatures remained quite low.

Detailed analysis of the performance of the collector over the heating season in 1988/89 gave the results shown in Table 15.1.

Table 15.1 Monthly energy collected and hours of operation in the active mode

Month	Solar radiation on the collector (kWh)	Collector gain (kWh)	Collector efficiency	Hours of fan operation	
				low	high
September	1730	587	0.34	28	40
October	1738	739	0.43	39	5
November	1535	627	0.41	32	34
December	591	257	0.43	27	4
January	989	459	0.46	37	12
February	1038	362	0.35	45	6
March	1062	349	0.33	30	16
Total	8683	3380	0.39	238	162

For the active mode, the energy collected amounts to 3380 kWh or 85 kWh/m$^2_{coll}$. However, because of significant storage losses to the ground and heat supplied to the office rooms when not needed, the useful energy supplied to the room was only one-fourth of the collected solar energy (850 kWh).

Energy consumption for the fan was 173 kWh, which is small compared to the collected solar energy of 3380 kWh.

15.3.2   Ekono office building, Otaniemi, Finland

Glazing:
U-value = 2.0–0.4 W/m^2 K depending on the air flow and blind position
Specific air flow rate: 45 m^3/h m$^2_{coll}$

Site and building
The EOKONO building in Otaniemi, Finland, consists of three blocks, each incorporating energy conservation ideas from construction phases during 1973 through 1988. Exhaust air windows are an essential feature in each of these blocks; the windows are aluminum framed in the first block and aluminum-cladded wood frames in the second and third blocks. The building has a total floor area of 18 000 m^2 and a volume of 66 000 m^3.

When designing these systems, the two most important criteria for the windows were both collection of the scarce winter solar energy and comfort provided at very low outdoor temperatures.

Fig. 15.12 EKONO office building in Otaniemi

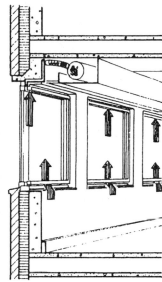

Fig. 15.13 Construction details of the exhaust air window

Solar strategy (OTA II)
- The typical exhaust air window has double glazing to the exterior, single glazing to the interior and venetian blinds in between.
- The effective U-value varies from 2.0 to 0.4 W/m²K depending on the air flow and blind position. It is negative if collected solar energy is calculated as a heat benefit.
- During hours of sunshine, a temperature rise of 15–20 K in the air flow of the south window is achieved. The temperature rise is much smaller for other orientations, and windows facing north always cool the air flow.

Summary of results
Energy fluxes during periods of high insolation levels are shown in Fig. 15.14 for the exhaust air window of the OTA II type. Approximately half of the incident solar radiation heats the air going into the recirculation system. Only a small fraction enters the room as direct radiation. This fraction may be larger depending on the construction and position of the blind.

15.4 SIMULATION STUDIES

Recommendations for design combine information from parametric studies on a hypothetical school building and from data and simulation results collected from the Haas office building.

The studies are restricted to air window collectors. The computer model TRNSYS was used for the simulations. Although the results

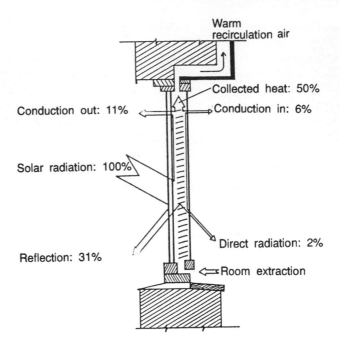

Fig. 15.14 Energy fluxes in exhaust air window

apply only for Swiss climate north of the Alps, they may also be used for other mid-European climates.

15.4.1   Building type characteristics used in parametric studies

For all parametric variations, including the reference case, a $70 \, \text{m}^2$ floor area classroom is used. The room is very well insulated, the specific heat loss coefficient being $0.9 \, \text{W/m}^2\text{K}$ for the heated floor area. Except for the south facade and the roof, all other walls are connected to adjacent rooms. The air change rate is $1.0 \, \text{h}$ during occupation and 0.25 during the rest of the day. The building site has full sunlight exposure with no shading by neighboring buildings or trees.

The occupancy pattern is from 9:00 to 12:00 in the morning and from 13:00 to 18:00 in the afternoon. Unoccupied rooms during school holidays and weekends are taken into account. When occupied, the heat setpoint is 20°C, whereas cooling starts at 26°C. The control of building services and operation of the air window collector respond to the incident radiation. The blinds close when a vertical south radiation of $350 \, \text{W/m}^2$ is reached. Artificial light is turned on when the radiation is less than $200 \, \text{W/m}^2$. The climate for the 1981 heating season in Geneva was used.

15.4.2 Base case (air window collector)

A base case was defined from practical experience. The total amount of auxiliary energy (heating including ventilation, and cooling; electricity consumption for lighting and fan operation) was calculated for different design variations. The building's auxiliary energy consumed with the air window collector system was compared to that of the same building with direct gain south facing windows (reference case).

The base case starts with 17 m² of glazed outer collector area per 100 W/K heat loss. The storage volume was chosen according to standards developed for residential applications.

Design proposal for base case (window air collector):

Active mode: above 350 W/m² global vertical south radiation

Glazed outer surface:
    17 m² per 100 W/K heat loss

Volume air flow rate: 65 m³/h m²$_{coll}$

Storage size: 0.8 m³/m²$_{coll}$

Passive discharge to heated room:
    $U = 1.2$ W/m²K

15.4.3 Reference case (direct gain)

The direct gain windows in the reference case have an area of 7.2 m² and are equipped with double, low emissivity glazing and appropriate shading.

Design proposal for reference case (direct gain)

Glazed window area: 7.2 m²

U-value: 1.6 W/m²K

Shading factor: 0.3 above 350 W/m²

15.4.4 System configuration

From experience with air window collectors in residential buildings, a number of factors determine the success of solar energy use. These parameters were selected for variation in this study, and are shown in Table 15.2.

15.4.5 Collector construction and size

The number of glazings and the characteristics of the air flow passing the absorber were studied with algorithms. The shape of the absorber and the air gap geometry could not be examined.

Table 15.2 Summary of parameter variations

Parameter		Base case	Variations*
Collector area (m²)		10.2	6, 8, 14, 18
Collector construction (Fig. 15.16)		venetian blind	roller blind†
Glazing	inner	2	1
	outer	2	1
Orientation		S	W, SW, SE, E
Air flow (m³/h m²$_{coll}$)		65	90, 50, 40, 25
Storage size (m³/m²$_{coll}$)		0.8	0.3, 0.6, 1.1, 1.35

*Only one parameter is varied at a time, other parameters are base case values
†The roller blind variation is run also with a varying collector area, i.e. 6, 8, 10.2, 14 and 18 m²

Figure 15.16 shows the heat consumed for different variations of the collector area. The figure shows only a small influence on heating consumption in the range studied for the standard configuration (2IV/2IV/Type A). The configuration (2IV/2IV/Type B) based on lower heat transfer properties of the absorber is of lower efficiency. Solutions with a single window pane, either on the interior or outer side, proved clearly less energy efficient than the standard configuration.

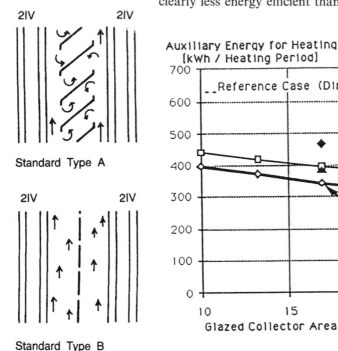

Fig. 15.15   Absorber construction

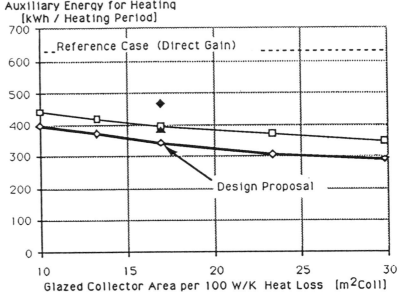

Fig. 15.16   Influence of collector size and construction on heating consumption

15.4.6   Collector orientation

Figure 15.17 shows the effect of varying the collector orientation, and that within ± 30° of south, useful solar gains will remain approximately constant. In some climates, the effect of morning fog must be considered.

As expected, the orientation of the collector also influences artificial light consumption to a great degree, as shown in Fig. 15.18. For east and west orientations, overheating in summer should receive special consideration, since protection at low solar elevation angles is difficult.

15.4.7   Air flow rate through the collector

Turbulent flow is desirable because it increases heat transfer. Air window collectors with venetian blinds provide turbulent flow on both sides of the absorber.

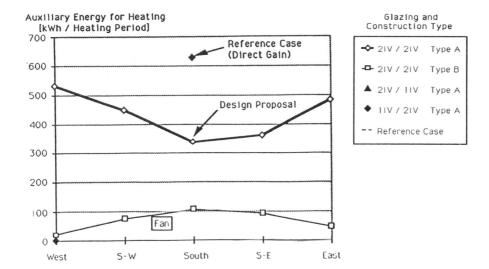

Fig. 15.17   Influence of collector orientation on heating consumption

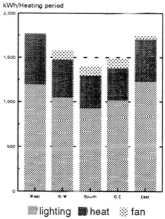

kWh/Heating period

lighting   heat   fan

Fig. 15.18 Influence of collector orientation on fan energy, heating and artificial light consumption

The efficiency of air window collectors is enhanced when the temperature of the air supplied to the collector is low. If air is recirculated to the collector from the heated space or if it is supplied from the return of a stratified rock bed storage unit, its temperature is approximately 20°C. At a flow rate of approximately 65 m^3/h m$^2_{coll}$ and a supply temperature of 20°C, an efficient collector will heat the air to 40–50°C with full sunshine. A typical temperature difference between the absorber and the air is 20 K.

Energy consumption for fan operation is also shown in Fig. 15.20. In the parametric studies, variation of heat removal factor F_R with air flow rate is factored with variation of the air flow rate. The influence of the heat removal factor on collector gains is larger than the effect on auxiliary energy shown in Fig. 15.21, which also includes the effect of the thermal storage. The designer must compromise between larger air flow rates (higher collector efficiency) and energy consumption for the fans.

Heat removal factor F_R

air flow (m^3/h m$^2_{col\ 1}$)	F_R
25	0.55
40	0.68
50	0.73
65	0.80
90	0.82

15.4.8   Influence of storage volume

Storage volume is determined by the collector area, hence the commonly used term 'storage volume/collector area ratio'. In the design proposal

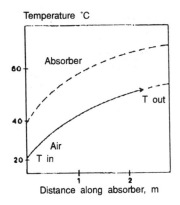

Fig. 15.19 Temperature along the absorber

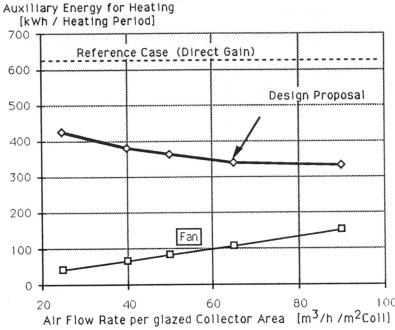

Fig. 15.20 Influence of air flow rate on heating consumption

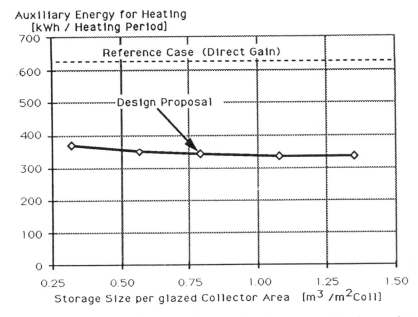

Fig. 15.21 Influence of storage volume on heating consumption for passive discharge mode

for the classroom, a storage volume/collector area ratio of $0.8 \, \mathrm{m^3/m^2_{coll}}$ was assumed. This ratio applies for a pebble bed storage with a heat capacity of approximately $400 \, \mathrm{W \, h/m^3 \, K}$.

The model used for parametric studies only allows storage volume to collector area ratios down to $0.25 \, \mathrm{m^3/m^2_{coll}}$. This limitation influenced the range of auxiliary energy for heating in Fig. 15.21, showing that the influence of storage volume on system performance is not very significant. Other computations on air collector systems, in Chapter 14, show that the storage capacity should not be less than $0.3 \, \mathrm{m^3/m^2_{coll}}$. For information about different storage configuration and discharge modes, see Chapter 19, Storage.

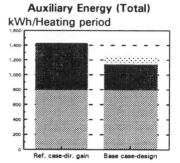

Auxiliary Energy (Total)
kWh/Heating period

Light Heating
Cooling Fan

Fig. 15.22 Energy consumption October through March

15.4.9 Energy and comfort

In the preceding paragraphs the influence of important design parameters on the heating energy consumption have been discussed. These conclusions are reflected in Fig. 15.22. Importantly, the air window collector system (base case) performs slightly better than the direct gain (reference case) in the schoolroom studied. Auxiliary heating consumption is further reduced, and with proper shading, no cooling is needed in the direct gain case.

Comfort is important when using air window collectors. Protection from glare is usually satisfactory and daylighting is only critical on overcast days. Generally thermal comfort with air flow windows is equal to or better than with ordinary windows, because the indoor glass cooled by the air flow radiates less than ordinary indoor glass. This applies when comparing clear ordinary glass with clear air flow windows, or shaded ordinary windows with shaded air flow windows. In these simulations, the room air temperatures were slightly higher when using air window collectors compared to the direct gain reference case, because no additional shading was used in the window collectors. In the reference case, a room air temperature level of 26°C was never reached.

Table 15.3 Number of hours exceeding comfort temperature level for the base case.

	Hours above	
	24°C	26°C
October	326	5
November	405	17
December	0	0
January	0	0
February	0	0
March	208	44
October to March	939	66

15.5 ANALYSIS

15.5.1 PC tools

LESO SAI-X

Capability The program provides monthly calculations of heating and cooling loads for buildings with direct gain, sunspaces, atria, building integrated air collectors, and double envelope and Trombe walls. It gives graphical output, which are optimal for solar components.

Available with handbook in French or German. Runs on IBM-compatible PCs with a minimum of 640 kbytes of memory and hard disk.

Contact: LESO-PB
        EPFL
        CH-1015 Lausanne, Switzerland

SIA-BEW-Doku 10

Capability The program offers monthly calculations of heating and cooling load for buildings with direct gain, sunspaces, atriums or air window collectors. There are ninety climatic stations in Switzerland. Output is in tables and graphs; with details on components available.

Available with handbook in German language. Based on Supercalc 5 spread sheet program. Runs on IBM-compatible PCs with a minimum of 2 Mbytes of memory.

Contact: EMPA-KWH
        CH-8600 Dübendorf, Switzerland

TRNSYS-PC-Version

Capabilities This program gives simulation of thermal (particularly solar) energy systems, with hourly time steps. TRNSYS is a modular program which offers users the option to add components. A set of components has been developed and validated for the simulation of air window collectors. A graphical front end, called PRESIM, supports the user to create the input file.

Operating language is Fortran 77, running on an IBM-compatible PC.

Contact: TRNSYS
        Solar Energy Laboratory
        University of Wisconsin, Madison
        1500 Johnson Drive
        Madison Wisconsin 53706, USA
        Cost: US $900

        Air Window Collector Modules

        Basler & Hofmann Energy Research Group
        Forchstrasse 395
        CH-8029 Zürich, Switzerland

15.5.2   Mainframe tools

TRNSYS
The mainframe version of TRNSYS offers similar capabilities to the

PC version. The only major drawback is that the graphics front end PRESIM only runs on a PC, so to use PRESIM, the TRNSYS input file must be created on a PC and then TRNSYS is run on the mainframe.

15.6 CONCLUSIONS

When an air window collector system is designed, several decisions must be made concerning the collector size and glazing, air circulation and storage. The decisions affect daylight transmittance, solar heat collection, overheat protection and dynamic insulation. These factors are briefly discussed below.

15.6.1 Natural light transmittance

In air window collectors the transmission factor may be adjusted by adjusting the tilt of the venetian blinds. At a 45° inclination approximately 7% of the incident radiation will pass through a collector facing south with double glazing on inner and outer side and a shading factor of the absorber of 0.15. Since in the active collection mode the incident radiation is higher than 350 W/m² there will be at least 25 W/m² behind the window with tilted blinds, enough to give 500 lux at 2 m from the window.

15.6.2 Solar heat collection

Measured data and TRNSYS simulations were used to determine the energy balance for an air window collector for the heating period. For domestic applications the value is approximately 140 kWh/m²$_{coll}$. For office buildings and schools, it is lower (105 kWh/m²$_{coll}$) because of the higher contributions of free heat from lighting and occupants (see Fig. 15.23). The times of occupancy also affect collector efficiency.

When sizing the collector, 1 m² of glazed collector area per 7 m² of heated floor area is a reasonable value. For good insulation, this gives 17 m² of collector per 100 W/K of heat loss.

15.6.3 Solar protection

The efficiency of shading is expressed by the shading factor. In air flow windows this factor can be adjusted, which is a great advantage. With venetian blinds inclined at 45° and double glazing on the inner and outer side, the shading factor is 0.07, which means that 7% of the incident energy is transmitted as light. Increasing the air flow rate will

Recommendations

1. Allow for sufficient natural light transmission

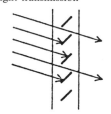

2. Use this ratio of collector area to heated surface area

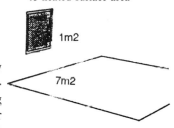

3. Include conventional windows for natural ventilation

4. Avoid overheating by using orientations other than west

5. Use either fixed or movable exterior solar protection

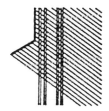

6. Use double glazing on inner and outer surface for better thermal insulation

7. Use this collector to storage ratio for passive discharge:

1 m²   0.8 m³

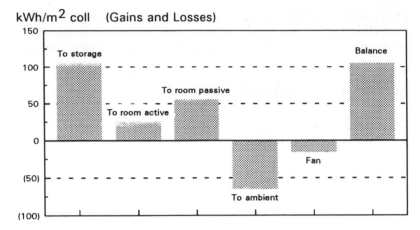

Fig. 15.23 Energy balance of air window collector in schools and office buildings in typical Swiss climate (Geneva) for October until April (all values are in kWh/m^2_{coll})

decrease the temperature of the internal glass, and therefore reduce the cooling load and improve thermal comfort. Additional external protection for summer months is recommended in mid-European climates.

15.6.4   Dynamic insulation

Air window collectors with double glazing on the inner and outside surface and a wooden frame have a U-value of approximately $1.4 \, W/m^2 \, K$. The air flow strongly influences the U-value and therefore no heat loss from the room to the outside occurs during active heat collection periods. The average effective U-value is approximately $0.9 \, W/m^2 \, K$ at an air flow rate of $65 \, m^3/h \, m^2_{coll}$ during all hours, including at night.

15.6.5   Applications

The analyses performed demonstrates that active solar heat collection with air window collectors and short-term storage is a good alternative to direct gain through windows. Applications for office buildings, schools and hospitals promise good results.

15.7 REFERENCES

15/1 Haas K., Brühwiler D., *Erdbedecktes Bürohaus*: *Ergebnisse eines Messprojektes*, Haas & Partner AG, Jona.

Contact: Solararchitektur
              ETH Hönggerberg
              CH-8093 Zürich, Switzerland

15/2 Seppänen O., Windows as cost effective solar collectors, *Proceedings of the National Passive Solar Conference*, American Section of ISES, 2400 Central Ave., Boulder, CO 80301, USA, 1981.

16 Mass Wall Systems

View into the mass wall at FUL auditorium building in Arlon, Belgium

A mass wall system combines collection, storage and transport of solar energy in one unit, a 'glazed wall'.

When a building also requires heat at night, an ideal solar strategy should include thermal storage. The mass wall allows the building to work simultaneously as a solar collector and as a storage device. Conversely, active solar storage strategies function independently of the solar collection function.

A mass wall is particularly well suited for commercial buildings that have a significant heat load during night-time compared to daytime because release of heat from the mass at night can help meet the night heat load, avoiding or minimizing the need for auxiliary heating.

16.1   INTRODUCTION

The mass wall is a passive solar concept providing three different functions simultaneously.

1. The mass wall collects solar energy, as a classic active solar collector, especially when well-oriented (see Fig. 16.1).
2. Solar energy is absorbed in the wall, and the surface temperature increases, thereby also raising the temperature of the buffer space.
3. The heat which is absorbed in the wall is slowly conducted through the wall to the heated rooms of the building. The short-term storage wall provides energy in the wall material. Simultaneously, the air can be transported from the buffer space to the heated rooms, either passively through natural circulation, or actively through mechanical ventilation. A vented mass wall is called a 'Trombe wall', after Felix Trombe, the architect who designed and built the system for the first time in southern France.

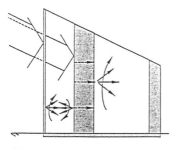

Fig. 16.1   Mass wall

16.1.1   Advantages

*   The mass wall is a simple solar collector, and glare problems are avoided inside the building when the solar gains are collected.
*   The high thermal inertia of the mass wall reduces the temperature extremes in the occupied part of the building.
*   The storage function of the device induces a time shift between energy collection and utilization. In commercial buildings this may mean that the building can go unheated at night.
*   The glass is a weather protection for the wall.

16.1.2   Disadvantages

*   Daylight may be reduced as the mass wall competes with window area.
*   If the windows are too small and the contrast is too great between the dark wall and glazing in the same wall, the mass wall can produce glare.
*   The large glazed area requires cleaning.
*   The mass wall complicates control of the auxiliary heating and cooling systems.

Fig. 16.2   Trombe wall

16.2   SYSTEM TYPES

16.2.1   Interior windows in the mass wall

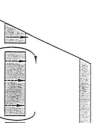

Interior windows in the mass wall (Arlon building) allow direct daylighting and solar gain via the mass wall facade; however, the effective area and storage volume decrease.

16.2.2   Orientation of wall

If the wall is not parallel to the glazing, absorption area and storage volume increase relative to the glass area. This may partially compensate lost mass wall area occupied by windows penetrating the wall.

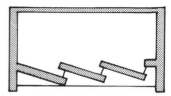

16.2.3   Vented mass wall (Trombe wall)

When the mass wall is vented naturally or mechanically, solar energy is transferred to the building faster and with greater efficiency. The storage effect of the system is decreased, and the time lag between collection and use of solar energy reduced. The Looe school has a naturally vented mass wall.

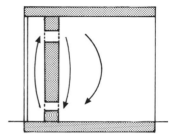

16.2.4   Dimensions of the buffer space

The buffer space can be made wide enough to allow easy cleaning of the glazing (Arlon building). The space can even be enlarged to form a sunspace, but often one that is expensive to maintain because it is a solar collector, which is normally either too hot or too cold in which to be comfortable.

16.2.5   Shading devices

Movable solar protection in front of the wall allows active control of the system to avoid overheating during hot days and to reduce heat loss during the night (Arlon building). Movable solar protection increases total costs, but it can be necessary for comfort.

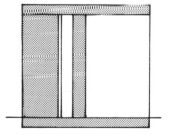

16.2.6   Insulated mass wall

In the case of a vented mass wall (Trombe wall), the wall may be insulated to reduce heat loss from the building. The active storage mass is the only mass on the outer part of the insulated material, but discharge of the mass can be controlled by regulating the air flow with dampers and possibly a fan.

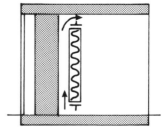

16.3   EXAMPLES

16.3.1   Auditoires FUL

Location: Arlon, Belgium

Building data

Volume: m³
  Gross   2260
  Heated   1988

Floor area: m²
  Gross   666
  Heated   570

Surface areas: m²
  Ground floor   425
  Roof   482
  Wall (excl. windows)   450
  Windows   154

66% of south facade is glazed

Degree-days (base 20)
Brussels:

Oct. to Apr. inclusive   3060
Annual: 3754

Horizontal solar radiation: kWh/m²
Oct. to Apr. inclusive: 320
Annual: 960

Installed space heating capacity:
                               190 W/m²

Insulation:

- N/E/W Walls 120 mm mineral wool
- Roof 200 mm mineral wool

Description of the building

The auditorium building of the Fondation Universitaire Luxembourgeoise in Arlon was completed in 1986. It is two stories high with amphitheaters, offices and meeting rooms. The building design includes a large glazed area facing south separated from a storage wall by a buffer space in the two side zones (mass walls), and a central zone in which a horizontal concrete slab allows accumulation of solar energy through direct gain (Fig. 16.3).

The heavy building structure reduces temperature extremes. Daylighting is achieved through the integration of interior windows within the mass wall and by choosing a design in which the wall and the glazing are not parallel. This allows daylight in without loss of mass wall area.

A gas-fired boiler supplies heat to the rooms by two independent radiator circuits. Three different levels of control are provided:

1. A thermostat controls the temperature of the boiler.
2. In each circuit, the temperature is controlled with a motorized three-way valve according to the temperature in the amphitheaters.
3. Each radiator is locally controlled by a thermostatic valve.

Heat usually runs continuously from 06:00 or 08:00 in the morning until 18:00 or 20:00 in the evening.

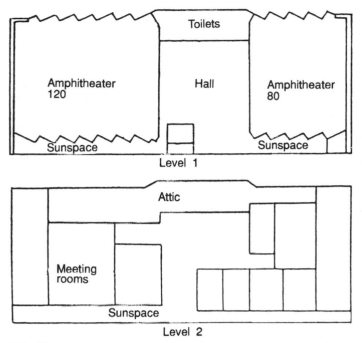

Fig. 16.3 Floor plan

Exterior roller blinds on the windows facing south reduce the problem of overheating in summer and keep the heat inside the building during the night in winter. These shading devices are activated automatically by a timer, and some can also be operated manually. The blinds are white painted aluminium. The U-value of the compound glazing and roller blinds is estimated to be $2\,W/m^2\,K$.

Three independent mechanical ventilation systems ensure sufficient air renewal when the building is fully occupied, and avoid overheating problems in summer. The first system works in the amphitheaters and it is controlled by both a temperature and a pollution sensor. The second works in the meeting rooms and is controlled by a timer. The third system is for the toilets, and runs throughout the day for hygienic reasons.

Mass wall
The building has two different mass walls facing south and extending up the full height of the building. A mass wall in the western part of the building is situated in front of a 128-seat amphitheater and meeting room; the eastern wall is situated in front of an 80-seat amphitheater and offices (Fig. 16.3).

The buffer space between the glazing and the concrete wall is an average of 1 m wide. The air ducts for the ventilation system are in this space, which also provides access to clean the glass. The buffer spaces are connected directly to the central hall of the building.

Roller blinds closed.

winter:	18:00 to 08:00
summer:	whenever overheating may occur.

Mass wall
Double glazing, 12 mm spaced
$$U = 3.0\,W/m^2\,K$$
Buffer space average 1 m wide
Concrete storage walls:

Thickness	0.25 m
Volume	$40\,m^3$

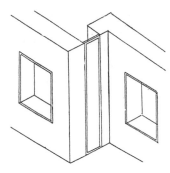

Fig. 16.4 Design of integrated windows

The wall is composed of a succession of L-shaped concrete elements, not parallel to the glazing and separated from each other by narrow interior windows. At the second level, in front of the meeting rooms and offices, additional windows are integrated in the wall itself to provide these rooms with additional daylight.

The mass wall is a completely passive system, unventilated and uninsulated. Solar energy in the rooms is controlled by using the exterior roller blinds. The roller blinds are always closed during the night in winter and during the weekend in summer.

The relationship between the mass wall of the FUL building and the roof is shown in Fig. 16.5. This design detail received special attention to avoid a thermal bridge between the wall and the roof and to avoid any passage of air between the buffer space and the heated rooms.

Results
Measurements of gas consumption and temperature levels were carried out during 1988 through 1990.

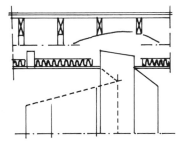

Fig. 16.5 Connection of exterior wall and roof

Heating load   The gas consumption for heating during 1988 and 1990 was stable at approximately 100 000 kWh per year, corresponding to an annual consumption of 150 kWh/m^2. (The figure is higher for 1987, which is attributed to the building being new and having to dry out.)

A closer look at monitoring results indicate that even with a thermostat control strategy, too much energy was consumed during nights and weekends. The building was partially heated during these hours when not required because a valve was improperly closed.

Furthermore, ventilation and infiltration losses are significant because air leaked through the roof. This weakness was identified in a pressurization test.

Annual gas consumption

	Year total (kWh)	Gross (kWh/m^2)
1987:	110 000	163
1988:	99 000	149
1989:	96 000	144
1990:	97 000	146

Table 16.1 Average temperature (DEGC) (June 1988 to May 1990)

Auditoria	19.5 ± 0.8
Hall:	21.5 ± 2.3
Offices:	21.7 ± 1.5
Meeting rooms:	20.7 ± 1.4
Visitors offices:	22.7 ± 2.0

Temperature levels   As shown in Table 16.1, the auditoria are the coldest rooms in the building with the lowest deviation from the mean. The central hall, which works as a direct gain zone, shows the highest temperature variation from the mean. For most rooms, the mean temperature is high, because it includes both day and night measurements.

Table 16.2 shows the extreme values of the temperatures in the same rooms. Maximum values usually result from too high solar radiation intensity while minimum values are usually associated with heating system set back at night. Indirect gain zones (auditoria) reach temperatures of 27.5°C while the direct gain areas reach 35.8°C.

Table 16.3 shows how often the temperature is above 24°C in the rooms. The auditoria are almost free from overheating, while all the other parts of the building overheat at least 25% of the time. The visitors' offices are rooms which are directly solar radiated, and also insulated from the hall. They are the most critical zones of the building.

Passive solar contribution

The passive solar contribution from a mass wall is difficult to evaluate. Nevertheless, the thermal contribution of the mass wall can be estimated by calculating the discharge flux in the auditoriums. The maximum value of this discharge flux is 8.3 W/m², recorded in August. Winter values are always negative, meaning that the wall always has a net heat loss during winter.

An estimation of the heat from solar energy in the building can be simulated. The comparison of the results of a simulation performed with complete climate data and another simulation performed with data modified to cancel the insolation yields an estimate of the gross heating load which is displaced by solar energy. The gross heating load also includes heat loss through the wall. In the case of the FUL building, 29% of the gross heating load is met by solar gains, which can be increased up to 33% by optimizing the design of the building. See Section 16.4. The average monthly values of the solar fraction are given in Fig. 16.6. Simulation results of the disaggregation of heat fluxes on a monthly basis are shown in Fig. 16.7.

Finally, an investigation of the response of the mass wall to external temperature is calculated with correlation coefficient between the mass wall temperature and external temperature, see Fig. 16.8. The correlations are shown in Figs 16.8 and 16.9, yielding the following regression coefficients for an average month:

Wall temperature/external temperature:	0.91
Wall temperature/solar radiation:	0.81

These results suggest that the wall responds to external temperature

Table 16.2 Temperature extremes (°C)

Auditoria:	13.5–27.5
Hall:	14.6–35.7
Offices:	14.3–31.3
Meeting-rooms:	13.5–30.1
Visitors Offices:	16.9–35.8

Table 16.3 Overheating frequency (percent of hours above 24°C)

Auditoria:	1
Hall:	24
Offices:	28
Meeting rooms:	15
Visitors offices:	35

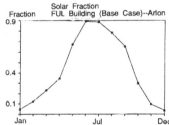

Fig. 16.6 Monthly solar fraction

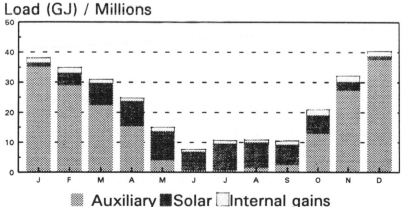

Fig. 16.7 Monthly energy flows

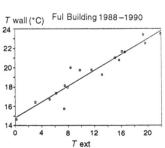

Fig. 16.8 Correlation T_{wall}/T_{ext}

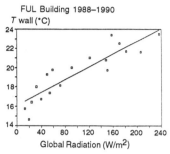

FUL Building 1988–1990

Fig. 16.9 Correlation T_{wall}/solar radiation

Location: East Looe, Cornwall, UK
Climate data:
(October through April)
Degree days, base 20:   2580 dd
Solar radiation, horizontal:
                                390 kWh/m²

Building data:
  Gross volume   3600 m³
  Gross floor area   1374 m²

Surface areas: m²
  Ground floor   1300
  Roof   1450
  Opaque wall   659
  Total window   335
  Roof lights   79

Installed capacities: W/m²
  Space heating   150
  Hot water   35
  Lighting   12

more than to solar radiation. The mass wall therefore works more as an insulating device than as a solar collection feature in the Belgian climate. This conclusion is supported by simulations in Section 16.4.

16.3.2   Looe School

Description of the building

The Looe School is situated on an exposed hilltop with open views to the south and southeast [16/2]. The region is one of the mildest in the UK but with high winds. The building is single storied, except for the staff area, and has ten classrooms radiating in four blocks from a central area.

The solar design allows a combination of direct and indirect use of both solar heating and daylight. The majority of glazing is kept to the south facades to maximize the potential for solar gains. Glazing accounts for 15% of the entire external wall area of the building. The south facades of the classrooms are 100% glazed; however, the lower 40% of the facade is essentially an 0.8 m high Trombe wall.

The opaque walls are generally constructed of traditional material and are highly insulated for British standards, with a U-value of 0.43 W/m² K. The main glazing units in the classroom are aluminum framed, horizontal-sliding, double glazed panels. Given the severe wind exposure, and assuming a 20% frame, the U-value of the double glazing is estimated to be 4 W/m² K.

Space heating is provided by a hot water system serving convectors in each classroom which are fan-assisted. Each convector is controlled individually using a thermostat in the classroom.

The school is naturally ventilated. Mechanical extract systems are supplied only in the kitchen area, staff toilets and showers. A low infiltration rate is achieved by a combination of the high quality glazing frames and draft lobbies on all entrances and exits.

The Trombe wall

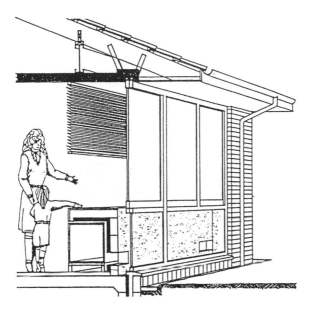

Fig. 16.10   The Trombe wall of Looe School

The Trombe wall is intended to store and release solar energy to the classrooms. Air openings are provided at the top and bottom of the cavity to allow solar energy to be transferred to the room by natural convection. The massive tilted (0.8 m wide) work bench is intended to accumulate and moderate direct solar gains, as well as serve as a display surface and storage area. The color (and hence absorption coefficient) of the bench top was chosen as a compromise between the desire to absorb solar gain and the need to limit the peak surface temperature for safety. Shading further reduces potential overheating by direct solar radiation. The deep 0.75 m overhanging eaves limit the maximum angle of direct solar radiation to 45° from the bench top.

This provides noon solar protection from mid-April through early September, and during the full school day (09:00 to 15:00) in June and July. The extra width of the bench top safely distances the pupils from the extensive glazing area and from cold drafts and cold glass surfaces.

Venetian blinds are provided in each classroom for further control of solar gain and glare. Usually these are set back from the window and come down in line with the inner edge of the bench. This allows the bench top to continue absorbing and storing solar energy.

Glazing properties:
Double glazed
$U = 4.0 \, \text{W/m}^2 \, \text{K}$
(severe exposure)

Glazing areas:	m²
South facing:	259
North facing:	25

Results

Measurements were taken of fuel consumption prior to January 1987 and February 1988. Short-term intensive monitoring of energy flows

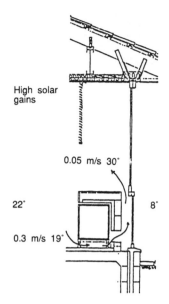

High solar
gains

0.05 m/s 30°

22°   8°

0.3 m/s 19°

Fig. 16.11 Natural ventilation
with high solar gains

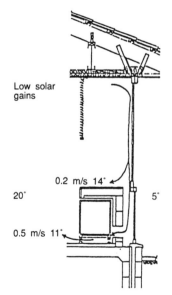

Low solar
gains

0.2 m/s 14°

20°   5°

0.5 m/s 11°

Fig. 16.12 Natural ventilation
with low solar gains

in the work bench area, air infiltration and lighting use was conducted in one classroom.

Table 16.4   Annual fuel use during three years

Year	Gas (MWh)	Electricity (MWh)	Degree days base 15.5°C
4-85/4-86	216	26	2047
4-86/4-87	270	25	2155
4-87/3-88	24	27	1882

Average specific energy consumption based on gross floor area was calculated to be $210 \, kWh/m^2 \, a$. Monthly values of fuel consumption show that the heating demand is strongly seasonal. A strong correlation coefficient (0.84) existed between the average weekly external temperature and weekly heating energy. A good correlation (0.75) was also found between the average amount of sunshine per week and heat used in a week, indicating that the building is responding positively to solar gains. With this correlation, the average solar contribution is estimated at 40% of the space heating demand.

During weekends when the school was unheated and no windows were opened, no people entered nor incidental gains accumulated, classroom conditions reacted significantly and quickly to solar irradiation, particularly when compared to the temperature of the central corridor.

The Trombe bench was intended to give three benefits:

1. To keep the seating area safely away from windows and to reduce problems caused by cold drafts, cold surfaces or too much heat from direct sunlight.
2. To moderate high solar gains through absorption and delay the release of solar gain through the massive work top area.
3. To improve the use of passive solar energy by the Trombe wall and thereby improve air circulation in the room.

The first objective is largely achieved, although difficult to quantify. The second objective was also fulfilled, based on a qualitative analysis. Monitoring showed a delayed (and reduced) gain of about two hours during peak hours with a long tail (eight hours) of slow release of stored energy into the classroom. Of the solar heat absorbed and delayed by the top of the Trombe bench, this estimate shows limited gains when compared to the total amount of solar energy entering the room. The contribution to reduction of peak temperatures in the classroom is less than 1°C.

The third objective was investigated and confirmed that during high solar gains and moderate external temperature conditions, a positive flow of warm air was emitted from the top of the cavity. However it was also observed that on days of low solar gains, a reversed air flow pattern could occur, and cooled air is injected from the bottom of the cavity into the classroom at floor level.

The temperature within the cavity, and so its ability to become a solar heat generator, was negatively affected by opening windows. This is unfortunate because windows are generally opened when the Trombe bench would operate most efficiently, i.e. at high solar radiation.

The general conclusion about the energy effectiveness of the Trombe bench is that it is insignificant to the building's use of energy. The solar response of the building is primarily from direct gain. The Trombe bench did not, however, introduce any apparent disadvantages and so it could be considered to be at least as effective as the equivalent area of simple glazing.

Table 16.5 Base case data

Orientation:	South
Glazing:	Double, High-e
Wall color:	White
Wall material:	Concrete
Wall thickness:	0.25 m
Climate:	Brussels
Glazing ratio:	0.65
Wall type:	Mass wall
Insulation:	
wall	0.28 W/m² K
roof	0.18 W/m²

16.4 SIMULATION STUDIES: FUL AUDITORIUM

Parametric studies were conducted to determine if the heating system could be improved. Two reference cases to compare with the building results are defined.

1. The base case design is the FUL Auditorium building design, data for which are summarized in Table 16.5. The comparison between a given variation and the base case leads to the optimization of the passive solar strategy.
2. The reference case design is the design of an equivalent building (of the same volume, floor area, and architectural shape, constructed with Belgian standards for insulation level, and fenestration) but without any special passive solar features. See Table 16.6 for data about the reference case.

Table 16.6 Reference case data

Orientation:	South
Glazing:	Double, High-e
Wall type:	Insulated
Glazing ratio:	0.3
Insulation:	
wall	0.53 W/m² K
roof	0.26 W/m² K

16.4.1 Program validation

The main tool used in the parametric studies is a Multi-zone Building Dynamic Simulation (MBDSA) program, developed by the University of Liège in Belgium. This PC tool is derived from the mainframe code LPB-1, which had never been validated with *in situ* measurements on a passive solar building before this Task XI study. A preliminary validation step was therefore required to ensure reliable results.

The period chosen for the comparison between model and measurement results of the passive solar feature of the building was August 1989, because it was a very sunny and warm month, requiring no auxiliary heating for the building. The comparison between measured and calculated temperatures shows strong agreement, especially in the hall where direct gain is expected. Figures 16.13 and 16.14 depict temperatures in the offices and halls respectively.

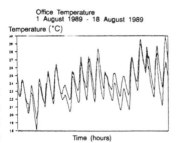

Fig. 16.13 Office temperature validation

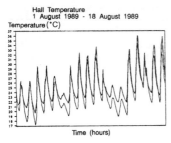

Fig. 16.14 Hall temperature validation

Moreover, the comparison of measured and calculated surface temperatures on the mass wall shows that MBDSA successfully models the wall's dynamic behavior. Consequently, MBDSA is an appropriate tool for parametric studies on the FUL building.

16.4.2 Parametric analysis

Energy savings and comfort criteria were used to compare the different designs as defined below.

Energy saving Total auxiliary load.
Comfort Hours of overheating during which overheating occurred (above 24°C) in the offices (the most frequently occupied zone of the building) and the temperature extremes in the auditoriums (the rooms behind the mass wall).

The results of the base case and reference case simulations are indicated in Tables 16.8 and 16.9.

Table 16.7 Parameters

- Orientation of the building
- Glazing type
- Buffer space geometry
- Mass wall absorption properties
- Mass wall thickness
- Roller blinds activation strategy
- South facade glazing area
- Climate

Table 16.8 Base and reference case results

Case	Heating load (kWh)	Overheating (h)	Swings Min (K)	Max (K)
Base	52 400	394	3.08	7.79
Ref.	54 750	411	3.40	7.63

Table 16.8 shows that the base case (or actual FUL building design) performs slightly better when compared to a reference building such as a state-of-the-art building in Belgium. With a lower level of thermal insulation, the design of the base case is far from optimal. A case where the different design variables are optimized is provided in Table 16.9.

Optimized design
Black mass wall
Low emissivity glazing
Narrow buffer space
Night roller blind
25% mass wall area

Table 16.9 Base case and optimized building

Case	Heating load (kWh)	Overheating (h)	Swings Min (K)	Max (K)
Base	52 400	394	3.08	7.79
Optimal	44 600	1148	2.75	7.89

A large potential for energy savings exists in the FUL building, if the design were optimized. The overheating of the offices would, however, become even more pronounced.

16.4.3 Building orientation

Three different orientations have been compared: south, for the base
case, west and east. Table 16.10 provides these results.

Table 16.10 Orientation variation

Orientation	Heating load (kWh)	Overheating (h)	Swings Max (K)	Min (K)
South	52 400	394	3.1	7.8
East	54 500	357	3.1	7.8
West	54 200	436	3.0	7.8
Reference	54 750	411	3.4	7.6

The south facade orientation is optimum to reduce the heating load,
but, as expected, leads to a higher level of overheating in the offices.

16.4.4 Glazing type

Six different glazing types are compared in Table 16.11, with the base
case in bold print.

		$(W/m^2 K)$
●	Single glazing	$U = 5.6; \tau = 0.9$
●	**Double high-e glazing**	$U = 3.0; \tau = 0.7$
●	Double low-e	$U = 1.6; \tau = 0.6$
●	Triple high-e	$U = 2.0; \tau = 0.6$
●	Triple low-e	$U = 1.5; \tau = 0.5$
●	Super glazing	$U = 0.6; \tau = 0.3$

Table 16.11 Glazing type variation

Glazing type	Heating load (kWh)	Overheating (h)	Swings Max (K)	Min(K)
Single	60 600	273	3.3	7.6
Double H	52 400	394	3.1	7.8
Double L	48 500	424	3.0	7.8
Triple H	50 200	395	3.0	7.3
Triple L	48 800	294	3.0	7.7
Super	48 300	255	3.1	7.7
Reference	54 750	411	3.4	7.6

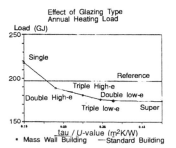

Fig. 16.15 Load (GJ) versus glazing type

Figure 16.15 shows a direct correlation between the total heating
load of the building and the transmittance/U-value ratio of the glazing.

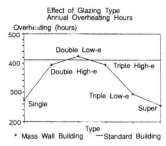

Fig. 16.16 Overheating (hours) versus glazing type

The higher the ratio, the lower the heating load. A double low-e glazing (ratio = 0.375) is optimal for the Belgian climate.

Figure 16.16 shows the effect of glazing type and hour of overheating. The risk of overheating is reduced by using either single glazing or glazing with low transmission (triple low-e or superglazing).

16.4.5 Variation of buffer space geometry

Two different configurations of buffer space geometry have been compared (Table 16.12). The base configuration provides a buffer space of 1 m width and a wall with windows. The classical mass wall configuration contains an opaque black wall with no interior windows, which is parallel and close to the glazing. Furthermore, this classical mass wall is assumed to be black.

Table 16.12 Buffer geometry variation

Geometry	Heating load (kWh)	Overheating (h)	Swings Max (K)	Min (K)
Base	**52 400**	**394**	**3.7**	**7.8**
Classical	50 300	638	2.9	76
Reference	54 750	411	3.4	7.6

When the wall is placed just behind the glazing and excludes any interior windows, the heating load is substantially reduced. This configuration optimizes energy used in the building; however, this also increases overheating.

16.4.6 Absorption coefficient

Five different absorption coefficients, each associated with a different color, have been compared to the mass wall in Table 16.13:

- Black walls: $\alpha = 0.9$
- Brown walls: $\alpha = 0.7$
- Grey walls: $\alpha = 0.5$
- White walls: $\alpha = 0.3$
- **White walls plus shading effects:** $\alpha = 0.1$

The heating load decreases continuously when the absorption coefficient increases; more solar energy is collected and subsequently transmitted to the rooms. Overheating increases as well, however.

Table 16.13 Wall absorption variation

Color	Heating load (kWh)	Overheating (h)	Extremes Max (K)	Extremes Min (K)
Black	50 600	562	3.0	7.8
Brown	50 900	542	3.0	7.8
Grey	51 250	502	3.0	7.8
White	50 700	457	3.1	7.8
White + shade	**52 400**	**394**	**3.1**	**7.8**
Reference	54 750	411	3.4	7.6

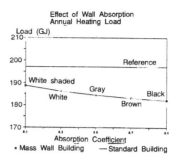

Fig. 16.17 Load (GJ) versus absorption factor

16.4.7 Wall thickness

The effect of the mass wall thickness is shown in Table 16.14. The 250 mm wall is the base value.

Table 16.14 Wall thickness variation

Thickness	Heating load (kWh)	Overheating (h)	Extremes Max (K)	Extremes Min (K)
50 mm	52 400	465	3.6	8.5
100 mm	52 600	429	3.3	8.3
150 mm	52 600	416	3.2	8.0
200 mm	52 500	403	3.1	7.9
250 mm	**52 400**	**394**	**3.1**	**7.8**
Reference	54 750	411	3.4	7.6

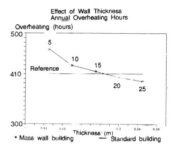

Fig. 16.18 Overheating (hours) versus thickness (cm)

The mass wall thickness has little impact on performance of heating. The effect is pronounced on the comfort indices: when the walls are made thicker, the risk of overheating is reduced and temperature extremes in the auditorium continuously decrease. This should reduce the morning peak load as well.

16.4.8 Glazing ratio

Different glazing ratios were compared to determine the optimal balance between solar collection and heat loss. The ratios are defined as the glazed fraction of the southern facade and the values are the following: 0% (opaque facade), 65% (base case), 100% (glazed facade).

In Table 16.15 the lowest heating load is achieved with a glazing ratio of 25%. The sensitivity of the heating load is small between 0.25 and 0.65 and allows the architect to select any value to meet the requirements of an aesthetic design. The risk of overheating increases with the glazing ratio, as expected.

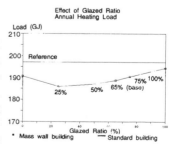

Fig. 16.19 Load (GJ) versus glazed ratio

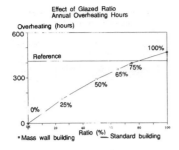

Fig. 16.20 Overheating (hours) versus glazed ratio

Table 16.15 Glazing ratio

Ratio	Heating load (kWh)	Overheating (h)	Swings Max (K)	Min (K)
0	52 900	0	3.3	7.7
25	51 600	160	3.1	7.8
50	51 90	291	3.1	7.8
65	**52 400**	**394**	**3.1**	**7.8**
75	52 900	395	3.1	7.8
100	54 000	468	3.1	7.8
Reference	54 750	411	3.4	7.6

16.4.9 Roller blind operation

During winter, the roller blinds are closed during the night and weekends to reduce heat loss. In summer, they are only set during weekends (from Friday night to Monday morning) except for special events such as meetings and conferences. In Table 16.16, the effect of changing the control strategy of the blinds is shown: the first strategy with no activation at all, the second with night activation for an entire year.

Table 16.16 Roller blind activation strategy variation

Strategy	Heating load (kWh)	Overheating (h)	Extremes Min (K)	Max (K)
Inactive	51 800	670	3.0	7.8
Night/WE	52 400	394	3.1	7.8
Night only	50 300	709	2.9	7.8
Reference	54 750	411	3.4	7.6

The present strategy of closing the blinds during the night and on weekends in the FUL building is the worst one because, on an annual basis, the reduction of solar gains is accompanied by an increase in heat load. Night operation, with the set time depending on the season, would result in a substantial energy saving, but would increase the number of hours the building is overheated.

16.4.10 Mass wall material

The FUL building was designed with reinforced concrete as the material for solar storage. Concrete is characterized by a high conductivity value (1.7 W/m K) and a high density (2400 kg/m^3). This produces a diffusivity value of 8.5×10^{-7} (m²/s K). Table 16.17 shows values for other storage materials: masonry (bricks) with a diffusivity of 1.4×10^{-6} (m²/s K) and water with a diffusivity of 1.4×10^{-7} (m²/s K).

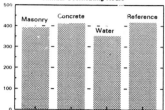

Table 16.17 Storage material variation

Material	Heating load (kWh)	Overheating (h)	Swings Max (K)	Min (K)
Concrete	**52 400**	**394**	**3.1**	**7.8**
Masonry	51 900	411	3.2	8.1
Water	51 200	349	3.1	7.5
Reference	54 750	411	3.4	7.6

Fig. 16.21 Overheating (hours) versus material

The results show that the heating load is not very sensitive to the type of storage material. The number of hours of overheating, however, can be reduced by using material with a high thermal capacity.

16.4.11 Climate

The performance of the base case mass wall building was modeled for the following climates:

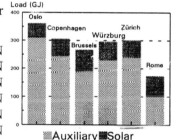

- Oslo: 60.0°N
- Copenhagen: 55.6°N
- **Brussels:** **50.8°N**
- Würtzburg: 49.8°N
- Zürich: 47.4°N
- Rome: 41.9°N

Fig. 16.22 Load (GJ) versus climate

The results in Table 16.18 and in Figs. 16.22 and 16.23 show that the contribution of passive solar to gross heating load (Fig. 16.22) is insensitive to climate in absolute terms; however, it is obviously largest in Rome where solar energy provides almost half of the gross heating load.

Table 16.18 Climate variations

Climate	Heating load (kWh)	Overheating (h)	Extremes Min (K)	Max (K)
Oslo	85 800	845	3.1	8.4
Copenhagen	67 400	236	3.2	7.4
Brussels	**52 400**	**394**	**3.1**	**7.8**
Würtzburg	63 100	621	3.1	7.7
Zürich	64 400	706	3.3	7.8
Rome	26 400	2891	2.5	6.5

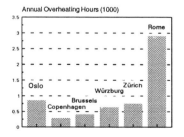

Fig. 16.23 Overheating (hours) versus climate

16.5 ANALYSIS

16.5.1 PC tools

MBDSA (Belgium)

General description MBDSA (Multi-zone Building Dynamic Simulator) performs an hourly based simulation of a building. The package MBDSA includes four modules:

- PRET: the meteorological preprocessor
- PREPA: the building preprocessor
- MBDS: the heat balance dynamic calculator
- POSTA: the results postprocessor.

The heat balance calculation module has been built as a TRNSYS-type component. This module is still developed at the University of Wisconsin at Madison, and delivered within the TRNSYS package as type 56.

Language and operating system Fortran 77; MS-DOS.

Application to mass wall modeling The program MBDSA does not model the mass wall as a built-in component. Consequently, the user has to build the model using standard types: walls, glazing, zones. The following features, relevant when modeling a mass wall, can easily be introduced:

- solar collection (direct, diffuse)
- absorption by the wall
- total convective plus radiative exchange between air and walls
- convective coupling between rooms
- conduction through the wall
- shadowing and scheduled transmission properties.

The following features cannot be taken into account by the MBDSA model:

- direct infrared exchange between the glazing and the wall
- thermal stratification of the buffer zone
- relative position of the wall versus glazing
- interior windows.

16.5.2 Mainframe tools

LPB-1 (Belgium)

General description LPB-1 performs a multi-zone dynamic (hourly based) simulation of a building. The LPB-1 program is in fact an earlier

Developed by:
Université de Liège (ULg)
Laboratoire de Themodynamique
Lisianne Cotton
rue Ernest Solvay, 21
B-4000 Liege
Belgium

Contact: ATIC
Paul Jacqmin
rue Brogniez, 41
B-1070 Brussels
Belgium

mainframe version of MBDSA (see Section 16.5.1). No significant differences appear between the two programs except that in LPB-1:

- a convolution method is used instead of the Z-transform approach to calculate the wall conduction processes
- the data-input only proceeds with numerical values rather than key words.

As the PC-version (MBDSA) now exists, the LPB-1 program has not been developed further by the authors. However, the program remains a reference tool for comparison with other models.

Language and operating system Fortran 77. Can be adapted to several mainframe operating systems (UNIX, PRIMOS, VMS, etc.).

Developed by:
Université de Liège (ULg)
Laboratoire de Themodynamique
Jean Lebrun
rue Ernest Solvay, 21
B-4000 Liège
Belgium

16.6 CONCLUSIONS

Careful optimization is required to gain a positive energy performance of a mass wall in a climate like Belgium. The research shows that the mass wall concept is unsuitable for the Belgian climate, a conclusion which is probably also valid for similar temperate climates with relatively little sun.

16.6.1 Building orientation

In any case, south orientation is the best orientation to save as much auxiliary heating energy as possible with a mass wall system. Reduction of overheating requires that the building be oriented more toward the east.

16.6.2 Glazing type

Maximum energy performance is achieved using double low emissivity glazing. A substantial reduction of overheating hours is possible using a poorly transparent glazing, such as triple low emissivity.

16.6.3 Glazed ratio

A glazed area of 25–50% offers optimal energy performances. To maximize comfort, the lowest glazing area is recommended.

16.6.4 Buffer space

A narrow buffer space improves the energy efficiency of the wall, but it also increases overheating. Ventilation ducts or other shading devices in the buffer space should be avoided.

16.6.5 Absorption coefficient

To maximize energy savings, the wall should absorb as much irradiation as possible, and therefore be of a dark color. To maximize comfort, it should reflect as much sunlight as possible.

16.6.6 Wall construction

Various materials can be used for the mass wall (such as concrete and bricks) without any significant variation in energy performance or comfort. A thick wall, i.e. 250 mm, improves comfort, but has little influence on energy savings.

  A mass wall with air circulation between the air gap and the building (Trombe wall) should be insulated in a Belgian or similar climate.

Optimum construction of mass wall
The mass wall which optimizes energy use is a black wall with double pane low emissivity glazing in front of it. In the actual Arlon building, the optimal mass wall area to gross south facade is 25%.

  For an optimal mass wall, the auxiliary energy consumption, 45 000 kWh/year, is close to what can be expected if the wall is replaced by a conventional wall with a good insulation.

16.7 REFERENCES

16/1 André, Ph., *Advanced Case Study*: Auditoires FUL – Arlon, IEA Task XI, Final Report, November 1990, Fondation Universitaire Luxembourgeoise, 185, Avenue de Longwy, B-6700 Arlon, Belgium.

16/2 Alexander D., Vaughan N., Jenkins H., and Jones P., under the direction of P. E. O'Sullivan, Looe Junior and Infant School. *EPA Technical Report*, April 1989. Welsh School of Architecture, Architectural Research and Development, University of Wales, College of Cardiff.

16.8 RECOMMENDED READING

Balcomb, D., *Rules of Thumb for Passive Solar Heating, Report LA-UR-80-702*, Los Alamos Scientific Laboratory, USA.

This book provides rules of thumb for the design of glazing areas and mass wall systems for 219 towns in the USA.

National Concrete Masonry Association, *Passive Solar Construction Handbook*, Energy Service Group, USA.

This book provides technical construction details about direct gain, storage walls and sun spaces. It shows building material for collectors (glazing) and storage systems and concludes with some examples.

Wray, W., and Balcomb, D., *Trombe Walls vs. Direct Gain. A Comparative Analysis of Passive Solar Heating Systems, Report LA-UR-79-116*

Contact: Los Alamos Scientific Laboratory, USA.

Using the simulation program 'PASOLE/SUNSPOT', two types of passive solar strategies are compared. The following parameters are varied: amount of thermal mass, glazing area, number of glazings, wall thickness, and night insulation.

Trombe, F., *Maisons Solaires, Techniques de l'Ingénieur*.

Contact: les Techniques de l'Ingénieur,
21, rue Cassette, 75006 Paris, France.

17 Transparent Insulation Systems

17.1 INTRODUCTION

The performance of the mass walls described in the previous chapter can be substantially improved through the use of transparent insulation (TI) as the glazing. This new material provides distinct advantages particularly in mild or cold and sunny climates, but it also requires special attention and therefore a special chapter is included.

The principal characteristics of walls provided with opaque or transparent insulation are illustrated in Fig. 17.1. Solar radiation is absorbed by a layer of plaster on the exterior. Insulation under the plaster impedes solar thermal gains by the masonry wall. On the

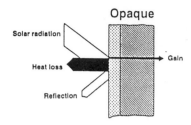

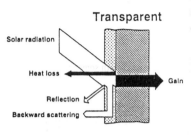

Fig. 17.1 Principal physical characteristics of an opaque and a transparently insulated mass wall

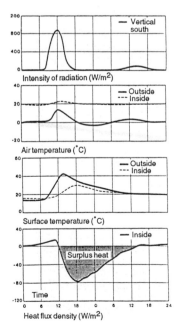

Fig. 17.2 48 hour measurement cycle of a 200 mm concrete wall with transparent insulation

contrary, with transparent insulation, solar radiation is partially transmitted through the insulating layer to be absorbed at the exterior surface of the wall behind the insulating layer. Transparent insulation permits a large part of the absorbed energy to be conducted into the wall. Depending on solar radiation, the wall heats up and temporarily transfers heat from the outside to the inside.

During periods of weak sun or no radiation at all, heat losses are minimized by the insulation of the material layer. During periods of solar radiation, the external wall absorbs radiation, stores heat, and can temporarily heat the surface of an adjoining space.

The thermal behavior of a wall with transparent thermal insulation is illustrated in Fig. 17.2, which shows data for a winter day and night. The time profiles of radiation intensity are indicated along with outside and inside air temperatures and wall surface temperatures. Other variables included are: the heat flux density measured at the interior wall surface of a 200 mm concrete wall provided with a transparent insulating system; U-value: $1.3 \, \text{W/m}^2 \, \text{K}$; and diffuse transmissivity: 0.6.

From the illustrations, one can see that the air temperatures inside rise only slightly after a strong peak of solar radiation, but inside surface temperatures rise substantially as the wall gains heat, peaking six hours after the solar peak. The maximum temperature of the exterior wall surface, 43°C, is reduced because heat is transferred to the interior surface, which reaches a maximum temperature of 30°C. At noon and during the night, the heat flux within the wall is directed to the inside.

17.1.1 Advantages

- The system provides heat gains from solar radiation in addition to insulation.
- The interior wall surface temperature is higher than conventional wall constructions, thus improving comfort in winter.
- Higher wall surface temperatures reduce the risks of moisture penetration and the occurrence of surface condensation and mold.
- Solar heat gains are delayed and therefore complement the direct gains from windows.

17.1.2 Disadvantages

- An inappropriately designed system may result in overheating of the insulation material and overheating of the rest of the wall.
- During warmer months of the year, it may be necessary to use costly solar shading devices to avoid overheating.
- Some TI materials are brittle so they must be fitted between glass panes or covered externally with glass panes. These materials then

must be mounted on the building facade with frame systems which are costly and may detract from the appearance of the building.

- Applications of the transparent insulation material to highly insulated walls or to thin walls with low heat storage capacity may cause high temperatures within the wall construction.
- Some of the materials may be fire hazards.

Physical characteristics
- Thermal insulation
- Time-delayed solar gains
- More comfortable interior temperatures
- Higher indoor surface temperatures

Design aspects
- 'Glass architecture'
- Careful design necessary
- Costs
- Risk of overheating in summer
- Inappropriate in some cases
- Fire hazards with some materials

17.2 SYSTEM DESIGN

The design and use of transparent insulation systems can be discussed under the following characteristics:

- Insulation material
- Installation
- Frame system
- Shading device
- Use of surplus heat.

17.2.1 Transparent insulation materials

Transparent insulation systems can be made from organic plastics materials such as polycarbonate honeycombs, capillary structures or acrylic foam, or inorganic glass fiber materials and aerogel as seen in the photos in Fig. 17.3.

The degree to which heat is conducted by the different transparent insulation materials is strongly dependent on temperature. A low value of $0.02\,W/m\,K$ is obtained for aerogel, and a relatively high value of $0.09\,W/m\,K$ for honeycombs.

The temperature limit of PMMA (polymethyl methacrylate) material is approximately $80°C$ and that of polycarbonate about $125°C$. The densities of the different plastic materials and of glass fibers range from 10 to $40\,kg/m^3$, and that of aerogel from 100 to $200\,kg/m^3$.

Aerogels (SO_2-gels) are made by hydrolyzing and polymerizing silicon alcoholates (alcogels) in alcoholic solutions. Drying these gels is performed in an autoclave under supercritical conditions. When alcohol is removed, alcogel becomes aerogel with an extremely porous microstructure. This structure gives the material its characteristic optical and thermal behavior. It is extremely brittle, so that for practice use it must be sandwiched between glass panes.

The effect on the transmission factor by the thickness of the transparent insulation is indicated in Fig. 17.4. With capillary diameters of $1–1.5\,mm$ and layers of $25–60\,mm$ for capillary materials, the transmission factor decreases to about 65%. In the case of materials enhancing scattering effects, for instance PMMA-foams or granulated aerogel, the transmission factor amounts to 0.3 that of granulated

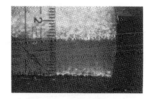

Capillary structure

PC-honeycomb

Glass fiber

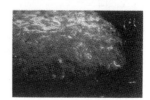

PMMA-foam

Fig. 17.3 Photos of various transparent insulating materials

Granulated aerogel

Homogeneous aerogel

Fig. 17.3 *continued*

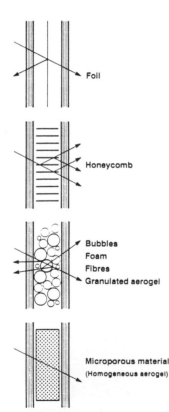

Fig. 17.5 Examples of transparent insulation materials inserted between glass panes. Arrows indicate light propagation characteristics

aerogel between 2 mm panes to 0.45, that of capillary materials to more than 0.6, and that of honeycombs to nearly 0.8 at the same *U*-value. The transmission factor equals almost the total energy transmission of ost of the transparent insulation materials, since their absorption is low.

To furnish those products with sufficient mechanical properties and to ensure good weather and fire protection, they are used behind single glass or placed between double glazing. Schematic drawings of the double-glazed types are given in Fig. 17.5. Convection-reducing materials like honeycombs, capillaries, foams, fibers, microspheres or granulates, partly scatter transmitted light. The transmittance is more or less influenced by the thickness of the material, but scattering light prevents looking through a window. There are also microporous, quasihomogeneous thermal insulation materials available which are fully transparent.

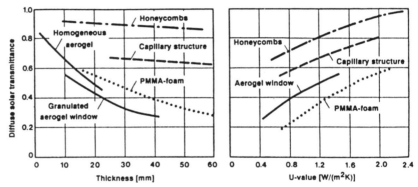

Fig. 17.4 Transmission factor (%) as a fraction of layer thickness and *U*-value for various materials (granulated aerogel is inserted between 2 mm glass panes)

17.2.2 Frame system

Normally, a frame is used to contain the transparent insulation unit, much the same as for a conventional window. There are two types of frame system:

1. A frame is first mounted on the wall and the transparent insulation unit is subsequently inserted (Fig. 17.6).
2. Prefabricated frame system (Fig. 17.7).

In addition to the above framed system, a frameless system is currently being developed. This system has an insulation layer bonded directly to the wall. Glazing is applied on the outside to provide weather protection.

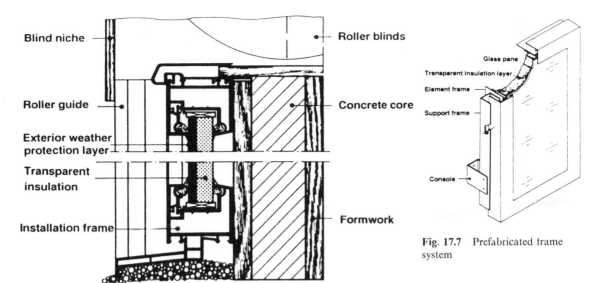

Fig. 17.6 Frame system with separate insertion of transparent insulation and external shading

Fig. 17.7 Prefabricated frame system

17.2.3 Ventilated system

If space is left between a layer of insulation and a wall, it is possible to ventilate the system and use the warm air for heating (Fig. 17.8).

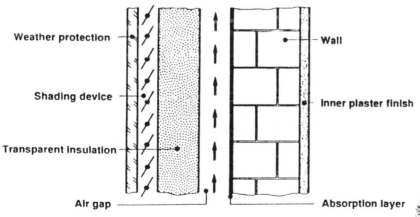

Fig. 17.8 Transparent insulation system with air gap between insulation layer and wall

In an open circuit, heated air flows directly to the rooms, whereas in a closed circuit, it flows in cavities within the structure (Fig. 17.9). Such systems are currently being developed. A detailed description of this type of system is also given in Chapter 19, Storage Systems.

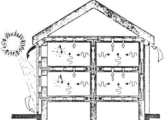

Fig. 17.9 Schematic of a closed circuit ventilated system

Weather protected

Weather protection
Shading device
Insulating layer

Wall
Air gap — Absorptive layer

With air gap

Without air gap

Fig. 17.10 Shading device installation

17.2.4 Water-cooled system

Water can be pre-heated by running it through water pipes laid along external wall surfaces. Since hot water is usually required throughout the year, such systems can be installed without shading devices, making the installation more cost-effective. Also, the pipes enhance the storage capacity of the external wall, and reduce the thermal stress on the wall. For this reason, lighter building materials may be employed; however, this requires careful design.

17.2.5 Solar shading devices

Roller blinds, venetian blinds and awnings can be used as active solar shading devices. Depending on the system, they can be mounted externally, if necessary, behind an additional pane that serves as a weather protection, or in front of the layer of weather protection. Schematic drawings of various solar shading installations are shown in Fig. 17.10.

Shading devices mounted on the exterior of buildings need frequent servicing because they are exposed to the weather. Alternatively, protected roller blinds or venetian blinds that are mounted behind glass panes are exposed to higher temperatures than external ones.

Transparent

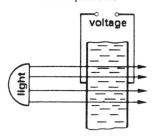

voltage

light

Translucent

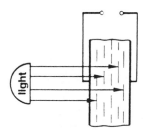

light

Fig. 17.11 Characteristics of electrochromic switchable glazing (liquid crystal type)

17.2.6 Switchable glazing

Solar shading is also possible with optically switchable glazing to exclude undesired solar energy. There are three basic types of glazing, chromogenic, physio-optic and electrodeposition systems. Chromogenic sheet materials, also called optical shutters, change the absorption or reflection of the glazing in response to heat, electricity or light. Windows will darken or lighten to vary the amount of solar radiation and heat entering the building. The material is classified as thermochromic if it responds to heat by changing color; thermotropic if it responds to heat or temperature by a change of transmission; electrochromic if the change of color is the reaction to an applied electric field or current; and photochromic if it responds to light only.

Electrochromic systems and entirely passive thermotropic shading systems are currently being developed. The characteristics of these glazing types are illustrated in Figs. 17.11 and 17.12. With electrochromic switchable glazing, the glass is coated with a flexible polymer film encapsulating tiny spheres of liquid crystals. The liquid crystals scatter incoming light when the spherical walls of the cells are unaligned. Light passes uninterrupted through a panel when a rheostat-controlled electric field aligns crystals within cells.

The most cost-effective technology is the thermotropic 'TALD' gel.

In a ground state at low temperature this material is transparent. With increasing temperature, clouding occurs from dissolved water molecules and increasing molecular chains within the gel. The clouding point can be regulated within a wide temperature range.

17.2.7 Other shading devices

In some cases, protruding structures or natural vegetation are sufficient as shading devices.

17.3 EXAMPLES

After its first application in housing, transparent thermal insulation is now being employed in commercial buildings.

17.3.1 Commercial buildings

Given the present state-of-the-art, and to be cost-effective, transparent thermal insulation systems should be applied under two conditions:

1. When solar shading devices are not required.
2. When large frame elements of uniform size can be applied: first, to reduce the portion of wall surface covered by frames, which do not produce an energy gain area and also have a lower insulating effect; and second, to lower construction costs through series production.

Commercial buildings, which often have large windowless facades, frequently meet those conditions. If, for reasons of image, steps are taken to improve the aesthetics of facades, transparent thermal insulation should also be considered. Boundary design conditions require careful review, however.

Supermarkets are buildings usually not characterized as architecturally noteworthy. The following case study demonstrates how this type of building can be made more attractive through cost-effective renovation.

17.3.2 A supermarket

A typical supermarket chosen to illustrate the use of transparent insulation for renovation is a $25\,000\,m^2$, one-storey building situated in southern Germany (Würzburg). The building was modeled using the programs SUNCODE and SUPERLITE linked with SUPERLINK.

The building is of reinforced concrete frame construction with a distance of 3 m between frames. Spaces are filled with 17.5 cm cavity

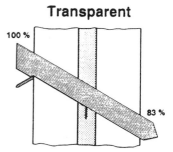
Transparent

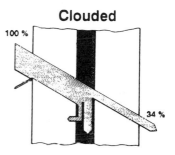
Clouded

Fig. 17.12 Physical characteristics of a glazing element with thermotropic solar protection

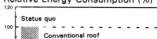
Relative Energy Consumption (%)

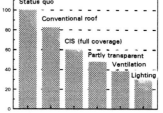

Fig. 17.13 Energy consumption for different retrofit measures on a supermarket

brick work. The roof is flat and consists of 12 cm reinforced concrete slabs and insulated externally with a 3 cm layer with gravel covering.

Improving thermal insulation must start with the roof, which has the largest external surface. Increasing the thickness of the insulation layer to 20 cm reduces the annual heating energy consumption by 20%. Completely opaque insulation on the 950 m^2 of exterior wall surface with a 10 cm insulation layer would further reduce the current demand to 60%. However, if 340 m^2 of the external southern wall surface were equipped with transparent thermal insulation, the annual heating energy consumption could be reduced to 45%.

The high air change rates (in the range of 1.5 to 3 h^{-1} during opening hours for the supermarket) make transparent thermal insulation with a ventilated insulation layer a good heating system. Calculations show that the annual heat consumption could be reduced to 20% of the current demand (Fig. 17.13). The remaining heat requirement could then be gained from internal gains from lighting and the refrigeration system.

If the roof were provided with improved thermal insulation, the temperature indoors would be lower in this supermarket even if transparent thermal insulation were applied (Fig. 17.14). Compared with housing, it is easy to save large quantities of energy in a commercial building. The same amount of energy could be saved only with a large number of apartments, necessitating more material and higher costs.

Annual energy consumption

Fuel	600 000 kWh
Electricity	500 000 kWh
● Illumination	30%
● Cooling	24%
● Ventilation	22%
● Others	24%

Total consumption based on floor area 44 kWh/m^2

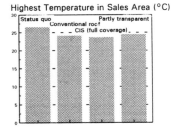

Highest Temperature in Sales Area (°C)

Fig. 17.14 Absolute maximum of air temperatures within sales area of supermarket for different retrofitting measures

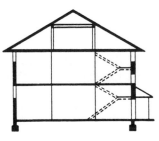

Fig. 17.15 Section of the two-story recreation building

17.3.3 Recreation building

A fictitious recreation building of an industrial company with about 100 employees will further demonstrate the advantages of transparent thermal insulation. Assume the building is situated near Cologne, Germany, and has a floor area of 24 m by 12 m and a north–south axis. In the two-story building, half the ground floor is taken up by technical installations, the other half by social rooms. The ventilation system is installed in the roof.

Shifts change at 14:00 and 22:00, respectively. Conventional design requires a heating system with an output of 40 kWh and a ventilation system with an output of 70 kWh. Hot water consumption for showering is 6000 l/d. During shift changes, air change rates of 4 h^{-1} and 10 h^{-1} are assumed for dressing rooms and showers respectively. Water preheating starts 2 h before the shifts change. The walls of the building are made of concrete, with a thickness of 20 cm for external walls, and of 12 cm for interior walls. A standard building has 6 cm thermal insulation mounted externally.

The total building surface to be insulated is 304 m^2. The window area is 60 m^2. Those are ideal conditions for transparent thermal insulation. Solar shading devices are unnecessary if damage to wall construction and the insulation system is avoided using careful design.

During shift changes, large internal gains occur from illumination, people and consumption of hot water. High air change rates almost completely extract those heat gains. On the whole, ventilation heat accounts for 94% of the total amount of heat consumed.

With transparent thermal insulation on the building's south facade and opaque thermal insulation on the remaining surfaces, the annual heating energy consumption is reduced to approximately 30% of the demand of a similar building constructed to a conventional design (i.e. the actual building as built) because surplus heat stored and released by the transparently insulated walls partially compensates for transmission heat loss and thermal energy needed to heat ventilation air.

The following section contains a selection of results on material properties and system characteristics.

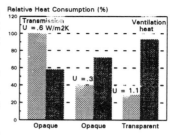

Fig. 17.16 Annual heat consumption of the building (relative figures as compared to usual construction) for additional opaque or for transparent insulation

17.3.4 Insulation materials

Some structures (such as honeycombs, capillaries, foams, fibers, and microspheres or granulates) reduce convection heat loss and partly scatter transmitted light. The transmittance is affected by material thickness.

Figure 17.4 shows the impact of the layer thickness on the diffuse solar transmittance, as well as the dependence of U-values on diffuse solar transmittance.

The thermal conductivity of the different transparent insulation materials is strongly dependent on temperature. Table 17.1 presents mean values suitable for use in calculations. Low values of 0.02 W/m K are obtained for aerogel, and relatively high values of 0.09 W/m K for honeycomb materials.

Table 17.1 Thermal conductivity of transparent insulation materials (mean values for about 20°C average temperature)

Material	Density (kg/m^3)	Thermal conductivity (W/m K)
Capillaries	40	0.07
PC-honeycomb	32	0.09
Glass fiber	18	0.04
PMMA-foam	15	0.06
Granulated aerogel	110	0.02
Homogeneous aerogel	180	0.02

Table 17.2 shows the influence of the insulating system on the thermal behavior of a 200 mm concrete wall facing south. Modeling was done

using the SUNCODE simulation program. An ambient temperature of 0°C was assumed. With transmission factors ranging from 0.2 to 0.6, and U-values between 0.9 and 1.6 W/m² K, the exterior wall surface temperature lies between 32°C and 52°C.

Table 17.2 Influence of transmission factor on the thermal behavior of a 200 mm south-facing concrete wall

Transmission factor	U-value (W/m² K)	Max. surface temp (°C) Exterior	Interior
0.6	1.0	52	33
0.6	1.1	46	32
0.5	1.1	44	30
0.5	1.6	38	29
0.4	0.9	40	29
0.3	1.2	32	26
0.2	1.0	33	26

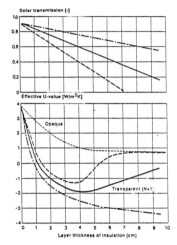

Fig. 17.17 Influence of layer thickness of different transparent insulating materials on transmission factor and effective U-value (example: a 200 mm concrete wall)

Of course, while thicker layers of insulation offer greater protection from heat loss, they also transmit less heat and decrease solar gains. The interdependence of the two effects leads to climate- and material-dependent optimum values of insulation thickness.

Figure 17.17 identifies various materials applied to a south-oriented, 200 mm concrete wall with a moderate, central European climate. In cases where the degree of radiation transmission varies strongly with the variation in layer thickness, optimum thickness for materials with high scattering effects range even below 50 mm, under moderate climate conditions. In climates with stronger radiation, a higher degree of radiation transmission can compensate for lower levels of insulation and vice versa.

17.3.5 Wall material and thickness

The thermal capacity of the wall diminishes the temperature from the outside to the inside and creates a phase shift between the solar gains outside and the heat transmitted into a room. Table 17.3 shows measured phase shift and ratio of amplitudes for five different materials and various wall thicknesses. The maximum surface temperatures of the wall are also given, for a U-value of the insulation system of 1.1 W/m² K, and transmission factor of 0.5 in the insulation layer.

17.3.6 Influence of climate

The heat flux through the wall is shown in relation to monthly insolation normalized by degree-days (kWh/m² dd) for different insulation systems

Table 17.3 Phase shift and temperature amplitude damping for several test wall constructions

Wall construction material thickness (mm)		Phase shift (h)	Ratio of amplitudes	Max. surface temperature (°C)	
				Exterior	Interior
Porous brick	365	14.0	0.04	73	24
	240	6.8	0.11	64	27
Limestone	240	6.2	0.14	53	26
Floating brick	240	5.6	0.19	51	27
Heavy concrete	200	4.0	0.46	43	31
	50	0.8	0.78	51	45
Cellular concrete	50	1.2	0.65	103	67

and wall constructions, compared to opaque insulation in Fig. 17.18. Positive heat flux denotes a transmission loss to ambient and negative heat flux denotes a solar gain. The hatched section separates the limiting values with and without surplus heat.

Idealized interior boundary conditions are assumed, i.e. a constant temperature of 20°C. In the heating period, the mean monthly heat loss of the opaquely insulated reference wall is $13\,kWh/m^2$, or more than $100\,kWh/m^2$ per year. The walls equipped with transparent thermal insulation lose heat each month in the range between 2 and $6\,kWh/m^2$, counterbalanced by heat gains between 3 and $12\,kWh/m^2$.

The external wall has a limited heat capacity and heat gains can only be stored for one or two days. These gains are given off to the interior as surplus heat. Heat losses occur during prolonged periods of weak radiation, although in theory there is more than enough surplus heat to offset them. Even in Shetland, where weak radiation predominates, negative U-values can be obtained during the mean heating period. During the heating period, more heat is transmitted into the interior than given off through the wall.

The kind of insulation system, wall material and wall construction that is selected influences the way surplus heat is used. The amount of surplus heat generated and its usability depends on the storage capacity of the external walls, the phase shift of temperature amplitudes and the maximum interior wall surface temperature. Usability requirements must be considered when determining the dimensios of insulation systems.

Figure 17.19 displays the effective U-value of the 200 mm concrete wall, which depends on the insolation/degree-day fraction according to climate. Values for locations ranging from Shetland to Sicily are given. These values have been calculated for a transparent thermal insulation layer with a U-value of $1.1\,W/m^2\,K$ and a transmission factor of 0.5.

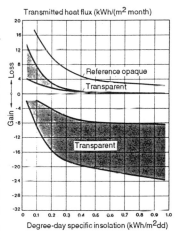

Fig. 17.18 Influence of climate on monthly heat gains and losses of transparently insulated mass walls

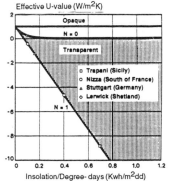

Fig. 17.19 Influence of climate on the effective U-value of a transparently insulated wall (200 mm concrete wall)

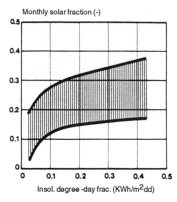

Monthly solar fraction (-)

Insol. degree -day frac. (KWh/m²dd)

Fig. 17.20 Influence of climate on the monthly solar fraction for different wall constructions and insulation systems

17.3.7 Monthly solar fraction

This is defined as

$$f = \frac{\text{exploited insolation}}{\text{total insolation}}$$

Figure 17.20 shows the influence of climate conditions on monthly solar fraction. Monthly solar fractions of more than 0.1 and up to nearly 0.4 are observed.

Table 17.4 presents effective U-values of various wall constructions equipped with south-oriented transparent thermal insulation with a U-value of 1.1 W/m² K and a transmission factor of 0.5. The effective U-values were obtained through experiments.

Table 17.4 Influence of different construction materials on the effective U-value of walls with transparent insulation

Construction material	Wall thickness	U-value	Effective U-value (W/m² K)	
	(mm)	(W/m² K)	$N = 0$	$N = 1$
Vertical core brick	365	0.5	0.25	-0.30
Light brick	240	0.7	0.3	-0.15
Limestone	240	0.8	0.32	-0.22
Pumice concrete hollow block	240	0.8	0.31	-0.22
Heavy concrete	200	1.0	0.41	-0.30
Normal concrete	50	1.3	0.54	-0.16

If the surplus heat is disregarded, the effective U-values amount to half the normal values. With surplus heat, gains are obtained for all constructions, the effective U-values being negative. The respective influences of different insulation layers are presented in Table 17.5. A reduction in the effective U-value is observed for transmission factors as low as 0.3.

17.3.8 Orientation

Table 17.6 shows the influence of orientation on surface temperatures. The time of year chosen gives a maximum temperature difference between interior and exterior surfaces.

The temperature difference is a measure of the thermal stress in the wall. The thermal stress on the wall is approximately the same for walls facing south, east and west, but occurs at different times.

The performance of a wall with transparent insulation and different orientations is given in Fig. 17.21. It presents the mean effective

Table 17.5 Influence of transparent insulating layer on the effective U-value of a 200 mm south facing concrete wall

Transparent insulation		Effective U-value (W/m^2 K)	
Transmission factor	U-value (W/m^2 K)	$N = 0$	$N = 1$
0.6	1.0	0.14	-0.88
0.6	1.1	0.27	-0.84
0.5	1.1	0.41	-0.30
0.5	1.6	0.58	-0.13
0.4	0.9	0.35	-0.28
0.3	1.0	0.48	-0.26

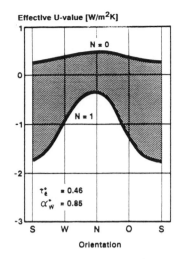

Fig. 17.21 The influence of orientation on the energetic performance of a wall with transparent thermal insulation (example: a 200 mm concrete wall)

Table 17.6 Influence of orientation on the thermal behavior of a wall with transparent insulation (200 mm concrete wall)

Orientation	Season	Max. surface temperature (°C)	
		Exterior	Interior
South	Autumn	43	31
East	Summer	39	29
West	Summer	42	30

U-values for the heating period with surplus heat ($N = 1$) and without surplus heat ($N = 0$) of the 200 mm transparently insulated concrete wall. The calculations are based on a U-value of 1.1 W/m^2 K and a transmission factor of 0.46 for Stuttgart. The fewest losses and the largest gains were observed with south facades, the effective U-value being reduced from 1.0 to -1.7 m^2 K. Significant reductions in heat losses were also obtained in the north walls, but with only small gains.

17.3.9 Color of absorption layer

The color of the insulation material also influences the performance of transparently insulated facades. The absorption factors are 0.39 for white, 0.91 for lack and 0.98 for selective black. Differences in selective tint influence the absorption factors. The impact of the absorption factor on the transmissivity of insulation material is illustrated in Fig. 17.22 for the 200 mm concrete wall.

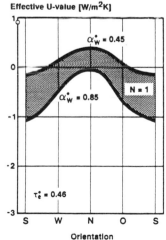

Fig. 17.22 The influence of solar absorption on the energetic performance of a wall with transparent thermal insulation (example: a 200 mm concrete wall)

17.3.10   Uncontrolled systems

Careful detailing and design can preclude damage to wall construction and thermal insulation under severe thermal conditions. In old buildings, wall constructions must be checked for homogeneity. In modern buildings, the phase change of temperature amplitudes and the variations of amplitudes in time may be chosen with an operating strategy. Either of two strategies can be adopted to create the system:

1.   Optimization of solar gains related to facade area.
2.   Minimizing specific heating energy related to floor area.

In general, optimizing heat gains in relationship to facade area always results in partial coverage with transparent thermal insulation. The smaller the area of transparently insulated facade surface, the larger the heat gains related to facade area. With or without opaque thermal insulation, the same energy consumption may result.

17.3.11   Controlled systems

The application of controlled systems is without risk, since overheating of construction and interior spaces is prevented by solar shading devices. Figure 17.23 shows a typical, controlled transparent insulation system with roller blinds.

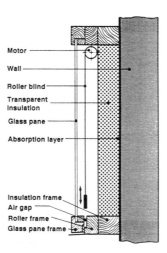

Fig. 17.23   Controlled transparent insulation system with roller blinds (schematic presentation)

17.4 REFERENCES

17/1 Schreiber, E., Boy, E. and Bertsch, K.: Aerogel as a transparent thermal insulation material for buildings, *Proceedings of the First International Symposium on Aerogels*, Springer Verlag, Berlin and Heidelberg, 1985.

17/2 Wittwer, V. *et al.*, Translucent insulation materials, *Proceedings of INTERSOL 85*, Montreal, 1985.

17/3 Hollands, K. T., Designing honeycombs for minimum material and maximum transmission, *Proceedings of the Second International Workshop on Transparent Insulation*, pp. 40–42, Freiburg, 1988.

17/4 Tewari, P. H., Advances in production of transparent silica aerogels for window glazing, *Proceedings of the First International Symposium on Aerogels*, pp. 31–7, Springer Verlag, Berlin and Heidelberg, 1985.

17/5 Rubin, M. and Lampert, C. M., Transparent silica aerogels for window insulation, *Solar Energy Materials*, **7**, 393–400, 1983.

17/6 Boy, E. and Meinhardt, S., Self-regulating temperature-dependent solar screens: TALD — a temperature controlled variable transparent glass, *Building Research and Practice*, **16**, 227–30, 1988.

17/7 Lampert, C. M. and Omstead, T. R., *Solar Energy Materials*, **14**, 161, 1986.

17/8 Boy, E., Experimental investigations of passive solar energy utilization of transparent insulated walls, *Proceedings of the ISES Solar World Congress*, Hamburg, 1987.

17/9 Boy, E. and Bertsch, K., Transparente Wämedämmung: Wärmedämmung und passive Solarenergienutzung in einem System, *WKSB 32*, **22**, 29–33, 1987.

17/10 Goetzberger, A., Gertis, K. A. *et al.*, Transparente Wärmedämmung, Final Report on BMFT Project 03E-8411-A. IRB Verlag, T 1830, Stuttgart, 1988.

17/11 Ortmanns, G. and Fricke, J., Moderne Fenster, *Physik in unserer Zeit*, **19**(1), 1–7, 1987.

17/12 Krochmann, J., Lichttechnische und strahlungsphysikalische Daten von Isoliergläsern, XXX-I/85 A, Berlin University, 1985.

17/13 Grochal, P., Hegen, D., Boy, E., Entwicklung eines fugenlosen transparenten Wärmedämmsystems. BMFT-Statusbericht, *Energetische Optimierung der Solarapertur*, pp. 301–13. Fachinformationszentrum, Karlsruhe, 1989.

17/14 Werner, H., Zwillingshäuser des Fraunhofer-Instituts of Bauphysik, Untersuchung energiesparender Massnahmen, *TAB*, **1**, 15–19, 1983.

17/15 Boy, E., Transparente Wärmedämmung im Praxistest — Zwischenergebnisse aus einer zwei-jährigen Untersuchungsperiode, *Bauphysik*, **11**(2), 93–9, 1989.

18 Absorber Walls

Fig. 18.1 Arsenal solar house, view from south-east

18.1 INTRODUCTION

An absorber wall uses the exterior walls, roofs, balcony parapets, etc. of a building as heat exchangers (Fig. 18.1). The source of energy for these heat exchangers is the combination of the sensible and latent heat content of the outdoor humid air and of the global radiation on the surface of the building.

To extract this ambient energy, the absorber element must be cooled by fluid that transfers heat from the environment to the building. The liquid is usually a mixture of water, anti-corrosion and antifreeze agents. A heat pump is used in the cooling system which uses power (usually electrical) to raise the low-temperature heat from the absorber to the required usable temperature level for space heating.

18.1.1   System design and operation

Absorber systems are usually employed in combination with:

• a conventional heat source (oil or gas fired), and/or
• with a low temperature storage unit (foundation slabs, ground heat exchangers), Fig. 18.2.

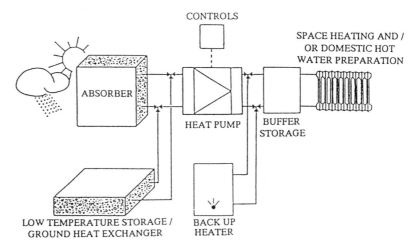

Fig. 18.2 Combination of absorber, low-temperature storage system, heat pump and conventional heat source

The heat output per square meter of the absorber surface depends on the difference in temperature between the surface of the absorber and the transfer fluid.

The favorable climate conditions which permit relatively high temperatures of the absorber surface and high heat transfer to a heat pump are:

• high wind speed, which improves convective heat transfer between the air and absorber surface;
• high humidity, causing evaporation so that any heat can be used if surface temperatures fall below the dew point;
• solar radiation on the absorber surface; and
• frequent precipitation.

18.1.2 Advantages and disadvantages

Integral absorbers, such as concrete elements, are economic alternative absorber walls for new buildings. The additional cost for desining an exterior wall to function as a mass absorber is approximately US $30/m², which includes piping, but excludes the heat pump.

The heat pump is normally electric, and produces 2–3 times more thermal energy than electric energy consumed by its operation. If, however, the cost of energy produced from oil or gas is significantly less than energy produced by electricity, an absorber wall would be relatively costly.

Metal absorbers are far more costly than concrete walls, and are currently used only in special cases, such as expensive commercial buildings.

Test results in [18/1] have show that absorber walls have the same service life as normal exterior walls. While the heat loss through the wall increases, this can be compensated by increasing the insulation thickness in the wall. The only negative aspect of an absorber wall is that if the temperature drops below the dewpoint, water stains form on the surface of the wall. If the design of the system is incorrect, or if it is not correctly operated, the following problems may occur.

Fig. 18.3 Extreme condensation stains/spots (after temperatures dropped extremely below dewpoint for several hours)

- Concrete that does not meet specifications may absorb a high degree of moisture and cause construction damage.
- When the operating temperature of the heat transfer fluid is more than 6–8 K below ambient air temperature, the heat pump coefficient of performance drops too much, causing the pump to work harder. Also, construction damage becomes more likely, especially if the concrete used did not meet specifications.

18.2 SYSTEM TYPES

Two types of absorber system are currently available:

1. integral absorbers (such as concrete absorbers) with high specific mass and correspondingly high thermal storage capacity/high thermal inertia;
2. lightweight metal or plastic absorbers with low specific mass and low thermal inertia.

In integral absorbers, the transfer fluid pipes are embedded in a concrete element. Because the concrete is also used to store heat, integral absorbers are particularly suitable if the heat pump is operated intermittently.

This chapter describes integral absorbers, which are cost-effective, and more often used. Figure 18.5 shows typical absorber constructions.

Exterior wall Massive absorber

Exterior wall Metal absorber with air gap on the reverse

Fig. 18.4 Absorber wall constructions

Balcony parapet Massive absorber

Supporting wall Massive absorber

Fig. 18.5 Absorber constructions

18.2.1   Transparent covers

The absorber can have a transparent cover; however, covers are advantageous only if the heat gained from solar radiation is higher than from the latent heat of the surrounding air. This is certainly not the case in central European climates in winter.

18.2.2   Combination with ground heat exchangers

As described above, a heat pump can be designed to provide all the heat required if the absorber system is combined with a low-temperature storage device. This concept is possible in new buildings, by designing the foundation slab to serve both as a storage unit and as a heat exchanger. During periods of low heat demand, surplus heat from the absorber is transferred to the foundation slab. When the temperature within the absorber wall drops below that of the storage unit, the heating system switches over to extracting heat from the storage.

18.3   EXAMPLES

18.3.1   Natter Knitwear Factory, Lustenau, Austria

The Natter factory, Fig. 18.6, was one of the first commercial buildings in Austria equipped with an integral absorber system. The building was commissioned in January 1982, and data monitoring took place from 1982 through 1987.

100% of both the heat for the factory and hot water for the entire building is provided by the integral absorber pump system. But space

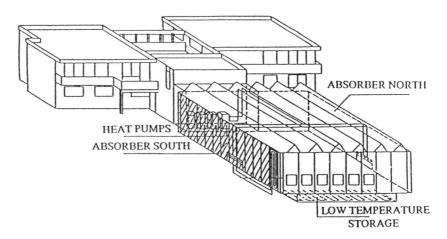

Fig. 18.6   Natter factory

heating in the living quarters and office space is provided by the absorber/heat pump system combined with a conventional oil boiler for domestic and office use.

Ambient energy is extracted by the heat pump from a foundation storage unit and 310 m² absorber walls, evenly distributed between the south and the north facades. The absorber wall is made of exposed aggregate concrete.

A total of 1950 m heat exchange piping is embedded in the 370 m³ foundation heat storage unit. The foundation is in direct contact with the ground water, since the water level is 2 m below the ground.

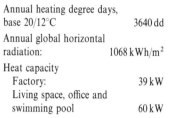

Annual heating degree days, base 20/12°C	3640 dd
Annual global horizontal radiation:	1068 kWh/m²
Heat capacity	
Factory:	39 kW
Living space, office and swimming pool	60 kW

Thermal performance

This system has been operating since 1982, demonstrating that the service life of a concrete absorber can equal that of normal concrete walls, if the absorber system is designed and operated as specified in Section 18.4

The average heat production of the system over the five years was 238 000 MWh/a. The average electricity consumption including electricity for the heat pumps, was 99 100 MWh/a. The coefficient of performance, defined as thermal energy production divided by electricity consumption, is 2.4. The output of the absorber is 405 kWh/m² a.

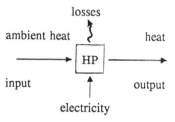

18.3.2 Arsenal solar house, Vienna, Austria

The Arsenal solar house is situated in Vienna, Austria. It is a testing and research facility designed to develop active and passive solar energy systems. It is also used as an office building for guest researchers and staff. Figure 18.1 shows the solar house viewed from outside.

The main purpose of this solar house is to examine the dynamic operating characteristics of two types of heat absorbers, copper and integral concrete absorbers. Data obtained for almost identical air and heat transfer fluid temperatures indicates that the thermal performance of an integral absorber is superior to that of a copper absorber on days with sufficient radiation (greater than 600 Wh/m² d). Integral absorbers perform better than the copper system because concrete absorbers retain more available solar radiation, which can be used during standstill periods, whereas copper has a lower capacity to store and transfer solar heat.

During the heating season, the integral absorber system alternated with the heat pump using heat extracted from the transfer fluid after standstill periods of at least half an hour.

Figure 18.7 shows the mean specific thermal performance of both types of absorbers as a function of the global radiation per day on the absorber surface. The data clearly shows the advantage of integral absorbers on sunny days.

The disadvantage of copper absorbers can be offset by using a buffer

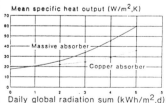

Fig. 18.7 Specific heat output as a function of global radiation yield

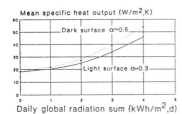

Fig. 18.8 Specific heat output as a function of global radiation sums and color of the surface

storage unit on the cold side of the heat pump and an advanced control system. This solution, however, increases energy costs for copper absorber systems.

On cold and cloudy days or during the night, the copper absorber system may be operated continuously. Because of its higher thermal conductivity, the copper absorber provides a slightly higher heat output than integral absorbers.

To achieve the same absorber heat output, the integral absorber requires a lower temperature transfer fluid temperature, which increases electric consumption, resulting in a reduced coefficient of performance.

The average coefficient of performance of the system tested in Austria during the last few years ranges from 2.3 to 2.9. The high performance values were measured in systems using both a heat pump and a back-up heating system.

The thermal performance of the system employing solar radiation is certainly influenced by the color of the surface. Figure 18.8 shows the specific heat output of the integral absorber as a function of daily global radiation when varying the color of the surface. The color of the facade does not influence specific heat output.

Figure 18.10 is an infrared photo showing the temperature distribution typical during operation of absorber systems.

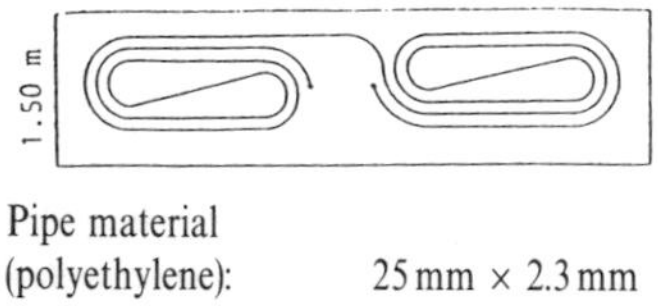

Fig. 18.10 Temperature distribution in a system of four integral absorber elements (infrared photo)

Pipe material
(polyethylene):   25 mm × 2.3 mm
Distance between parallel
pipes: 0.1 m
Shortest bending diameter: 0.4 m
Total pipe length installed: 20 m

Fig. 18.9 Integral absorber element

18.3.3 A garden wall application

Monitoring took place between 1982 and 1987. A garden wall provides the heat source for this system in Rankweil, Austria, which was monitored from 1982 to 1987. The garden wall consists of prefabricated elements which serve as supporting walls. The absorber and storage pipes were installed so that the visible wall surfaces function as absorbers, and the earth-covered part of the wall serves as a storage unit, as shown in Fig. 18.11. The system provides all the hot water required by the occupant. Both the garden wall and absorber plate face south.

When the ambient temperature drops below $+3°C$, the conventional backup heating system operates with the heat pump system. The total heating capacity installed is 29.6 kW.

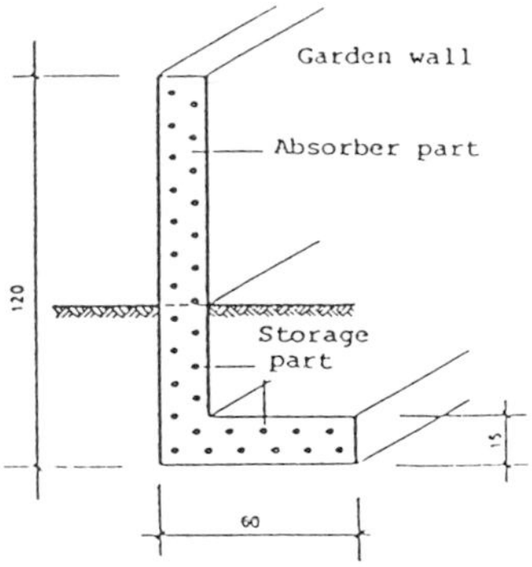

Fig. 18.11 Section in the garden wall in Rankweil, Austria

Thermal performance
The average output of the system is 32 MWh/a. Electricity consumed, including that for pumps, was 12 MWh, giving a coefficient of performance of 2.7. The specific output of the absorber is 550 kWh/m^2 a.

Conclusions
The higher value coefficient of performance shows that the application of an absorber with two active surfaces is more cost-effective compared to a facade system. The results indicate that physical separation of the absorber and storage functions is unnecessary.

Annual heating degree days, base 20/12°C:	3700 dd
Annual global radiation:	1016 kWh/m^2
Design ambient temp.:	$-16°C$
Absorber wall	
Length:	32 m
Surface area:	10 m^2
Pipe length:	180 m^2

18.4 DESIGN INSIGHTS

18.4.1 Construction requirements

Concrete in the wall of a mass storage system, as well as metal absorbers, must withstand mechanical and thermal stress tests. Increased stress must be met for metal absorbers to prevent problems wherever absorber plate and transfer fluid pipes are joined by welding or hard-soldering.

Moisture in concrete absorbers
Measurements of moisture in concrete absorber elements conducted at the Fraunhofer Institute of Building Physics, in Germany [18/4] have given the following results:

- There are small differences in moisture content within a concrete absorber element. However, no significant increase of moisture was found in the immediate vicinity of the transfer fluid pipes.
- There was no evidence of significant moisture absorption in the concrete absorber elements. The mean moisture content of concrete absorber elements was found to be 6% in weight, i.e. an increase of 1% in weight over standard exterior concrete walls.

Required air contents in fresh concrete (after vibrating)	
Maximum grain size (mm)	Air content in consolidated fresh concrete (%)
8	6.0–8.0
16	4.5–6.5
25	4.0–6.0
32	3.5–5.5
63	3.0–4.5

Freezing

In the surface layers of concrete absorbers, stresses result from frequent freezing and melting of moisture. The cooling process may cause condensation and frost on the surface of absorber elements. Since freezing has a strong effect on concrete if there is water on its surface, porous concrete must be used: air-entrained concrete having numerous air pores (less than 0.3 mm diameter) resists frost more than normal concrete. When water freezes and expands in the capillary pores of the concrete, it can escape into the numerous air pores so that the concrete does not crack. Before concrete is mixed, a sufficient amount of an air entraining agent should be added.

Piping

Since the absorber heating system is integrated in the building's wall, the system must have the same service life as the building structure. Consequently, the absorber pipe materials must function for at least 50 years under operating conditions. Success has been achieved with HDPE (high density polyethylene) piping with 25 mm diameter and 2.3 mm wall thickness.

Proper venting of the absorber pipes must be secured; air accumulation can be critical because of the way pipes are installed, as shown in Fig. 18.9.

18.4.2   Heat pump system

Good performance, long service life and low maintenance costs of the absorber wall and the heat pump system depend on the design and maintenance of both. The following remarks refer to design of the heat pump system.

- The power consumption of the circulation pumps should not exceed 5% of the heat pump to achieve a high thermal energy production per used kilowatt-hour.
- Special attention should be given to reduce the noise emission from the heat pump. Often, heat pump systems with good thermal performance are hampered by an unacceptably high noise level.
- The pipe system between the heat pump and the absorber will be very cold and should be insulated accordingly. The insulation material must prevent water condensation on the surface of the pipes, and it must prevent humidity absorption through diffusion.
- Additional heat output can be achieved if the connecting pipes between absorber and heat pumps are installed in the ground because they will act as ground heat exchangers.

Design

When designing the absorber and heat pump systems, the challenge is to optimize the temperature of the absorber surface and admissible cooling (difference between ambient air temperature and transfer fluid temperature). Figure 18.12 shows the coefficient of performance of a typical absorber wall heat pump as a function of the temperature of the cooling gluid (water/glycol) in the absorber wall. The bigger the difference, the higher the specific heat output of the absorber will be. The required absorber surface decreases but it has a negative influence on the performance.

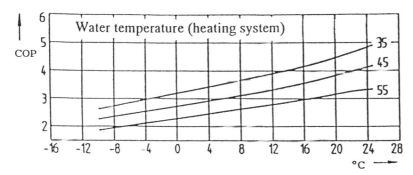

Fig. 18.12 The coefficient of performance as a function of the temperature of the water–glycol cooling fluid (Source: Siemens)

The minimum water–glycol temperature is usually in the range of about −5°C to 0°C. The correct determination of the minimum operating temperature is not merely a technical but a cost–benefit problem.

- If electricity is relative inexpensive compared to thermal energy, a lower minimum operating temperature can be allowed, giving a lower coefficient of performance.
- A typical operating temperature of the water/glycol fluid will be 5–7 K below ambient temperature during continuous operation. In a central European climate, this will provide an output for the integral absorber of 80–200 W/m^2.
- There is a direct relationship between the specific performance and global radiation on the absorber surface.

The size of the absorber is calculated on the basis of the lowest ambient air temperature at which the required heating capacity can be provided by the system. In this calculation, it is assumed that the absorber is operated under extremely unfavorable heat absorption conditions: or heat absorption is only from ambient air with no radiation or condensation and at a low wind speed.

Experience and simulations have shown that a safe design is 15 W/m^2 K at a 6 K temperature difference between ambient air and mean transfer fluid temperature. Consequently, the specific heat output is 90 W/m². To this heat output one must add the electricity use of the heat pump. The sum is the output of thermal energy from the heat pump.

If the design temperature is $+3°C$ and the coefficient of performance is three at this temperature, the electrical power used is 45 W/m² absorber surface.

$$\frac{90_{\text{thermal}} + Q_{\text{el}}}{Q_{\text{el}}} = \frac{90\,\text{W/m}^2 + 45\,\text{W/m}^2}{45\,\text{W/m}^2} = 3 = \text{COP}$$

The design heating capacity available is $(90 + 45)\,\text{W/m}^2 = 135\,\text{W/m}^2$.

18.4.3   Heat loss through an absorber wall

When the exterior walls of a building are used as absorbers in a heat pump system, transmission loss will increase. This can be compensated, to a large degree, if extra thermal insulation is installed between the heat exchanger zone and the inner parts of the wall. Without such compensation, the U-value of a wall increases about 30%, given a temperature difference of 5–7 K between the ambient air and the fluid in the wall. This increase of the U-value happens when the heat pump is operating, primarily by cold temperatures.

18.5   ANALYSIS TOOLS

Two programs for analysis and design of absorber systems are currently used in Austria: the SONNWAND (sunwall) program and the absorber program. Both programs permit a dynamic simulation, and were developed as a part of a thesis [18/2]; they are published but not commercially sold. They were validated on the basis of the data acquired in the Arsenal solar house project, and they can be run on an AT personal computer with DOS.

The concept of radiation air temperature was used for the representation of the heat sources on the absorber surface that result from the absorption of global radiation, long-wave radiation exchange, and convection. Time steps of ten minutes allow a good representation of dynamic effects in copper absorbers with low thermal inertia, particularly swift changes of global radiation intensity. The programs may be used to study a variety of possible construction types, such as transparent protective layers in front of the absorber, different colors, different kinds of thermal insulation in the wall, etc.

Both programs provide the following output: temperature profiles over wall cross section, heat flows, and effective heat output (amount of heat received by the transfer fluid per unit time unit). Required meteorological data are: test reference years including hourly values of direct and diffuse radiation, ambient air temperature, and humidity.

18.6 CONCLUSIONS AND RECOMMENDATIONS

Constructing an absorber wall involves considerable risk, particularly in the case of integral absorbers, which necessitate concrete quality specifications. Prefabricated absorber elements should be used.

Absorbers should be placed on southern, eastern, or western orientations to use as much solar radiation as possible.

If the absorber is operated in combination with a storage unit, such as the foundation slab of the building, the storage unit must be loaded whenever there is a heat surplus in winter. In spring, there is usually no need for the stored heat, so it should go unused.

The mean difference between transfer fluid temperature in the wall and ambient air temperature should not exceed 5–7 K.

The temperature fluctuations in absorbers, especially in metal absorbers, is much greater than that of other heat sources commonly used for heat pumps. This is primarily the result of solar radiation, which may raise the absorber temperature to a relatively high level.

The required absorber area should be determined through dynamic system simulation. Rough average values for systems with storage units with a central European climate are: 5 m² absorber surface plus 5 m² storage surface (foundation slab surface) per kilowatt heat capacity.

If about 50% of the absorber area is in direct contact with the ground, 7 m² absorber surface per kilowatt should be chosen. In this case a storage unit is superfluous.

In the near future, one can expect that capacity modulated, highly efficient heat pumps with improved refrigerants (such as R 134a) will appear on the European market, providing an increased coefficient of performance and avoiding ozone depletion.

One can also expect prefabricated wall construction (especially lightweight construction) to increase its share of the market. At least some of these will be used for ambient energy heat exchange.

Table 18.1 Calculated COPs by climate. Absorber facing south, without back-up system

Oslo	2.4
Vienna	2.7
Zürich	2.8
Brussels	2.9
Copenhagen	2.9
Rome	3.4

18.7 REFERENCES

18/1 Bayer, R., Massivabsorber-Heizsystem, *Forschungsbericht des Bundesministeriums für Bauten und Technik*, Wohnbauforschung, Wien 1982. Bundesministerium für Bauten und Technik A-1010 Wien, Schubertring 1.
  This book demonstrates the uses of integral absorbers. Fundamental concepts are explained and results of experiments are discussed.

18/2 Lingner, S., Dynamische Simulation von Absorber-Wärmepumpen-Systemen, Diplomarbeit, TU Wien, Institut für Allgemeine

Physik, TU Wien, A-1040 Wien, Wiedner Haupstr. 8-10.
This thesis is a detailed simulation, validated by measurements. The influence of absorber construction, operating modes and climatic conditions are discussed.

18/3 Bruck, M., Spangl, W., Weinguny, S., Resch, R., Standardisiertes Abnahmeverfahren für Sole/Wasser-Wärmepumpenheizungsanlagen und Solaranlagen zur Warmwasser-Erwärmung, Bundesministerium für Wissenschaft und Forschung, A-1010 Wien, Freyung 1.
This report describes a detailed acceptance test for heat pump systems with concrete or metal absorbers and ground heat exchangers as heat sources.

18/4 Prüfbericht über Feuchtigkeitsverhältnisse in Beton-Absorberelementen Fraunhofer-Institut für Bauphysik, Aûenstelle Holzkirchen, November 1982.
A compilation of Austrian, Swiss and German references on absorber walls is given in:
Massiv- und Wandabsorber, IRB-Literaturauslese Nr 665, IRB-Verlag, Informationszentrum Raum und Bau der Fraunhofer Gesellschaft, Nobelstr. 12, 7000 Stuttgart 80, Tel: 0711-6868-500, Telex: 7-255-167.

19 Storage Systems

19.1 INTRODUCTION

This chapter explores the use of short-term thermal storage in combination with various types of solar air collectors in commercial buildings. It also discusses the system configuration for short-term storage, active charge by air flow and passive discharge. This type of system is also known as a hybrid system.

The thermal storage requirements for commercial buildings (where night thermostat setback may occur at 18:00) are different from residential buildings (where setback may not occur until 22:00). The

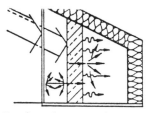

Passive charge and
discharge

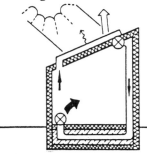

Active discharge from
storage (open loop)

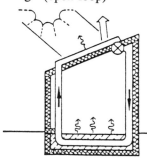

Passive discharge from
storage (closed loop)

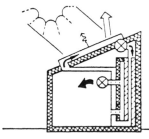

Active discharge from
storage

later thermostat setback of residential buildings results in the release of heat from thermal storage immediately after sunset being useful to meet the continued heating demand. In commercial buildings this immediate release of heat is less useful as the building is no longer occupied at that time. Accordingly, either of two strategies must be chosen: (1) discharging is finished at 18:00; or (2) discharging is optimized to reduce morning peak heating loads. To better control the release of heat, an active discharge of the storage (i.e. by fan) is advantageous.

19.1.1   Benefits

Thermal storage increases the usability of solar gains because it stores heat from the hours of the day when the sun is strong until it can be used during a time when the sun is weak. Thermal storage systsems can also reduce peak heating loads in the morning provided that the temperature of the storage which is exposed to the room (i.e. passive discharge) has not fallen below daytime room temperature set point. An additional advantage is that building elements can have several uses: structural, fire protection, and thermal storage.

19.1.2   Disadvantages

Unfortunately, using thermal storage systems requires energy input (electricity) when the storage system is charged or discharged. As with all storage systems, the building structure will require extra volume. The fans may create noise. Open loop systems require filters and are mostly untried in Europe.

19.2   SYSTEM VARIATIONS

Both charge and discharge of the storage can be passive, as with mass wall systems (see Chapter 16). Passive discharge is shown in the Meteolabor building, which is discussed later in this chapter. Active discharge of the storage is also exemplified later in this chapter in the section on the Schopfloch Kindergarten. Passive discharge is always closed loop. In fan-driven systems, discharge may be part of either a closed or open loop system. In open loop systems, the air from the room is used as a heat transfer medium. In closed loop systems, the air flows in a sealed circuit and does not contact room air.

19.3 TEST CASES

Four examples have been analyzed: the Meteolabor building, the Nautilus building with a solar chimney at Ispra, the test house in Essen, and the Schopfloch Kindergarten. The main system characteristics of the four examples are shown in Table 19.1.

Table 19.1 System characteristics

Example	Storage type	Collector	Distribution
Meteolabor:	hollow core	facade	fan driven
Ispra:	concrete slab	facade	thermosyphon
Essen:	pebble-bed	sun trap	fan driven
Schopfloch:	rock bed	roof	fan driven

19.3.1 Meteolabor

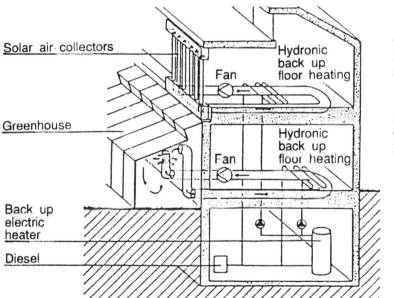

Greenhouse glazing area: 110 m²
Air collector area: 27 m²
Storage:
  Volume 317 m³
  Thermal capacity 210 kWh/K
Building transmission heat loss
coefficient: 320 W/k
Installed fan capacities
    15 × 80 W = 1200 W

Fig. 19.1 Energy system of Meteolabor building

Storage system and auxiliary heating
The Meteolabor building is heated by solar energy from a greenhouse and an air collector. Storage discharge is passive. (A description of the Meteolabor is also given in Section 14.3.2.) The rooms are heated from the hollow floor (Fig. 19.2) through which solar heated air is fan-forced

from the greenhouse and the collectors. The air is circulated through metal ducts which are 150 mm in diameter and embedded in the concrete floors.

The system incorporates nine fans at ground level and six fans at the upper level. Hydronic auxiliary heating is provided by a copper tube grid embedded in the floor. The rooms are constantly kept at 20°C, without night setback.

Storage system construction

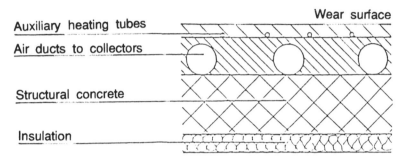

Fig. 19.2 Cross-section of the floor

Solar energy from the greenhouse and the air collectors produces 60% of the annual gross auxiliary heating load. Because auxiliary heating is integrated in the concrete floor which also acts as thermal storage, it is impossible to make a detailed evaluation of the storage system. The performance of the system is discussed in Chapter 14, Air Collector Systems.

Collector efficiency is highest when the temperature difference between collector and storage is large. Since the heating system also heats up the concrete slab, the slab accumulates heat with reduced efficiency. Such a system works well only if the auxiliary heating mode and storage charging mode are separated. To do this, a data acquisition and temperature control system predicts future weather conditions and charges the storage accordingly. This system is effective under most conditions; however, if cloudy weather is predicted by the control system and sunny conditions prevail, back-up floor heating will begin and the collector efficiency is reduced.

The efficiency of solar collection and storage would be increased by separating the auxiliary heating from the floor using radiators or air heating.

19.3.2   Nautilus building, Ispra, Italy

This building makes use of various passive solar strategies, all incorporating vertical thermosyphon solar chimney type collectors (Fig. 19.3).

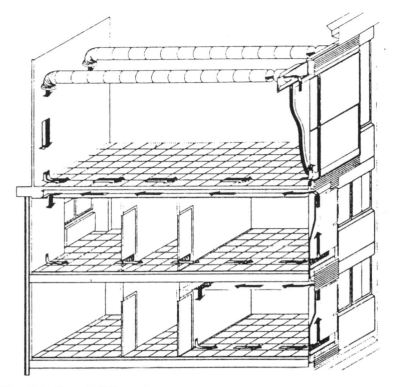

Fig. 19.3 Ispra building solar strategy

Storage discharge is passive.

Three different storage and distribution systems were installed:

1. On the ground floor, collector air passes through an uninsulated suspended metal ceiling which acts as a plate heat exchanger and radiating surface.
2. On the first floor, four ducts are embedded in the concrete ceiling. Each duct is connected to a solar chimney.
3. On the second floor, metal pipes suspended below the ceiling are supplied directly from the collector.

Monitoring data from only a few days is available for analysis of this interesting building. During the monitoring period, the back-up system was shut off.

System variations monitored
For monitoring and analysis, the building was divided into three separate sections corresponding to the ground, first, and second floors. Four distinct distribution and storage systems were studied:

1. Offices on the ground floor with a 3 m high solar chimney collector connected to a suspended metal ceiling.

2. Offices on the first floor with a 3 m high solar chimney collector connected to a hollow-core concrete slab. The 10 m long channels have a cross-section of 32/30 cm (height/width), through which heated air is transferred to the north rooms.

3. Offices on the first floor use the same system as in number two; but the length of the hollow-core concrete slab is only 4.2 m. Thus the solar preheated air is recirculated to the collector from the south instead of from the north room.

4. Laboratories on the second floor use a 5 m high solar chimney connected to three non-insulated suspended metal tubes, each with a diameter of 49 cm and a length of 9.5 m.

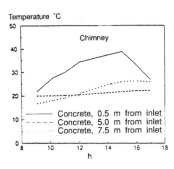

Fig. 19.4 Temperatures in and between the air ducts (9 March)

Results

The air velocities in the ducts of the storage system during a sunny day reach 0.075 and 0.1 m/s by 11:00 h. Velocities peak at 0.175 to 0.20 m/s between 14:30 and 15:00 h. The ducted system of the second floor consistently experiences the lowest air flows. The reason for this is that channel 4 is uninsulated and conducts heat to the room. It is also somewhat longer than the others.

The temperatures of the air in the chimney and of the concrete mid-distance between the air ducts at three different distances from the inlet is shown in Fig. 19.4. The temperature in the concrete close to inlet starts low because this section of the floor is poorly insulated. This area needs 2.5 h of heating before it reaches room temperature (20°C) to compensate for the lack of insulation.

The temperature 5.0 m and 7.5 m away from the warm air inlet increases very slowly, indicating that the thermal mass is higher than necessary given the actual collector area. Actual solar gains are stored completely within a length of 5.0 m on this sunny day which reaches a maximum global horizontal radiation of 650 W/m².

Recommendations

If most solar gains are to be delivered to the south zone of the building and only additional gains are to be moved to the north zone, the air outlet of the channel should be placed in the first part of the north office close to the partition wall between the north zone and the south zone. This reduces the channel length and thus air flow resistances are reduced.

If, however, the first half of the long channels are insulated, a major part of the solar gains will be discharged in the north zone, which can be desirable, since the south rooms profit from direct solar gains.

19.3.3   Test house, Essen

In this example, a solar attic collector and a rock bed storage system were tested as a combined thermal storage strategy. The test house is

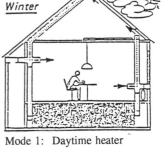

Winter

Mode 1: Daytime heater

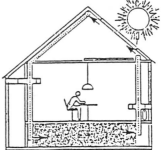

Mode 2: Storage mode

divided into two identical halves; one serves as an area for testing, the other as a control. The hybrid system consists of a solar attic collector integrated in the roof attic and a rock bed storage in the cellar. Heating is provided either directly from the collector or by active discharge from storage.

The solar collector is a $10 \, m^2$ glazed area on the roof facing south. The walls and the floor of the attic are painted black to absorb solar energy. The rock bed storage has a gross volume of $1.5 \, m^3$. During the night, movable insulation panels are inserted in the windows. A fan with a power rating of 120 W drives the distribution air flow from the attic to the room or to the storage.

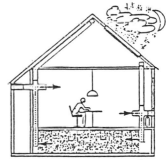

Mode 3: Discharge mode

Operating mode
The hybrid solar strategy operates in three modes.

1. *Daytime heating* When indoor air temperature is too low and the attic is warm enough, the room is heated directly by the collector.
2. *Storage mode* If the room and the collector have a higher temperature than the heating setpoint (20°C), then changing the storage starts.
3. *Discharge mode* When space heating is required, and the collector can not provide heat then storage discharge starts, provided that the storage temperature is above 23°C.

Fig. 19.5 Hybrid system operation modes

Results
The control room is influenced by the same user profile as the test room; it has the same passive gains as the test room through a south

window. All important parameters were recorded from December to May. Data were analyzed to evaluate the amount of auxiliary energy which is substituted by the hybrid system. The energy changes from heat gains and losses of the test room and the reference room are shown in Fig. 19.6. Auxiliary heating (*H*) is reduced by 915 kWh or 41% using the hybrid passive solar strategy.

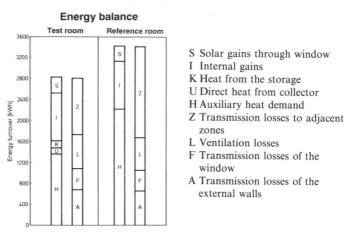

S Solar gains through window
I Internal gains
K Heat from the storage
U Direct heat from collector
H Auxiliary heat demand
Z Transmission losses to adjacent zones
L Ventilation losses
F Transmission losses of the window
A Transmission losses of the external walls

Fig. 19.6 Gains and losses from December through May

Heat loss through vertical walls and ventilation is identical for the two zones; however, the heat loss to the attic and cellar is considerably lower in the test area than in the reference area.

The solar contributions directly from the attic (*U*) and from the storage (*K*) are both low. Together, they account for only 135 kWh or 14% of the total energy saving. Seventy percent of the total energy savings (645 kWh) is from a reduction in heat loss to attic and cellar. These two spaces act as an envelope warming the building.

The data does not address the volume of the rock bed storage. A parameter study was conducted (using the SUNCODE program) varying the length of the rock bed storage and the insulation of the storage envelope.

Simulation results are presented in Fig. 19.7. Various insulation thicknesses were assumed as well as an adiabatic case with no heat losses from the storage. As expected, the auxiliary heating load is lower for the adiabatic case. For storage volumes greater than about 1 m³, no improvement is obtainable. For the purposes of comparison, a storage volume of 0.5 m³ was assumed, which may be near optimum when the cost is taken into account. A 10 m² collector area corresponds to a ratio of storage volume to collector area of 0.05 m³/m².

More auxiliary heat is used in the room without a storage system because a considerable amount of heat is lost to the cellar.

The calculated passive heat loss to the ground is 296 kWh when the

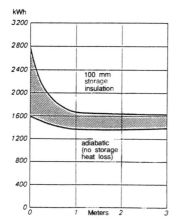

Fig. 19.7 Auxiliary heating versus rock bed length

storage system is $0.5\,m^3$. Some of this lost heat could be utilized if the storage were situated within the heated space.

Recommendations

Tests on the solar energy attic collector in the house in Essen indicate that only a small storage volume ($0.05\,m^3$ per m^2) collector is needed. Most energy saving is from the attic solar collector and the storage in the cellar, which create a warm envelope around the heated space, thereby reducing heat loss.

An alternate design for the storage system is a hollow core concrete floor or ceiling (150 to 200 mm thick) or an internal cavity wall facing two heated zones. An even simpler design to consider is an attic sun collector with a massive concrete ceiling, which is then irradiated directly by solar energy. The glazing would have to be effectively insulated during the night to prevent heat loss. Efficient glazing with transparent insulation might be simpler than movable insulation.

19.3.4   Schopfloch Kindergarten

In the Schopfloch Kindergarten, a $38\,m^2$ solar air collector is connected to a $20\,m^3$ rock bed thermal storage. A detailed description of the building is given in Section 14.3.1. Solar heating is provided by passive storage discharge.

The storage area is positioned in the center of the building. It is placed on the ground floor facing an atrium, between the toilet and material room, as shown in Fig. 19.8. Any losses of heat through the storage walls (with insulation of 10 cm) are passive gains for the building.

The kindergarten is heated by a hot air floor and a wall hypocaust heating system, diagrammed in Fig. 19.10. Auxiliary heat is supplied by a gas heater, which is also connected to the air heating system. The control system is described in Chapter 14, Air Collector Systems.

Performance

Figure 19.11 shows the temperature through a period of four days with sunshine. No active discharge occurred during this period.

The air velocity is evenly distributed in the cross section of the inlet to the storage, with variations from 2.5 to 2.9 m/s. During charging the storage demonstrates good temperature stratification and efficient heat transfer over the whole storage volume.

The monthly performance of the strategy is shown in Fig. 19.12. The heat delivered directly from the solar collector to the building is the major solar contribution of the system. The electrical consumption used for the fans of the hybrid solar system is very small. The electricity used for the fans in the daytime mode is only 3–4% of the energy

Air collectors
Absorber area   28 m²

Storage
Gross volume   20 m³
Thermal capacity   54 kWh/K

Installed capacity
Auxiliary heater   100 W/m²

Hypocaust fan
  low   0.50 kW
  high   2.50 kW
Collector fan   0.25 kW

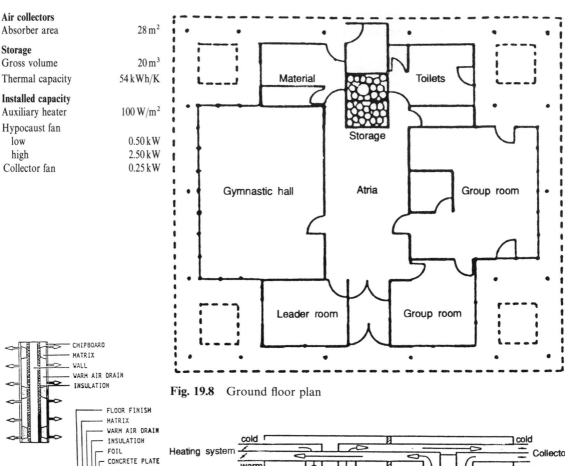

Fig. 19.8 Ground floor plan

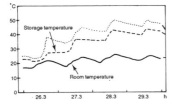

Fig. 19.10 Cross-sections of the hypocaust wall and floor elements

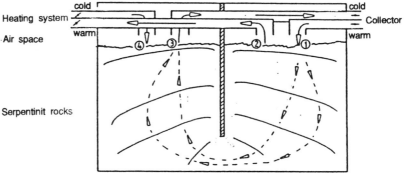

Fig. 19.9 Sketch of storage element illustrating the charging mode

delivered. The total electricity consumed to transport air to and through the storage is 9–25% of the thermal energy depending on the month.

Storage volume

In Chapter 14, the performance of the system is modeled in detail. The parameter study shows that a system with 20 m³ of storage volume

Fig. 19.11 Storage temperatures 26–29 March, with no discharge

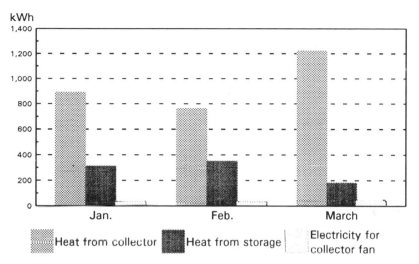

Fig. 19.12 Monthly performance

and $36\,m^2$ of air collector provides 25% of the gross heating load of the building. Of this total, 12% is gained in the direct heating mode (daytime heating), whereas the remaining 13% is supplied from the storage.

In Fig. 19.13, the solar contribution from the storage system is shown for different volumes of storage. The solar fraction in Fig. 19.13 is a percentage of the difference in heating load of the building, with and without storage.

With a $40\,m^2$ collector area, a storage volume of $4\,m^3$ is appropriate. Generally, a storage volume to collector area (RSC) of $0.1–0.2\,m^3/m^2$ is appropriate.

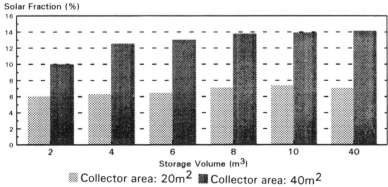

Fig. 19.13 Used solar energy versus gross storage volume (rock bed) for collector areas of $20\,m^2$ and $40\,m^2$

A storage system for a hybrid solar strategy need not occupy a significant amount of volume. If the $4.0\,m^3$ rock bed storage area had been constructed as a vented cavity concrete wall, it would occupy $0.6\,m^2$ of floor space, compared to the actual $20\,m^3$ pebble bed storage occupying $7.6\,m^2$ floor space.

19.4 DETAILED RESULTS

Studies of the systems used as examples in this chapter show that the optimum volume of thermal storage would be considerably smaller than what was actually built in the buildings discussed. This section shows the results of a parameter study performed for a $17\,m^2$ office room.

The program SERIRES 2.1-IBP, an enhanced mainframe version of SUNCODE, was used to simulate the office. Changes to the model allowed detailed simulation of hollow core storage elements including calculation of channel mass flow and three-dimensional thermal conduction.

19.4.1 Storage placement

The effects of storage placement on auxiliary heating load and overheating are simulated. The control case is an office unit without storage, but with a ceiling and a floor exposed to the ambient. Three locations of the hollow core storage elements were investigated:

1. Slab in the ceiling
2. Slab in the floor
3. Slab with both sides facing the heated zone.

Table 19.2(a) Specification of hybrid system

Wall collector:	
Collector area:	$5.0\,m^2$
Orientation	South
Inclination:	vertical
Air flow rate:	$35\,m^3/h\,m^2$
Control temperature difference:	3.0 K
Hollow core concrete element:	
Volume	$0.4\,m^3$
Thermal capacity	1.0 MJ/K
Passive discharge area:	$2.7\,m^2$
Insulation from ambient:	100 mm
Constant ground temperature:	10°C

Table 19.2(b) Placement of hollow core storage

Storage placement	Auxiliary energy (kWh/m²a)*	Overheating hours ($t > 24°C$)	
		Nov.–Mar. (h)	Oct.–Apr. (h)
Reference	85.0	3	81
Ceiling	73.9	13	139
Floor	73.2	13	158
Internal	72.8	15	163

*Relative to the floor area

Among the three systems with storage placing internal storage is marginally more effective than storage exposed to the environment. The differences are not as great as expected, but overheating must be guarded against.

Less heat is gained from a storage system connected to the ambient compared with a system with an internal store, though the warm envelope effect partly counterbalances the heat loss through the storage floor or roof.

19.4.2   Storage size and control strategy

The size of the storage is varied from zero (i.e. a system with daytime solar heater only) to a storage with a $0.25\,m^3$ per m^2 collector. In all cases, the storage system is assumed to be an internal cavity wall with both sides facing the heated area, as in Table 19.2(a).

Case 1: Daytime heating in operation only when there is a heating load.

Case 2: Daytime heating in operation even if the room temperature exceeds 20°C.

Table 19.3 Variation of storage volume and control strategy

Case	Storage volume	Ratio of storage volume to collector area (RSC)	Discharge area
	(m^3)	(m^3/m^2)	(m^2)
1	0	0	0
2	0	0	0
3	0.25	0.05	1.6
4	0.50	0.10	2.7
5	1.00	0.20	5.9
6	1.25	0.25	7.6

The wall collector is controlled so that it works whenever the collector temperature exceeds the storage temperature by 3 K, except for case 1, where the collector works only if there is a heating load; i.e. the room temperature does not exceed 20°C. The results of the parametric study are shown in Table 19.4.

For the storage systems, cases 3–6, Table 19.4 shows that increasing storage volume generally benefits energy saving but leads to more overheating hours. The effect is small when the ratio of storage volume to collector area exceeds about $0.10\,m^3/m^2$.

Case 2 allows some discomfort with the daytime heater, when the facade collector operates even if the room temperature exceeds 20°C. Compared to case 1, the number of hours with more than 24°C increases significantly in the second case. The total number of 158 hours from October through April, inclusive, comprises 11% of working time (10 hours per day).

Table 19.4 Performance of a storage system in an office

Variation (Table 19.3)	Storage vol/col area (m³/m²)	Auxiliary energy (kWh/m² a)	Overheating hours (t > 24°C)	
			Nov.–Mar. (h)	Oct. –Apr. (h)
Reference	0.00	85.0 —	3	81
case 1	0.00	78.0 8	5	139
case 2	0.00	73.6 13	89	158
case 3	0.05	73.5 14	14	156
case 4	0.10	72.8 14	15	163
case 5	0.20	71.8 16	11	161
case 6	0.25	71.6 16	11	161

*Energy saving relative to reference system (%)

The preferred system, both for energy saving and comfort, is Case 3, the system with the small storage unit. Little is to be gained with a larger storage system.

19.5 ANALYSIS

19.5.1 PC tools

SUNCODE-PC
Available with language and operating system:
Fortran 77 MS-(DR-)DOS

Capabilities SUNCODE is a simulation model for hourly energy analysis and temperature simulation in multizone buildings. Solar features like Trombe walls, rock bed and phase-change-material (PCM) storage are provided explicitly by separate input sections and calculation subroutines. Hybrid systems are modeled implicitly by input tricking.

Description A building is represented by a thermal resistances network. Non-steady-state heat transfer through walls is solved by an explicit forward-difference method. The equipment-controlled zone temperatures are determined by a Jacobi iteration executed with constrained optimization.
  Building envelope integrated air collector and construction integrated storage elements are defined as additional zones (subzoning), which are connected by a temperature-controlled fan specified in an extra input section. The weakness of the program in modeling the storage element, e.g. a hollow core concrete slab, is that it is limited to one-dimensional thermal conduction and air flow is modeled as air change between zones.

Contact:
BEST
Katzenbachstrasse 44
D-7000 Stuttgart 80
Germany

19.6 CONCLUSIONS

The analysis of test cases for air collector systems with passive and active storage discharge showed that the solar contribution to the total heating requirement can be as high as 60%. However, storage systems with passive discharge increase the likelihood of overheating in the spring and summer, so that some means of controlling the discharge from storage would be an advantage.

The simulations indicate that storage volume was mostly larger than necessary. An optimum ratio of gross storage volume to collector area was found to be in the range of 0.05 to $0.20 \, \text{m}^2/\text{m}^3$. This applies to both active and passive systems and to various storage materials. A comparison with optimum values quoted in the literature is given in Table 19.5. The literature values are for the most part higher. Slight differences in the definition of gross storage volume (i.e. with or without envelope volume and air spaces) are insufficient to explain this discrepancy. The investigations were based on the climate of central Europe, so that the results might have to be adjusted for other climates.

Table 19.5 Ratio of storage volume to collector area (RSC)

References	Optimum RSC (m^2/m^3)	Storage material
Essen	0.05–0.10	Concrete slab
Schopfloch	0.10–0.20	Rock bed
[19/5]	1.00–1.50	Rock bed
[19/6], [19/7]	0.30–0.70	Pebble bed
[19/8]	0.20	Pebble bed

Surprisingly, a storage system internal to the building is only marginally more effective in reducing auxiliary heating than storage exposed to ambient or the ground. This is because although internal storage delivers more useful heat than storage exposed to ambient, the buffer effect is lost.

Similarly, a rock bed storage system in combination with a solar trap collector is mainly effective in reducing the transmission losses to the attic and the basement. Thus, about 70% of the savings achieved are due to reduced transmission heat losses and only about 30% to the solar energy actually delivered.

A direct collector system without storage was found to provide slightly more than half the total saving obtained with systems incorporating storage. Since a direct system is considerably cheaper and incurs less risk of overheating than a storage system, this may be a real option in many practical cases.

A daytime heater system (with no storage, and the collector delivers solar energy directly to the building) provides more than half of the energy savings achieved from a solar strategy with storage given average German climate conditions.

Investigation of an optimal storage volume was made. In this context, storage volume is defined as the gross volume, including the storage envelope and including the air between the storage material (rocks, pebble bed, hollow core concrete). The optimal storage volume to collector area for the conditions studied in Germany is 0.1–$0.2\,m^3$ gross storage volume per m^2 collector area; this value is based on two examples analyzed in this sourcebook, the Essen test house and the Schopfloch Kindergarten, and two parameter studies. The optimal storage volume takes both energy performance and comfort into account.

Furthermore, this conclusion is valid for both active and passive discharge systems, and for various storage materials, such as pebble bed storage or rock bed storage systems (active discharge), or hollow core concrete slabs (passive discharge). The optimal storage volume = 0.1–$0.2\,m^3$ per m^2 solar collector is based on analyses done with German weather data. In extreme climates, (cold or very sunny) these conclusions are probably invalid.

19.7   REFERENCES

19/1 *IEA Seminar on the Status of Solar Air Systems*, Utrecht (NL), March 1–3, 1988.
Contact: NOVEM BV
PO Box 8242
3505 Utrecht, Netherlands.

19/2 Contadini, G., De Giorgi, G., Ferrario, A., Fumagalli, S., Rossi, G. (IUAV), Silvestrini, G., *Monitoring of a Solar Chimney and Different Ceiling Storage/Distribution Systems in an Office Building Located in Northern Italy*, CNR-Ieren.

19/3 Gertis, K., Erhorn, H., Rath, J., *The Heating System as a Building Component*, HLH 36, H. 12, S. 559–563, 1987.

19/4 Schuler, M., *The Schopfloch Kindergarten*, Advanced Case Study Report, IEA Task XI, Institut für Thermodynamik und Wärmetechnik, Universität Stuttgart.

19/5 Zimmermann, M., *Handbuch der passiven Sonnenenergienutzung*, SIA Dokumentation D010, 'Planungsunterlagen zu Energie und Gebäude', Schweizerischer Ingenieur- und Architekten-Verein, Zürich, December, 1986.

19/6 Kurer, T., Filleux, C., Lang, R., Gasser, H., *Passive und aktive Sonnenergienutzung bei Gebäuden*, Final Report of the Research Project, 'Solar Trap', Nationaler Energie-Forschungs-Fonds, PO Box 4001, Basel, August, 1982.

19/7 Filleux, C., Riniker, W., Kurer, T., Gasser, H., *Untersuchungen an einem Latentspeicher für Sonnenanlagen mit Luftkollektoren*, Separate Report on the Research Project, 'Solar Trap', Nationaler Energie-Forschungs-Fonds, PO Box 4001, Basel, December, 1985.

19/8 Fisch, N., Hahne, E., *Nutzung der Sonnenergie in Luftheizungsanlagen*, Klima-Kälte-Heizung 12, Part 6, pp. 1396–1401, 1984.

19.8   RECOMMENDED READING

IEA Conference Paper on Air Collectors, Utrecht, 1988.

Contact: NOVEM BV
PO Box 8242
3505 Utrecht, Netherlands

Garg, H. P., *Advances in Solar Energy Technology*, Vol. 1, *Collection, and Storage Systems*, D. Reidel Publishing Company, ISBN 90-277-2430-X, 1990.

Bloss, W.H., Pfisterer, F., Advances in Solar Energy Technology. *Proceedings of ISES Solar World Congress*, Hamburg, Vol. 1–4, Pergamon Press, ISBN 0-080343155-5, 1987.

Volumes 1 and 2 of the proceedings provide an extensive overview of the worldwide state of the art in active storage and collector systems. Volume 4 discusses the interaction between passive solar energy use and solar architecture.

Fisch, N. M., *System Analysis for Using Solar Energy for Room Heating with Air as Heat Transfer Medium*, ISBN 3-922-429-10-6, 1984.

Contact: Institut für Thermodynamik und Wärmetechnik
Universität Stuttgart
Pfaffenwaldring 6
D-7000 Stuttgart 80

Kublin, W., Krüger, E., Schuh, K., *Handbook*: *Passive Use of Solar Energy*, Schriftenreihe 04, 'Bau- und Wohnungsforschung', Heft Nr. 04.097, Munich, 1984.

DAYLIGHTING

CONTRIBUTORS

Part 4 Editor and Chapters 20, 22, 23, 24 and 25
N. Hopkirk
Swiss Federal Laboratories for Materials Testing and Research
Überlandstrasse 129
CH-8600 Dübendorf
Switzerland

Chapters 22 and 24
B. Andersson, B. Erwine, R. Hitchock and R. Kammerud
Building Systems Analysis Group
Lawrence Berkeley Laboratory
University of California
Berkeley, CA 94720
USA

Chapters 21, 23 24 and 26
O. Aschehoug
Department of Architecture
Norwegian Institute of Technology
N-7034 Trondheim
Norway

Chapter 23
M. Boisdenghien
Architecture et Climat
Université Catholique de Louvain
Place du Levant 1
B-1348 Louvain-la-Neuve
Belgium

Chapters 22 and 24
J. E. Christensen
Thermal Insulation Laboratory
Technical University of Denmark, Building 118
DK-2800 Lyngby
Denmark

Chapter 24
J. Christofferson
Thermal Insulation Laboratory
Technical University of Denmark
Building 118
DK-2800 Lyngby
Denmark

Chapters 22, 24
R. Colombo
CEC, Joint Research Center
Ispra
Italy

Chapters 23 and 24
E. Gratia
Architecture et Climat
Université Catholique de Louvain
Place du Levant 1
B-1348 Louvain-la-Neuve
Belgium

Chapter 22
P. E. Kristensen
Esbensen Consulting Engineers
Havnegade 41
DK-1058 Copenhagen
Denmark

Chapters 22 and 24
C. Paludan-Müller
Esbensen Consulting Engineers
Havnegade 41
DK-1058 Copenhagen
Denmark

Chapters 21 and 23
M. Schiler
University of Southern California
Los Angeles, CA 90089
USA

Chapters 22 and 24
A. Seager and A. Hildon
Databuild
4 Venture Way
Aston Science Park,
Birmingham
B7 4AP
United Kingdom

Chapters 22, 23 and 24
M. Szerman
Fraunhofer Institut of Building Physics
Nobelstrasse 12
D-7000 Stuttgart 80
Germany

Chapters 23 and 24
M. Thyholt
Department of Architecture
Norwegian Institute of Technology
N-7034 Trondheim
Norway

20 Introduction

Commercial and institutional buildings often consume large amounts of electrical energy for lighting, cooling and equipment. Efforts to economize electrical energy are at least as important as conserving space heating energy.

One effective means of reducing electric consumption is to make use of daylighting. This can lead to lighting energy savings and less overheating. Daylighting offers higher luminous efficacy (lm/W) than most artificial lighting systems. Hence, less cooling energy is needed, and a higher proportion of the expended energy is converted to light.

Different daylighting strategies include increasing daylight penetration, improving the uniformity of daylight distribution and introducing automatic lighting control systems.

Use of daylight affects heating and cooling energy consumption, as well as electric consumption for lighting; therefore savings of both aggregates of energy and lighting energy must be considered. The optimization of a building design must accordingly consider all end uses of energy as well as the sources of energy and their respective costs. For example, 1 kWh of saved electric energy may be more valuable than 1 kWh of saved thermal energy.

At least as important as energy conservation are the quality of light, the view and contact with the exterior, which bring psychological and physiological benefits, all of which are reasons for optimizing the use of daylighting.

Part 4 of the sourcebook, Daylighting, first describes standard and advanced daylighting strategies, illustrated by a few short examples from existing buildings. The importance of daylighting strategies and automatic lighting control systems is then demonstrated by three detailed case studies.

A daylighting and an energy analysis program were linked by two newly developed computer programs, Daylink and Superlink, enabling simulation analysis of daylighting and of the thermal behavior of a building simultaneously.

A parametric study, using these coupled programs, was made for various daylighting strategies and automatic lighting control systems. The effect of these daylighting strategies and automatic lighting control systems on the total energy consumption (lighting, heating and cooling) was analyzed.

21 *Classification of Strategies*

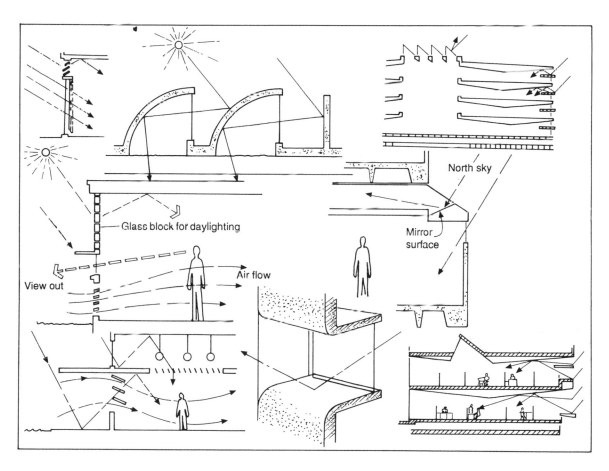

Section 21.1, Classical Daylighting Strategies, describes strategies frequently used in architecture, including sidelighting, toplighting, and light distribution strategies.

Section 21.2, New Daylighting Strategies, describes new methods which can introduce and control daylight in buildings. Examples are innovative glazing, innovative sidelighting systems, and core daylighting systems.

21.1 CLASSICAL DAYLIGHTING STRATEGIES

Admitting light into buildings has been a design consideration for as long as buildings have existed; and certainly ever since the invention of glass, which prevents the weather from entering a building, but allows light in. The advent of electric lighting gave additional lighting options, but these are still relatively inefficient and can cause overheating.

Toplighting predominates in warehouses, factories, markets and other public or single-story buildings, primarily because these buildings are deep. Sidelighting exists in offices, apartment buildings, and multi-story buildings.

21.1.1 Sidelighting

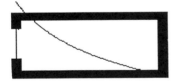

Fig. 21.1 Room aspect ratio

Room aspect ratio
Early architects understood that the depth of a room away from a window is limited by the need for natural light. The height of the window sill, the overall height and width of the window are all critical dimensions. The higher the window, the deeper the light penetration into the room, and the more even the distribution.

Fig. 21.2 Footprints

Building footprints
Similarly, the overall width of a building is limited by the depth of two rooms and a hallway between them; thus, buildings tend to have typical footprints. (Frank Lloyd Wright actually stated that the ideal width of a wing in a building is about 13 m.) To increase the area, the minimum width is convoluted into various shaped floorplans, such as E, H, F, L, U and O.

Room reflectivity
The amount of light reflected to the back of the space, and thus the comparative illumination levels between front and back for any given amount of light admitted, is affected by the reflectivity of interior surfaces. The higher the reflectivity, the more light at the rear of the space and the more even its distribution.

Ever since fluorescent lighting became common, these basic daylighting strategies were ignored. Expensive commercial space dictated that every square meter in a building should be utilized. Typical depths of rooms no longer allowed the use of daylight, and daylight was thus ignored.

Clerestories

In many early public buildings, and most notably in churches, a strategy which combined toplighting and sidelighting, namely the clerestory (CL), was used. Clerestories were usually parallel to the primary axis of the space, and combined with the structural order in the building to produce fantastic lighting effects. Opportunities to use clerestories in such dramatic ways still exist in some public buildings, such as convention centers, sports arenas, and other large open spaces. The same strategy may be used on a smaller scale, or clerestory windows may be above the normal window line in a sidelit space.

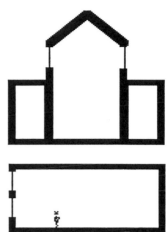

Also, placing clerestory windows on an axis perpendicular to the major axis provides infill lighting where sidelighting might be dim, or where internal configurations would block light from parallel clerestories. For example, bookshelves tend to block light from parallel axis clerestories; then, it is often better to use a perpendicular design on end walls (or overhead) even though this seems counterintuitive (see the Meteolabor example in Part 3, Solar Heating, Fig. 14.14).

Fig. 21.3 Clerestories

21.1.2 Toplighting

Sawtooth

A sawtooth (SW) roof uses a series of single exposure clerestories. This building profile is typical of industrial buildings of all sizes in Europe dating from the turn of the century, and large industrial buildings (such as airplane construction, etc.) in America dating from the 1930s.

In colder climates, it may be appropriate to face sawtooth glazing to the south, to increase solar gains. Controls may be necessary to limit glare and sharp shadows or veiling reflections, and a proper overhang, diffusing glass, or internal baffles may control such problems.

Fig. 21.4 Sawtooth roofs

Monitors

Monitors (MO) are a version of a stepped roof which may allow light to enter simultaneously from two or more directions. With a proper overhang on the southern exposure and a stepped roof, the distribution of the illumination below is surprisingly uniform.

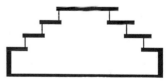

Fig. 21.5 Monitors

Skylights

Skylights (SKY) are horizontal openings in the ceiling surface, which bring in a great deal of light with a minimum amount of glazing area. However, almost all roof constructions are less expensive and better insulators than even the best skylights. Also, the integration of skylights which avoid all leakage can be expensive.

The other drawback of skylights is the possible higher summer heat gain than winter heat gain, since summer sun angles are higher. Also in most cases, glare control and distributing light necessitate the use of diffusing glazing, thereby losing much of the psychological benefit

Fig. 21.6 Skylight with light well

of the visual connection with the sky.

The depth of the roof construction strongly affects skylight performance. In warehouses and other low budget construction, there is often simply a roof surface of minimum depth, with minimum insulation, and open web construction underneath. Most of the light which enters the skylight enters the space below. As construction depth increases, especially with mechanical systems typical in office or more expensive building construction, the construction penetration becomes important. The sides of the penetration are known as the light well, and both the depth and the surface reflectance of the light well are important to the net transmission of light. The shape of the well can influence the distribution of light, and also the glare seen from below. Using a diffusing glass and comparatively wide spacing between skylights demands careful design to avoid the underside of the ceiling becoming dark, especially in comparison to the surface luminance of the underside of the diffuser (see Chapter 26 of [21/1]).

The variation of the skylight strategy which tilts the skylight along with whatever roof angle is present, typically one on each side of a gable, is known as the shed strategy. A shed strategy differs from a skylight in that it provides a slightly different light distribution and solar radiation collection.

Fig. 21.7   Shed roof

21.1.3   Light distributing strategies

Sloped or reflective ceiling
One of the simplest light distribution ideas is the sloped ceiling. It should offer equivalent daylight to a room with a high ceiling. The introduction of ducts in the ceiling construction at the back of the room maintains the height of the window. An extreme version of the increase in internal reflectance is to use a specular, or extremely high reflectance, ceiling surface. This is called a reflector ceiling (R). A variation of this is to place internal ceiling blades or reflectors to reflect light onto the floor or work surface near the rear of the space.

Fig. 21.8   Sloped ceiling

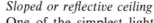

Fig. 21.9   Ceiling blades or baffles

Overhangs
Overhangs are necessary to control sunlight, but invariably hinder daylight penetration. A reflective surface provides an interesting alternative, however.

Light shelves
An innovative light distribution strategy is a horizontal fin above eye level but below the ceiling, often protruding both inside and/or outside of the glazing. Such fins are light shelves (LS) and may have a different glazing above and below the shelf.

The effectiveness of such shelves clearly depends on orientation, and

Fig. 21.10   Light shelves

may create more even light distribution by decreasing the illumination level at the front without decreasing the level at the rear.

21.1.4 Summary

Several of the daylighting strategies evaluated in the following chapter decrease heating loads, which makes them interesting, even if they do not directly increase the daylight levels in the space. Others increase the level of light. The resultant drop in the electrical lighting load and internal heat gains associated with that lighting load is beneficial.

Some of the daylighting strategies merely improve the quality of light within the space, which is more difficult to evaluate, but should also be considered.

Indeed, some daylighting strategies may decrease the quality of light in the space, and this must certainly be considered. Glare, contrast ratios, veiling reflections and light color and variation with time are all to be considered; improvements in energy use at the cost of human comfort and productivity are worthless gains.

The strategies considered in any design application must always be considered with an overall perspective. It is not just a question of illumination available on a horizontal surface, but the interactions between light quality, climate, building function and orientation, and building materials and equipment for overall energy usage, and occupant comfort.

21.2 NEW DAYLIGHTING STRATEGIES

New technologies increase opportunities for introducing and controlling daylight in buildings. The following overview of new daylighting systems relies heavily on a similar overview by P. Littlefair [21/2].

21.2.1 Functions and classification

A daylighting system is generally described as a collector, a transport system, and a local distribution system. New daylighting technologies perform all or some of these tasks, distinguished below by methods used:

- Innovative glazings which reduce U-value or control solar gain, daylight levels, and glare;
- Innovative sidelighting systems; and
- Core daylighting systems.

Only direct sunlight can effectively be focused and concentrated with existing technology; but diffuse skylight can be redirected to project a more beamlike distribution.

21.2.2   Innovative glazings

Recent developments in glass and glazing systems offer new possibilities in the design of conventional windows and skylights, thereby offering a potential for improved daylighting. They can be divided into superinsulating glazing and glazing with control capabilities.

Superinsulating glazings
Superinsulating glazing reduces the heating penalties normally associated with fenestration and thus enables an increase in daylight apertures, giving more daylight to deep perimeter areas. Better insulation also affects the optimum skylight aperture area.

A prerequisite is, of course, that the increased insulation is not associated with a decreased daylight transmission (Fig. 21.11). Increased solar gains associated with increased aperture area must be controlled with appropriate shading systems.

New methods with a potential for superinsulation with center-of-glass U-values below $1.0 \, \text{W/m}^2 \, \text{K}$ include:

- glazing with aerogel (transparent) insulation
- vacuum glazing
- translucent (not transparent) insulation
- multiple-layer glazing with improved spectral selectivity and gas fillings.

Aerogel is porous silica material with cavities smaller than the wavelength of light. The material is now available commercially in panels of up to $0.5 \, \text{m} \times 0.5 \, \text{m}$ and in granular form. The solid panels will, when sealed in a glass unit and evacuated, give a center U-value of around $0.4 \, \text{W/m}^2 \, \text{K}$ for a 20 mm thickness. Similar or even lower values can be reached with vacuum glazings which are still being developed. Research continues on maintaining a hard vacuum over time.

Several translucent insulation materials have recently been introduced. They can be employed in daylight apertures where visual contact is less important, such as clerestory windows and skylights, because translucent material diminishes any view. The thermal conductivity of the insulation is comparable to conventional opaque insulation materials, but the optical properties are different from clear glazing materials, offering lower transmission and higher angular sensitivity.

Recent innovations have been successful in insulating windows with multiple glazing layers with low emissivity coatings and inert gas cavity fillings. With inert gases such as krypton, and thermal breaks in spacers, these glazings can reach U-values below $1.0 \, \text{W/m}^2 \, \text{K}$.

Several new types of transparent and translucent materials will

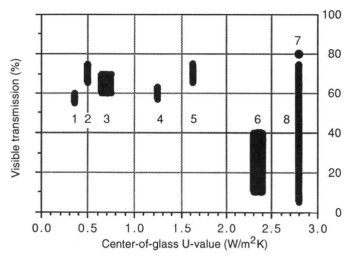

1: Evacuated 20 mm aerogel, low-*E* glass (type: monolithic)
2: Vacuum glazing
3: Multiple glass/film layers with low-*E* coating, krypton gas
4: Double glazing with one suspended plastic film with low-*E* coating
5: Double clear glazing, low-*E* coating
6: Double solar control reflective glazing
7: Double clear glazing
8: Double glazing with electrochromic coating for visible radiation.

Fig. 21.11 Visual transmission and center-of-glass *U*-value for innovative and conventional glazing types

thermally out-perform conventional opaque building envelope elements. These offer new possibilities for daylighting, such as solar windows facing north, and translucent ceilings and walls.

Glazings with control capabilities
Switchable glazings, that is, glass capable of dynamically varying the transmission of light and radiation, can adjust automatically to outside conditions and control the admission of daylight and solar energy.

By reducing the transmission, switchable glazing can also reduce glare and overheating, which is particularly useful in the perimeter zone close to the window where daylight illumination often exceeds design values for long periods of the day and year. A scheme that gives switching capability for the daylight aperture for this zone, independent of the daylight apertures for the deeper zones, also helps reduce the illumination contrast across the depth of the room. Switchable glazing can also be used as solar shading and to provide privacy.

Switchable glazings fall into three categories:

• electrochromic glazing whose transmission is changed by applying an electric field,
• photochromic glazing whose transmission depends on a change in light level, and
• thermochromic glazing whose transmission can change with a change in temperature.

Of the options described, electrochromic glazing offers the best control and the largest potential for saving energy. Only small-scale applications are currently available, such as rear-view mirros in automobiles that adjust to day and night conditions. However, an electrically controlled liquid crystal film which changes from transparent to translucent is also available.

21.2.3   Innovative sidelighting systems

The challenges in using daylighting in sidelit interiors are controlling daylight levels and solar gain in the zone closest to the windows, enhancing daylight levels in the deeper zone, and extending the depth to which daylight may replace artificial lighting.

Conventional light shelves (described in Section 21.1) can solve some of these problems by reducing the daylight levels and insolation close to the window and perhaps by increasing daylight levels to a small degree at the back of a space.

New materials and components, typically incorporated in the upper part of the side windows or in separate clerestory windows possibly above a light shelf, offer additional options for sidelighting.

New sidelighting systems include solar shading which admits diffuse light and redirects diffuse light and sunlight to the back of the room. Systems which redirect sunlight to deeper zones inherently work also as shading systems for the zone close to the windows (beam daylighting or beam sunlighting systems).

Several technological options exist for such applications:

- prismatic glazing or prismatic panels
- reflective blinds, mirror panels
- holographic glazing, and
- lens systems.

Glass with parallel prisms on the interior face, and prismatic glass blocks, redirect diffuse skylight to the deeper parts of the room, to a limited degree, from where the sky is not visible. The same type of prisms can, however, also be used to redirect sunlight to the ceiling, giving shading in the front of the room, and generally increase daylight levels by diffuse reflection from the ceiling. For this purpose, the tilt of the prismatic elements should adjust to changing solar altitudes during the year.

A new sidelighting system uses acrylic panels, where one set of the prism faces has a reflective metallized surface to reflect sunlight out. The panel is positioned at an adjustable angle to the window face so that sunlight is reflected out and diffuse skylight is refracted upwards onto the ceiling (Fig. 21.12). A version with vertical prisms, especially useful for windows facing east and west, is also available.

Venetian blinds with specular reflective upper surfaces function much the same as prismatic glazing (Fig. 21.13). Depending on tilt, sunlight can be reflected out or up on the ceiling, where it can be redistributed after diffuse reflection. Adjustment to varying solar positions is easier with blinds; both tilt and spacing should ideally vary to accommodate both diurnal and seasonal variations in solar position.

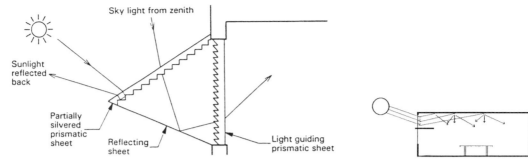

Fig. 21.12 Prismatic plastic panel system that rejects sunlight and redirects skylight

Fig. 21.13 Reflective louvers above a light shelf direct sunlight onto diffusing ceiling

Other uses of mirror systems exist. The upper face of a light shelf can reflect sunlight onto the ceiling. An outside mirror at window sill height will function the same way, but gives more glare. A novel solution to the problem of adjusting the tilt of such mirrors is incorporated in the Variable Area Light Reflecting Assembly (VALRA) (Fig. 21.14). A reflective plastic film is rolled along a tilted surface, so that a small steeply tilted mirror is created in summer and a larger, nearly horizontal mirror in winter. Hence sun rays are reflected to the rear of the room both in winter and summer.

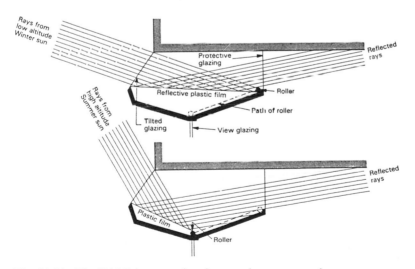

Fig. 21.14 The VALRA system in winter and summer mode

Lenses which concentrate and relay sunlight to deep interiors, bringing daylight into spaces far from the perimeter zone, are correctly considered core daylighting systems.

Holographic diffraction gratings [21/5] imbedded in glazing perform form similarly to adjustable reflective louver systems. By combining several gratings, holographic glazing can handle a range of solar angles. The potential of such systems is promising because they eliminate bulky and expensive systems for diurnal and seasonal adjustments, but holographic glazing is still in the development stage.

21.2.4   Core daylighting systems

To daylight deeply set spaces, some type of light piping [21/4] must be utilized. However, pipelines for diffuse daylight tend to be bulky and consume space (i.e. light wells); therefore almost all core daylighting systems rely on sunlight exclusively. This again implies that a tracking system is necessary to accommodate changing sun positions.

The main elements involved in such systems are:

- a collector/concentrator system,
- a pipeline or transport system, and
- a distribution or emitter system.

Several technological options exist to meet each of these functions. The collector system is based either on mirrors or lenses that concentrate sunlight falling on the system's aperture and direct it onto the aperture of the transport system. With delicate tracking equipment, most collector systems are housed in a transparent shelter, and filters or infrared-transparent mirrors remove the invisible parts of the solar spectrum.

For the transport system in a core daylighting system there are several options (Fig. 21.15):

- open light wells or atria,
- lens guides,
- hollow reflective light guides,
- prism light guides,
- optical fibres, and
- liquid-filled light guides.

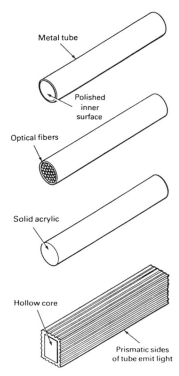

Metal tube

Polished inner surface

Optical fibers

Solid acrylic

Hollow core

Prismatic sides of tube emit light

Fig. 21.15 Some examples of different types of light guides for core daylighting systems

Open light wells require lenses and mirrors to direct the light along a path, which can consume a great deal of space. Each lens in a lens guide is place in the focal point of the preceding lens, and mirrors are required to change the direction of the light path.

A hollow reflective light guide is essentially a pipe with an internal mirror surface. In a prism light guide, the pipe is made of a transparent material with small prisms parallel to the pipe axis on the outside of the pipe wall. Light falling on the guidewalls is reflected back from prism surfaces; the glancing angle of incidence results in total internal reflection in the pipewall material.

Optical fibers and liquid-filled light guides are based on the principle of internal reflection in a transparent material. Water in the light guide could possibly serve the double function to filter out infrared radiation by circulating the water. Similarly, an open light well could also serve as a ventilation duct.

Optical fibers are the most costly transport system, but require little space and easily adapt to existing building structures. Figure 21.16 shows how other types of core daylighting systems require pathways through the building, just like any other services. At each floor in a multi-story building; a light tapping point exists to carry light from vertical guide collectors leading from the collector mounted on the roof.

Little development is reported with emitter and distribution systems. Light input varies greatly with solar altitude, requiring an output control in the distribution system. Artificial back-up lighting for overcast periods can also be incorporated in the distribution system. This would allow the removal of heat from lights in the occupied space.

A couple of commercially available core daylighting systems merit special mention. The Japanese Himawari (Sunflower) system uses an array of Fresnel lenses as a collector, each feeding into an optic fiber. The whole unit is housed in an acrylic sphere which also protects the tracking system. The bundle of fibers comprises the transport system for the Himawari system.

The Canadian Light Pipe produced by Total Internal Reflection (TIR) uses a prism light guide housed in a rectangular duct (Fig. 24.17 and reference [21/7]). The bottom side of the housing can be translucent and emit light for the unit. The light is input from one end, and a mirror in the other end reflects light back into the prism pipe, which is made of a thin plastic film with prism backing. The input light leaks evenly from the bottom diffuser, making the light pipe both a transport and a distribution system. An example of its application is described in the case study in Section 22.1.

Since almost all core daylighting systems rely on direct sunlight, they promise the most cost-effectiveness in climates with a high probability of sunshine, which are also cooling-dominant climates.

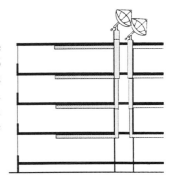

Fig. 21.16 Vertical and horizontal distribution of sunlight from roof-mounted tracking collector

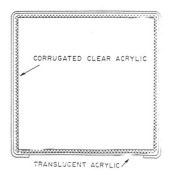

CORRUGATED CLEAR ACRYLIC

TRANSLUCENT ACRYLIC

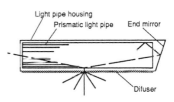

Light pipe housing
Prismatic light pipe   End mirror

Diffuser

Fig. 21.17 Section of the TIR light pipe and schematic principle of operation

Acknowledgements

Most of the figures used in this report were taken from reference [21/2] with the kind permission of the Building Research Establishment, Building Research Station, Garston, UK.

21.3 REFERENCES

21/1 Selkowitz, S., Skylight Handbook,
21/2 Littlefair, P., Innovative daylighting systems — a critical review, *National Lighting Conference*, The Chameleon Press, 5–25 Burr Rd, London SW18 4SG, UK 1988.

21/3 Ruck, N.C., Letting in the daylight, Batiment International, *Building Research and Practice*, **14** (4), 294–300, 1986.

21/4 Johnson, K. & Selkowitz, S., Light guide design principles, *1986 International Daylighting Conference*, Long Beach, 1986, 11-4/7. *Proceedings* II, ASHRAE Publication Sales, 1791 Tullie Circle, N.E., Atlanta, GA 30329, USA.

21/5 Ian, R. & King, E., Holographic solar access, *1986 International Daylighting Conference*, Long Beach, 1986, 11-4/7. *Proceedings* I, c/o 1508 Emerson Avenue, McLean, VA 22101.

21/6 BRW, *Sunlight Distribution in Remote Interior Locations Using Multi-Axis Suntracking as a Light Source*, Minneapolis, 1987.

21/7 Gilmore, E., Piping light, *Popular Science*, Box 54965, Boulder, CO 80322-4965, USA, May 1988.

21/8 Gilmore, E., Sunflower over Tokyo, *Popular Science*, Box 54965, Boulder CO 80322-4965, USA, May 1988.

22 Examples

The results presented in Chapter 22 are based on:

- base case studies made within the framework of the IEA Task XI,
- short independent studies for the sourcebook,
- advanced case studies made within the framework of the IEA Task XI.

The examples offer brief highlights of daylighting strategies in existing buildings used to replace conventional electric lighting. A building's characteristics, its location, costs, control strategies, user reactions, if possible, the energy saved and simulation work effectuated, are given.

The case studies in the last three sections describe in detail three commercial buildings, which utilize daylighting strategies. A building description, measurements taken during IEA Task XI, results and implications, modeling and possible parametric studies are also included. All cases are in northern climates. Three topics are described in the case studies: daylight factor measurements with rooflights, interior illuminance and power measurements with light shelves, and occupant usage of lights and blinds. The know-how gained through modeling these relatively complex buildings is included in Section 24.3.

22.1 EXAMPLES OF STRATEGIES

22.1.1 Rooflights for core daylighting

Climate:

Latitude:	55°N
Ac. sun hours:	596
Ac./theoretical:	0.28
Degree days (base 20°C)	4344

Building: The Copenhagen School of Economics and Business Administration
Client: Dansk Ingenierforenings Pensionskasse
Architect: Henning Larsens Tegnestue
Consulting Engineer: Birch & Krogboe (Installation Seitzberg & Neltoft (Construction)

Summary
The Copenhagen School of Economics and Business Administration is a three-story 30 000 m^2 building. The circulation area is daylit by

rooflights. The interior walls are primarily white to reflect daylight. The building is 242 m long and built around three atria — a central atrium and two smaller ones at each end of the building.

Control strategies
Automatic exterior shading curtains are mounted on the east, south and west facades, and are controlled both by solar cells and manual control. If the wind is too strong, the curtains are automatically retracted to protect them. The rooflights open centrally to avoid overheating the building. Automatic lighting control works in the circulation areas, turning off electric lights when there is adequate sunlight, and turning on lights when it becomes too dark for comfort.

User reactions
The occupants are completely satisfied with the daylighting strategies and the automatic shading curtains.

Cost:
Total: approx.
DKK 180 000 000
(ECU 750/m²). Shading curtains are mounted at all east, south and west facades, at a price of approx. DKK 1 200 000.

Simulation:
The building indoor climate and the energy consumption have been simulated by: BLAST, SUNCODE and tsbi 2.1.

Contact:

Birch & Krogboe,
Teknikerbyen 34,
DK-2830 Virum, Denmark.

22.1.2   Rooflights with diffuse glazing

Building: Sportshall, Waldenbuch, Germany
Client: Community of Waldenbuch
Architect: Horst Haag

Climate

Latitude	49°N
Altitude	420 m
Ac/theoretical	0.40
Degree days (base 20°C)	3434

Cost: 4 395 000 DM (2 200 000 ECU) equal to 1760 DM/m²

The sportshall in Waldenbuch is the main center for indoor sporting activities in the town. The building is used for training and competitions, and can seat up to 500 spectators. The sports ground of the hall is daylit by diffuse glazing in the rooflight and additional clear glazed windows in the facade facing north.

Summary
The sportshall has a total floor area of 2500 m² and a total volume of 19 000 m³. A linear rooflight, 45 m long (width 5.75 m), with diffuse glazing exists over the sports ground of equal length and 1215 m². The top ridge is east–west oriented. A clear glazed window 2.5 m high, giving additional daylighting, is included along the total length of the north facade. The internal surfaces are covered by bright reflecting wood.

Lighting control
Manual on/off control of an additional lighting system is possible, and during competitions, the artificial lighting system is always used.

User reactions
Occupants are generally pleased with the daylighting features. The uneven daylight distribution on the floor can, however, disturb the athletes, and the clear glazed windows facing north often cause glare.

Climate

Latitude	52°N
Degree days, (1987)	1956
20 year ave.	2115

Architect: James Stirling

22.1.3   Louvered roof monitors

Building: Clore Gallery, London, England

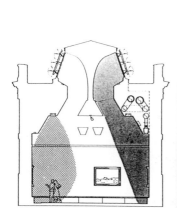

Fig. 22.1   Monitors with louvers

Photograph by M. David Clarke

The gallery design brief required as much natural lighting as possible within the gallery so that outside variability of light could be reflected inside. This variability would make the internal environment of the gallery more pleasant and also show different perspectives of the pictures on display.

Summary

Monitors were designed to deflect daylight on to the gallery walls. Daylight falling onto the hanging zone had to be reflected at least once to minimize harmful ultraviolet radiation.

External adjustable louvers on the monitors are programmed to meet preset positions each hour of the day throughout the year, based upon a typical day for each month. Fixing the louvers in set positions each hour enables variable external daylight to be reflected within the gallery, but at a reduced level.

Control systems

The total amount of daylight falling on each wall, along with the maximum and minimum levels, is recorded by a control system, which then uses this information to modify the louver control algorithms so as not to exceed an average exposure of 0.5 million lux hours per year. If the internal light levels fall below a present minimum for a given period of time, then the computer activates artificial lighting.

Further reading

For more information on the Clore Gallery, see ⌊22/1, 22/2⌋.

22.1.4 Internal and external light shelves

Building: South Staffordshire Waterworks Company, Walsall, England

Summary

Continuous fenestration bands of low emissivity glazing ($U = 1.6 \, W/m^2 \, K$) around the waterworks building reduce solar gains and heat losses without greatly reducing daylight penetration. The shelves and the building's overhang provide summertime shading to perimeter areas, but also allow light penetration during winter or on dull summer days. The polished stainless steel shelves, set at an angle of 20° to the horizontal, combined with white painted internal shelves, form a complete light shelf, which produces increased uniform daylight throughout the offices. An automatic lighting control system turns the improved daylighting into an energy saving by turning off unwanted lights.

Climate

Latitude	53°N
Altitude	162 m
Degree days base 20 (1987)	4008
20 yr. avg.	3560
Architect:	Harry Bloomer Partnership
Service Engineer:	King Cathery Partnership
Energy Consultant:	Databuild Ltd.

Cost: The building, which was principally newly built at a cost of £1 790 000 (£467/m², ECU 286/m²) compares well with typical offices of similar size (between £420–£500/m²). The window shading and shelf system was approx. £36 000 (or 2%) of the total cost.

Energy savings

Office lighting use was monitored and extrapolated to be about 9 kWh/m² a, an acceptably low figure. Electric lighting could however be further reduced by decreasing the unnecessarily high base level of electric lighting during the day.

Control strategy of lighting

An Energy Management System (EMS) allows light to be turned on manually, depending upon external light levels and time of day. Switching the lights off is automatic at a preset time or when predetermined external daylight limits are exceeded.

User reaction

Occupants are pleased with the daylight features, but there is some dissatisfaction with the automatic lighting controls and with glare through the upper sections of windows.

22.1.5   Clerestory daylighting

Building: CEC: Passive Solar Laboratory, JRC, Ispra, Italy
Design team: Colombo & H. Bloem

Climate

Latitude	45°N
Longitude	8°E
Ac. sun hours	945
Ac/theoretical	0.46

Summary

The Solar Laboratory at the Joint Research Center (JRC) in Ispra, Italy, is a rectangular single-story building designed as an experiment to study the possibility of storing excess heat for use in colder periods

with a heat pump. Daylight is adequately introduced into the conference room, behind the sunspace, using only clerestories.

The building has a main section and a sun space, with a total area of 260 m², with 80 m² of clerestories facing south inclined at 60°, and about 7 m² of vertical clerestories in the wall of the main building facing north. Also see Fig. 24.7.

Energy saved
The energy savings are mainly from heating and cooling gains, as the clerestory system is part of the passive solar strategy.

Control strategy
Fixed and movable shading devices are mounted on the south façade to control solar insolation and daylight. The lighting design criteria provide sufficient natural light with efficient comfort. Under normal conditions, artificial lighting is unnecessary anywhere in the building, although a manually operated fluorescent lighting system exists. A data acquisition system was used to monitor temperature, waterflows, solar radiation and daylight illumination. The existing daylight values within the room were measured.

22.1.6   Heliostats with light pipes for core daylighting

			Climate	
Building:	Victoria Park Place, Toronto, Canada			
Design team:	TIR System Ltd		Latitude	43°N
	L. Whitehead, President		Ac. sun hours	720
	J. Scott, Chief Engineer		Ac./theoretical	0.61

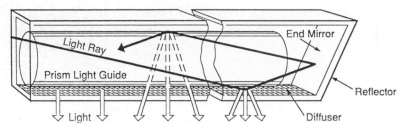

Fig. 22.2   Plastic light pipe

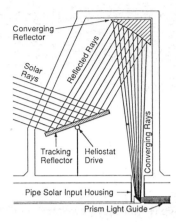

Fig. 22.3   Sun tracking system

Plastic tubes with moulded-in prisms, transport light by internal reflection. Some light escapes due to microscopic defects in the tubes so that the whole tube emits light. This light then passes through a diffuser.

Summary
There are eight systems, each capturing sunlight on the roof with a heliostat in a solarium, transmitting it, via a converging mirror and an aperture; then distributing it evenly in the core area using a defocusing mirror elbow system placed beneath each aperture leading to the light pipes.

A heliostat (flat mirror 2.2 m²) reflects the sunlight via a converging mirror into light pipes. These distribute the light into the offices.

Energy saved
An estimated 51.6 kWh/m² a or 30% of electric lighting energy of the core office space was saved from the heliostats and light pipes. There is also less cooling cost because sunlight offers better luminous efficacy than luminaries, and because heat from the sun is removed in the piping process. In addition, 40% of the cost of operating artificial lights was saved primarily from cleaning and changing bulbs.

Floor area:
● Gross: 2000 m²
● Core: 186 m²

Capital costs of 8 heliostats and light pipes: $200 000 Cdn.

Special features
Good light distribution and illuminance levels of approximately 700 lux are achieved with no glare. A 1.2 m diameter sunbeam can illuminate 23 m² of office space at over 1000 lux, decreasing overheating. The pipes perform better in hotter climates where more sunlight enters and the light pipe system transports light well, but the pipes are a poor thermal transport system. The efficiency of the light transporting ability is about 25–30% of the light input level.

Control strategy of electric lights
The electric lights are programmed to respond to external illuminance.

User reaction
The passing by of clouds, a pleasant and natural effect, is noticeable when using the light pipes.

22.2 CASE STUDY: BRF BUILDING

Site data

Location:	Copenhagen, Denmark
Latitude:	56°N
Climate data:	
October–April	
Degree days	
(base 20):	3719
G_H (kWh/m²):	305
Actual sun hours:	596
Ac/theoretical:	0.28
Annual:	
Degree days	
(base 20):	4344
G_H (kWh/m²):	1018

22.2.1 Introduction

The main daylighting features of the BRF building are the rooflights illuminating the circulation areas. Automatic control of both the electric lighting and blinds using exterior sensors was studied. The purpose of monitoring the building was to study the benefits from daylighting and daylit circulation areas.

Illuminance, electric lighting and daylight factor measurements were taken and show good performance of the daylighting system [22/11, 22/3].

The amount of lighting energy saved was calculated to be approximately 18 kWh/m² a if the corridor lighting was controlled automatically. The correlations between savings and important parameters were also studied, showing that continuous dimming increases savings, higher design illumination levels obviously give higher potentials for saving and the ratio of glazing area to floor area of 0.36 was satisfactory. More glazing would not substantially affect light savings.

22.2.2 Building description

The BRF building is a four-story office building with a total floor area of about 17 000 m². Daylight through the rooflights creates a pleasant

Fig. 22.4 Characteristics of the three-story arcade rooms

atmosphere (see Fig. 22.4). All the long office blocks have a glass covered arcade room for circulation, stretching lengthwise between the two ends of the building. The rooflights are double glazed 4 mm float glass and cover 85% of the roof area. The walls and ceiling are white, the floor dark brown and the railings opaque acrylic. Individual electric lighting for each floor is controlled by one light sensor placed on the roof, giving desired minimum illuminance on all three floors of the circulation areas.

This results in 100 lux on the second and third floors but only 50 lux on the first floor at the standard positions, i.e. 1 m above floor level and 0.6 m from the side wall. The blinds, used to avoid overheating and glare, are controlled automatically by four light sensors. The lighting schedule is from 5:00 to 18:00 with a lighting power density of 7.8 W/m^2. Adjacent offices are not daylit by the circulation corridors.

U-values (W/m^2 K)

Roof:	0.15
Wall:	0.23
Floor:	0.24
Window	2.20
and	1.90 (office)

Glazing in arcades: (double glazing)

U-value (W/m^2 K):	3.10
Daylight transmission:	79%
Solar transmission:	76%

Desired lighting level in circulation

area:	100 lux
Installed power:	7.8 W/m^2

22.2.3 Measurements

Measurements were made to answer the following questions. What fraction of the working day could daylight replace electric lighting; what levels of daylight factors existed in the corridors; and finally, how good is the automatic control of the electric lights and blinds?

The measurements are divided into three groups.

1. For ten working days, observations were made of weather conditions, and continuous measurements were taken of exterior and interior illuminances, electric light and blind status (whether on or off and up or down), and duration of electric lighting/day.

2. Daylight factor measurements for a complete set of locations in the circulation area were made. The daylight factor measurements, which were made at the standard positions, at various heights along the corridor center line and at various distances from the side wall, are valid for an overcast day.

3. The transmission coefficient of the glass in the circulation area was measured, as were other optical properties, such as reflectivity of the surfaces under diffuse light conditions, etc.

22.2.4 Results

1. The weather during the ten days was presumed to be typical for the time of year (mean exterior horizontal illuminance = 20.1×10^3 lux). The measurements gave daylight utilization factor (DUF) values, or the fraction of the work day during which the daylight replaces electric light, for each day and floor [22/3, 22/11]. The mean values of the DUF per floor were $DUF_1 = 0.61$, $DUF_2 = 0.62$ and $DUF_3 = 0.85$, which are good considering the long occupancy

time from 5:00 to 18:00. DUF_1 and DUF_2 are equal because the desired illuminance on the first floor is only 50 lux, while on the second floor it is 100 lux. Hence daylighting can replace electric lighting for about 70% of the work day. No clear correlation exists between the mean daily exterior illuminance and the DUF values because the DUF values depend primarily on the available daylight in the morning, whereas the mean illuminance is dominated by the conditions during the intervening hours.

The arched rooflights could have high losses. Also, DUF values depend on the length of the working day. Unfortunately no global measurements or calculations were made to determine the influence of the thermal losses and gains through the rooflights.

2. The daylight factors along the center line of the corridor vary from 24 at the top of the third floor to 2.5 on the first floor (see Fig. 22.5a). Figure 22.5(b) gives daylight factors as a function of the distance from the sidewall of the corridor. The daylight factors remain low and constant for the first and second floors up to 1.2 m from the side wall (at the railing). From there to the center, the daylight factors increase quickly. Daylight factors of 0.4, 0.9 and 5.1 are obtained at the standard positions (0.6 m from sidewall) on the three floors respectively (see Fig. 22.5b). A lighter color floor could increase the daylight factor near the wall. The measurements were made during two days with a completely overcast sky.

With a mean measured exterior illuminance of 6.1×10^3 to 12.2×10^3 lux for overcast skies, despite the low design illumination level of 50 lux on the first floor, lighting is needed there. Mean daily daylight utilization factor values of 0.35–0.61 were measured for such overcast conditions.

3. Turning on and off lights automatically was found absolutely acceptable by the occupants in the corridor. This was not the case for the automatic control of the blinds in the offices, which was disturbing. The blinds were activated at a global horizontal illuminance of about 30×10^3 lux (about $270\,W/m^2$).

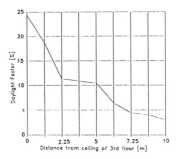

Fig. 22.5(a) Daylight factors measured in the vertical direction, from the ceiling of the third floor, in the middle of the space

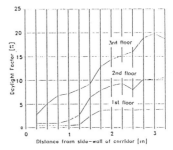

Fig. 22.5(b) Daylight factors measured in the horizontal direction on all three floors, 1 m above floor level

22.2.5 Simulations

An important question to answer was: how difficult is it to simulate such a highly complex building with an existing daylighting program to calculate the energy savings and run a parametric study? Also, what approximations were required and what accuracy could be expected? The program Daylite 2.2 was used. The detailed simulation and assumptions are described in Section 24.3, on Daylite 2.2. The program was only usable if one compared measured and predicted daylight factors to adjust the model, which then gave results comparable with other measurements.

Table 22.1 Mean monthly daylight utilization factors (DUF) values for the three floors (DUF$_1$, DUF$_2$, DUF$_3$)

	DUF$_1$	DUF$_2$	DUF$_3$
Jan.	0.31	0.31	0.54
Feb.	0.39	0.53	0.69
Mar.	0.58	0.77	0.85
Apr.	0.66	0.93	1.00
May	0.61	1.00	1.00
Jun.	0.74	1.00	1.00
Jul.	0.63	1.00	1.00
Aug.	0.60	0.94	1.00
Sep.	0.51	0.79	0.85
Oct.	0.49	0.60	0.69
Nov.	0.38	0.38	0.54
Dec.	0.28	0.28	0.43
Year	0.52	0.71	0.80

Parametrics

Based on calculations with the program Daylite 2.2, 68% or 18 kWh/m² a (i.e. 14 kW/m² a, 19 kW/m² a and 21 kWh/m² a for the first, second and third floors respectively), of lighting energy was saved in a year compared to the values if lights were on during the entire work day. The savings were determined from the mean yearly calculated daylight utilization factors (DUF) and the lighting power density, hence the installed lamp type affected the savings (see Table 22.1).

Continuous dimming   If a continuous dimming system for electric lights was used with a minimum power of 15%, then an increase in savings of 25% (3.4 kWh/m² a) on the first floor, 9% on the second floor and 1% on the third floor could be obtained. Hence, there was significant improvement on the two bottom floors where the daylight factors were rather low. Overall, there was a 10% increase in lighting energy savings.

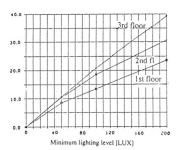

Fig. 22.6   Energy savings as a function of the minimum lighting level

Working day length   The 13 h work day is longer than average; so energy savings for a 10 h day, from 07:30 to 17:30 were investigated. The result was as expected, an increase in the DUF values, but also with less energy finally saved as the lighting energy consumed for the artificially lit case also decreased. The largest decrease (14% or 2.8 kWh/m² a) was for the third floor, where the DUF value hardly changed. A 4% decrease was obtained for the first floor.

Required lighting level   The near-linear relationship between energy savings and the minimum required lighting level is shown in Fig. 22.6. If the minimum lighting level is low, little energy is saved, but little is used.

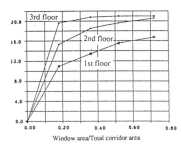

Fig. 22.7   Energy savings as a function of relative window area to the total floor area of the corridors (0.36 for the actual building)

Window size   The importance of window size is shown in Fig. 22.7. For ratios of window area to the total floor area greater than 0.2, only the first and the second floor (to a lesser extent), have a significant increase in savings. The actual area of the windows was about 36%. Doubling that window area increases the savings by 11% (6 kWh/m² a). These results are applicable to lighting energy only and to corridors with a low design illuminance (100 lux) and not to the total energy required (lighting, heating and cooling).

22.2.6   Conclusions

The measurements demonstrate the good performance of the daylighting system. The daylight factors are always above 2% in the center and along the balconies a bit further than 1 m from the wall for the two top floors; however, they drop to 0.4% on the first floor near the wall.

The simulations indicate that 68% of the lighting energy can be saved, that the optimum window size for lighting is near the actual value of 36%, and that another 10% savings is obtainable with continuous dimming.

This design could probably be used in other climates because of the low illuminance levels required and the diminution of solar gains by blinds facing south. The single sensor which controls lighting is responsible for a low design illuminance value on the first floor. This would have to be corrected in another building. Also, if rooflighting is used, automatic lighting control is essential to save lighting energy.

22.3 CASE STUDY: SOUTH STAFFORDSHIRE WATER COMPANY BUILDING

Site data

Location: Walsall, England	
Latitude:	53°N
Altitude:	162 m

Climate data

October–April (incl.)	
Degree days (base 20):	3470
Solar rad G_H (kWh/m²):	317
Actual sun hours:	508

Annual

Degree days (base 20):	4008
Solar rad G_H (kWh/m²):	963

Dimensions

Floor to ceiling height:	3 m
Size (m²)	
Gross:	3833
Heated:	3208
Unheated:	
Attic space:	625
Second floor:	645

Building cost (1985): £467/m² gross

Typical cost (1985): Medium height and quality £420 to £500/m²

U-values (W/m² K)

floor:	0.35
wall:	0.20
window:	1.60
frames:	1.60

22.3.1 Abstract

The South Staffordshire Water Company building is 3200 m² (four stories) high, and utilizes light shelves to provide shading from summer solar gain and to improve daylight distribution in rooms [22/3, 22/8]. The shelves allow large areas of glazing, with heat loss reduced by low-emissivity double glazing (see Section 22.1).

The results of monitoring confirm that the light shelves modify illuminance levels, rather than redistribute daylight, with a consequent improvement in light uniformity. This effect may reduce demand for electric lighting. The automatic control system appears to inhibit optimum energy savings, as it keeps the innermost group of lights on permanently throughout work days.

22.3.2 Daylighting

The principal daylighting feature is the use of internal and external light shelves to prevent overheating while maintaining the quality of daylight within the offices. The light shelf design was developed based on work done in the 1950s by the Nuffield Foundation Hospital Trust.

The high level shelf (interior and exterior) which acts as a solar shade, reduces light levels near the window and possibly increases light levels at the back of rooms.

Solar heat gains in summer are limited by the shelves and the overhangs, without large reductions in either winter solar gains or daylight deep within rooms. A deep concrete window sill at desk level works as a solar absorber and reflector to further diminish summer peaks in solar gains and enhance daylighting (see Figs. 22.8 and 22.9).

Envelope heat loss (kW/K)

Transmission:	2.1
Infiltration/ventilation:	3.0

Glazing properties

Double glazed, low emissivity, argon filled (12 mm).

U-value:	1.6 W/m^2 K
Daylight transmission:	60%
Solar transmission:	59%
or if reversed:	69%

Lighting
Installed capacity

Offices; ceiling:	10 W/m^2
Task:	16 W/desk

Design condition

Offices:	350 lux
Circulation:	250 lux

Ceiling luminaires

600 mm recessed fittings each including three T8 linear fluorescent tubes (correlated color temperature 4000 K, color rendering index Ra 85). Power use is 75 W per fitting.

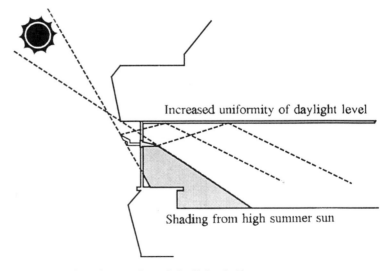

Fig. 22.8 Designed operation of the light shelf

Office ceiling lights on all floors are automatically controlled by the building energy management system (BEMS). The control allows lights to be turned on manually according to the time of day and information from roof-mounted photoelectric cells (two on each facade). This logic also determines when luminaires are automatically turned off, although lights can be manually turned off at any time.

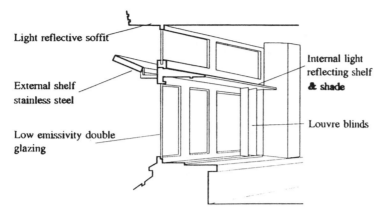

Fig. 22.9 Light shelf and window assembly

22.3.3 Monitoring

The objectives of monitoring the building were to determine how much the energy demand is reduced by the passive solar features and how much the working environment is improved.

In a joint venture between the United States and United Kingdom, data monitored from (1) and (2) below were used to validate the Daylight Performance Evaluation Methodology (DPEM) (see reference [22/9] and Section 24.1).

Two second-floor offices 9344 m^2 and 135 m^2) were selected as representative spaces. Figure 22.10 shows the selected offices and their electric lighting groups. Monitoring was performed from April 1987 to June of the same year, in two stages:

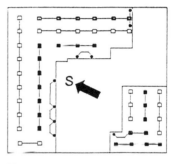

Fig. 22.10 Second-floor offices

1. Long-term monitoring of the passive solar features, interior illuminance, power used by the lights on the second floor, and irradiance data were performed to determine their contribution to overall lighting performance.
2. A one-time test was performed overnight to reduce the effect of external lighting. The test was made to calibrate the individual effects of the BEMS-controlled electric lighting groups on the individual light sensors and the power consumption. The illumination from daylight alone, during the long-term monitoring period, could then be obtained.

Monitored results

Lighting Figures 22.11 and 22.12 illustrate typical data showing how lighting energy use responds to available solar irradiance. Energy use is low relative to the maximum possible, and the majority of energy used is a base load when supplementary electric lighting is unnecessary. It was confirmed that the lighting control software provides for one

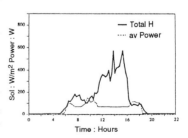

Fig. 22.11 Lighting power and irradiance

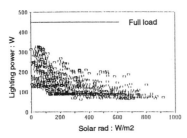

Fig. 22.12 Lighting power vs irradiance

group of lights in the rear of room to be on permanently during office hours regardless of available daylight and user wishes. This unsatisfactory arrangement inhibits the full realization of energy savings.

22.3.4 Modeling

Daylight performance evaluation methodology (DPEM)
(see also Section 24.1)
The DPEM uses both mathematical simulation and measurement to identify annual effectiveness of the daylighting system. Short-term measurements (one to four weeks) were made of global horizontal and diffuse radiation, internal light levels, and electric lighting power.

This data is used to adjust mathematical models for daylight and lighting energy use in the selected spaces. The key relationships are internal light levels as a function of daylight, and electric lighting energy use as a function of internal illumination and the lighting control strategy.

These models, once established and calibrated for a short period of monitoring, were extrapolated using annual climate and building use data to yield annual performance data.

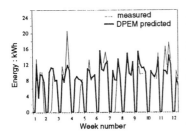

Fig. 22.13 Measured vs DPEM predicted lighting

Modeling results
The DPEM used four weeks of measured data to adjust the results from the SUPERLITE daylight model and the structured lighting control model for the 344 m^2 office. The DPEM used monitored climate data, so that the predictions could be compared with monitored lighting use over the same period.

The DPEM predictions show strong agreement for the entire measurement period, excluding holidays (see Fig. 22.13). The predicted total lighting energy over this period differed from the monitored value by only 5%. The annual projection of energy use, using DPEM for the Kew 1964/5 standard weather year, was 9.3 kWh/m^2 a. This value is less than the observed average of 21 kWh/m^2 a for the whole floor; this latter figure, however, includes the service core and circulation areas, neither of which are daylit. Rescheduling the base load lighting would make possible approximately 25% additional savings.

These observations, taken together with the apparent sensitivity of energy use to available daylight, suggest that the northwest and northeast offices may use significantly more energy than a southeast office, but further analysis is required. A simple explanation for the increased energy use could be that the northwest and northeast offices have windows in two rather than three walls as in the southeast office.

Visual appraisal

The overall effect of the light shelves is to distribute daylight with greater uniformity between front and rear of the room compared with a simple window system. Moreover, an even greater light uniformity exists in offices from front to rear at eye height than at desk height as shown in Fig. 22.14. In particular, the higher uniformity of daylight at eye height could well affect users' perceptions of the interior and consequently their desire for supplementary electric light.

These analyses support the idea that it is more accurate to say that the daylight has been modified rather than redistributed. Redistribution is more apparent than real. Energy use may be related to perceived relative daylight levels which might trigger a desire for electric lighting.

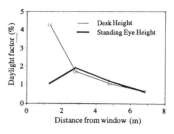

Fig. 22.14 Daylight factors profile

22.3.5 Conclusions

Overall, this appraisal confirms the worth of daylighting as a passive solar strategy in non-domestic buildings where lighting energy costs are comparable to those for space heating.

The building design allows large glass areas with permanent shading to eliminate summertime overheating while promoting good daylight penetration and distribution.

The DPEM is a promising technique for energy analysis which provides a deeper understanding of the correlation between electric lighting and the available solar resources.

Data suggest that the daylighting strategy should be more accurately referred to as apparent redistribution of daylighting.

22.3.6 Acknowledgements

Much of the data used in the preparation of this paper was collected by Databuild under contract to the Energy Technology Support Unit. The views expressed are those of the authors.

22.4 CASE STUDY: TECHNOLOGIEZENTRUM, STUTTGART

The building has a two-story linear atrium with adjacent office space and additional north and south outside-facing office spaces. The rooflight in the linear atrium is oriented east and west. No other special daylighting features exist.

Measurements were made to clarify the potential for energy saving of lighting control equipment and the reduction of daylighting potential by use of shading devices. In an office suite with one room facing the

atrium and another facing south outside, measurements of the manual
on/off lighting control and the use of shading devices were carried out
by the Fraunhofer Institute of Building Physics, Stuttgart [22/3, 22/10].

22.4.1 Introduction

The atrium supplies adjacent office rooms with daylight and fresh air.
The adjacent rooms have double glazed windows facing the atrium.
The atrium itself is glazed with 7 mm wired clear glass. The rooflight
is oriented to the east/west and has a width of 5.5 m. It has painted light
wells 4 m high and reflects direct sunlight into the space. Overhangs, 2 m
wide, are placed above the windows of the adjacent spaces. A desired
design illuminance of 500 lux is planned in all office rooms and of 150
lux in secondary rooms.

The office rooms facing the exterior have adjustable blinds as shading
devices, which are adjusted manually by occupants. The rooms adjacent
to the atrium do not need shades.

22.4.2 Measurements

The measurement equipment was installed in the occupied office
presented in Fig. 22.15. In zones I and II, a chemical laboratory was
installed, while zone IV was used for ordinary office work. Zone III
was used as an entrance.

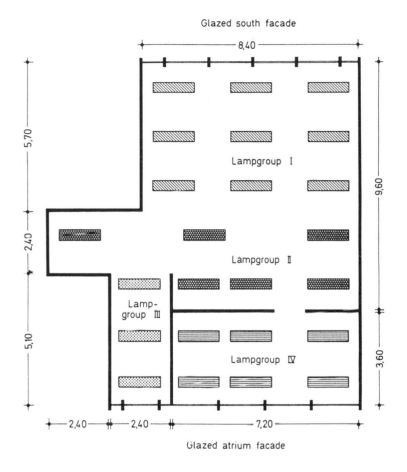

Fig. 22.15 Floor plan of monitored office

During 10 weeks in autumn 1989, the following measurements were monitored every 15 minutes:

- On/off position of switched lamps, for manual lamp control;
- Electric consumption of all lighting circuits; and
- Position of venetian blinds (south façade).

22.4.3 Results

Use of artificial lighting
The use of artificial lighting in the monitored office is shown in Fig. 22.16 for a week in October 1989. During that week, the weather was sunny and warm. The figure illustrates a regular pattern of when the lights were manually switched on and off for the four different lamp circuits.

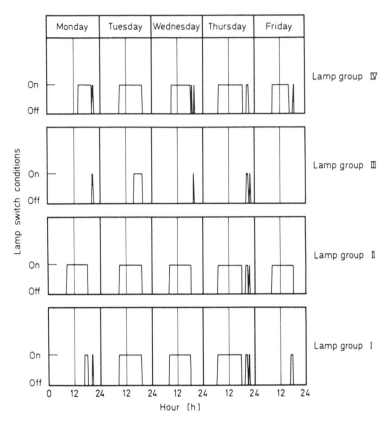

Fig. 22.16 Status of the artificial lighting in the monitored office of the Technologiezentrum, Stuttgart in the week from 23 to 27 October 1989. Four different zones are presented

Of interest are some regular peaks in all zones which occur during the late afternoon when cleaning staff are in the office. If the lights are off when the staff arrives, cleaning staff switch on all circuits; when the offices are cleaned, all lights are switched off.

In lamp group I (closest to the south facing window), lamps are switched on less often compared to lamp group II. In lamp group II, the lamps remain on nearly all day. Zone I, then, is sufficiently daylit when people start working, so that they do not need additional light at this time. There is no indication that a specific quantity of light makes people turn off artificial lighting when enough daylight is available. In zone III (the entrance), lighting is seldom used, indicating not that it is sufficiently daylit, but that it is an entrance with no representative character. In zone IV (the ordinary office connected to the atrium), lights are on nearly all day during the week of monitoring. This room may not be sufficiently daylit by the atrium.

Table 22.2 shows the number of hours when artificial lights are turned on in the Technologiezentrum, Stuttgart, and the resulting internal heat gains in the week of monitoring, from 23 October to 27 October. Values of the four different zones shown in Fig. 22.15 are presented. The mandatory weekly flexible working time was 39 hours.

Table 22.2 Number of hours artificial lights were on, and internal heat gains from 23 to 27 October 1989

	Hours per week (h)	Specific weekly internal gains by lighting (Wh/m^{2}W)
Daylit office:		
Near window	36.75	510
Daylit office:		
Far from window	53.50	660
Entrance	6.50	110
Office connected to atrium	47.50	840

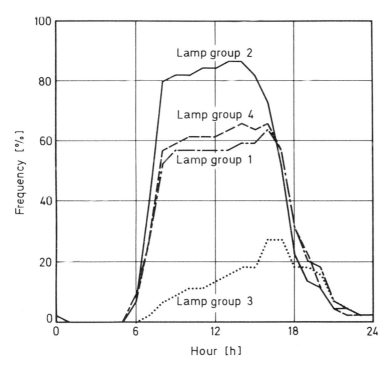

Fig. 22.17 Percentage of switched-on lamps in the four zones for the whole monitoring period (weekends excluded)

Figure 22.17 shows that in zone II (the inner zone), lamps were switched on during 80–85% of all hours during the monitoring period, excluding weekends.

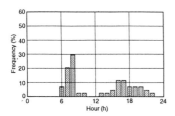

Fig. 22.18 Hourly switch-on frequency of lamp group IV in the Technologiezentrum, Stuttgart for the whole monitoring period in autumn 1989

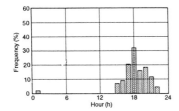

Fig. 22.19 Hourly off frequency of lamp group IV in the Technologiezentrum Stuttgart for the whole monitoring period in autumn 1989

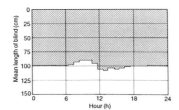

Fig. 22.20 Mean length of the venetian blind before window I at the south facade of the monitored office as observed for the whole monitoring phase

Zone I (near the window facing south) and zone IV (connected to the atrium) show surprising agreement; however, in zone IV the lights are turned on more often than in zone I, which is explained by the lower daylight levels in the zone connected to the atrium compared to the zone connected to the environment. During the day, lights are only switched on, not off.

This leads to higher internal heat gains from lighting in the afternoon when overheating is most likely. This tendency can be seen in detail in Figs. 22.18 and 22.19 for zone IV, connected to the atrium.

Clearly, from Figs. 22.18 and 22.19, artificial light is mainly turned on twice during the day (in the morning and in the afternoon), whereas only in the afternoon is the light turned off. Apparently, in the monitored office, users do not care about wasted lighting energy, or they would turn off the light when the available quantity of daylight is adequate, or at least during lunch. When arriving at the office, the occupants then consider whether they need additional light. During the day, more and more artificial light is turned on, particularly in the afternoon when the intensity of daylight becomes inadequate, if the lights are not on already.

Use of shading devices

All windows on the south façade have aluminium venetian blinds as shading devices with adjustable tilts. In Fig. 22.20, the use of shading devices for the windows on the south facade is illustrated with window I. The figure shows the mean lowered length of the venetian blind during monitoring. The total window height is 1.5 m. The figure shows that in this office room, an average of nearly two thirds of the window is shaded by the venetian blind. Only at the bottom of the window, about 50 cm of the glass is uncovered to maintain visual contact with the environment. In the morning, the blind is usually pulled up, whereas in the afternoon it is pulled down. When the occupants leave the office, the length of the blind remains as it is in the afternoon. The frequency of moving the manual blind is shown in Fig. 22.21.

The three main periods when blinds are moved is identified in Fig. 22.21. Interestingly, in each period, the occupants may have different motivations for moving the blind.

1. In the morning (even in summer and autumn) the occupants arrive, open the window for a while to let in fresh air and raise the blind somewhat.
2. At noon (especially in autumn and winter when the noon sun is low) the occupants experience glare and lower the blind.
3. In the afternoon, when overheating may occur (particularly in summer and autumn), the blind is lowered without concern about internal heat gain from artificial lighting, often switched on at the same time.

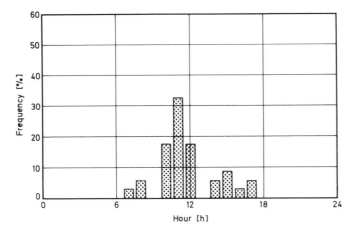

Fig. 22.21 Mean hourly frequency of manual blind moving before window I at the south façade of the monitored office during the whole monitoring phase

Use of the venetian blinds as daylighting devices by manual adjustment of the tilt of the single blinds was not monitored.

22.4.4 Conclusions

The measurements indicate that in the offices, artificial lighting is switched on for a majority of the day. In zones which are either directly daylit or adjoin the atrium, lights were switched on for approximately 60% of all monitored work hours, while in zones with poor daylighting, lights were on during approximately 85% of all work hours.

Lights are switched on primarily in the morning when work starts, and during the afternoon.

The shading devices were used for different purposes during the day, mostly to avoid glare at noon and/or avoid overheating in the afternoon while artificial lights were on.

A general conclusion is that manual light and shading device control seldom leads to adequate, energy-efficient use of lighting or shading systems.

22.4.5 Acknowledgement

This investigation was funded by the German Ministry of Research and Technology in the framework of the German participation in the IEA-TASK XI project.

22.5 REFERENCES

22/1 Wilson, P., A New light on Turner: reconciling conservation and display, *The Clore Gallery — An Illustrated Account of the New Building for the Turner Collection*, The Tate Gallery, 1987, pp. 39–44.

22/2 Carver, M.N., The control of daylighting in the Clore Gallery for the Turner Collection, *National Lighting Conference*, The Chameleon Press, 5–25 Burr Rd, London SW18 4SG, UK, 1988.

22/3 Passive and hybrid solar commercial buildings, *Advanced Case Studies Seminar*, The Renewable Energy Promotion Dept., Energy Technology Support Unit, Harwell Laboratory, Oxfordshire OX11 0RA, UK.

22/4 *EPA Solar Building Study*: ETSU 1160/SBS/4.

22/5 *IEA Task XI Basic Case Study*, REPG, Energy Technology Support Unit, Harwell Lab., Oxfordshire OX11 0RA, UK, 1988.

22/6 Van Hattem, D., Colombo, R., and Actis Dato, P., *The Passive Solar Heating System of the Solar Laboratory in Ispra*, CEC: Passive Solar Lab. J.R.C., Ispra, Italy, 1987.

22/7 Littlefair, P.J., Innovative daylighting systems — a critical review, *National Lighting Conference Proceedings*, The Chameleon Press, 5–25 Burr Rd, London SW18 4SG, UK, 1988.

22/8 Heap, L.J., Palmer, J., Hildon, A., Redistributed daylight – a performance assessment, *National Lighting Conference*, The Chameleon Press, 5–25 Burr Rd, London SW18 4SG, UK, 1988.

22/9 Andersson, B., Erwine, B., Hitchcock, R., Kammerud, R., Seager, A., Hildon, A., *Daylighting performance evaluation methodology — Summary Report*, Report No. 24002, Lawrence Berkeley Laboratory, University of California, Berkeley, CA 94720, USA, 30 September 1987.

22/10 Szerman, M., *IEA-Task XI Project*, National Report, Fraunhofer Institute of Building Physics, Nobelstr. 12, D-7000 Stuttgart 80, Germany, 1989.

22/11 Paludan-Müller, C., Kristensen, P.E., *Daylighting through Rooflights in the BRF Headquarter*, Esbensen Consulting Engineers, Havnegade 41, DK-1058 Copenhagen, Denmark, 1991.

23 Detailed Results

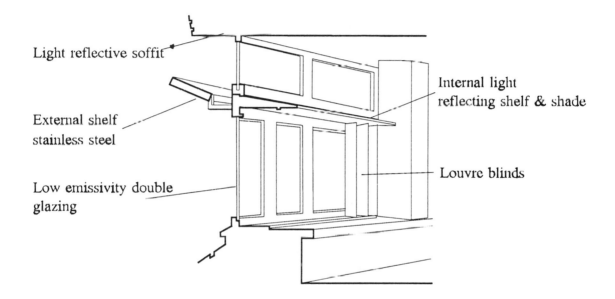

Light reflective soffit

External shelf
stainless steel

Low emissivity double
glazing

Internal light
reflecting shelf & shade

Louvre blinds

Chapter 23 presents simulation results for various daylighting strategies, linking for the first time the daylighting program, Superlite, to an energy program, DOE-2 or MBDS. The link, 'Daylink', was developed by LBL, USA, for Task XI. The simulation results report only energy values; glare and illuminance distribution are excluded in the analysis, but are obviously also important topics. In addition, this chapter presents physical model measurements under an artificial sky to determine Daylight Factors in an office adjoined to an atrium.

Section 23.1, Introduction, describes input/output data.

Section 23.2, Results of Parametric Study, analyzes lighting plus heating, lighting, and lighting plus a third of heating, based on parametric results for Zürich, Brussels, Rome and Oslo. The cooling load is a measure of discomfort, and no mechanical cooling is considered.

Section 23.3, Daylighting, Air Conditioning and Energy Costs, considers air conditioning and energy costs for offices with various heating and cooling systems in Zürich and Brussels.

Section 23.4, Daylight Factors in Rooms Adjacent to an Atrium, describes the physical modeling to obtain daylight factors and the derived nomogram for an adjacent room.

Section 23.5 presents Conclusions from monitoring and simulation.

The Appendix (Section 23.6) contains assumptions and the differences between climates and module inputs.

23.1   INTRODUCTION

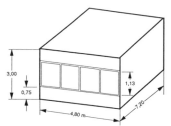

Fig. 23.1   Module 1, an office with three occupants during a working day

Daylighting strategies for an office and a classroom with specific boundary conditions were simulated. Energy savings were quantified for lighting, heating and cooling in the climates of Rome, Zürich, Brussels and Oslo [23/1].

Detailed energy consumption data were computed for daylighting through a side window and for simple daylighting strategies added to this window. Despite the limited number of cases studied, interesting relationships became apparent between the daylighting strategies, artificial lighting, heating and cooling.

23.1.1   The modules

Surface reflection:
Walls = 60%
Roof = 80%
Floor = 30%

Work plane height
= 0.75 m

Glazing area
= 5.2 m^2
   (15% of floor area)

Base cases for an office (module 1) and a classroom (module 2) are defined in Figs. 23.1 and 23.2. The office has only one exterior facade, the other five surfaces being embedded (adiabatic). Two situations were considered, one completely unshaded and one with partial shading from a neighboring building. The neighboring building is across a street and 18 m away, 15 m high and 30 m wide (case: SH). For the classroom, two situations were examined: one classroom with an external wall and exposed roof with no shading from neighboring buildings, and the other classroom on the ground floor, with one external wall, no roof exposure (ceiling), and partially shaded by a neighboring building (case: SH).

Details of the assumptions, construction and occupancy schedules are provided in the Appendix, Section 23.6.

Uncontrolled and base case definition
An uncontrolled case for all climates, (referred to as NIX) has no blinds and the lights are always on when people are present. It is the worst possible case because no solar or artificial light control is assumed.

A base case for all climates assumes an automatic lighting control. Daylighting strategies are added to the base case which is already energy efficient. In this manner the effect of the daylighting strategies can be compared.

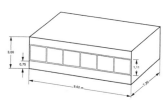

Fig. 23.2   Module 2, a classroom with 20 occupants with different national, daily and holiday occupancy schedules

For Belgium and Switzerland, the base case (BASE) activates blinds between 1 May and 31 October and has automatic continuous dimming lighting control with a minimum of the continuous control of 16%.

For Norway and Italy, the base case (referred to as ST) has an automatic on/off lighting control system (as continuous dimming is rare in Norway and Italy). Blinds are active between 1 May and 31 October.

Surface reflection:
Walls = 60%
Roof = 80%
Floor = 30%

Work plane height
= 0.75 m

Glazing area
= 10.4 m²
(15% of floor area)

23.1.2 Daylighting strategies

Sidelighting
The side window with 15% glazing area relative to floor area is present with all sidelighting concepts.

The *clerestory* (CL) is above the lower window with the same physical properties. The glazing areas are 5%, 10%, and 14% of the floor area.

An *overhang* (O), used in conjunction with sidelighting concepts, is in the form of a balcony 1.3 m deep. The reflectance of the opaque overhang is either 25% (concrete), or 80% for reflective material.

Fig. 23.3 Skylights (SKY)

Light shelves (LS), interior, exterior or combined (added to the 10% clerestory), have a depth of 1.0 m (equal to the height above the window). The reflectance of the opaque light shelf surfaces is 80%.

Toplighting
The side window with 15% glazing area relative to the floor area is also present with toplighting concepts.

The diffuse *skylight* area in the sensitivity study is 2% (and 4%) of the floor area. It is off-centered with its center above the back illuminance reference point. Only in the skylight case were different glazing properties used (Fig. 23.3).

$$\tau_{\text{visible}} = 59\%, \ U = 2.0\,\text{W/m}^2\,\text{K} \text{ and solar transmission } (g) = 45\%$$

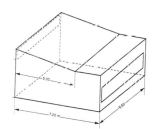

Fig. 23.4 Sawtooth (SW)

The *sawtooth* glazing with overhang (13% of the floor area, roughly corresponding to a large clerestory), is in the wall opposite the window. Glazing areas of 5% and 10% were also studied (Fig. 23.4).

The *monitors* are glazed in two directions with a total glazing of 13% of the floor area. This is the same glazing area as the sawtooth. Again, overhangs are added (Fig. 23.5).

23.1.3 Input data

- Minimum interior temperatures (for heating) of 20°C and maximum (for cooling) of 26°C during occupancy.
- A night set back to 16°C after school or office hours.
- External blinds are activated when the transmitted direct radiation

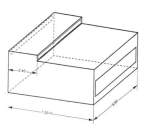

Fig. 23.5 Monitor (MO)

(or global for Belgium) exceeds 150 W/m², during the non-heating season.

- Illumination levels (350 and 500 lux) are recommended standard values for the classroom and office given by the various countries.
- Occupants adjust their exterior window blinds to avoid switching on lighting.
- Glazing coefficients of thermal transfer are 1.6 W/m² K for Zürich and Brussels, 2.0 W/m² K for Oslo, and 2.72 W/m² K for Rome.
- In Section 23.3, baseboard heating with a thermostatic control and a 1°C throttling range for the temperature control was simulated. Simulations for cooling during the day were made using an enthalpy-type economizer and a variable air volume cooling system (VAVS) with minimum outside air flow of 30 m³/h per person, a minimum supply temperature of 14°C and supply flow of six air changes per hour. No cooling occurred during the night.

The main assumptions made are given in the Appendix, Section 23.6.

Table 23.1 Classroom: percentage savings relative to the uncontrolled case for lighting (L), lighting plus heating (L + H) and cooling (C)

Orientation	Energy use	cont. dim. (%)	on/off (%)
S	L	69	66
	L + H	29	30
	C	68	70
		36*	
N	L	66	60
	L + H	19	19
	C	61	65
W	L	68	63
	L + H	21	21
	C	72	74
		36*	
E	L	68	
	L + H	21	
	C	74	
		44*	
SH	L	60	50
	L + H	32	30
	C	56	56
		40*	

*No blinds

23.1.4 Output data

The heating and cooling energy reported in Section 23.2 are the quantities of heat to be added to or extracted from the module to maintain interior temperatures set in the input schedules. No mechanical system is simulated because its efficiency, which depends on weather conditions, could mask the influence of the daylighting strategy. The energy quantities are given by the 'system' output SUM in DOE-2.1C.

Throughout the analysis of Section 23.2, the sum of lighting energy plus heating energy (L + H) is the main criterion for ranking because lighting energy alone is an insufficient criterion. Useful* heating energy is coupled with lighting, depending on the quantity of useful heat given out by the lights. Lighting plus a third of heating energy ($L + H/3$) corresponds to a heat pump or energy costs (electricity costing three times as much as oil).

The calculated cooling load is a measure of venting necessity or discomfort index for all classrooms, which are normally not mechanically cooled, and for offices in northern climates. The cooling load is relatively high because it represents an entire year. Finally, the blind trigger value is high, allowing a high admittance of summer solar gains. If cooling is too high, then air conditioning has to be integrated, and cooling energy will intervene in the total energy. Air conditioning the offices is treated in Section 23.3.

In Section 23.3, a baseboard heater, a variable air volume cooling

---

*Useful energy: quantity of energy actually used to satisfy a given need (lighting, hot water, room heated to 20°C), exclusive of distribution losses and plant efficiencies

system (VAVS) with an economizer and a chiller were simulated during the heating and cooling periods. Different aggregates of energy (e.g. lighting plus a third of heating and cooling) are considered, representing both energy and costs.

23.2 RESULTS OF PARAMETRIC STUDY

23.2.1 Results for Switzerland

Both the classroom and office were simulated. First, automatic light controls were studied, then the effect of the addition of up to twelve daylighting strategies to the base case. Hence, their separate effects are obtained.

Automatic light control
For the classroom, adding an automatic lighting control system to the uncontrolled case gives high energy savings for the four orientations of about 65% for lighting and 40% for cooling. The savings for lighting plus heating are much lower, at about 25% because the heating must be augmented to counterbalance the loss of heating from the lights. Similarly high savings occur for the office, namely 55% for lighting, 45% for lighting, plus heating and 27% for cooling with automatic dimming (see Tables 23.1 and 23.2).

Automatic dimming vs. on/off light control
For lighting in the classroom, continuous dimming (BASE) is better than on/off (ST) (Tables 23.3 and 23.4). The weather conditions dictate that often only a little extra rather than full on lighting is required to reach the design illuminance level of 350 lux. There is no significant difference between on/off (ST) and continuous dimming for lighting plus heating as extra heating is required with dimming (see Table 23.3).

For the office, continuous dimming lighting control is always better than the on/off system, especially for the shaded south for both lighting and lighting plus heating (Table 23.5). Lighting dominates the lighting plus heating balance.

Table 23.2 Office: percentage savings relative to the uncontrolled case

Orient-ation	Energy use	Control strategy cont. dim (%)	on/off (%)
S	L	61	52
	L + H	55	49
	C	49	47
		27*	
N	L	55	32
	L + H	36	25
	C	38	29
W	L	58	43
	L + H	44	35
	C	52	48
		27*	
E	L	58	42
	L + H	43	34
	C	50	47
		27*	
SH	L	43	21
	L + H	36	19
	C	45	35
		17*	

*No blinds

Table 23.3 South classroom: energy for different lighting control systems (continuous dimming with 16% base load, zero base load, on/off, and with no system)

Energy (kWh/m^2 a)	Cont. to 16% (BASE)	Contin. to Zero	On/off	NIX
Lighting	9.7	6.4	10.4	30.8
Lighting + heating	34.2	32.0	33.9	48.5

Installed power: 17.5 W/m^2

Table 23.4 Classroom: percentage change in energy consumption for various daylighting strategies relative to the base cases given in kilowatt-hours. Maximum savings are flagged

Daylighting strategies		South				North				West				Shaded south			
		L	H	C	L+H	L	H	C	L+H	L	H	C	L+H	L	H	C	L+H
Base, cont. dimming		668	1696	535	2364	714	2928	268	3642	690	2445	431	3135	847	1319	972	2166
no blinds, no dimming	(%)	218	−28	211	42	198	−19	156	24	208	−24	263	27	151	−19	130	48
blinds, no dimming	(%)	218	−26	103	43	198	−19	156	24	208	−23	130	28	151	−18	66	48
no blinds, dimming	(%)	0	−4	98	−3	0	0	8	0	0	−1	131	−1				
on/off light control	(%)	7	−4	−7	−1	21	−5	−10	0	18	−6	−4	−1	25	−10	1	4
low ceiling refl.	(%)	7	−1	1	1												
overhang	(%)	1	1	−9	1	1	0	−1	0	1	1	−3	1	2	0	−7	1
refl. overhang	(%)	1	1	−9	1												
10% clerestory w/o blind	(%)	−22	−13	153	−15	−24	12	80	5	−23	3	171	−3	−23	7	89	−5
10% clerestory w blind	(%)	−22	−10	95	−14									−23	8	45	−4
10% cler. + overhang	(%)	−18	3	58	−3												
exterior light shelf	(%)	−20	−2	122	−7	−22	12	78	5	−21	6	190	0	−23	9	75	−3
int. + ext. light shelf	(%)	−20	−8	154	−11					−21	5	181	−1	−22	8	89	−4
13% sawtooth	(%)	−27	37	47	19	−33	−19	327	−22								
13% sawtooth + overhang	(%)					−26	−15	183	−17	−36	14	122	3				
monitor + overhang	(%)	−25	12	76	2	−32	3	137	−4	−16	11	138	5				
2% skylight	(%)	−26	7	26	−2	−29	5	48	−2	−27	4	44	−2				
skylight + well	(%)	−23	7	26	−2												
4% skylight	(%)	−30	19	54	5												

Table 23.5 Office: percentage change in energy consumption for various daylighting strategies relative to the base cases (given in kWh). (Maximum savings are flagged)

Daylighting strategies		South				North				West				Shaded south			
		L	H	C	L+H	L	H	C	L+H	L	H	C	L+H	L	H	C	L+H
Base	(kWh)	471	83	1058	554	540	369	594	909	500	247	826	747	682	133	1056	815
no dimming, no blinds	(%)	153	−70	96	120	121	−36	62	57	138	−38	108	80	75	−32	81	57
blinds, no dimming	(%)	153	−70	52	120	121	−36	62	57	138	−38	55	80	75	−33	45	57
no blinds, dimming	(%)	0	0	43	0	0	0	0	0	0	0	52	0	0	0	50	0
on/off light control	(%)	21	−33	5	13	50	−28	16	19	36	−22	8	17	39	−30	17	27
low ceiling refl.	(%)	7	−7	2	5	10	−5	4	4	9	−4	2	5				
overhang	(%)	1	0	−4	1	1	−1	0	0	2	0	−2	1	5	−2	−2	3
refl. overhang	(%)	1	0	−4	1	1	−1	0	0	2	0	−2	1	4	−2	−2	3
10% clerestory w/o blind	(%)	−24	23	71	−17	−29	60	28	7	−26	45	67	−2	−22	43	61	−11
10% clerestory w blind	(%)	−24	23	44	−17									−22	43	36	−11
exterior light shelf	(%)	−22	54	53	−11	−27	58	27	8	−24	51	76	1	−22	51	50	−10
ext. light shelf + blind	(%)	−22	54	26	−11												
int. + ext. light shelves	(%)	−20	34	66	−12	−24	56	29	8	−22	47	72	1	−19	44	59	−9
int. + ext. light sh. + blind	(%)	−20	34	39	−12					−22	47	38	1				

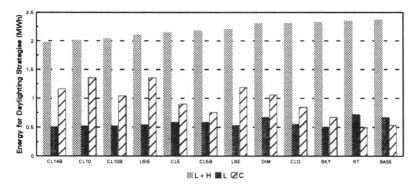

Fig. 23.6 South classroom: lighting plus heating, lighting and cooling yearly energy consumption in ranking order for lighting plus heating

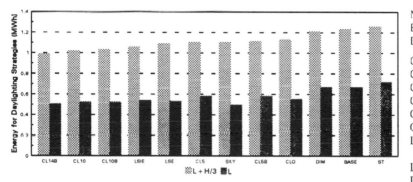

Fig. 23.7 South classroom: lighting plus a third of heating (ranking order), and lighting yearly energy consumption

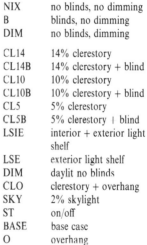

NIX	no blinds, no dimming
B	blinds, no dimming
DIM	no blinds, dimming
CL14	14% clerestory
CL14B	14% clerestory + blind
CL10	10% clerestory
CL10B	10% clerestory + blind
CL5	5% clerestory
CL5B	5% clerestory + blind
LSIE	interior + exterior light shelf
LSE	exterior light shelf
DIM	daylit no blinds
CLO	clerestory + overhang
SKY	2% skylight
ST	on/off
BASE	base case
O	overhang

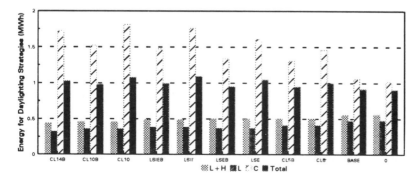

Fig. 23.8 South office: lighting plus heating (ranking order), lighting, cooling and total (with cooling system) yearly energy

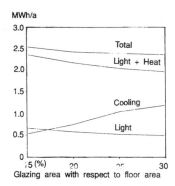

Fig. 23.10 South classroom: energy as a function of glazing area (with blinds)

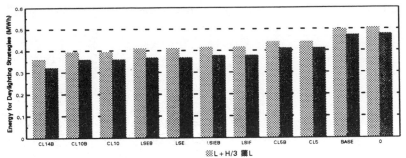

Fig. 23.9 South office: lighting plus a third heating, and lighting yearly energy consumptions in ranking order for L + H/3

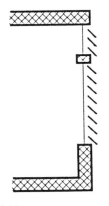

Fig. 23.11

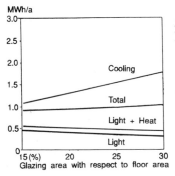

Fig. 23.12 South office: energy as a function of glazing area (with blinds)

Clerestory glazing area

Adding a clerestory and thereby increasing the glazing on the south side of the classroom from 15 to 29% of the floor area decreases the lighting energy by 25% (Fig. 23.10).

Heating energy is also reduced (Table 23.4). Lighting plus heating energy is then decreased by 17%. Including mechanical cooling in the energy total makes the total consumption decrease only slightly with increasing glazing area (Fig. 23.10, see Total).

For the west/east classroom orientations, simulations show that lighting plus heating remains insensitive to glazing area with a slight minimum for 20–25% glazing area. For the north orientation, the smaller the glazing area, the lower the lighting plus heating energy consumption.

In the case of the office, the lighting energy decreases by 32% if the glazing area increases from 15 to 29% of the floor area. Auxiliary heating increases in compensation for heating from the lights and the solar gains are poorly used, so that the lighting plus heating energy decreases by only 21% (which is small in absolute value) (Fig. 23.12, Table 23.5).

The absolute lighting energy savings with increased glazing are still greater for the shaded south office than for the unshaded office. Absolute lighting plus heating savings are roughly the same for both the shaded and unshaded offices (Fig. 23.12, Table 23.5).

The total energy including mechanical cooling increases slightly with increasing glazing area for both the shaded and unshaded offices (Fig. 23.12). It is therefore important to know whether air conditioning shall be included or not before deciding on the daylighting strategy.

Overhang

The overhang outside the classroom has no influence on the lighting energy because the zone near the window is not considered separately for electric lighting and the overhang is not directly above the window. Furthermore, the overhang decreases the cooling by at most 9%.

Without the overhang, the blinds are closed three times more often because of the inside blind sensor, providing similar cooling. Lighting plus heating energy is unchanged as the winter solar gains are not reduced much by the overhang. Therefore, the two systems, blinds or overhang, are more similar than expected. Cooling can be approximately halved if an overhang and blinds are introduced together (see Table 23.3).

Also for the office an overhang has minimal effect on energy consumption except when the office is shaded by a neighboring building. In that case, the overhang causes an increase in lighting energy use (see Table 23.5).

10% clerestory and light shelves
For the classroom, the 10% clerestory and added light shelves save between 20 and 24% of the lighting energy relative to the base cases, depending on the orientation. (See Figs. 23.6 and 23.7.)

The savings are due to the increased glazing area from the clerestory and not the light shelf. Different light shelf systems show no significant lighting differences. Light shelves improve visual comfort by equalizing the illuminance levels in the room. The 10% clerestories save lighting plus heating energy for the south, shaded south and west orientations (savings of 5.2, 1.6, 1.4 kWh/m² a, respectively), but they can cause high cooling loads (Table 23.3). Heating demands are in fact reduced as well as the lighting as solar gains are well used for the south unshaded case.

Adding a light shelf to a south window with clerestory increases heating demand, especially if the light shelf is exterior. The 15% saving in lighting plus heating of the clerestory drop to 11% for the interior/exterior light shelf and 7% for the exterior one. However, the exterior light shelf decreases the cooling by 12% (compared to 23% decrease by adding exterior clerestory blinds). See Figs. 23.6 and 23.7. For the west, the clerestory and light shelf save no lighting plus heating compared to the base case, but lighting savings are still about 20%, hence savings of 6% are possible for L + H/3.

In the case of the office, where required illumination is high, the 10% clerestories and added light shelves are recommended for all orientations to save lighting energy, and savings of 22–29% are possible (Table 23.5).

The clerestories are slightly better without light shelves except for the shaded south. In the exposed south, clerestories save 17% (2.7 kWh/m²) of lighting plus heating, but the savings are small in absolute values compared to the classroom, as the solar gains are poorly used. Cooling loads are high and therefore blinds must be used. (See Figs. 23.8, 23.9 and 23.12.)

If an exterior light shelf is introduced, then the saved lighting plus heating energy is reduced from 17% to about 11%. Cooling loads are decreased by 10% but remain higher than if a clerestory blind is used or for a small clerestory without blinds.

Clerestories and light shelves are added to the side window

- 15% window glazing
- 10% clerestory glazing (6.9 m² for the classroom)
- exterior clerestory blinds available

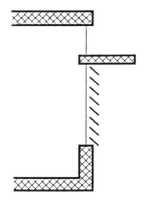

- 15% window glazing
- 10% clerestory glazing
- 1 m deep at head

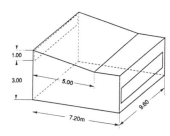

Table 23.6 Classroom: percentage change in energy for different sawtooth glazing areas relative to the base case (given in kilowatt-hours)

Saw-tooth glazing area		South		
	L	H	C	L+H
Base (kWh)	668	1696	535	2364
5% (%)	−10	16	17	8
10% (%)	−24	30	36	15
13% (%)	−27	37	47	19
		West*		
Base (kWh)	690	2445	431	3135
5% (%)	−6	7	38	4
13% (%)	−36	14	122	3

*The sawtooth facing east has an overhang

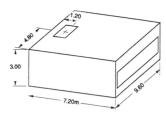

As lighting energy savings remain high for the office facing west, savings of 12–16% are possible for clerestories with or without a light shelf for L + H/3. For the north orientation, although no energy savings are possible for L + H, savings of up to 13% are possible for a medium clerestory for L + H/3, primarily from lighting savings and because heating demand is not too high.

In offices and in reality, the lights are often left on all day unlike the base case, which assumes dimming. An exterior light shelf with automatic light control then saves about 50% of the total energy and 70% of the lighting energy compared to the uncontrolled case. Other advantages of light shelves over the base case are that electricity, which is more expensive, is saved and the illuminance levels are more homogeneous. (See also assumption (b) in the Appendix.)

Sawtooth

The sawteeth considered (5%, 10% and 13% glazing areas) are recommendable, if saving lighting energy is important. In that case they are a good solution for all orientations with savings of up to 36%. Illumination from a window and sawtooth glazing facing opposite ways gives good natural lighting. In the analysis of lighting plus heating, of the cases examined, only the classroom facing north with the large sawtooth glazing facing south is recommended. If L + H/3 is considered, then the large sawtooth window facing east with an overhang can save some energy. The sawtooth facing north offers no savings. (See Tables 23.3 and 23.6.)

Skylights

Translucent skylights directly above the rear sensor (with 2% and 4% glazing relative to the floor area) save lighting energy for all classroom orientations when added to the existing window. Savings of between 26% and 30% are possible depending on window orientation and skylight size as shown in Table 23.3, and Figs. 23.6 and 23.7.

More heating is required by the skylight than by the base case partly to compensate for less lighting, and because horizontal solar gains in winter are much smaller than the heat losses ($U = 2.0 \, \text{W/m}^2 \, \text{K}$). Hence, although lighting demands decrease, lighting plus heating savings are negligible (2%) or even negative for the bigger skylight.

For the classroom facing south, although extra winter solar energy (9%) is gained from the small skylight, these gains are not comparable to those through the large vertical unshaded south clerestories. Clerestories admit more winter solar energy because the glazing area is larger, vertical glazing is more favorable than horizontal in winter, and the clerestory has a better solar transmission and U-value. If skylights are desired for the classroom, then small units are possible.

If L + H/3 is considered, then the small skylight offers potential energy savings (10%) for all basic window orientations (Fig. 23.7). Overheating is not frequent in the Zürich climate because the skylight glazing area is small, the solar transmission coefficient is low and there are school holidays in midsummer.

Monitors
For lighting energy alone, south-facing monitors are good for north-facing classrooms (32% savings) and quite good for south-facing classrooms. For lighting plus heating, they are only advantageous for the classroom facing north (savings of $2.0\,kWh/m^2\,a$).

Conclusions
Daylighting strategies and especially automatic lighting control must be considered for classrooms and offices, whether or not mechanical cooling is present. The major part of the savings for lighting and consequently for lighting plus heating are due to automatic lighting control. It saves between 40% and 70% of lighting energy and between 20% and 55% of lighting plus heating energy.

If daylighting strategies are integrated with automatic lighting control, additional savings of lighting plus heating energy (11% to 21%) are possible for the modules facing south, but only small savings are possible for modules facing east or west, and no savings are possible for modules facing north (except with a sawtooth or monitor facing south). This result is due to the cold winter in Zürich. Shading by a neighboring building shows the difficulty in saving energy in the embedded classroom compared to an exposed classroom with a roof and the high potential for energy saving for a deep office.

Higher percentage energy savings are possible for lighting plus a third of heating for the south modules, and considerable savings of 6% to 16% are possible for modules facing east or west and for the office facing north. For the classroom facing north with rooflights even higher savings occurred.

Overheating is primarily a problem in the embedded classroom and offices. For a module facing south, light shelves with a medium clerestory provide a compromise, saving lighting plus heating energy while avoiding overheating. They have the advantage of equalizing daylighting levels in the room. Overheating can also be avoided by closing blinds earlier, or opening windows. It is important to determine if air conditioning will be installed in a building before deciding which daylighting strategy will be used. (See Section 23.3, Daylighting, Air Conditioning and Energy Costs.)

23.2.2   Results for Belgium

For the Belgian climate, the office module was simulated for the four orientations south, north, east and west; and the classroom module was simulated for the south facade alone. The design illuminance level for the classroom is lower than for the office. The heating load is higher because the roof is exposed and ventilation losses are high. Consequently, the heating load (H) is higher and the cooling load (C) is lower than in the office. For the Belgian simulations, the blinds are activated when global transmitted radiation exceeds $150\,W/m^2$. (In Zürich the blinds were lowered when direct radiation exceeded $150\,W/m^2$.) Consequently, the computed cooling load is much lower than results in Zürich.

The simulations for lighting, heating and cooling energy consumptions, performed with DAYLINK and MBDS, take into account the Belgian climatic data (Uccle).

Five lighting control systems are analyzed:

BASE continuous dimming with base power load of 16%
MIN continuous dimming with base power load of 0%
ST1 on/off stepped light control (one step: 0 to 500 lux)
ST2 on/off stepped light control (two steps: 0 to 250 lux, 250 to 500 lux)
NIX no blinds and non dimming of lights

Effect of increasing the glazing area (from 15 to 25% of floor area)
When placing a clerestory above the window of the base case lighting energy decreases by 17 to 23%, according to the orientation (see Table 23.7). The effect on heating for different orientations is:

● south: reduction of 21%
● north: increase of 16%
● east and west: slight increases
● shaded south: heating does not change.

The cooling load rises sharply when a clerestory is placed above the window, double for the north facade, and is five times as high for the south facade. In absolute values, however, the cooling loads are all small relative to Zürich.

If blinds like those on the window are placed in front of the clerestory (CLB) or if an overhang (CLO) is added, the increase in cooling is significantly reduced. The cooling load then is three times as high as that of the base case for the south windows. A light shelf between the window and the clerestory does not save much energy. It reduces direct solar radiation on the work surface, while its high reflectivity allows even distribution of daylight in the room.

Effect of the lighting control system
The introduction of lighting control systems plays a major role in the office. Predictably, the ideal lighting control system is a continuous dimming system with electric power dropping to zero when the interior illumination of the work plane reaches 500 lux (MIN). Then, lighting requirements are reduced by 16 to 20% compared to the base case

(Figs. 23.13 and 23.15). Three independent control circuits, in the front, center and back of the office, instead of two circuits would reduce the lighting load by about 12%.

Also of importance, a light control system capable of being turned on or off in two steps (ST2) offers energy consumption values for lighting plus heating similar to base case (continuous dimming with 16% base load) values except for the shaded south cases (Fig. 23.15). The same tendency which occurs for the office is observed for the south classroom (see Table 23.8). The best lighting control system is continuous dimming with no base load. The two-stepped lighting control reduces lighting and consequently cooling loads with respect to the base case (Fig. 23.17).

Possible savings using daylighting strategies
Various daylighting strategies in the office are compared to a base case which is taken as a reference (using the same blinds and same dimming lighting system) to give the following results (see Table 23.7 and Fig. 23.16).

An exterior light shelf for the shaded south facade slightly increases the performance of the clerestory. The increase of daylight penetration in this deep office is appreciable.

The overhang (O and OR) has only a limited influence on artificial lighting (excluding the zone close to the window). The increase in the glazed area from the clerestory (applicable to CL and CLO because the overhang does not influence the results) provokes a reduction of the lighting load of between 17 and 23%. Installing an exterior or interior light shelf (LSE, LSI) leads to a small increase in lighting energy compared to the clerestory alone, but the clerestory with light shelf still offers a reduction in lighting of 14–21%, compared to the base case.

An overhang (O and OR) analyzed with two fixed reference points, has only a limited negative effect on lighting plus heating or lighting plus a third of heating. Despite this negative effect, the usefulness of an overhang should be carefully considered for the south facade, because beam solar radiation can fall directly on the work plane close to the window during summer, causing visual discomfort without an overhang.

Daylighting strategies which are valid for the office provide similar benefits in the south classroom. The overhang barely influences the level of artificial lighting while the increase in the glazed area (clerestory, exterior and interior light shelves) provokes a reduction of lighting of 12–18%. The best results are obtained by the rooflighting, where the reduction in lighting loads varies from 22–25% for the classroom (see Table 23.8).

When L + H loads are considered for the classroom, the best results are obtained by sidelighting; when L + H/3 loads are examined, both sidelighting and rooflighting give good results (see Fig. 23.18).

Table 23.7 Office: annual loads relative to the base case (BASE). (Maximum savings are flagged.)

DL strategies		South				North				East				West			
		L	H	C	L+H	L	H	C	L+H	L	H	C	L+H	L	H	C	L+H
Base	(kWh)	664	260	108	923	739	613	100	1352	701	513	114	1215	703	493	111	1196
no blinds, no dimming	(%)	105	−32	634	67	84	−17	215	38	94	−20	333	46	94	−22	696	46
on/off light. control 1 step	(%)	18	−10	16	10	37	−14	45	14	29	−13	21	11	27	−11	27	11
on/off light. control 2 steps	(%)	3	−5	−9	0	12	−7	10	4	8	−6	−5	2	7	−6	−5	2
dimming base power load 0	(%)	−20	7	−17	−12	−16	4	−18	−7	−18	4	−16	−9	−18	5	−25	−9
no blinds, dimming	(%)	0	−3	376	−1	0	0	27	0	0	0	132	0	0	−4	500	−1
low ceiling reflection	(%)	5	−3	19	3	7	−2	22	3	6	−3	15	2	6	−3	15	2
overhang	(%)	1	1	19	1	1	0	6	0	1	0	7	1	1	1	−4	1
reflective overhang	(%)	1	1	18	1	1	0	6	0	1	0	8	1	1	1	−5	1
10% clerestory	(%)	−18	−21	392	−19	−23	16	134	−5	−21	10	211	−8	−20	6	402	−9
clerestory + overhang	(%)	−18	−3	193	−14	−23	16	121	−5	−21	14	115	−6	−20	12	188	−7
exterior light shelf	(%)	−17	−10	372	−15	−21	16	133	−4	−20	12	203	−6	−19	9	376	−7
interior light shelf	(%)	−16	−23	398	−17	−18	14	135	−3	−17	8	217	−7	−16	5	406	−8
10% clerestory + blind	(%)	−18	−19	166	−19	−23	16	122	−5	−21	10	121	−8	−20	8	120	−9
exterior light shelf + blind	(%)	−17	−8	139	−14	−21	16	122	−4	−20	12	114	−6	−19	11	92	−7
interior light shelf + blind	(%)	−16	−21	171	−16	−18	14	124	−3	−17	8	125	−7	−16	6	123	−7
interior light shelf + blind + reflective overhang	(%)	−14	−5	155	−12												

Table 23.8 Annual loads relative to the base case (BASE). Maximum savings are flagged

Daylighting strategies		South				
		L	H	C	L+H	L+H/3
Base	(kWh)	810	1642	89	2453	1358
no blinds, no dimming	(%)	149	−17	719	37	81
on/off light. control 1 step	(%)	8	−3	−13	1	4
on/off light. control 2 steps	(%)	−6	−1	−19	−2	−4
dimming base power load 0%	(%)	−28	4	−25	−7	−15
no blinds, dimming	(%)	0	−5	426	−3	−2
reflective overhang	(%)	1	0	6	0	1
10% clerestory	(%)	−18	−12	421	−14	−16
exterior light shelf	(%)	−16	−8	390	−11	−13
interior light shelf	(%)	−12	−13	425	−13	−13
10% clerestory + blind	(%)	−18	−9	158	−12	−14
exterior light shelf + blind	(%)	−16	−5	115	−8	−11
interior light shelf + blind	(%)	−12	−10	161	−11	−13
interior light shelf + refl. overhang	(%)	−12	−4	131	−7	−9
sawtooth	(%)	−25	35	94	15	−1
monitor + overhang	(%)	−22	13	25	1	−8
skylight	(%)	−24	5	57	−4	−12
skylight + well	(%)	−22	5	57	−4	−11
skylight + reflective overhang	(%)	−24	6	65	−4	−12

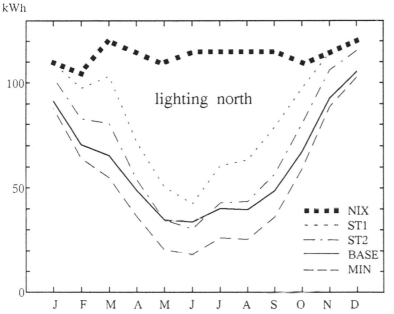

Fig. 23.13 Monthly lighting load L for the north-facing office

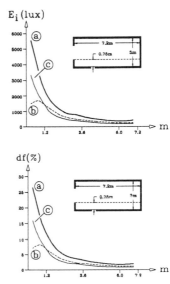

Fig. 23.14 Illuminances and daylight factors on the work plane: 15 June, 1 p.m.: (a) south clear sky; (b) north clear sky; (c) overcast sky

South Office: Lighting Control Systems

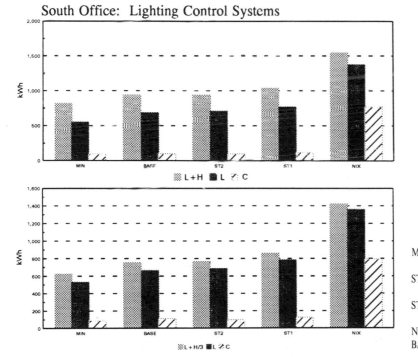

MIN	dimming base power load 0%
ST2	o/off light. control 2 steps
ST1	on/off light. control 1 step
NIX	no blinds, no dimming
BASE	base case

Fig. 23.15 Annual energy consumption in ranking order for lighting plus heating

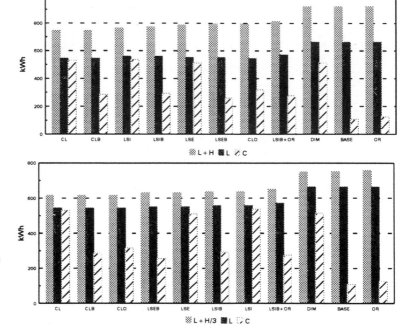

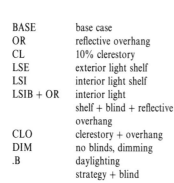

BASE	base case
OR	reflective overhang
CL	10% clerestory
LSE	exterior light shelf
LSI	interior light shelf
LSIB + OR	interior light shelf + blind + reflective overhang
CLO	clerestory + overhang
DIM	no blinds, dimming
.B	daylighting strategy + blind

Fig. 23.16 Annual energy consumption in ranking order for lighting plus heating

23.2.3 Results for Italy

Only the south classroom was studied. Daylighting strategies were added to the base case, already an energy efficient design. The new base case has blinds and automatic on/off lighting control which is better than the continuous dimming. Mechanical cooling is generally unacceptable for classrooms; hence cooling energy becomes a discomfort index and lighting plus heating energy is considered crucial for classrooms. Lighting plus a third of heating is also examined. All cases except the continuous dimming case employ an on/off lighting control system.

Automatic light control

Three factors allow the very large lighting (L) savings of 60–85%. First, the uncontrolled case is the worst possible situation and possibly unrealistic. Second, the school schedule is from 8:00 to 14:00, so that lighting is hardly needed. Third, Rome has a sunny climate (Table 23.9).

The savings in lighting plus heating (L + H) remain large (70–80%) for the south, as lighting is more important than heating in Rome. The savings drop to 30% for the north, where the lighting energy

Table 23.9 Percentage savings compared to the uncontrolled case

Or.	Energy	Control strategy	
		Continuous dimming (%)	On/off (%)
S	L	78	85
	L + H	73	80
	C	41	46
N	L		64
	L + H		30
	C		50
SH	L		60
	L + H		59
	C		45

South Classroom: Lighting Control System

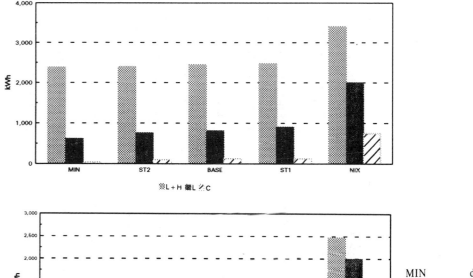

MIN   dimming base power load 0%
ST2   on/off light. control 2 steps
ST1   on/off lighting control 1 step
NIX   no blinds, no dimming
BASE   base case

Fig. 23.17 Annual energy consumption for lighting plus heating (ranking order) (kWh)

Table 23.10 Classroom: percentage change in energy for various daylighting strategies relative to the base case

Daylighting strategies		South			
		L	H	C	L + H
base	(kWh)	194	59	706	253
uncontrolled case	(%)	545	−61	84	404
contin. dimming	(%)	43	7	8	35
overhang	(%)	3	2	−9	2
10% clerestory	(%)	−49	−83	180	−57
10% clerestory + blind	(%)	−49	−83	119	−57
clerestory + blind + overhang	(%)	−45	−8	40	−37
exterior light shelf	(%)	−47	−17	107	−40
exterior light shelf + blind	(%)	−47	−17	46	−40
int. + ext. light shelf + blind	(%)	−46	−59	88	−49
sawtooth	(%)	−61	217	12	4
skylight	(%)	−55	29	22	−36

South Classroom: Daylighting Strategies

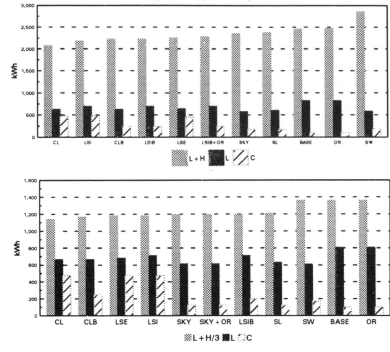

CL	10% clerestory
LSE	exterior light shelf
LSI	interior light shelf
LSIB + OR	int. light
	shelf + blind + refl.
	overhang
SKY	skylight
SL	skylight + well
BASE	base case
OR	reflective overhang
SW	sawtooth
SKY + OR	skylight + overhang
.B	daylighting
	strategy + blind

Fig. 23.18 Annual energy consumption for lighting plus heating (ranking order) (kWh)

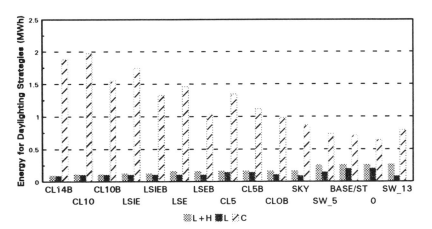

Fig. 23.19 South classroom: lighting plus heating, lighting and cooling yearly energy consumptions in ranking order for lighting plus heating

consumption is less than heating. Cooling energy savings from an automatic control and blinds are about 50% for all three cases.

Automatic dimming versus on/off light control

An on/off lighting control system offers better results than the dimming system for lighting and lighting plus heating in the Rome climate for the base case classroom facing south. Daylighting levels exceed the design illumination levels during much of the day, so no artificial lighting is required. It is then better if the lights can be completely off with an on/off control, rather than at 16% of the maximum power with a continuous dimming system. The lighting energy per unit area is low at 2.81 kWh/m² a, which is partly due to the school schedules. It increases with continuous dimming to 4.02 kWh/m² a (Table 23.10).

Overhang

An overhang is required to minimize cooling. Calculations show that the overhang has surprisingly little effect on lighting (3%) because there is no light reference point near the window. With the overhang present, the blinds only close in October when sufficient direct radiation enters the room (see the discussion in the Swiss example); therefore the overhang's effect on cooling loads is small. The overhang is interesting if mechanical cooling is required and is important for comfort near the window (Table 23.10).

Clerestory glazing area

Increasing the glazing area from 15 to 29% with clerestories for the classroom facing south provides high savings for lighting and lighting plus heating (55% and 63% respectively) because lighting dominates (see Fig. 23.21). 2.3 kWh/m² a are saved, compared to a saving of 5.7 kWh/m² a for Zürich. Clerestory blinds do not affect heating consumption, because blinds are raised in midwinter and the heating season is short. Energy consumption hardly decreases for glazing areas above 25%.

As lighting energy dominates in the Rome climate, substantial lighting savings give high savings for L + H/3. Computations show a decrease in lighting plus heating energy consumption that decreases with increasing glazing area for the classroom facing west and east. A minimum for lighting plus heating energy is observed at 15–20% glazing for the north classroom.

CL14	14% clerestory
CL14B	14% cler. + blind
CL10	10% clerestory
LSIE	int. + ext. light shelf
LSE	exterior light shelf
CL5	5% clerestory
CLOB	10% cler. + overhang + blind
SKY	skylight
O	overhang
BASE/ST	base case w. on/off
SW–5	5% sawtooth
SW–13	13% sawtooth
.B	plus blind

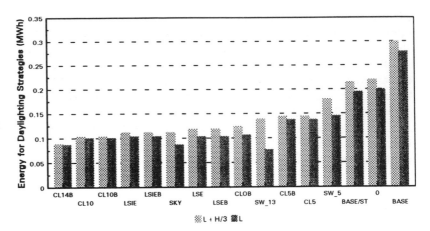

Fig. 23.20 South classroom: lighting plus a third of heating, and lighting yearly energy consumptions in ranking order for L + H/3

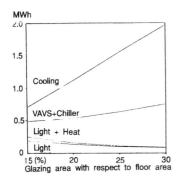

Fig. 23.21 South classroom: energy as a function of glazing area (with blinds)

- 15% window glazing
- 10% clerestory glazing
- 1 m deep at head height
- exterior clerestory blinds available

Table 23.11 Classroom: percentage change in energy for different sawtooth glazing areas relative to the base case (given in kWh)

Saw- tooth glazing area	South			
	L	H	C	L + H
Base (kWh)	194	59	706	253
5% (%)	−25	73	3	−2
13% (%)	−61	217	12	4

10% clerestory and light shelves

Large clerestories decrease lighting energy, but cause overheating. If low lighting energy and small cooling loads are important, then consider interior and exterior light shelves with clerestory blinds, or an exterior light shelf without blinds. Interior and exterior light shelves with blinds are also recommended to economize lighting plus heating. (See Table 23.10 and Fig. 23.19.)

Ten percent clerestories halve lighting energy and reduce heating demands to near zero. Adding an overhang directly above the medium clerestory reintroduces nearly all heating requirements, because of loss of solar gains through the clerestory; cooling loads have, however, acceptable values (below 1 MWh/a).

The three daylighting strategies, a 10% clerestory with exterior light shelf and blinds, a 5% clerestory with blinds or a 10% clerestory with overhang and blinds, all save about the same lighting plus heating energy (1.4 kWh/m^2 a) while keeping the cooling loads low (1 MWh/a). Finally, for overall comfort, the exterior light shelf is recommended.

Sawtooth

A sawtooth facing north (added to the base case) maintains acceptable lighting plus heating (-2%) energy consumption values for a classroom facing south, but the sawtooth must be small because it increases heating demand (Table 23.11). Low lighting energy means that L + H/3 is lower for both sawtooth areas than for the base case. In fact the large sawtooth provides interesting results, as shown in Fig. 23.20. Cooling levels also remain low, mainly due to the summer holiday schedule.

Skylight

A skylight added to a room with a front window is effective any time that low lighting and cooling energy requirements predominate. The small translucent skylight (with 2% glazing area) is a reasonable solution for Roman schools. The 5% extra winter solar gains partly offset the reduced heat gains from lighting and heat losses of the skylight glazing (high U-value).

If lighting plus heating are considered, the total energy consumption decreases (-36%). Cooling demand with the small skylight is actually less than with the clerestory because of the low solar transmission coefficient of the skylight (0.59), its small area, and because summer holidays reduce the amount of time when horizontal glazing is detrimental. If L + H/3 is considered, the skylight becomes particularly attractive since 55% of lighting energy is saved (Fig. 23.20).

- 15% window glazing
- 2% skylight glazing
- above rear light sensor
- translucent

Conclusions

A 60–80% saving in lighting energy is possible using an artificial lighting system that responds to daylight from windows. On/off lighting control gives somewhat larger savings than continuous dimming control (with a 16% base load) for lighting and lighting plus heating in the south classroom. Added rooflighting or sidelighting offer even higher lighting savings.

For this study, medium clerestories with or without exterior light shelves or overhang or a small clerestory save substantial lighting plus heating energy, and avoid too much overheating. A clerestory, added light shelf, or small skylight can save from 2.1 to 1.3 kWh/m² a. Large clerestories are inadvisable because they increase the overheating. Use of blinds, light shelves or an overhang with clerestories is important to prevent overheating.

23.2.4 Results for Norway

Only the classroom module was studied for the Oslo climate (60° northern latitude). Results presented here are for a continuous dimming and on/off lighting system, four sidelighting and three toplighting strategies. The energy results are annual lighting (L), heating (H), lighting plus heating (L + H) and cooling (C) load, in kWh. Norwegian schools are never equipped with mechanical cooling. The calculated cooling load should therefore be considered a measure of venting necessity, or discomfort when overheating, if the venting capacity is inadequate. Schools are often heated electrically, so heating and lighting energy use are directly comparable. All cases except the continuous dimming control system assume an on/off lighting control system.

ST	on/off
BASE	base case
NIX	uncontrolled case
DIM	daylit + no blinds
O	overhang
CL	10% clerestory
LSE	exterior light shelf
LSIE	ext. + int. light shelf
SW	sawtooth
MO	monitor
SKY	skylight

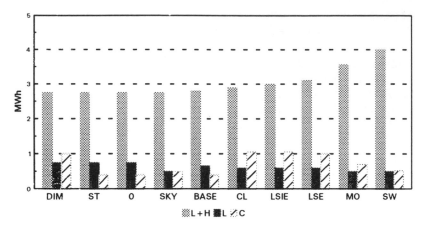

Fig. 23.22 South classroom: lighting plus heating, lighting and cooling yearly energy consumption in ranking order for lighting plus heating

Automatic lighting control

Table 23.12 gives the percentage energy savings of the lighting controls relative to an uncontrolled case (lighting is on all day when the classroom is used). The uncontrolled case is without blinds, while conventional daylighting cases (continuous dimming and on/off control) have blinds. Hence the case with no daylighting is the worst case.

A large fraction of lighting energy can be saved when an automatic lighting control system is used. However, much lighting energy is also useful heat and with the long heating season, the combined savings of lighting plus heating energy are modest.

Lighting control reduces the lighting energy by 57% and the combined heating and lighting energy by 23% for the south. The annual saved consumption is 815 kWh with electric heating, which does not warrant the extra investment in an automatic control system when considering current prices for energy (Table 23.12).

Large lighting energy savings are even possible for the classroom facing north.

Table 23.12 Percentage savings compared to the uncontrolled case

Energy		Control strategy	
		Continuous dimming (%)	On/off (%)
S	L	62	57
	L + H	22	23
	C	71	74
			30*
N	L	55	52
	L + H	−18	−16
	C	85	87

*Without blinds

Automatic dimming versus on/off light control

Only 12% lighting energy is saved when using the dimming system instead of the on/off control. With electric heating there are no savings, which indicates that a more expensive dimming system is less cost-effective than an on/off control (Table 23.13).

Overhang

The results using an overhang are surprising. The expectation is that the overhang significantly reduces daylight and increases the lighting load but the reduction is insignificant (1%). More importantly, the

Table 23.13 Energy demands in kWh/a for the base case (on/off control with blinds), and percentage change for various daylighting strategies in Oslo

Daylighting strategies		South			
		L	H	C	L + H
base	(kWh)	733	2011	369	2744
uncontrolled case	(%)	134	−8	282	30
daylit + no blinds	(%)	0	0	167	0
continuous dimming	(%)	−12	6	11	1
overhang	(%)	1	0	10	0
10% clerestory	(%)	−24	18	186	7
exterior light shelf	(%)	−23	24	164	11
exterior + interior light shelf	(%)	−24	21	191	9
sawtooth	(%)	−36	76	40	46
monitor	(%)	−31	51	76	29
skylight	(%)	−36	14	28	1

overhang reduces the cooling load, as efficiently as automatic blinds with conventional sidelighting (Table 23.13).

Clerestory and light shelves
A clerestory window is effective in bringing daylight into the deeper part of the classroom, but energy requirements for both heating and cooling increase considerably, partly due to the poor glazing used normally in Norway. To avoid the cooling problem, clerestory windows facing south must have blinds, and the windows should have highly insulating glazing.

Light shelves are ineffective in reducing the cooling energy because of the low solar altitude (Fig. 23.22 and Table 23.13).

Rooflighting strategies
Rooflighting provides quality daylighting with smaller increases in cooling loads compared to sidelighting strategies such as clerestories because of the low sun angles of this latitude. Lighting savings are, however, offset by increased heating demand for the monitor and sawtooth because of their glazing orientation and only the skylight remains a reasonable proposition.

Conclusions
Only a classroom facing south was studied.

A 50–60% saving in lighting energy is possible by using a lighting control system. The continuous dimming gives 5% larger savings than an on/off system.

Introducing a light control system without blinds, alone saves 30% cooling load because the lights are turned off during periods with large solar gains.

When lighting and heating energy are combined, monitors and sawtooths perform worse than windows, because heat losses are greater.

Because much of the lighting energy is useful heat, the energy benefits of daylight are diminished.

The special daylighting strategies increase cooling loads compared to sidelighting with blinds.

In a classroom facing north, the lighting energy is typically 15% higher, and the heating energy is approximately 60% higher than a south-facing orientation, but classrooms facing north have no cooling problems.

23.2.5   Comparison across climates

Two aspects were considered for the south classroom.

- the effect of climate alone on energy consumption, using a constant input (Swiss base case facing south).
- the effect of climate, local school schedules and construction on the energy consumption.

Effect of climate alone (*constant input*)
The climates studied were Rome, Zürich, Brussels and Oslo. Results are surprising in that Brussels requires more yearly lighting and heating than Oslo, Zürich or Rome. Tables 23.14(a, b) present the results and Table 23.20 the climatic statistics.

Table 23.14(a)   Winter energy consumption for different climates (constant base case input)

Energy (MWh/a)	Rome	Zürich	Brussels	Oslo
Light	0.26	0.41	0.56	0.62
Heat	0.00	1.41	1.73	1.75
L + H	0.26	1.82	2.29	2.37

Winter: November, December, January and February

Table 23.14(b)   Annual energy consumption and solar gains for different climates (constant base case input)

Energy (MWh/a)	Rome	Zürich	Brussels	Oslo
Light	0.32	0.72	0.91	0.80
Heat	0.01	1.63	2.09	1.95
Cool	2.67	0.50	0.21	0.64
L + H	0.33	2.35	3.00	2.75
L : H	32	0.44	0.44	0.41
Solar*	3443	1816	1225	902

*Winter solar gains through window in Wh

Lighting Brussels has the least solar radiation on the south facade; leading to the highest annual lighting energy consumption. The three northern countries have similar lighting energy (20% range). In winter, Oslo requires the most lighting with its short days and low irradiation.

Heat Conduction losses dominate in Oslo, which has the lowest outside temperatures. For Brussels, the infiltration losses dominate with high winds (double the Oslo values). For Zürich conduction and infiltration losses are of roughly equal magnitudes, while for Rome, both values are small. High infiltration losses for Belgium are unfortunate as winds are local and independent of latitude. Although the Oslo weather year used in the study was exceptionally warm, winter heating energy is still highest for Oslo. On an annual basis, however, Brussels required more heat because of the spring winds.

Lighting plus heating Annual energy consumption is finally higher for Brussels than Oslo and Zürich because of the high lighting loads and infiltration losses.

Cooling Cooling values are misleading for Oslo because the summer temperatures used are high. The cooling throttling range of 1°C also introduces an uncertainty range.

Effect of local schedules, constructions and climate on lighting, lighting plus heating, and cooling

Lighting This is affected by shorter school schedules in Rome, Oslo and Brussels than in Zürich. The decrease is most marked for Rome (see Table 23.15).

- Lighting and heating are treated in the ratio 1:1. Heating is assumed to be electric or with baseboard heating at the system's level. (For a discussion on aggregate energy see Section 23.3)
- No heating set-back possible during holidays with MBDS

Table 23.15 Annual energy consumption for different climates and local input data for the on/off base case

Energy (MWh/a)	Rome	Zürich	Brussels*	Oslo
Light	0.19	0.72	0.88	0.73
Heat	0.06	1.63	1.59	2.01
Cool	0.71	0.5	0.08	0.37
L + H	0.25	2.35	2.47	2.74

*Program MBDS used

Heating This is increased, due to U-glass and U-wall for Rome, and due to U-glass and shorter winter holidays for Oslo. Finally, for lighting plus heating, the effects cancel out for Oslo, a decrease is observed for Rome (lighting is dominant), and a very approximate decrease for Brussels. The highest energy consumptions are observed for Oslo when both school schedules and construction data are considered.

Cooling This is significantly less than could be expected in Rome, because there are 13 weeks of summer holidays, and less in Oslo, which has eight weeks of holidays, compared to five for Zürich. Brussels has low cooling loads because of the control of blinds assumed and also summer holidays.

Conclusion

Saving lighting energy by using daylight is possible for all climates analyzed in this study. Northern countries use similar quantities of energy for the base case because of compensating occupancy schedules. Lighting plus heating energy is saved in Brussels, Zürich and Rome if daylighting strategies are integrated; however, all four countries can save lighting plus a third of heating energy (L + H/3) for nearly all orientations.

Knowledge of the weather, the local construction and the schedules are important to be able to compare results of different countries.

23.3 DAYLIGHTING, AIR CONDITIONING AND ENERGY COSTS

The applicability of daylighting strategies depends on the resulting cooling loads, which affect either total energy use or comfort. The magnitudes of the cooling loads determine the need for air conditioning.

23.3.1 Cooling system

The cooling load (C) or cooling energy for a module is respectively either the amount of heat to be removed from the module, or the amount of electric energy required by an efficient air conditioning system. DOE-2 simulations for the Swiss classroom and office base cases, assumed an optimized cooling system (VAVS with an enthalpy economizer and chiller during the cooling period of May to October). The total cooling reduction factor (cooling energy/cooling load) is about 0.34 or C/3 for the cooling energy required, giving a total energy of about L + H + C/3.

23.3.2 Energy costs

Assuming that in middle European regions the ratio of electricity costs to oil costs is 3 : 1, then, as an example, the total energy costs with oil heating and air conditioning can be represented by L + H/3 + C/3.

23.3.3 Example: Swiss Office

The office is modeled using the reduction factor for cooling, of 0.68 for a variable air volume system (VAVS) and economizer during the cooling period rather than a year, and of 0.34 for a VAVS, an economizer and a chiller. The ranking order for daylighting strategies changes depending on whether lighting plus heating energy or air conditioning (total energy) is considered.

The cooling loads rise quickly when daylighting strategies such as clerestories are employed, so that electric cooling energy required becomes important, despite efficient cooling systems.

The cooling loads will be lower for Brussels than Zürich because the blinds are closed when the transmitted global radiation exceeds $150 \, W/m^2$, as the diffusion is very important there. For Zürich, the blinds are closed when the direct radiation exceeds that limit. Cooling is anyway lower in Brussels.

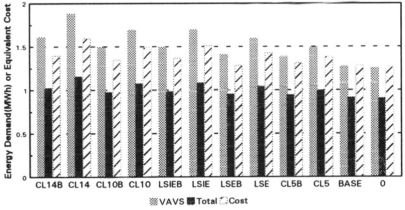

CL14	14% clerestory
CL14B	14% cler. + blind
CL10	10% clerestory
CL10B	10% cler. + blind
LSIEB	ext. + int. light shelf + blind
LSIE	int. + ext. light shelf
LSE	exterior light shelf
LSEB	ext. light shelf + blind
CL5	5% clerestory
CL5B	5% cler. + blind
BASE	base case
O	overhang

Fig. 23.23 Zürich south office: annual energy consumption for lighting plus heating plus cooling, L + H + C/3 (total energy), L + H/3 + C/3 (costs) in ranking order for L + H

For the Zürich climate, the south clerestories with blinds offer the most energy efficient lighting plus heating strategy. If air conditioning with a chiller (total energy) and energy costs are examined, the exterior light shelf with 10% clerestory is slightly better than the clerestory alone. Also, the small clerestory is better than the bigger one. The base or overhang cases remain good solutions for saving energy or costs (Fig. 23.23).

For the west orientation, of the cases studied, the 10% clerestory with blinds (CLIOB) is the best daylighting strategy after the base and overhang cases if total energy and costs are considered. The exterior light shelf offers insufficient window shading in summer, hence cooling loads remains high. A small clerestory with blinds would probably also be a solution.

If air conditioning is required, a simulation of the exact building with proposed cooling system and daylighting strategies is recommended. Note that cooling loads are high in this study due to the blind strategy.

In conclusion, daylighting strategies are still interesting in Zürich, even if air conditioning is used. Strategies to consider are those which limit cooling loads, such as the base case with or without an overhang, or limit cooling and save lighting energy, such as a medium clerestory with an exterior light shelf and blinds for the south orientation or a small clerestory and blinds. The medium clerestory with light shelf saves the most lighting energy. These strategies also save total energy costs.

23.3.4   Example: Belgian office

The more the glazed surface increases, the more the cooling load increases for south and west facades, and the more the heating load increases for the north and east facades in Belgium.

If air conditioning is considered, then a clerestory with or without an interior light shelf or an exterior light shelf with blinds is a recommendable solution. These strategies are also applicable if energy costs are considered (Fig. 23.24).

The total energy for lighting, heating and cooling for four different systems and the four orientations are summarized in Table 23.16 for the proposed daylighting strategies. These are determined according to the interior comfort as well as to the amount of saved total energy or costs. Note that the blinds were closed much earlier in the Belgian study ($G_{H,trans} > 150\,\text{W/m}^2$) giving lower cooling loads. It could mean a slight increase in artificial lighting energy.

Table 23.16   Proposed daylighting strategies and energetic effect for the Belgian office

System type	Proposed daylighting strategies				Global load (kWh/m²)			Load reduction			
	S	N	E	W	Reference		Proposed daylight strategy	Compared to NIX (4 Mod.)		Compared to BASE (4 Mod.)	
					NIX	BASE		(kWh)	(%)	(kWh)	(%)
L + H + C	LSIB + OR	BASE	BASE	LSEB	68.1	37.0	37.6	−4212	−44.7	+81	+1.6
L + H + C/3	LSIB + OR	CLB	CLB	LSEB	56.1	34.9	33.7	−3101	−40.0	−176	−3.6
L + H/3 + C	OR		CLB	CLB	LSEB	61.0	28.0	28.0	−4555	−54.0	+6	+0.2
L + H/3 + C/3	LSIB + OR	CLB	CLB	LSEB	49.0	25.9	23.7	−3496	−51.6	−303	−8.5

NIX	uncontrolled base case
BASE	base case
CLB	10% clerestory with blinds
OR	reflective overhang
LSEB	exterior light shelf + blinds
LSIB + OR	interior light shelf with blinds + reflective overhang

23.4   DAYLIGHTING IN ROOMS ADJACENT TO AN ATRIUM

23.4.1   Artificial sky measurements

Preface

An artificial diffuse sky for conducting model measurements was designed and built at the Fraunhofer Institute of Building Physics in

South Office: Daylighting Strategies

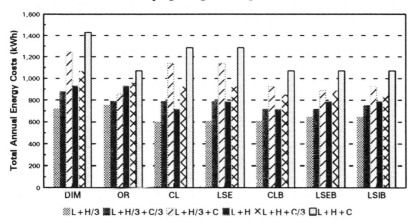

Fig. 23.24 Total annual energy costs (kWh)

Stuttgart, Germany [23/2]. The measurements were planned to answer the question of how the performance of atria influences the amount of daylight available in adjacent rooms.

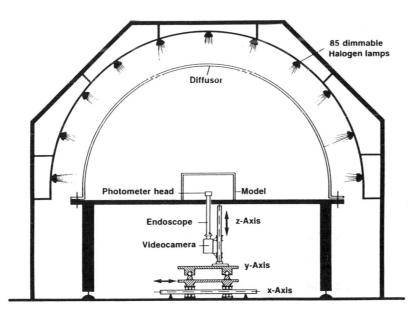

Fig. 23.25 Schematic drawing of the artificial sky. Each halogen lamp is individual dimmable by a PC. Luminance and illuminance measurements within the models are carried out automatically

Artificial sky

The artificial diffuse sky that was set up at the Fraunhofer Institute of Building Physics is represented in Fig. 23.25. Under the table is a robot unit which drives the floor. The photometer head and the endoscope video camera unit are also visible. The artificial sky consists of 85 halogen lamps with diffuse radiation characteristics. Each light source is independently dimmable by a PC, so that different sky luminance distributions can be modeled. The models of rooms or of whole buildings can be placed on a table under the sky. The models may have no floors, as the floor is in a movable connection with the table. On this operable floor, different measuring instruments can be installed. During measurements, the floor is moved inside the model by a computer-controlled robot unit. The robot drives the measurement instrument to defined coordinates inside the room. Thus, it is possible by comparative tests to obtain measured data at the same geometrical position. This is useful for comparing different systems or boundary conditions under the same sky conditions.

Measurement technique

A miniature photometer can be installed on the movable floor to record the illuminance distribution on any plane in the room. In practice, the measurement is carried out for a horizontal plane at the height of a working place. The miniature photometer head is connected to the robot unit which moves it across the room. The measurement data is recorded when the defined geometrical position is reached. It is possible to execute measurements on a very fine grid ($> 1/200\,\mathrm{mm}$). For a plane in a normal room, the whole procedure takes only a few minutes and is carried out completely automatically.

Besides measuring the illuminance distribution with photometer heads, it is possible to record it on the surfaces by means of an endoscope connected to a black and white video camera. The endoscope camera unit is mounted on the robot and movable along three axes. The video signal is analyzed by a video processing image computer system installed on a PC. By means of a calibration function the luminance of the surrounding surfaces can be measured. The total of 256 grey steps of an image can be processed with a false color routine, so that different areas with the same luminance with respect to the endoscope lens have the same color. Areas with a different luminance have different colors.

Parametric study

The sensitivity study performed is aimed at investigating the influence of the performance of atria on daylighting conditions in adjacent office rooms. This linear type of atrium is commonly used; hence it is suitable for investigations on the influence of different atrium parameters on the daylighting performance of office rooms. The measurements were

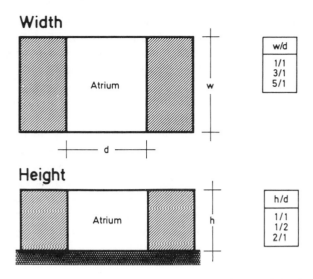

Fig. 23.26 Parameter variations of atrium height, width and depth

performed in the artificial sky under CIE standard overcast conditions.

In the present sensitivity study the ratio of atrium height (h) to width (w) is varied. In addition, the distance (d) between the two linear office buildings is also varied. These variations can be seen in Fig. 23.26.

Another parameter under investigation is the glazing type of the atrium roof and the office room windows. Here, normal double glazing (double) and IR coated/gas-filled glazing (low-emissivity) are considered variations. Moreover, the reflectances of the floor and the walls inside the atrium are modified. The different variations are compiled in Table 23.17.

Table 23.17 Parameter variations of atrium glazing types and reflectives

Glazing type	
Office	Atria
IR-coated/gas-filled	Double
IR-coated/gas-filled	IR-coated/gas-filled
Double	IR-coated/gas-filled

Reflectance (%)		
Surface	Atria	Office room
Floor	20–70	15
Walls	20–70	50
Ceiling	—	70

The adjacent room connected to the atrium is a common office with a window/facade ratio of 60%. The dimensions of the room are

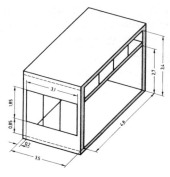

Fig. 23.27 Geometry of the measured office connected to the atrium

presented in Fig. 23.27. The geometry of the adjacent office is fixed for the sensitivity study. The reflectances of all surfaces inside the room are fixed (15% floor; 50% walls; 70% ceiling). For each variation, the illuminance distribution was measured on the working plane at 0.85 cm above the floor.

Results

The daylight factor distribution on a horizontal plane inside an office connected to an atrium is derived from these measurements. For ease in handling, the data was compiled to give mean daylight factors to describe the result for one single set of variations for a room. All values are condensed into a nomogram (Fig. 23.28). Even this nomogram was derived from a limited number of measurements. From the nomogram it is possible to read the mean daylight factor of a room connected to an atrium for a wide range of variations.

Nomogram

An example of how to use the nomogram follows.

The mean daylight factor of an office connected to an atrium can be read from the nomogram for the following boundary conditions.

- Office at center level of atrium
- Atrium depth   15 m
- Atrium width   50 m
- Atrium height   12 m
- Reflectivity of opaque atrium wall   0.50
- Reflectivity of atrium floor   0.50
- Glazing type:
    office–atrium   double
    atrium–outside   low-ε
Resulting mean daylight factor   2.30%

Summary

A nomogram derived from artificial sky measurement data was developed to predict the mean daylight factor in office rooms connected to a linear atrium. This nomogram can easily be used by architects and designers to obtain information about the influence of different design parameters on the usable daylight in office rooms which are daylit through an atrium.

23.5 CONCLUSIONS

23.5.1 Introduction

It is important to address daylighting at the beginning of a project as it deals with the basic structure of the building. Sections 23.2 and

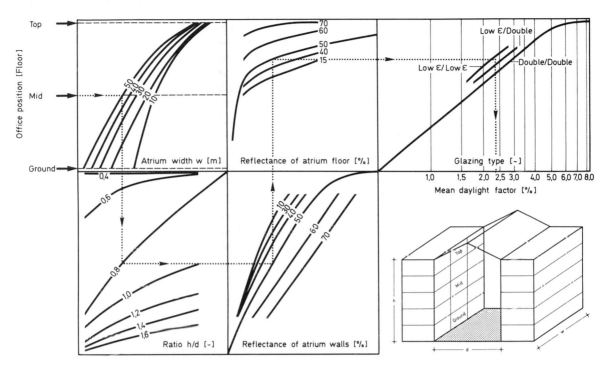

Fig. 23.28 Nomogram for deriving mean daylight factors of rooms connected to atria. The graph has been constructed from a set of measurements carried out for a wide range of variations in the artificial sky at the Fraunhofer Institute of Building Physics

23.3 provide information on which daylighting strategies influence daylighting inside, how these strategies, and the resulting artificial lighting, are coupled to the heating and cooling, and how they affect the total energy consumptions. Interesting daylighting strategies can then be investigated by simulating the building to be built, with its own restrictions and boundary conditions (such as the heating and cooling systems envisaged). Computer programs now available are described in Sections 24.1 and 24.2. The final decisions about daylighting should be made by an expert.

The parametric study addresses energy savings. An important criterion concerning possible savings with daylighting strategies is the type of energy to be economized: electric lighting, lighting plus heating or a combination of lighting, heating and cooling. Simulations of the classrooms facing south were conducted for all climates. All classroom orientations in Zürich and all office orientations in Zürich and Brussels were examined.

Added to energy considerations, visual comfort and glare are important in reality, but these were not studied separately. Although glare was not studied, it would not often occur in the simulated situations as ventian blinds were lowered when the radiation transmitted through the windows was above a certain level, removing glare at the same time. In reality, blinds were assumed to be adjustable lamellae, which can be adjusted to remove glare. However, in the DOE-2 thermal simulations, the lamellae had to be assumed fixed, as DOE-2 can not simulate adjustable lamellae. Glare could be important for clerestories without blinds with direct sunlight falling on a blackboard or a PC screen. This is partly avoided with a light shelf, as the sunlight is reflected to the ceiling.

23.5.2   Automatic lighting control systems

Automatic lighting control systems (whether on/off, stepped or continuous dimming) obviously nearly always save energy for both lighting and lighting plus heating, compared to the uncontrolled case (lights on during occupancy, and no blinds). The major part of the savings that can be achieved comes from introducing automatic lighting control. Daylighting strategies produce only small additional savings.

Lighting energy
For lighting, 50–85% of the consumed energy can be saved for shallow classrooms, depending on climate and orientation. Maximum savings occur for the unshaded south.

For the south, possible savings are greatest for Rome, then Zürich then Oslo and Brussels climates which are of the same order of magnitude. Less savings are possible for deeper offices. Maximum savings (for the south) of 50% and 60% are possible for Brussels and Zürich, and decrease (by approximately 20%) if the office with continuous dimming is shaded.

For both classrooms and offices, a continuous dimming system is more advantageous for Oslo, Zürich and Brussels. Only Rome requires on/off light control because daylight is readily available.

Lighting plus heating energy
For lighting plus heating energy in classrooms facing south, energy savings remain high for Rome as lighting energy dominates, but decrease to 30% of the consumed energy for Zürich and lower for Brussels and Oslo. Heating from the lights is replaced by normal heating. The percentage savings possible for offices are 20–55%, with a maximum for the south office in Zürich. Energy savings do not decrease as much for the office when heating is included in the energy balance because the heating demands are low and partly provided by the computer. Much of the heat from the lights caused overheating.

When heating is included in the analysis, the type of optimum lighting control system changes, as the extra lighting energy with on/off control contributes to the heating. For all classrooms, except for Rome, on/off or continuous dimming (with 16% base load) yield similar savings. The deciding factors are then purely comfort (due to sudden or overly frequent changes in illuminance levels) or installation and amortization costs. For Rome the on/off system is clearly better.

On the other hand, for the offices in Zürich and Brussels, continuous dimming is better by a large margin, with the extra lighting energy from the on/off system now causing overheating. Considering that the simulated continuous dimming lighting control system is conservative with its 16% base load which can not be cut off, then it is clear that for all offices in similar climatic regions, continuous dimming should be seriously considered.

Finally, if 'manual switching' were used as the uncontrolled case, the savings would be lower, but still significant, as measurements show that occupants often do not switch off lights when the daylighting exceeds the design level (Section 22.4, Technologiezentrum, ACS).

Cooling energy

Savings are high (approximately 70–88%) for the three northern climates when automatic lighting control and blinds are introduced, but are smaller for Rome (about 45%). This is partly because the Roman school schedules exclude hot summer months. For the northern climates, half the savings are from the automatic lighting control and the other half are from blinds (except modules facing north), if the module is not shaded by a building. Lower savings result for the shaded office as lights are on more often.

23.5.3   Daylighting strategies

(See Tables 23.18 and 23.19.) As possible energy economies obtained by introducing daylighting strategies (e.g. clerestories, sawteeth) vary with the kind of energy considered, conclusions are presented separately for each. The results obtained for lighting plus heating are very different from those obtained for lighting alone. It is therefore important to know whether combined energy consumption or just lighting will be considered.

As mentioned before, savings from daylighting strategies may appear small as strategies are added to the base case which already has an automatic lighting control system. It is difficult to establish a valid reference case, as occupancy behavior varies tremendously. Final savings are the sum of energy saved from the automatic lighting control system and daylighting strategies. These savings would be maximum values as the uncontrolled case is the worst situation.

For the base case with or without daylighting strategies, blinds are always available for the window. The 10% clerestory (simulated for all climates) increases the glazing area from 15 to 25% of the floor area. The large sawtooth glazing is larger than the 10% clerestory, and

Table 23.18 Classroom: possible proposed daylighting strategies based on lighting plus heating energy savings and visual comfort

	Rome	Zürich	Brussels	Oslo
South	med. cler. + overhang + blind med. cler. + ext. light sh. + blind small cler. + blind	small or med. cler. (+ blind) med. cler. + ext. light sh. (+ blind)	med. cler. + int. light sh. + refl. overhang	on/off or skylight
North		S-facing sawtooth + overhang		
West		skylight/base case		
East		skylight/base case		
Shaded south		med. cler. + ext. light sh. (+ blind) small clerestory med. cler. + blind		

Table 23.19 Office: possible proposed daylighting strategies based on lighting plus heating energy savings and visual comfort

	Rome	Zürich	Brussels	Oslo
South		small or med. cler. + blind med. cler. + ext. light sh. + blind	med. cler. + int. light sh. + blind + refl. overhang	
North		base case	cler. + blind	
West		med. clerestory (+ blind), base case	med. cler. + ext. light sh. + blind	
East		base case	cler. + blind (base case)	
Shaded south		med. cler. + ext. light sh. + blind med. cler. + blind	med. cler. + ext. light sh. + blind	

facing the opposite direction. The diffuse skylight, simulated for all climates, is off-centered and covers only 2% of the floor area. The total light shelf depth (whether exterior, interior or half in and out) remains constant. The following results apply to possible savings with respect to the base case (room with 15% glazing of the floor area).

Lighting
Saving electric lighting energy is possible for all orientations and all four climatic regions by introducing a daylighting strategy, other than an overhang, compared to the base case with a side window.

Classroom   Maximum savings vary from about 25 to 30% for mid- and northern European climates to about 60% for Rome. For the three northern countries, rooflights (large sawtooth and the skylight with 2% glazing) are optimal, followed by clerestories, with and without light shelves. With rooflights, daylight from another orientation or the zenith is allowed in reducing lighting requirements. This is the best solution for climates without much sun. For Rome, little lighting is required anyway, and extra daylight from any direction is good.

One should note that medium clerestories or interior and exterior light shelves for the embedded classroom in Zürich or for the exposed classroom in Rome probably cause overheating, and therefore need clerestory blinds and perhaps an overhang or an exterior light shelf (with or without clerestory blinds).

If the classroom is shaded by a neighboring building in Zürich, lighting energy increases by almost one quarter for the base and clerestory case. For Rome, the electric consumption more than doubles.

Office   Clerestories alone followed by clerestories with light shelves are best for all orientations, for Zürich and Brussels (except the Brussels shaded office). Savings of about 25% of the consumed energy were possible for Zürich and a little less (20%) for Brussels. Zürich also has the problem of overheating.

Shading the base case office by a neighboring building increases the lighting energy required by about 45% for Zürich and 40% for Brussels.

Potential absolute lighting energy savings with increased glazing area are greater for the shaded classroom or office than for the unshaded case.

Lighting plus heating

Generally, classrooms have no air conditioning, hence lighting plus heating is a crucial energy determinant.

Classroom   Daylighting strategies are ineffective for Oslo as too much extra heating is required when they are introduced. This is due partially to the glazing used which is representative of current standards.

Brussels and Zürich climates enjoy energy savings of up to 15% of the base case for the south classroom with medium clerestory, and Rome can save about 40% with an appropriate strategy, i.e. an exterior light shelf. Savings of up to $6 \text{kWh/m}^2 \text{a}$ are possible with side daylighting strategies (large glazing area) for the south classroom in Zürich, which is large when compared to measured energy consumptions of $34–50 \text{kWh/m}^2 \text{a}$ for two existing daylit schools in Switzerland.

The ranking orders for the daylighting strategies for Zürich and Brussels are similar even when computations are made with two different programs. For the south classrooms, rooflights considered are no longer optimal, as was the case for lighting alone. Clerestories, followed by light shelves, now offer the greatest benefit. As mentioned earlier, overheating can be a problem, especially for the embedded and shaded case in Zürich where the savings are actually small. If one considers a classroom facing south in Zürich, then a small or medium clerestory with blinds or an exterior light shelf with a medium clerestory (with or without clerestory blind) is recommended because lighting plus heating energy is saved without overheating. If an overhang is placed above the clerestory rather than introducing an exterior light shelf, then nearly all the benefits of the clerestory are lost.

For Brussels, clerestories give the highest energy savings, but similar savings are possible with an exterior light shelf which avoids overheating. The latter is, however, not so critical. An interior light shelf with overhang is recommended to avoid direct radiation in the classroom in summer.

For Rome, clerestories (large or medium) facing south provide large energy savings, but also cause overheating. Consequently, an exterior light shelf could be added, or a small (less than or equal to 5%) clerestory with blind could be used to eliminate solar radiation. Another solution, acceptable for Rome, is to place an overhang above the clerestories.

Results for other orientations only exist for Zürich. Daylighting strategies offer no significant savings for west and east orientations. Sawteeth facing south remain the best solution for classrooms facing north and give the best savings of the cases studied in Zürich.

Because solar gains are utilized in the classroom facing south, savings are double those for the office for Zürich. This is not the case for Brussels, where equal savings, per unit area, for the classroom and office were calculated because of limited solar gains available and poorer insulated construction.

Overhangs are less effective than expected because blinds and overhangs interact, as they do in reality, when no exterior automatic control for blinds is employed.

Office Simulations exist for Brussels and Zürich and were conducted with different thermal programs.

Reasonable savings with daylighting strategies are only possible for the south orientation for Zürich because of cold winters. All clerestories facing north, west and east lose too much heat, but this may improve with glazings with higher insulation values. For Brussels, which has milder winters, savings above 5% still exist, for orientations which are not south, although the savings drop for the orientations other than south to a half or less of the ones for the south orientation. However, for both classroom and office, the exterior lightshelf has the advantage that it reduces overheating, without blinds being closed, allowing visual contact with the outside and equalizing illuminance levels in the room. Generally, for the south orientation, medium clerestories, with or without blinds, offer good solutions to save energy, followed by light shelves added to clerestories. Maximum savings of 17% for Zürich and 19% for Brussels are realized.

Larger clerestories do save more energy but may introduce unacceptable cooling loads. In Zürich, smaller clerestories are equivalent to exterior light shelves with medium clerestories.

Classroom and office Shading by a neighboring building generally increases the energy consumption for the base cases. Simulations show the difficulty of saving lighting plus heating energy in the shaded classroom with only one exterior surface and a long heating season in Zürich (sole simulation). The potential for saving lighting plus heating energy exists for deep shaded offices in Brussels and Zürich where the heating seasons are shorter. When shaded by a building, an exterior light shelf loses its effect on the lighting plus heating energy balance.

Lighting plus a third of heating
Percentage energy savings of lighting plus a third of heating, which represents costs for many countries, are possible in many more cases than savings of lighting plus heating.

Classroom Strategies that save large amounts of lighting energy are attractive, such as the skylight with 2% glazing or the large sawtooth facing north in Rome, which are ineffective for lighting plus heating savings. Reasonable savings (approximately 9%) are now also possible for classrooms facing east and west, while high savings are possible for classrooms facing north in Zürich with rooflights.

Office For both Brussels and Zürich, savings are possible for all orientations, which is not the case for the lighting plus heating balance of Zürich. For a medium clerestory facing west, savings of 5 and 16% relative to the respective base cases are achieved for Brussels and Zürich, respectively.

Cooling
Overheating is an important problem. It is clear that introducing daylighting strategies may increase the cooling requirements with respect to the base cases; however, if large glazing areas are avoided, cooling loads stay below those of the uncontrolled case.

If cooling loads are high, different daylighting strategies may be recommendable. Overheating in classrooms, where air conditioning is inapplicable, must be overcome with an appropriate choice of daylighting strategy, such as: an exterior light shelf added to a medium clerestory with or without blinds, a small clerestory only, including an overhang above the medium clerestory (which can lose nearly all benefits acquired with the clerestory, depending on the climate), introducing an overhang with an interior light shelf (not so efficient), using a small diffuse skylight to introduce the extra daylighting (but avoiding overheating) and having blinds.

Passive cooling methods are also a potential solution to overheating, such as: extra window openings (which could not be simulated), closing blinds as soon as direct radiation enters a room (which could also require more artificial lighting), appropriate school holidays (as in Italy) or other passive cooling systems. The final choice will depend on many factors, such as the climate, possible shading by neighboring buildings or trees, the building's architecture etc.

If a building is an office, air conditioning can be included. This leads to the last part of the simulation analysis (Section 23.3).

Daylighting, air conditioning and energy costs
If air conditioning is introduced, then different daylighting strategies may be advantageous as the cooling loads are removed mechanically. The higher the cooling load, the more critical the applicability of daylighting strategies. For Brussels, which has low cooling loads, nearly the same daylighting strategies are recommended with or without mechanical cooling; whereas in Zürich, which has much higher cooling loads, proposed daylighting strategies differ. In Zürich, the exterior light shelf with medium clerestory and blinds or the small clerestory with blinds remain energy efficient compared to the base cases for the south orientation. Of course, the psychological advantages of the light shelf compared to the base case must be considered. The cost analysis with air conditioning shows that the daylighting strategies mentioned above are now economical.

If the introduction of daylighting strategies requires the addition of air conditioning, then fan energy required for the cooling system must also be included in the total energy consumption balance. If air conditioning is already planned, then the fan energy may increase only slightly if daylighting strategies are introduced. Lastly, it is clear that a good air conditioning system is required.

23.5.4   Nomogram

A nomogram can be used to determine daylight factors in an office of fixed dimensions and adjacent to a linear atrium and to study the effect of various design parameters. The office can be at various levels and the dimensions and glazing of the atrium varied.
Appendix

23.6   APPENDIX

The following assumptions, input data and remarks are supplemental to Section 23.1.

23.6.1 Assumptions

(a) SUPERLITE is unable to simulate movable blinds. This introduces the following assumptions: when the blinds are simulated as closed in DOE-2 due to high direct transmitted radiation ($> 150\,W/m^2$), the occupants regulate the blind lamellae to avoid switching on the lights. The values from SUPERLITE can then be used directly. This means that no increase in lighting energy is allowed due to the blinds closing. (Previous simulations with DOE-2 and external blinds show that this is acceptable.)

(b) The light reflected from light shelves is assumed to be diffuse by SUPERLITE. If in reality semi-specular reflection occurs, the lighting energy for the rear zone of the office might be less than calculated.

(c) Cooling loads vary between Belgium and Switzerland because of the different blind controls (see Section 23.1.3). They can also vary due to the throttling range of $1°C$ and the magnitude of the maximum cooling rate.

(d) All heat from the lights goes into the room using appropriate weighting factors.

23.6.2 Input

- All construction data and occupancy schedules are country and module dependent (see Tables 23.21 and 23.22).
- The external blinds are simulated by schedules with a value of 0.2 for the shading coefficient and a reduction factor of 0.85 for the thermal coefficient.
- The visible transmission for the blinds is scheduled at 1.0 (see Section 23.6.1).
- The minimum power of the continuous dimming lighting control system is 16% of the maximum power. The illuminance sensors are placed at two reference points situated at 1/2 and 5/6 room depths centered on the window.
- The workplane is at table height (0.75 m).
- The air-infiltration was based on the recommended air exchange rate of $30\,m^3/h$ per person.
- Sidelighting and rooflighting strategies are considered for the classroom and sidelighting strategies for the office.

23.6.3 Remarks concerning the output data

The main information concerning output data is treated in Section 23.1. In addition to this information, the cooling load will be relatively high as it refers to the entire year, rather than the cooling season, and the set point is low (26°C). The system would also not necessarily be

Table 23.20 Climatic statistics for Zürich, Oslo, Brussels and Rome

	Rome	Zürich	Brussels	Oslo
Yearly values:				
Average temperature (°C)	15.3	8.7	10.1	5.6
No. of days below zero	17	96	41	156
Ave. wind speed (m/s)	1.7	2.3	3.8	1.6
Ave. daily total hort. (kWh/m² day)	4.5	3.0	2.6	2.8
Ave. daily dir. normal (kWh/m² day)	4.7	2.4	1.8	2.9
Ave. daily total vert. S (kWh/m² day)	3.6	2.7	2.4	2.8
Winter values: (Nov./Dec./Jan./Feb.)				
Ave. winter temperature (°C)	9.1	0.5	4.0	−4.3
Ave. daily dir. normal (kWh/m² day)	2.5	1.0	0.7	0.6
Ave. daily tot. vert. S (kWh/m² day)	3.2	1.8	1.3	0.9
Hours of daylight/day (h/day)	9.6	9.1	8.7	7.1
General data:				
Max. solar altitude in DOE-2 (°)	72	66	63	54
Latitude (°N)	41.5	47.3	50.5	59.6

Table 23.21 Input differences between the two modules

Input	Classroom	Office
External surfaces	2	1
Infiltration rate* (ac/h)	2.89	0.87
Person gains† (W)	1600	360
Equip. gains† (W/m²)	none	5.2
Module depth: width	0.75	1.5
Schedule	school	office
Occupants	20	3
Lighting type	fluorescent (3 rows + board)	HID lamps
Light. power (W/m²)	17.45	15.1
Ill. design level (lux)	350	500

*30 m³/h per child/occupant
†Scheduled

sized to handle all peak cooling demands. Finally, the blind trigger value ($I_{trans,dir} > 150\,W/m^2$) is high, allowing a large admittance of summer solar gains. If cooling is too high then air conditioning will have to be integrated and the cooling energy will intervene in the total energy.

Table 23.22 Input differences between the countries

Input		Classroom				Office	
		Rome	Zürich	Brussels	Oslo	Zürich	Brussels
Attendance (h/day)		6	8	8	6	8	9
Lights (h/day)		6	9	9	7	9	10
U_{wall}	(W/m² K)	0.36	0.28	0.40	0.29	0.28	0.40
U_{roof}	(W/m² K)	0.47	0.19	0.26	0.17		
U_{glaz}	(W/m² K)	2.72	1.6	1.6	2.0	1.6	1.6
g } glazing		0.76	0.67	0.67	0.65	0.67	0.67
τ_{vis} }		0.82	0.78	0.78	0.77	0.78	0.78
Lighting system		o/f	con	con	o/f	con	con
Holidays: summer	(weeks)	13	5	9	8		
Holidays: winter	(weeks)	5	8	6	4.5		

con: continuous dimming
o/f: on/off
g: solar radiation transfer coefficient (transmission, absorption and emission)
τ_{vis}: visible transmission
U (W/m² K): coefficient of thermal transfer

U and g apply to the view glazing and the clerestory glazing for all cases

23.7 REFERENCES

23/1 Hopkirk, N., EMPA, Uberlandstrasse 129, CH-8600 Dübendorf, 1988.
23/2 Szerman, M., *Scale Modelling of Adjacent Rooms to Atria: Artificial Sky Measurements and Recommendation, Curves*, Fraunhofer Institut of Building Physics, Noblestr. 12, D-7000 Stuttgart 80, 1989.

24 Analysis Tools

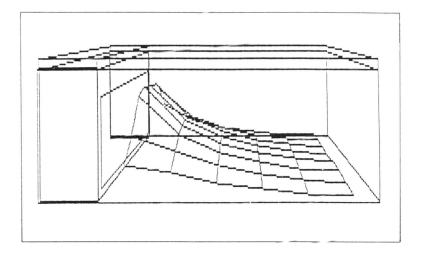

Chapter 24 is divided into three sections.

Section 24.1, Tools Used in Task XI, describes computer programs (three purely daylighting computer programs and three linked energy analysis programs). Two of the energy programs (DOE-2 and tsbi3) have their own simple daylighting routines. A comparison of DOE-2 and MBDS and the Daylight Performance Evaluation Methodology (DPEM) are also included.

Section 24.2, Links, provides information about the linking programs (DAYLINK and SUPERLINK) developed in Task XI. They link SUPERLITE (a daylighting program) to an energy analysis program. This allows the interaction between daylighting and the thermal behavior of a building to be studied.

Section 24.3, Experience in Using Daylighting Tools, compares computed results with measurements for SUPERLITE, DOE-2.1C and Daylite 2.2

24.1   TOOLS USED IN TASK XI

24.1.1   Description of tools

Six analytical tools were used by researchers in the IEA Task XI [24/1]:

Daylighting programs	*Linked energy analysis programs*
SUPERLITE	DOE-2.1C
Daylite 2.2	tsbi3
Daylit	MBDS

Tables 24.1 and 24.2 summarize the input and output possibilities of these programs. Further information concerning SUPERLITE, Daylite 2.2 and DOE-2 is available in Section 24.3.

Windows & Daylighting Group
Building 90-3111
Lawrence Berkeley Laboratory
University of California
Berkeley, CA 94720, USA

SUPERLITE

SUPERLITE is an accurate, well-validated [24/2, 24/3], complex public-domain research program. It calculates daylighting levels for detailed room geometries, seven standard daylighting strategies, shading from external and internal obstructions but no energy consumptions (Table 24.2). In the newest version, light levels can be determined due to a combination of daylighting systems and electric lighting systems. Obviously, a room having only daylighting systems or electric lighting systems can be modeled. SUPERLITE requires a mainframe or PC computer and has an unfriendly input. The latter has been simplified by the development of a menu input, with a graphical check. Its run time is about 1/2 minute for a one hour calculation of a complex room on the mainframe. As output, one has daylight factors, hourly illuminances on work surfaces and/or luminances of indoor or outdoor surfaces. However, it treats only a uniform sky, a standard CIE overcast sky or a clear sky with or without sun and not real weather data. The input weather data is the sky model plus irradiance data and luminous efficiencies, or geographic data, date and time, or sun position and atmospheric data. A diffuse reflectance is assumed for every interior surface.

The main philosophy is to be accurate, not impose too many limits and allow the grid dimension to be specified by the user. The calculation method is the flux transfer method including the Monte Carlo method for the direct illumination on external surfaces and numerical integration for direct illumination on indoor surfaces and work planes.

Its advantages are its flexibility and user-friendliness when combined with the program package, ADELINE. The obvious disadvantages are its lack of energy calculations, limitation to standard skies and inability to simulate movable blinds. ADELINE overcomes some of these constraints.

Daylite 2.2

Daylite 2.2, a privately owned program, is aimed at design work. It includes a menu-drive input with extensive input and output graphics. One rectangular room with no external shading can be simulated for one or all hours of one design day per month (21st). One obtains either isolux plots for a standard CIE sky for one specified hour or illuminances at one reference point for the design day. From these results the lighting energies for the month then for the whole year are extrapolated. Nine standard daylighting strategies plus complex skylights, glare, comfort index and contrast ratios can be simulated. Limited European weather data is available within the IEA or from Solarsoft (USA).

Mrs C. Ashton
Solarsoft
1406 Burlingame Ave., Suite 31
Burlingame, CA 94010, USA

The main philosophy is the interactive process to enable checking and the calculation of electrical lighting. The accurate flux transfer method is also used accounting for direct sunlight, externally and internally reflected light. The main advantages are the large variety of strategies and combinations of strategies one can study, the graphic outputs and the electric lighting energy. The disadvantages are the rectangular room, no simulation of blinds, no external shading and the non-availability of the coding.

A user guide, in addition to the standard manual, is also available.

Daylit

Daylit is a fast, design tool with a friendly interface, but with English units, aimed at architects and to be used at the start of a project. It is not clear whether the program has been validated or not. On a PC, it requires 30 s for a yearly calculation. It can treat a rectangular room, venctian diffusing blinds with impinging direct sunlight in an elementary way, translucent shades and four daylighting strategies. Based on average monthly weather data, it can calculate illuminance levels at three fixed reference points along the central line of the room. Outputs exist (in table and plot form for a quick overview) for various hourly and yearly configurations, for total and lighting annual energy consumptions. The latitude, number of clear and overcast days per month, average, maximum and minimum outdoor temperature and the lowest and highest indoor comfort temperatures are required as input.

Mr M. Milne
Graduate School of Architecture
& Urban Planning UCLA
405 Hilgard Avenue
Los Angeles, CA 90024, USA

This easy-to-use program is based on the LOF Manual Illumination Calculation Method. The Coefficient of Utilization Factor, based on the room geometry and surface reflectances, is multiplied by the available sky and reflecting ground daylighting. Illuminances for a mean sky, an overcast sky, and a clear sky with and without sun are calculated. Added to the normal daylighting strategies, there exists the possibility of having a scheduled design illuminance level. The main advantages are the output plots, simulated blinds and cost analysis.

The disadvantages are that only three fixed points can be studied, that the window size is fixed by the room and working plane heights and that the window can not be perpendicular to another window.

DOE-2.1D

Mr F. Winkelmann
Building Energy Simulation Group
Building 90-3147
Lawrence Berkeley Laboratory
University of California
Berkeley, CA 94720, USA

DOE-2.1D is an energy analysis program which is well validated. It was developed for energy conservation in buildings. The added daylighting part calculates hourly interior illuminance levels for up to two light zones, the resulting electric lighting consumption and total energy consumptions (electrical, heating and cooling). Monthly and yearly total energy consumptions are obtained. Six daylight strategies can be simulated as well as shading from external obstructions. Both the input and program are fairly large. A huge variety of outputs, both hourly and global, cover detailed daylighting results (e.g. interior or window illuminances, daylight factors) as well as radiation data, statistics and of course global energy consumptions. All the calculations are for real weather data, which has to be input as a standard hourly TRY tape.

The program is split into four parts: loads, systems, plants and economics with a fixed interior temperature in 'loads' which is then allowed to vary in 'systems'.

Micro DOE-2.1C
Gene Tsai
Acrosoft International Inc.,
3120 South Wadsworth Bld.,
Suite No. 1,
Denver
Colorado 80227, USA

The daylighting is calculated using the daylight factor method for 20 sun positions for a clear sky with and without sun and one overcast sky position. Intermediate values are interpolated. The program's advantages are mainly its versatility (e.g. glare, heat recovery), its complete energy analysis and detailed reports. It can also be linked to SUPERLITE. The main disadvantages, as a daylighting program, are the limited number of daylighting strategies it can simulate and the overestimated illuminances at the rear of the room.

tsbi3

Jorgen Erik Christensen
Keld Johnsen
Danish Building Research Inst.,
Postbox 119,
DK-2970 Horsholm, Denmark

This program has been developed by the Danish Building Research Institute for research and for commercial use by consulting engineers. tsbi can be used for analyzing indoor climate, energy consumption, daylighting, passive solar energy, automatic control functions, etc.

It is user-friendly and operated by a combined window/menu system interface using keyboard and mouse. The simulation of the loads and the systems is done simultaneously. The program is complex and has many facilities, including being linked to SUPERLITE via SUPERLINK/DAYLINK. tsbi3 calculates hourly interior illuminance levels and energy consumption in order to evaluate the variations of lighting quality and electricity demand over the year. The daylight level is calculated for up to four reference points. Different artificial lighting systems are available if the design illumination level is not covered by daylighting.

The daylighting is calculated using the sunlight factor method and is very roughly as follows. The sunlight factor is calculated for four different types of illuminance distribution for the window: sky illuminance, reflected illuminance, direct sun and solar devices. The sunlight factor describes the luminance for a reference point in the room according to how much natural daylight strikes the window. This means that the natural daylight can vary with different window orientations, skies and direct sun.

The output from the program provides indoor temperature and humidity, energy balances, heating and cooling demands, internal loads, solar radiation, infiltration, venting by windows, ventilation, heat loss by transmission, illuminance at the reference points, glare, fractional output of lights, electric lighting etc. all on hourly, daily, weekly, monthly or yearly basis.

MBDS

The MBDS computer program was developed by the University of Liège (ULg). It was constituted from the 'TYPE 46' of the program TRNSYS, and was designed for providing full information on the dynamic behavior of a multi-zone building under the effect of cooling and heating loads, solar radiation and infrared losses, outdoor temperature changes and free gains such as occupancy and lighting. The available daylighting, leading to hourly lighting loads, can not be accounted for directly. To study its effect, MBDSA, a modified version of MBDS, can be linked to SUPERLITE via a modified version of DAYLINK.

Lisianne Cotton,
Université de Liège
Lab. de Thermodynamique,
Rue Ernest Solvay 21,
B-4000 Liège, Belgium

MBDS's possible outputs per zone contain detailed hourly information as to what is happening physically (e.g. net heat and cooling demands, surface temperatures, the gains through convection with adjacent zones, the absorbed radiation by each wall). If any heating or cooling power is insufficient for the satisfaction of a prescribed set-point temperature, the program switches automatically to free floating temperature calculation in the concerned zone.

The meteorological hourly data used in the MBDS program is a typical mean year. Irradiation data and the sunshine period integrated over the day to calculate infrared losses are available.

Comparison between MBDS and DOE-2

MBDS was used as energy program by Belgium instead of DOE-2. The main differences between DOE-2 and MBDS are:

- The shadowing effects by neighboring buildings have to be calculated by hand in MBDS, whereas they are automatic in DOE-2.
- No 'holiday set-back' for heating (as in DOE-2) can be included in the program MBDS, so that the assumption taken for the holidays is that the heating is shut off.
- Different calculation methods exist for the solar direct transmission coefficients.

Daylight Performance Evaluation Methodology (DPEM)

The methodology employs both simulation and measurement. Data recorded over a limited time period is extrapolated to predict the annual effectiveness of the daylight system.

Through simulation, a model is developed to represent the energy performance of the daylighting system. Short-term measurements identify the degree and character of discrepancies in the simulation model. After adjustment for such discrepancies, the calibrated model can be used to predict the annual performance of the daylighting system.

24.2   LINKS

24.2.1   DAYLINK

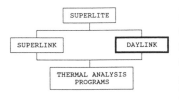

Advantages
Complex variable interactions may be studied.

Disadvantages
The program is a linkage of programs, which may need to be adapted to the computers being used.

Nicole Hopkirk
EMPA
CH-8600 Dübendorf
Tel: +41 1 832 4791

DAYLINK links a daylight simulation program (SUPERLITE) with a building thermal system and energy simulation program (at the moment, DOE-2 or MBDS). Although any moment in time can be calculated, an entire year is of greatest interest. The DAYLINK outputs are the files necessary to run the energy simulation (e.g. DOE-2). DAYLINK can also be used alone to calculate the daily electrical energy required by different lighting systems (e.g. dimming or stepped) and the illumination on the 3rd and 18th of each month at a given reference point. If a building simulation program is used the final output is that of the energy simulation. The original Lawrence Berkeley Laboratory version runs for one reference point, and each of the three steps involved (i.e. running SUPERLITE, DAYLINK and DOE-2) must be individually initiated. A modified version for two reference points and requiring a batch job exists at EMPA, CH.

The philosophy of the program is to model daylighting accurately, using a good daylighting model, and then use that output as input to a good energy model available. Daylighting information is transferred as a matrix of daylight factors for a grid of sun positions and sky conditions, which is then interpreted into lighting power reduction factors based on circuit groups, lighting demand schedules and the same real weather data as used for the thermal analysis. The reduction factor file is then passed on to the energy simulation program. A complete yearly simulation of a room takes approximately an hour and a half of VAX 11/780 time.

24.2.2   SUPERLINK

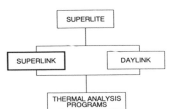

SUPERLINK [24/4] has been developed at the Fraunhofer Institute of Building Physics to obtain realistic estimates of the interactions between daylight, artificial lighting and the dynamic thermal building performance.

The link program SUPERLINK also couples two detailed, validated calculation programs. The program SUPERLITE 1.0 is currently used as preprocessor for the daylighting calculation. The dynamic thermal simulation of the building can be carried out by any thermal simulation program which allows variable hourly internal gains, due to lighting, to be incorporated into the thermal balance.

The link program SUPERLINK is a menu-driven program system which manages all calculation processes by itself.

Michael Szerman
Fraunhofer Institute of
Building Physics
Dept. of Heat/Climate
Tel: +49 711 9703 380

The work surface illuminance is calculated for standard sky conditions (overcast sky, clear sky with sun, clear sky without sun) for 24 hours on the 15th day of each month for the defined room and building site. With these values the program calculates the energy needed for artificial lighting to provide the desired illuminance level on the work surface under the specified conditions. These results of hourly internal lighting loads under defined sky conditions for one day per month are coupled by means of an overlay function which considers the actual sunshine probability at the considered weather station for each hour of the whole year. As a result, hourly internal heat gains due to lighting are produced over the whole year and can be used by any dynamic thermal building simulation program.

SUPERLINK can calculate up to 25 reference points in a room. On/off or different dimming strategies of the lighting system can be investigated in both links.

24.2.3 Comparison of lighting energy using SUPERLINK and DAYLINK

The two link programs, SUPERLINK and DAYLINK, were used to calculate the lighting energy required for the classroom base case. It has two reference points to control the artificial lighting, with a minimum lighting base power of 16% of the maximum power. Zürich weather data were used.

A good agreement exists for the monthly saved lighting energy computed by SUPERLINK and DAYLINK (Fig. 24.1). The main discrepancies occur in the four winter months where DAYLINK predicts more savings than SUPERLINK. Figure 24.2 illustrates that the yearly lighting energy consumptions can differ by 5% when comparing the SUPERLINK and DAYLINK calculations, if a 16% base load is given. Considering that the methodologies are completely different, this is a reassuring result.

Conclusion
Despite very different approaches to the linking procedures, quite similar results are obtained for the continuous dimming lighting control. The discrepancies occur mainly in winter.

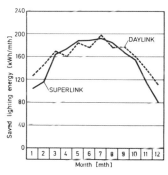

Fig. 24.1 SUPERLINK–DAYLINK monthly comparison

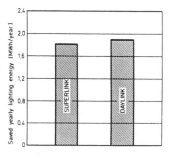

Fig. 24.2 SUPERLINK–DAYLINK yearly comparison

24.3   EXPERIENCE IN USING DAYLIGHTING TOOLS

24.3.1   SUPERLITE

Possibilities and limitations of the calculation of daylighting with the program SUPERLITE

The German Standard, DIN 5034/1/, provides a simple semi-graphical method to evaluate and optimize the efficiency of daylighting strategies. The daylight factors at fixed positions in standard rooms have been calculated. Since then, computer programs have been developed for the rapid and exact analysis of daylight conditions in rooms. This discussion presents the possibilities and limitations of the calculation of daylighting of the calculation program SUPERLITE and compares the daylight factors calculated with it and with the DIN method.

SUPERLITE is briefly described in this section (see also Section 24.1). Detailed information is available in the original study [24/5]. For standard sun and sky conditions, the program computes the illumination conditions of an arbitrary room that is illuminated by daylight. SUPERLITE can model rooms of arbitrary geometry, as long as they consist of plane and trapezoidal walls and windows. See Tables 24.1 and 24.2 for modeling capabilities.

SUPERLITE has several shortcomings. The reflection characteristics of all building component surfaces are assumed to be ideal diffuse. The influence of mirror systems and materials with non-ideal diffuse

Table 24.1   General information, input and output for five daylighting programs

Program	Origin	Machine	Manual	Daylight analysis	Energy analysis	Hourly data	Typical day	Monthly illum.	Other	Uniform sky	Overcast sky CIE	Clear sky CIE	Direct CIE	Ground reflection	Building shades	Building geometry	Internal partition	Electric light	Grid illuminance	Reference pt. illum.	Glare	Hourly report	Isolux	Other	Heating	Cooling	Lighting	Inside temp.	Daylight/elect.	Hourly	Other
	General					Weather				Sky model				Input							Output Daylighting				Output Energy						
Daylit	U	P	—	x	x	—	—	—	x	—	x	x	x	x	—	R	—	x	—	3	—	x	—	x	x	x	x	—	—	x	x
Daylite 2.2	S	P	x	x	e	—	—	x	x	—	x	x	x	x	—	R	—	x	49	x	x	x	x	CR	—	—	x	—	x	x	x
DOE-2.1D	L	A	x	x	x	x	—	—	—	—	x	x	x	x	D	C	—	x	—	2	x	x	—	x	x	x	x	x	x	x	x
SUPERLITE 2	L	A	x	x	—	—	—	b	x	x	x	x	x	x	D	C	x	x	x	x	—	x	x	d	—	—	—	—	—	—	—
tsbi3	B	P	x	x	x	x	—	—	—	—	x	x	x	x	x	C	—	x	x	x	x	x	—	x	x	x	x	x	x	x	x

U = UCLA	b = see text	R = 1 rect. room	P = PC
S = solarsoft	d = daylight factors	C = complex	A = mainframe/PC
L = LBL	e = electric lighting	D = diffuse	
B = thermal		CR = contrast ratio	
Insulation Lab, DK.			

reflectance are not taken into consideration. Up to now, arbitrary luminance distributions of the sky cannot be handled by the program. Neither is it possible to determine the direct impact of the use of daylight in rooms on heating and cooling loads.

Comparison: SUPERLITE–German Standard DIN   The calculation and measurement procedures for the determination of the indoor illumination with daylight are laid down in German standard DIN 5034 Annex 1/2 [24/5]. The daylight factor is computed using a semi-graphical method, which computes the sky component and the reflectance on outdoor enclosures employing the diagram of luminance. When the reflectance on the indoor enclosure has been determined, the daylight factor (DF) can be calculated. This method can be applied to rooms with windows or with skylights. Computation examples of several rooms are included in the regulation to simplify the application of the method.

To compare SUPERLITE and the DIN 5034 method, the following standard pre-calculated room (Fig. 24.3) was used for overcast conditions. It is a study with two windows on one side. Two buildings of different height are opposite the room (Fig. 24.4). At a point which —

Table 24.2   Daylighting and lighting information for five daylighting programs

Program	Window room					Daylight techniques									Lights			General		
	Glazing type	Tilted	Blinds (diff.)	Ceiling tilt	Surface refl.	Reflectors	Light shelves	Sawtooth roof	Clerestories	Overhang/fin	Skylight	Atria	Light well	Monitors	Design illum. level	Type ON, S, Dm	Control strategy	Neighboring building	Building geom. shade	Blind control
Daylit	C															od				
	D	x	x	—	x	—	x	—	—	O	x	—	x	—	x	S	x	—	—	—
Daylite 2.2	C															od				
	D	x	—	x	x	—	x	x	x	Op	x	—	x	x	x	S	d	—	—	—
DOE-2.1D	C		M													od				
	D	x	F	x	x	—	a	—	x	x	x	b	—	x	x	S	x	x	x	x
SUPERLITE 2.0	C									T										
	D	x	F	x	x	x	x	x	x	Op	x	—	—	x	—	—	—	x	x	—
tsbi3	D	x	F	x	x	—	—	x	x	x	x	x	x	—	x	od / S	x	x	x	x

C = clear, heat absorbing, refl.   a = not accurate   S = stepped
D = diffuse   b = daylighting in atria only   od = on/off + dimming
T = translucent   d = total of 6 options   M = movable
O = overhang only   Op = opaque   F = fixed

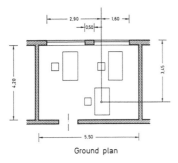

Ground plan

Fig. 24.3 Ground plan of room
according to DIN specifications

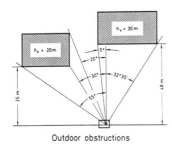

Outdoor obstructions

Fig. 24.4 Outdoor obstructions
for the same room

given the arrangement of the furniture — is the most ill suited as a
working surface, the daylight factor is approximately 1.8% according
to standard DIN 5034.

Figure 24.5 shows the daylight factor contour on the work surface
of the same room under completely overcast sky. As with other
examples, the values of the DF obtained with DIN 5034 and with
SUPERLITE agree closely with each other at the most unsuitable
working place. The DF contour is asymmetric, since the obstruction
in front of the window is asymmetric, too. The DF in the darkest
corner is less than 1%. Near the windows, it is above 15%. One should
note that SUPERLITE calculates up to 400 points on the working
plane whereas the DIN method deals with one point only. The
illuminance contour can also be calculated for direct sunlight, giving
the sun patch on the working plane, to improve furniture arrangement.

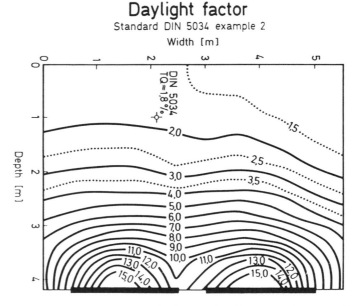

Fig. 24.5 Daylight factor distribution and reference point according to
SUPERLITE and the DIN method

Conclusion The German standard DIN 5034 enables planners to
determine already at the design stage whether a room is sufficiently lit
with daylight. It is possible to determine whether the daylight factor
reaches the recommended minimum value. The method is, however,
complex for a non pre-calculated room. With SUPERLITE, investigations in relation to daylight can be conducted, such as variations in
building construction or fenestration, something which cannot be
examined with the standard DIN 5034.

Simulation of the ELA atrium with SUPERLITE

The mainframe version of SUPERLITE was used to model one of the linear atria in the extension to the Electrical Engineering Department at the Norwegian Institute of Technology in Trondheim (see Part 6, Atria, for a description of the building, Section 36.6 [24/11]).

The program was used to find daylight factors under CIE overcast sky conditions in the atrium, on the floor and on the lower part of the two parallel walls on the north and south side of the atrium. But the number of different types of wall surfaces proved to be greater than the number that could be handled by SUPERLITE, so some manual averaging had to be done. Likewise, the real number of glazed surfaces is six (pitched overhead glazing equal two, each gable a rectangle and a triangle), but the program can only handle five. The roof glazing size also resulted in larger final elements (0.85 m × 0.85 m) than recommended for accuracy (0.25 m × 0.25 m). As a result of the surface complexity, the program was stretched to its limits in accepting input surfaces.

More serious, however, was that the real atrium in many respects incorporated features that could not be modeled at all. In the center of the atrium, a staircase, an elevator shaft and connecting bridges constitute severe obstructions that were not taken into account.

Each gable wall was partly obscured to the outside by heavy greenery, making educated guessing on reflectance and transmission necessary.

Given all these uncertainties, it is surprising to see how the results conform to measured values (Fig. 24.6). One should not take this at face value as a proof that SUPERLITE performs well in this case, as

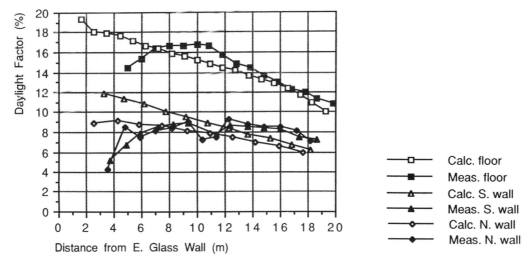

Fig. 24.6 Daylight factors measured and calculated in ELA atrium away from the east wall

there are also many uncertainties connected to the measurements. But we can at least draw the conclusion that the general level and general trend are in very good agreement. The decrease in measured values as one approaches the gable wall (Fig. 24.6) is caused by the greenery covering the lower part of the glazing; this detail could not be handled by the program.

As a conclusion, modeling this case with SUPERLITE was cumbersome and involved many approximations in comparison to the real situation. Even so, the program gave us results which are very useful and within reasonable accuracy.

A serious limitation in SUPERLITE in atrium calculations is the inability to handle more than one set of glazings. In most cases one would like to investigate conditions in rooms facing the atrium, but in order to model this situation, one would have to consider the atrium an unglazed open obstruction outside the room, and do manual corrections for the light loss in atrium glazing and overhead obstructions.

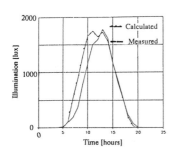

Fig. 24.7 Sunspace roof

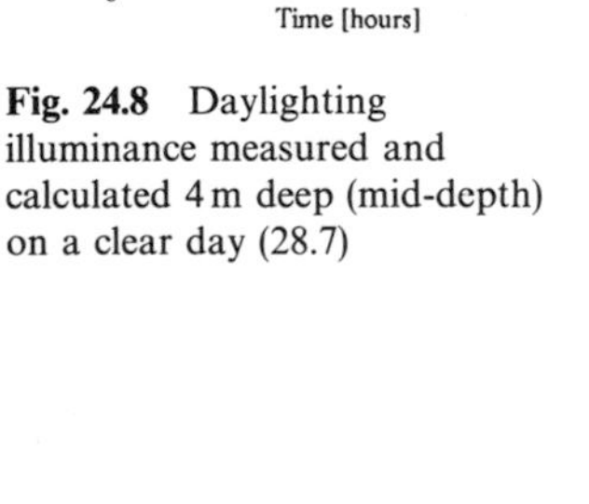

Fig. 24.8 Daylighting illuminance measured and calculated 4 m deep (mid-depth) on a clear day (28.7)

24.3.2   DOE-2.1C

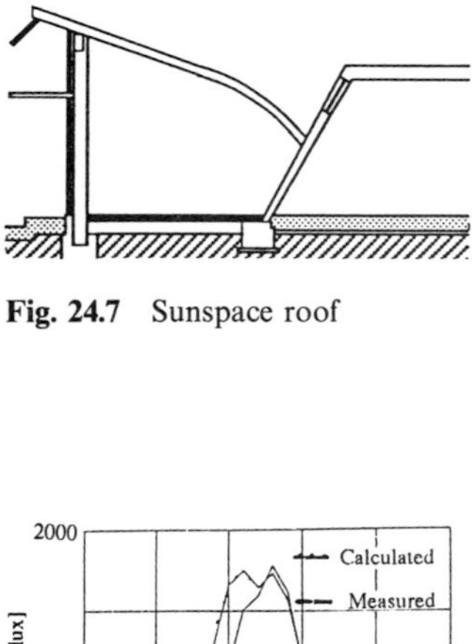

Simulating of the Ispra Laboratory with DOE-2.1C
The modeled meeting room has a complex geometry with inclined south-facing clerestories (see Section 22.1). Sunlight is reflected into the room from the sunspace roof attached to it on the south (see Fig. 24.7). Small clerestories face north also. Measured wall, floor, ceiling and furniture reflectances were used as input, as well as the exact room dimensions. The locally measured radiation data was used as weather data input and the cloud ratio was calculated from the ratio of diffuse to global horizontal radiation [24/6]. The calculated illuminances at reference points 4 m and 6 m deep (measured from the south wall) were compared to the measured values.

Despite the complex geometry of the Ispra lab, with its sunspace, fairly good results (Fig. 24.8) were obtained for the first reference point 4 m deep and at table height (depth of room = 8.1 m at floor level). The higher calculated illuminance values for the morning are probably due to the difficulties encountered when simulating the east door. It had to be simulated using a measured visible transmission value. The calculated levels were too high for the 6 m deep reference point (Fig. 24.9). Comparisons done for the day 26 July 88 showed similar results but with a greater discrepancy.

This trend seems to be in partial agreement with comparisons of the illuminance calculations made with SUPERLITE/DAYLINK and

DOE-2, that is, that DOE-2 generally overestimates the illuminance at the rear of the room. (This was found using cloud covers recorded by human obseration, which are accurate enough but do not necessarily correspond to the amount of diffuse and direct radiation present.) The higher calculated illuminance values (Fig. 24.9) are probably due to the split-flux method used. Maybe a European luminous efficacy rather than the American value used in DOE-2 would give better results.

A second outcome of this simulation is that if a reference point is in the direct sun for one of the 20 pre-calculated fixed solar positions used by DOE-2, then this affects many other hourly results because of the linear interpolation made between these values. Avoiding this direct sun on the reference point still includes reflected direct sun correctly. This outcome does not affect the lighting energy consumption as no electric lighting is required when direct sun is available.

DOE-2 should not be used as a daylighting model but as an energy analysis program. This study shows that the calculated lighting energy may be underestimated. Nonetheless, the daylighting model incorporated in DOE-2 allows a reasonable integration of hourly daylighting levels to calculate the lighting loads and provides a realistic total energy figure.

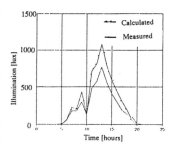

Fig. 24.9 Daylighting illuminance measured and calculated 6 m deep (3/4 depth) on a cloudy day (27.7)

24.3.3 Daylite 2.2

Simulation of the BRF building with Daylite
The modeled arcade corridor was 13.2 m high and 9.45 m to the ceiling of the third floor (Section 22.2 and [24/7–24/9]). It included three floors with rooflights covering 85% of the half-cylindrical roof. The transmittance of the rooflights ($\tau_{vis} = 0.78$) and that of the various surfaces were measured.

The 'equivalent' reflectances of the open areas between the 1st and 2nd, as well as between the 2nd and 3rd stories were determined. The measurements indicate that about 16% of the light, hitting the horizontal plane of the opening from above, was reflected back from the underlying surfaces.

The corrected and calculated daylight factors were compared to the daylight factors measured along the vertical central axis of the arcade and at 11 points in a horizontal direction across each of the circulation corridors. Additionally during 10 working days the exterior illuminance and the status of the electric lights on all three floors were monitored to obtain the daylight utilization factors (DUF) for each floor for September. The DUF is the fraction of the working day during which the daylight replaces electric light.

Since it was not possible to describe the overall geometry of the arcade room in the Daylite program, a model for each of the three floors was set up. In each case a 'sawtooth' description with a light

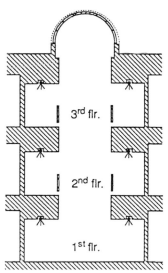

well was used for the roof. For the 2nd and 3rd floors, the opening to the underlying stories was regarded as being part of a uniform floor space.

The reflectance of this floor was an area-weighted mean value of the real floor and 'equivalent' reflectance of the opening. One of the modeled 'rooms' consisted of all the 2nd floor plus the central part of the 3rd floor up to the rooflights, this acting as a well. For the 1st and 2nd floors, the space between the ceiling of the corridor and the rooflight was modeled by specifying an equivalent large thicknes for the roof structure. The illuminance on the 1st and 2nd floors was reduced by adjusting the light well wall reflectance coefficient (R_{wall}) in order to account for the losses due to distribution of light to the corridors of the above stories. The estimated R_{wall} was simply derived as the appropriate adjustments that would give a reasonable agreement between the measured and calculated daylight factors distribution. The measured and the corrected calculated daylight factors are given in Fig. 24.10. Finally, the movable blinds could not be modeled.

Three main points arise from the results:

1. *Available daylight comparison*: comparisons of the monthly lux-hours calculated by Daylite and the measured global illuminance values (irradiance $\times$ 110 lm/W) indicated that the calculated values were too optimistic (40%) for January, February and March. This does not however affect the studied September results.
2. *Daylight factor comparison*: Fig. 24.10 shows that for the 1st and 2nd floors at 2.4 m and 3.3 m from the sidewall the calculated daylight factors seem to be very slightly reversed in magnitude. At 1.5 m they are much too low compared to the measurements for the 1st and 2nd floors. The third floor calculations, however, give good results. The fact that blinds could not be simulated would explain too high calculated values, but it is not clear whether the blinds were ever activated during the measurement period.
3. *Daylight utilization factor comparison for September*: Table 24.3 indicates the mean DUF for each floor averaged over 10 working days in September. The actual design illuminance levels per floor were 50 lux, 100 lux and 100 lux respectively.

Again, a very good agreement is observed for the third floor. The measured value for DUF1 is overestimated because of the low design illuminance level (50 lux).

The mean of the three calculated values for the daylight utilization factor, gives 0.72, which is very close to the mean value measured during September (0.7), indicating that the calculations are fairly reasonable. The measurements and simulations were the contribution of P. Kristensen and C. Paludan-Müller of Esbensen Consulting Engineers.

Table 24.3 Mean daylight utilization factors (DUF1, DUF2, DUF3) for each floor

	DUF1	DUF2	DUF3
Measured	0.61	0.62	0.85
Calculated	0.51	0.79	0.85

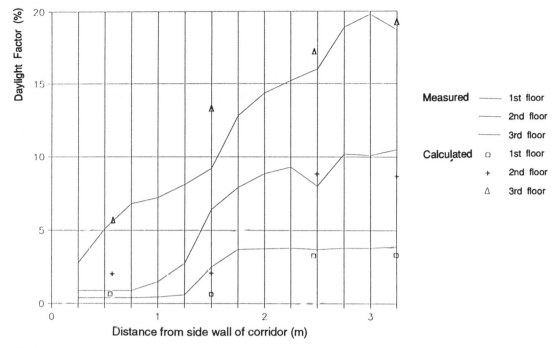

Fig. 24.10   Daylight factor comparison

24.4 REFERENCES

24/1 Hopkirk, N., *Proceedings of Workshop 2: Comparison of Daylighting Tools*, EMPA, Uberlandstrasse 129, CH-8600 Dübendorf, 1987.

24/2 Selkowitz, S., Kim, J. J., Navvab, M., Winkelmann, F., *The DOE-2 and SUPERLITE Daylighting Programs*, Lawrence Berkeley Laboratory, CA, 1982.

24/3 Spitzglas, M., Navvah, M., Kim, J. J., *Scale Model Measurements for a Daylighting Photometric Data Base*, Lawrence Berkeley Laboratory, CA, 1985.

24/4 Szerman, M., *SUPERLINK 1.0 Documentation Manual*, Fraunhofer Institute of Building Physics, Nobelstr. 12, D-7000 Stuttgart 80, 1990.

24/5 Szerman, M., Erhorn, H., *Möglichkeiten und Grenzen der Tageslichtberechnung mit dem berechnungsprogram SUPERLITE*, Fraunhofer Institute of Building Physics, Nobelsstr. 12, D-7000 Stuttgart 80, 1988.

24/6 Orgill, J. K. and Hollands, K. G. T., Correlation equation for hourly diffuse radiation on a horizontal surface, *Solar Energy*, **19**, 357 (1977).

24/7 Christensen, J. E., Christofferson, J., *Introduction User's Guide to Daylite*, Thermal Insulation Lab, Technical University of Denmark, Building 118, DK-2800 Lyngby, 1990.

24/8 Paludan-Müller, C., Kristensen, P. E., *Daylighting Through Rooflights in the BRF Headquarters*, Esbensen, Consulting Engineers, Havnegade 41, DK-1058, Copenhagen K, 1989.

24/9 *Advanced Case Studies*, The Renewable Energy Promotion Dept. Energy Technology Support Unit, Harwell Laboratory, Oxfordshire OX11 ORA.

25 Conclusions

An important criterion concerning savings with daylighting strategies is the type of energy to be economized: lighting, heating, cooling or combinations thereof. The reference case chosen will also be determinant for the magnitude of the savings.

The short examples of existing buildings illustrate how daylighting strategies can be used in buildings to profit from the available daylight. Three buildings show the usefulness of rooflighting. Adequate interior daylighting is obtained for about 70% of the time for a circulation space. A sports hall is comfortably lit by daylighting, and in a museum, not only is energy saved, but visible contact to the outside weather conditions is valuable to highlight the paintings. A conference room demonstrates the possibility of adequately daylighting a room with clerestories alone, where the normal walls are not free. Finally, a new technology for core daylighting with light pipes, which can bring both energy savings and psychological advantages, is presented.

The following conclusions are based on monitored data from three buildings and simulations of a classroom and office for a variety of daylighting strategies in various climates with local schedules and constructions.

25.1 AUTOMATIC LIGHTING CONTROL SYSTEMS

Integrating automatic lighting control systems is responsible for the major part of energy savings. Simulations indicate that lighting energy savings of 12–85% for a room are possible, depending on room type, orientation, shading by buildings, type of lighting control and climate. These energy savings are relative to the case where artificial lighting would be always on during occupation time. Rather lower savings are calculated for lighting plus heating energy as the heating energy increases to compensate the decreased lighting energy. This is not so marked if the lighting consumption dominates. The Technologiezentrum case study demonstrates that manual lighting and shading control were ineffective to save energy. Automatic control is therefore an advantage.

For both the simulated classrooms and offices we find that a continuous dimming system is more advantageous for lighting in Oslo, Zürich and Brussels. In Rome, where daylight is plentiful, on/off control is more advantageous for the simulated classroom facing south than continuous dimming with its 16% base load.

If lighting plus heating energy is considered, then the choice of continuous dimming or on/off control system depends on the use and geometry of the room. There were no significant differences between systems for the classrooms, except for Rome where on/off remained better. Continuous dimming rather than one step on/off was found profitable for offices in Zürich and Brussels. Parametrics based on the BRF building also indicate that introducing an automatic continuous dimming system rather than an on/off would save about 10% lighting energy.

25.2   DAYLIGHTING STRATEGIES

These included increased glazing area by using clerestories, adding light shelves to the clerestories or adding specific rooflights, all to a base case with 15% glazing area relative to the floor area, with blinds and automatic lighting control available.

25.2.1   Lighting energy

Introducing daylighting strategies in a room is beneficial in many cases. For lighting energy alone, any strategy which includes more glazing, especially skylights or a sawtooth, is profitable especially if the room is shaded by a neighboring building. The use of rooflights is demonstrated by the Danish building (BRF) where the center of the circulation area is satisfactorily lit by rooflights, saving a large amount of electric lighting (68%).

25.2.2   Lighting and heating

Possible savings of lighting plus heating energy decrease in colder climates or for glazing not facing south.

In climates like Zürich with cold winters and fairly hot summers, substantial savings for lighting plus heating energy are generally only possible for daylighting strategies on the south facades (about 17%). Minimal savings are possible with small extra horizontal or glazing facing west. Daylighting strategies which increase the glazing area facing east or, worse, north require extra heating energy which cancels the lighting economies. Glazing with a higher insulation value could change this. If the lighting contribution is weighted by a factor of three

(L + H/3) to represent cost or a heat pump, then reasonable savings become possible for glazing on the west, east or even the north facades for an office, or for a classroom facing north with rooflights.

Savings with daylighting strategies exist for all orientations in milder climates (up to about 20% in Brussels). The savings are higher for the south orientation, and drop to about a half or less for other orientations. For orientations not facing south, the various studied daylighting strategies yield similar economies.

The change in ranking order for lighting plus a third of heating (L + H/3) instead of L + H is insignificant for the office.

Savings of lighting plus heating energy become difficult in colder climates such as Oslo and would only be possible if good insulation of the building and good glazing are used. This was not the case in this study, in which typically rather poor values were used. If lighting plus a third of heating (L + H/3) is considered then savings are possible for certain strategies (skylights being best).

Hot climates, such as in Rome, show higher percentage savings for glazing facing south in a classroom. The high lighting energy savings dominate the results of combinations of lighting and heating as the heating demands are low.

It is recommended to use exterior light shelves with a clerestory facing south in Brussels, Zürich and Rome. Although the light shelves save a little less lighting plus heating energy than clerestories alone, they reduce cooling loads without closing blinds so often, allow better visual contact with the exterior and create more homogeneous illumination levels. If the room is shaded by a neighboring building, the savings of lighting plus heating energy hardly decrease with an exterior light shelf. Its effect is also small for west, east and north-facing glazing in offices. Extra glazing is recommended when the building is shaded (see Section 23.5, Tables 23.18 and 23.19). The monitored office building in England (SSWC) is an example where light shelves and overhangs eliminate summertime overheating while promoting good daylight penetration and distribution even in an overcast climate as well as saving lighting energy. The study confirms the worth of daylighting in offices, where lighting costs are comparable to those of space heating.

25.2.3 Energy costs (heating case)

Costs can be reduced with daylighting strategies more frequently than lighting plus heating energy can be saved. Generally, strategies which are favorable for lighting energy savings but not necessarily for lighting plus heating are also favorable when lighting plus a third of heating (L + H/3) is considered (e.g. skylights and glazing facing east or west). If the strategy includes glazing facing north in a cold climate, the above conclusion may not be valid (e.g. sawteeth).

25.2.4 Cooling

If the cooling load is high, different daylighting strategies will have to be recommended. When no air-conditioning is foreseen, as in European classrooms, then a good choice of strategy, such as an exterior light shelf with a medium clerestory, blinds, a small clerestory, or an overhang above the clerestory (which can lose nearly all the benefits acquired with a clerestory) or a small diffuse skylight can reduce overheating.

If mechanical cooling is included in the total energy calculation, the cooling magnitude can be decisive for the choice of daylighting strategy. If the cooling is high as in Zürich, the ranking order of strategies will be different from the case where only lighting plus heating energy without cooling is considered. For example, for an office in Zürich facing south, a medium glazing area (25%) with blinds is recommendable to save lighting plus heating energy. But the base case with 15% glazing area, with or without an overhang, is better energy-wise if an inefficient cooling system is installed. A clerestory with medium glazing area and an exterior light shelf or a smaller clerestory (5%), all with blinds, is also competitive energy-wise if an efficient cooling system is used. If the cooling load is low and an efficient cooling system is used, then roughly the same daylighting strategies as those for lighting plus heating are energy saving. Different strategies may, however, be recommendable, depending on orientation, if the cooling system is inefficient.

25.3 ANALYSIS TOOLS

Two new 'link programs', which link the daylighting program SUPER-LITE to an energy program such as DOE-2.1C or MBDS, were developed in the Task XI. They allow the calculation of the effect of daylighting on the thermal and energetic behavior of a building. Despite very different routines used, the differences in annual lighting energy between the two link programs are small, occurring mainly in winter.

Simulations were done using three daylighting programs: SUPER-LITE, Daylite 2.2 and DOE-2, although the latter is mainly an energy analysis program with a daylighting routine. Our experience shows that, whereas simple rectangular rooms are easily simulated, complex, real buildings need a great deal of thought, approximations and additional hand calculations or measurements to be simulated. If this is done, then reasonable results can be expected.

The new link programs have permitted sensitivity studies to be performed to show the importance of including automatic lighting control systems and daylighting strategies in commercial buildings. The advanced case studies have confirmed that lighting energy can be saved with daylighting strategies and that automatic lighting control systems are essential in offices.

26 Recommended Reading

Hopkinson, R.G., Petherbridge, P. and Longmore, J., *Daylighting*, Heinemann, London, 1966.

This is the classical 'bible' of daylighting, with a wealth of information, covering all aspects of the topic at that time: lighting criteria, the daylight source, all available methods of calculation, daylight photometry, physical modeling, regulations, design and planning. Some of the information is now obsolete, and other aspects of daylighting are today more in focus, but this is still a valuable reference book.

Evans, B.H., *Daylight in Architecture*, McGraw-Hill, New York, 1981.

This is one of the first books of the new generation of daylighting literature, spurred by the renewed interest for both architectural and energy reasons. Subjects covered are the need for light, how daylight behaves in architecture, the sky as light source, and how to evaluate design by model studies. A section presents case studies with several prominent buildings included. A major point stressed is that daylight solutions must be integrated with other design considerations — natural ventilation/cooling, solar energy, acoustics, electric lighting. The book relies heavily on simple figures and graphs that explain principles and concepts. Many real building examples are included throughout the text.

Lam, W.C., *Sunlighting as Formgiver for Architecture*, Van Nostrand Reinhold, New York, 1986.

The title of this book is somewhat misleading, as the text covers daylighting in general, not only direct sunlight. The book is aimed at architects, and is basically a catalogue of sun/daylighting concepts illustrated with a wealth of building examples. Principles are explained in graphic form, and some model results are presented. About half of the book is devoted to case studies — urban design, offices, schools, museums, and other building types.

Moore, F., *Concept and Practice of Architectural Daylighting*, Van Nostrand Reinhold, New York, 1985.

This is a comprehensive manual on daylighting, aimed at the practicing architect and the early stages of design. It covers basic concepts in lighting and vision with analogies and graphics, and requires little theoretical background. The fenestration of some famous buildings is explained. Both daylighting and sun protection are treated in detail, and most of the available methods for analysis are presented, many with examples.

Sundials, nomograms, etc. are given in large formats in appendices, ready to use. The book also gives surveys of computer models and instruments, and instructions on how to build a mirror-box artificial sky.

Robbins, C.L., *Daylighting, Design and Analysis*, Van Nostrand Reinhold, New York, 1986.

This book is an important recent reference on daylighting, with a coverage similar to Moore's book, but with a more engineering-oriented treatment. It goes from basic concepts in lighting, via the daylight resources to fenestration concepts and analysis. Necessary formulae and tables are given in great detail, and every chapter concludes with a comprehensive reference list. Both the lumen, the daylight factor and the flux transfer methods of analysis are explained, as well as physical modeling. The integration between daylighting and electric lighting is also included. Almost two-thirds of the book is very useful appendices, of which 450 pages give daylight and sunlight availability and daylight utilization data for 75 US cities.

Selkowitz, S. (ed.), *Skylight Handbook*, Lawrence Berkeley Laboratory/ Charles Eley Assoc., Berkeley, CA, 1986.

Skylights provide an effective way to illuminate horizontal surfaces with daylight. This handbook covers all the basics, building up the reader's understanding step by step on how they work and how they can be used. The emphasis is on skylights as sources of uniform task lighting in deep one-story buildings, where daylight can give considerable savings in lighting and cooling energy and electric peak load. The handbook covers design issues and explains all the basic concepts associated with skylights as indoor illumination. Worksheets are included that give step by step instructions on how to design a skylight system and how to calculate energy and power savings.

Schiler, M. (ed.), *Simulating Daylight with Architectural Models*, Daylighting Networks of North America.

For a complex geometry, physical modeling is the only available analysis method. This useful handbook covers all aspects of how to build models, using real or artificial skies, measurement methods and equipment, and presentation and evaluation of model measurement results. The focus is on energy conservation and how daylighting interplays with artificial lighting. The book also contains a section with illustrative case studies and an extensive bibliography. This is the only comprehensive manual within this field, unfortunately somewhat too limited to North American conditions (and units).

PART **5**

COOLING

CONTRIBUTORS

Part 5 Editors and Chapters 28, 31 and 32
B. Meersseman and A. De Herde
Architecture et Climat
Université Catholique de Louvain
Place du Levant 1
B-1348 Louvain-la-Neuve
Belgium

Chapter 29
S. Alvarez
Dept. Ingeniera Energetica y
Mecanica de Fluidos
Universidad de Sevilla
E-41012 Sevilla
Spain

Chapter 27
F. Butera
Dipartimento di Energetica ed
Applicazioni di Fisica
Universita di Palermo
I-90128 Palermo
Italy

Chapter 29
J. Lopez de Asiain
Escuela Arquitectura
Avenida Reina Mercedes S/N
E-41012 Sevilla
Spain

Chapter 29 Editor
A. Lauritano
Dipartimento di Energetica ed
Applicazioni di Fisica
Universita di Palermo
I-90128 Palermo
Italy

Chapter 30
G. Silvestrini
CNR-IEREN
Via C. Rampolla 8
I-90128 Palermo
Italy

Chapter 29
G. Silvestrini and G. Pecorella
CNR-IEREN
Via C. Rampolla 8
I-90128 Palermo
Italy

27 Introduction

27.1 BACKGROUND

Finding the best cooling strategy for many buildings poses significant challenges. In an urban area, for example, noise from traffic may be too loud to open windows for natural cooling. The incentive to find alternative cooling methods is, however, great as cooling costs in modern large buildings can be very high. Particularly challenging are climates where both high temperatures and humidity occur.

Natural cooling techniques have evolved over centuries, but their application has been very rare in recent decades. Energy-intensive mechanical air conditioning has been the standard solution. As a result, electricity consumption for cooling has drastically grown. This is especially true in threshold countries like Brazil, Korea, Taiwan, Malaysia, etc., where air conditioning in commercial buildings is essential and cooling loads are high.

For psychological, physiological and historical reasons, people are accustomed to working in an artificially heated environment rather than in an artificially cooled one. Heating methods that 'let the sun in' and 'keep the heat in' are comparatively easy to achieve but cooling requires more sophisticated approaches: for example, control of air temperature and velocity, wall and ceiling surface temperatures, as well as air humidity control. Cooling has not been as systematically studied as heating, and hence, there are fewer standard techniques available.

Part 5, Cooling, is organized according to the following chapter descriptions.

27.2 STRATEGIES

The goals and design principles of cooling strategies usually employed are discussed and methods for their practical application (separately, or in combination) are given. The five strategies are:

- solar radiation control
- heat avoidance
- reduction of internal gains
- passive cooling, and
- heat extraction.

27.3 EXAMPLES

Chapter 29 presents two examples: Seville Expo 1992, where outdoor cooling strategies along with measured and predicted results are given, and an office building in Sicily, where cooling techniques are described.

27.4 ANALYSIS TOOLS

The computer tools used to simulate cooling strategies are analyzed and presented in a matrix. Information about hardware needed, ease of use, cost and documentation is given for each tool. Attention is drawn to the lack of appropriate design tools currently available.

27.5 CONCLUSIONS

The need to combine active and passive cooling techniques for saving energy is stressed. Recommendations for promising new systems are given. A quantitative evaluation of combined systems was impossible within the framework of the present study.

28 Strategies

28.1 SOLAR RADIATION CONTROL

The primary method of controlling solar radiation is to size windows carefully relative to the dimensions of the rooms behind them, and to locate windows at positions appropriate to local insolation conditions. Considered separately, these methods rarely suffice to ensure adequate comfort. When necessary, the following methods may be applied.

Fig. 28.1 Day care enter in Charlottenburg, Germany

Fig. 28.2 Delahaye house in Waterloo, Belgium

Fig. 28.3 Office building, Copenhagen, Denmark

28.1.1 Window and roof protection

Window protection reduces solar insolation, thus avoiding an increase of both air temperature and mean radiant temperature, and avoids direct insolation on occupants. Movable devices, permanent devices and external environmental measures may all serve as effective window protection.

Movable devices

Interior blinds, exterior blinds or louvers, and blinds between two layers of glass offer effective protection against direct radiation. The disadvantages of movable interior devices are that they obscure the view to the outside of a building, and release absorbed radiation into the room. This phenomenon can be diminished with reflective blinds but external reflection from light colored blinds may cause visual discomfort when the sun shines on them.

Exterior blinds or louvers prevent solar radiation from entering a room and can be especially effective in shielding diffuse radiation. Louvers can be automated for maximum efficiency. However, exterior blinds are difficult to maintain and can obscure the view.

Blinds placed between two layers of glass can be either normal or venetian blinds with slats that tilt. They combine the advantages of both internal and external blinds in requiring less cleaning and preventing radiation from entering a room. They also shade diffuse radiation. On the other hand, blinds between glass present a few disadvantages. Access to the blinds for repair may be expensive. Vapor condensation between the two layers of glass sometimes occurs in winter if the blinds are inadequately vented to the outside. If the slats do not tilt, or if the blind is a shutter-type device, it can obscure the view.

Design considerations

- Blinds left down in winter reduce usable solar gains.
- They may modify or hinder natural ventilation.
- Blinds will increase the need for artificial lighting, especially if they are dark or made of coated aluminum.
- The use of light colored or metallic polished blinds may cause glare in nearby buildings.
- Blinds can slightly reduce heat transmission from windows.

Permanent devices

Overhangs and roof protection are common in hot climates and present the advantages of having little or no effect on views, and when placed above the top of a window facing south, they admit low winter sun while blocking high summer radiation. The main disadvantage of using permanent window protection is that effectiveness is limited to windows facing south. For windows facing east and west, other devices must be used because of the low solar angle of incidence. Vertical projections, or fins, offer a way to shade windows facing east and west, and can be used in combination with overhangs. The disadvantages of using fins are that they strongly frame the view, may be expensive, especially for multi-storied buildings, and may hamper window washing.

28.1.2   Design considerations

Permanent window protection can induce radical changes in air movement patterns within the building, especially when detached from the exterior wall. Thermal bridges to the interior should be avoided whenever possible.

Vegetation
When correctly selected and strategically placed, vegetation may prove an effective window protection. The use of vegetation is particularly useful to protect east and especially west windows. Issues to be considered are:

Fig. 28.4   Taliesin East, Taliesin, USA

- Vegetation contributes to air cooling through evaporation.
- Vegetation can modify wind direction and velocity, and can even funnel wind.
- Daylighting may be severely reduced.
- Vegetation diminishes usable solar gains in winter, since bare branches block 20–40% of the sun's direct radiation.

28.1.3   Special glazing

When using special glazing, the designer generally has two major options:

Fig. 28.5   Dellicour building, Brussels, Belgium

- using reflecting glass to decrease energy transmission by increasing reflection, or
- using absorbing glass to decrease total transmission of the glazing by decreasing direct transmission and increasing outward re-emission after absorption.

Photochromic, thermochromic and electrochromic glass, which changes optical properties according to external conditions, is being developed. Although a valuable future alternative, these types of glass are still in development and are too expensive for wide application.

Special glazings are advantageous because of the variety of properties they offer to reflect, absorb or transmit energy for each specific job. Reflecting and absorbing glass also works on east and west windows and they are fully effective on diffuse radiation. A major disadvantage of special glazings is that they may change the characteristics of daylight

Fig. 28.6   Bekaert Metalworks Company, Merelbeke, Belgium

in comparison with that transmitted through conventional glass.

Designers interested in special glazings should be aware of the side-effects. Non-selective reflecting and absorbing glass reduces solar gains in winter. Also, they sharply reduce the amount of daylight admitted to the building, thus, the need for electric lighting is increased.

28.1.4   Lattice devices

A superstructure in the form of a lattice can be used to intercept direct radiation to the roof. The lattice reflects part of the radiation, re-emits long-wave radiation, and can be cooled with cross ventilation. Even better results are observed if both faces of the interstitial air space between the superstructure and the roof are reflective, thereby hindering heat transfer across the gap by radiation. The disadvantages of a lattice are first the risk of attracting animals to nest, and second, the accumulation of debris.

28.1.5   Building protection

Building orientation
East and west walls are difficult to protect from direct radiation because low morning and afternoon solar incidence angles make overhangs ineffective. If a building is oriented on an east–west axis, then most apertures can be placed in the south wall, where they can easily be protected. The choice of east–west orientation may however conflict with required optimum ventilation, depending on prevailing breezes.

Fig. 28.7 Haas and Partners Office, Jona, Switzerland

Earth sheltering
Earth sheltering a building is a traditional solution to protect the interior from direct radiation from the sun. This has the advantage of decreased temperature extremes. Although single earth sheltered buildings tend to have low air infiltration rates, and thus lower cooling loads in hot climates, natural ventilation strategies are hampered. Moreover, spaces at the rear of the building may be insufficiently lit, necessitating skylights. For this type of building, air cooling using underground ducts may prove attractive.

28.1.6   Protection of outside spaces

Environmental cooling reduces the heat load of a building by cooling the immediate environment. Several techniques will achieve this objective as follows.

Ground vegetation

Vegetation protects the soil from direct solar radiation and can cool through evaporation. Vegetation may also strongly affect ventilation by channeling breezes and changing their direction or velocity according to the geometry of the planting.

Shading systems

Shading systems, such as canvas-covered streets and patios, offer the advantage of protecting the ground from solar radiation. If the shading devices are lightweight and highly reflective, they will stay cool, avoid heat storage, and reduce heat re-radiation from the ground. In combination with vegetation, the level of protection can be further increased. Systems employing the stack effect may also be used to improve ventilation.

Fig. 28.8 Expo '92, Seville, Spain

Typical of all fixed shading devices, they obstruct the view. Moreover, unventilated shading devices can accumulate heat in a confined area and create local overheating. The cost of installation and maintenance may be high. Finally, they inhibit heat re-radiation at night.

Urban compactness, mask effect and ventilation obstacles

In hot, dry climates, many cities are traditionally compact, providing natural shading between buildings and an acceptable climate within. The presence of nearby buildings, however, can completely alter the wind pattern and restrict sunlight in winter, increasing the need for winter heating and daylighting.

Fig. 28.9 Expo '92, Seville, Spain

28.2 HEAT AVOIDANCE

Heat avoidance denotes various methods for preventing exterior heat from reaching the interior of a building.

28.2.1 Reduction of transmission gains

External surface treatment

The color of a surface affects its absorption characteristics. Emission properties are determined by the nature of the material and the surface characteristics; for example, metals are characterized by low emissivity, while plastics have high emissivity.

In hot climates, it is important to use a highly emissive surface coating to encourage re-radiation at night.

Insulation

Insulation improves summer comfort by lowering the temperature of the inner surface of the building envelope. Roof insulation is particularly effective, since in summer, the roof is exposed to the highest radiation

Fig. 28.10 Piazza del Commune, Assisi, Italy

Fig. 28.11 Los Molinos School, Alicante, Spain

Fig. 28.12 Castel, Palermo, Sicily

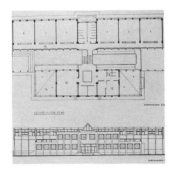

Fig. 28.13 School building, Almeria, Spain

levels. The main disadvantages are that insulation is relatively costly and demands carefully design and quality work to avoid thermal bridges and condensation.

Thermal inertia

If the building has sufficient mass, heat absorbed at the exterior surface during the day does not reach the interior of the building, but flows back to the surroundings when the exterior surface temperature drops at night. Thermal inertia is only effective where there is a wide diurnal temperature variation, and where the average ambient temperature is within the comfort zone. This is often the case in hot dry climates.

Sufficient means of cooling the mass at night must be provided, for example, through night re-radiation, and/or fan-forced ventilation. Otherwise peak cooling loads and equipment power rates will increase.

Shape and compactness

A building's surface area to volume (A/V) ratio is an important variable. Under appropriate climatic conditions, when considering isolated buildings, a high A/V ratio is advantageous for cooling because it facilitates natural ventilation. Also, lighting energy may be reduced if the potential for daylighting is fully exploited. However, a high A/V ratio contradicts the principle of grouping spaces to preserve a cool core in the building, and may conflict with heating strategies.

28.2.2   Reduction of infiltration

Reduction of infiltration through the envelope can lower heat transfer from the hot daytime surroundings, and avoid excess moisture accumulation in humid climates. Humidity entering a building may condense due to lower inside temperature. The infiltration rate depends not only on the wind velocity but also on the difference between indoor and outdoor temperatures.

Ventilation for cooling and hygienic purposes is always needed. The hygienic ventilation rate is set between 10 and 35 m³ per hour and per occupant, depending on the country and on the type of occupancy. Infiltration may or may not provide this ventilation.

28.2.3   Zoning

Rooms with the same level of thermal comfort should be connected and arranged in a ring around the core of the building. Occupation time can also determine the spaces which belong to the core and those that belong to the ring. This can be achieved, for example, by creating a ventilated, south-facing buffer space, to the north of which is a cool central courtyard, enclosed by a ventilated, and shaded access area in the form of a ring.

28.3   INTERNAL GAINS REDUCTION

28.3.1   Reduction of lighting gains

Reduction of lighting gains aims to reduce the cooling loads through the use of daylight instead of electric lighting and to reduce electricity consumed for lighting.

Light entering a building is composed of direct and diffuse sunlight, light from the sky and neighboring surfaces. Diffuse light is the only usable part of daylight, since direct sunlight generally creates unbearable glare. In hot climates, the problem of over-illumination is crucial. Views of bright exterior surfaces must be excluded. A detailed view of daylighting strategies and their relevance to total energy requirements (cooling, heating, and illumination) is provided in Part 4, Daylighting. Particularly when daylight enters from the roof, it is important to shade openings to avoid heat production.

Fig. 28.14   School building, Almeria, Spain

28.3.2   Reduction of casual gains

Avoiding high occupancy density, careful scheduling of room occupation, and, whenever possible, using outer spaces (e.g. in school buildings) will reduce undesired heat gain. Heat gains from equipment may be reduced with appliances that consume minimum energy and by locating them outside occupied areas on the leeward side of the building when there is pressure from prevailing wind, or in an area of high gains provided with a high rate of ventilation.

28.4   NATURAL COOLING

After all efforts are made to minimize heat production in a building, cooling strategies can be examined.

28.4.1   Physiological cooling

Physiological cooling creates a sensation of thermal comfort without changing either temperature or humidity of the room air. Instead, other parameters influence the feeling of comfort: metabolism, clothing, skin temperature, radiant temperature and air velocity. Those parameters can be combined to achieve the desired comfort level.

The easiest and most common physiological cooling strategy is air movement. A fan, for example, can increase comfort without changing

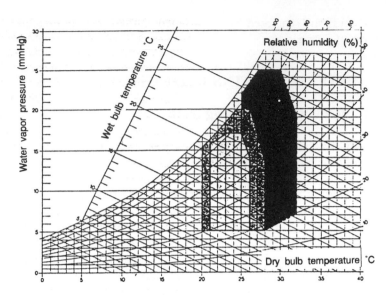

Fig. 28.15 Comfort chart showing the influence of ventilation

the air temperature. When the room temperature is lower than the skin temperature, air movement activates heat loss from the skin by convection. It also increases skin evaporation by breaking the saturated air envelope surrounding the body.

The comfort charts (Fig. 28.15 and 28.16) illustrate how ventilation and evaporative cooling can extend comfort zones. The comfort zone is indicated by the white areas of the graphics. In the grey area, comfort is reduced, but cooling is not absolutely necessary. The black area in Fig. 28.15 indicates how ventilation can extend the comfort zone, whereas in Fig. 28.16 the black area indicates the effect of evaporative cooling.

28.4.2 Building cooling

Careful arrangement of the building in its surroundings can facilitate ventilation by prevailing winds. Envelope cooling may be used to discharge accumulated heat. Different methods to achieve this are described below.

Envelope cooling
Envelope cooling mainly aims to cool the thermal mass of the building and diminish the mean radiant temperature of the envelope surfaces. Three ways exist to achieve this.

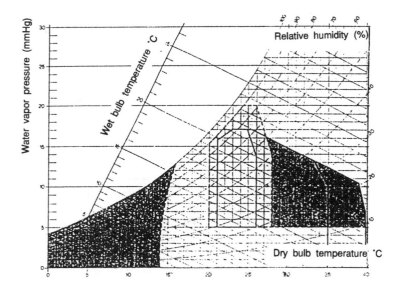

Fig. 28.16 Comfort chart showing the influence of evaporative cooling

Night radiative cooling When the sky is clear, the mean radiant temperature of the night sky is well below that of the air at ground level or the exterior surfaces of a building. Much heat accumulated during the day can be radiated from buildings to the sky, but overcast skies or high humidity make radiative cooling ineffective.

Convective cooling Cooling through convection is a common strategy in warm, humid climates; cross ventilation in the basement and the attic of a lightweight building can reduce the temperatures of the floor and ceiling. In hot, dry climates, convective cooling is used essentially at night, because night temperatures are lower. For maximum effectiveness, mass storage may be used to remove heat during the day, which is then discharged at night by forced ventilation. Under some conditions, a double envelope with night ventilation may be considered.

Conductive cooling This type of energy exchange is possible if the building envelope is in contact with a cooler mass, for example, the earth. This requires, of course, that the envelope in contact with the mass has good heat conductance and is uninsulated. A disadvantage of conductive cooling is the risk of contamination and water ingress, necessitating vapor barriers and drainage systems. Also, heat loss in winter can become a problem.

Fig. 28.17 Expo 1992, Seville, Spain

Fig. 28.18 Expo, 1992, Seville, Spain

Fig. 28.19 Castle, Palermo, Sicily

28.4.3 Air cooling

Evaporative cooling

The evaporation which occurs at the surface of water extracts heat from the air, and as the temperature of the air falls, its relative humidity rises. This process is called evaporative cooling. Although difficult to apply inside, it proves extremely efficient for external spaces.

To optimize evaporative cooling and movement of air and water, extensive water to air surface contact is needed. This can be achieved with landscape features, such as ponds, canals, and fountains. Water can also be micronized in the air or on hot surfaces; then it is important to carefully control the size of the drops and the cleanliness of the water. Other evaporative cooling devices include water circulation under a porous pavement, fountains, and cascades. Plants also evaporate water, producing a cooling effect.

Evaporative cooling is particularly efficient in hot dry climates, where air can absorb large quantities of vapor, significantly decreasing its temperature. This technique is inapplicable to hot humid climates with air near the saturation point. The large amount of water required during cooling restricts this technique to regions where water is plentiful. A further drawback of passive techniques is the difficulty of controlling the air humidity.

Design considerations for using evaporative cooling include:

- Water surfaces greatly add to thermal mass.
- With large open surfaces, night re-radiation proves extremely effective.
- Evaporative cooling is easily combined with natural ventilation by the use of the stack effect.
- Water area open to direct solar radiation can cause glare.

Underground ducts

Before entering the building, air can be cooled by channeling through an underground tunnel. This is recommended provided the ground substrata has sufficient cooling potential and pollutants from organic decomposition or radon will not enter the system. Alternately a tube can be installed in the ground and covered by white pebbles, and the ground cooled through evaporation of water dripping from a pipe.

28.4.4 Natural ventilation

Ventilation achieves three major functions:

1. Ensuring adequate indoor air quality by eliminating stale air and drawing in fresh air.
2. Increasing body comfort by removing heat through convection and evaporation of perspiration (see Section 2.8.4.1), and

3. Cooling the thermal mass of the building when the ambient temperature is lower than inside.

Temperature gradient effect

Indoor temperature gradients induce ventilation by drawing cool ambient air through inlets at the bottom of the building and exhausting it through vents at the top. This is known as the stack effect. In hot climates common applications of the stack effect are solar chimneys and wind towers. Solar chimneys are simple and effective, and can be applied to any building.

Heat extraction is enhanced by air movement between air masses of different temperatures; in the shade cast by a building, cool air pockets are created, while on the other side, the sun warms up the air. Thus when warm air from the sunny side of the building rises, cool air from the shady side can be drawn down through the building.

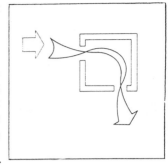

Fig. 28.20 Air flow pattern in a room without deflectors (wind perpendicular to an opening)

Wind pressure effect

When wind strikes a building, high pressure builds on the exposed surface and low pressure on the opposite face. Depending on the size and location of openings in the building envelope, air will flow from the high pressure to the low pressure areas extracting heat. Ventilation is best achieved in open plan spaces. Fixed wind deflectors may be used to alter the pressure patterns of the walls of a building. If ventilating different areas alternately is desirable, adjustable deflectors as in Fig. 28.21 can be used. The best ventilation is at body level, and should be the goal of these devices.

The venturi effect also induces ventilation. This is the case, for example, when wind flows through the space between the inner and outer roof coverings, inducing air movement in the room below, and is thus particularly useful for attics and other roof spaces and cellars. Wind towers, relying primarily on the stack effect, also incorporate wind-induced ventilation effects. Wind towers may also function as pure wind collectors in which the stack and venturi effects are negligible.

The main disadvantage of wind-induced ventilation is that increased air speeds may conflict with building utilization. Orientating the building to maximize the wind pressure effect may conflict with the orientation required by solar protection.

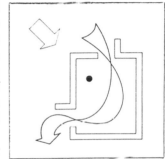

Fig. 28.21 Air flow pattern in a room with deflectors (wind at 45° to the openings)

29 Examples

29.1   SEVILLE EXPO 1992

29.1.1   Introduction

Between 20 April and 12 October 1992 the 500th anniversary of the discovery of America, Seville was the host city of the Universal Expo. Over 103 countries, 21 international organizations, 17 Spanish communities and 15 private firms participated in this event.

Over 18 million visitors were expected at the Expo, on an average day 290 000 visitors were planned for. The site of the Expo, named Isla de la Cartuja after the medieval monastery located there, was an island of 215 ha on the Guadalquivir river.

A major aspect of the Master Plan for the development of the site was the improvement of the climatic conditions of the outdoor spaces of the site, which represented about 50% of the total area. Climate conditions in Seville from June to September are extreme. During the summer of 1989 a maximum air temperature of over 40°C was recorded on 18 days. The extreme temperatures and intense solar radiation make staying in the open practically unbearable during mid-day. Despite this, the Expo organizers wanted the outdoor spaces to serve not only for access to the various pavilions, but also as rest and social activity areas.

The Master Plan used groups of pavilions around larger open spaces designated as high traffic public zones. These areas were environmentally controlled to provide desirable climatic conditions and unique ambience for rest and leisure activities. Major international pavilions faced these special areas.

29.1.2   The pilot

To assess the effectiveness of the proposed cooling strategies, a pilot experiment was approved by the Expo 1992 Executive Committee during July 1987. The area of 15 000 m^2 for the provisional Expo offices of the Expo was chosen for the experiment.

The site contained:

- a large pond to be used as a center of water circulation and evaporation;
- two types of pergolas, one for pedestrians only, with water-cooled pavement and canvas cover as a protection from sun and rain, the other for both pedestrians and vehicles, covered with an electro-soldered lattice for climbing vines;
- a bioclimatic Rotunda on the main axis of the experimental site, as a prototype for rest and recreation areas to be distribution throughout the main avenues of the Expo.

29.1.3   The bioclimatic Rotunda

The Rotunda was designed to capitalize on size, functionality and aesthetic appearance of the rest areas throughout the outdoor spaces. With three levels linked by stairways, the structure formed a square with sides of 31 m. Two lower levels were the area used by occupants, forming two concentric circles with diameters of 24 and 16 m, respectively. The difference in height between the various levels was 80 cm with cascades falling from level to level. The Rotunda was covered with a white polyvinyl chloride (PVC) pyramidal covering of 13% transmissivity, open at the top. Since the Rotunda was a full-scale pilot experiment, it employed various techniques and strategies to thermally condition outdoor spaces. Twelve cooling towers were placed in one of the Rotunda avenues. These towers were 30 m high, topped with wind traps which performed as fans in the Rotunda tower. Mist techniques employed in the Rotunda were also adapted to the remaining outdoor spaces. The palenque, an area of 10 000 m² where public festivities were held, is of particular interest. It contains: sprinklers for the covering; five air conditioning units, each with a sensible and a latent cooling section (the sensible sections are supplied with cold water from the fountains within the palenque); and wet barriers along the entire perimeter, consisting of a combination of water curtains and micronizers.

Experimental program

An experimental program was designed to evaluate the effectiveness of the suggested techniques, and to permit the validation of theoretical models. The experimental program was divided into two main phases.

Phase I (summer of 1989) evaluated natural air cooling techniques. Phase II (summer of 1990) evaluated the behavior of the Rotunda. Various subsystems were also re-sized and their operational strategies redesigned. An adaptive–predictive automatic control system was developed to decide which subsystem should operate and at what intensity depending on outdoor conditions and those in the Rotunda.

Phase I: Cooling techniques Various means of achieving cooling strategies used at the Expo are listed in Table 29.1.

Table 29.1

Strategies	Means
1. Solar radiation control	Covering (shading direct and diffuse solar radiation)
2. Heat avoidance	Reduction of infiltration
3. Natural cooling	
Ground cooling	Running water beneath the pavement (Fig. 29.1)
Envelope cooling	Cooling of the covering by sprinkling
Air cooling	Cascades (Fig. 29.1)
	Evaporative cooling

Cooling strategies and actions Evaporative cooling of room air was achieved employing the techniques described below.

● *Air conditioning unit*

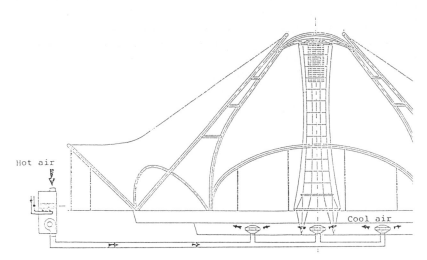

Fig. 29.1   Air conditioning unit, cool pavement and cascades

Concept: forced evaporative cooling

Fan-driven air passes through a permanently humid packing fill. At certain times of the day, the air is post-cooled in the underground ducting. To assure a suitable temperature in the material surrounding the duct, it is ventilated during the night, taking advantage of the lower air temperature.

● *Micronizers in trees (Fig. 29.2)*

Concept: droplet evaporation by natural convection of air

Nozzles placed in the foliage of trees create an artificial fog by injecting water at high pressure through minute orifices. The small droplets, having a volume median diameter (VMD) of around $20\,\mu$m, evaporate upon release into the surrounding hot air which becomes cooler. Since the cool air is heavier than the hot hair, a continuous descending flow of cool air is obtained.

● *Micronizers in towers*

Concept: droplet evaporation by fan-forced convection of air

Nozzles are distributed along the tower in different sections. Evaporation of the droplets cools the air blown by a fan placed on top of the tower, thus making it sink. Fresh air then arrives at the bottom of the tower and cools the Rotunda. The design variables and the control strategy were carefully selected to maximize the cooling capacity while protecting visitors from non-evaporated water droplets.

Fig. 29.2   Micronizers in trees

● *Micronizers in peripheral rings and towers*

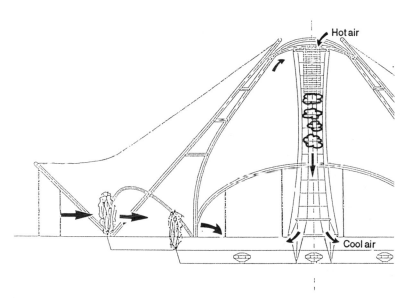

Fig. 29.3   Peripheral rings

Concept: droplet evaporation (air movement by forced convection driven by wind)

The only effective way to prevent the wind from neutralizing the air-cooling measures of air is to place a barrier which pre-cools the air before it enters an occupied area. The barriers are based on the evaporative cooling of the air passing through a micronizer bank.

Results of Phase I   A total of 41 sensors was located in the Rotunda plus five in the weather station, with a sampling period of one minute, and averaging and recording every 10 minutes. In addition, air temperature, relative humidity, global solar radiation on a horizontal plane, wind velocity and direction were measured at the weather station.

Figure 29.4 shows the temperatures of the covering at the least favorable (south-west) facing plane on 16 August 1990 with sprinkling and on 17 August without sprinkling along with outdoor air temperatures. The temperature of the surface covering decreases approximately 6°C with sprinkling.

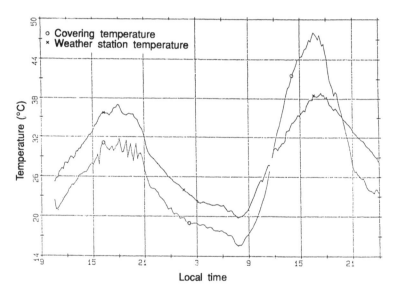

Fig. 29.4   Temperature at the plane facing south west of the covering compared with outside temperature

Group A

- Cooling the covering with sprinklers
- Cooling the air with micronizers in trees
- Operation of the wet barrier when necessary

Figures 29.5 and 29.6 show the air temperature and the relative humidity respectively at different heights of the Rotunda on 14 August 1990, using the subsystems listed in Group A (see Phase II below). The control set point was established to maintain 65% average relative humidity at heights between 0.5 m and 1 m from the ground.

Phase II: Comfort assessment   To obtain a given level of comfort in outdoor spaces, there are a total of five variables which can be adjusted:

First day: 11 August 1990

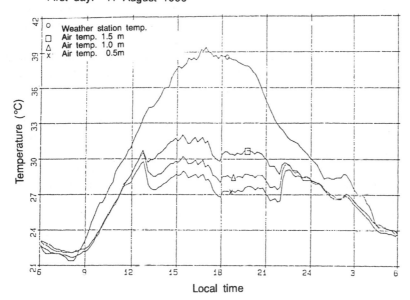

Fig. 29.5 Air temperature at different heights inside the Rotunda for Group A

First day: 11 August 1990

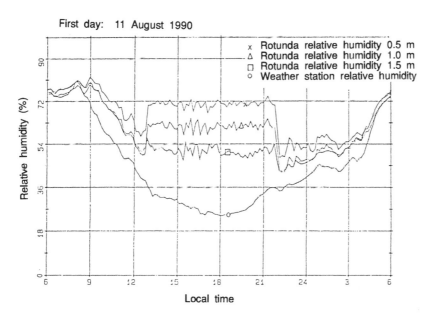

Fig. 29.6 Relative humidity at different heights inside the Rotunda for Group A

solar radiation, surface temperature, air temperature, air velocity, and relative humidity. The number of variables to be manipulated in any given situation and the degree of manipulation depend on the characteristics of the area to be treated (geometry, dimensions, level of confinement), the effectiveness and cost of appropriate techniques and on aesthetics. Furthermore, the level of comfort required in each space depends on the activity carried out by its occupants (in a walkway, rest area, restaurant, shopping center), and the length of time people remain there.

To evaluate the impact of these variables on comfort level, isocomfort graphs were developed. Isocomfort graphs show comfort level in terms of grams of sweat per hour. In the case of the Rotunda, surface temperature of the covering, air temperature, and air velocity were analyzed simultaneously.

Relative humidity is an implicit variable, since the efficiency of evaporative cooling depends directly on the relative humidity of the ambient air.

After preliminary calculations, cooling the pavement would be ineffective in reducing air temperature. Likewise, vertical wall cooling was unsatisfactory because the cascades were small and their radiant effect upon the occupants negligible.

Figure 29.7 shows the resulting isocomfort graph for a sweat rate of 60 g/h (MET = 1) and outside design conditions (38°C, 30% relative humidity), for various air movement velocities within the pavilion.

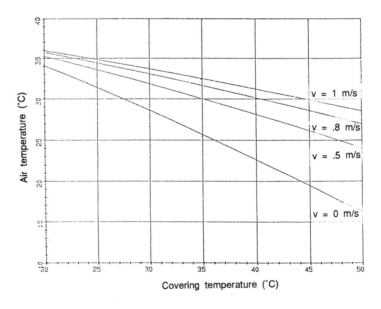

Fig. 29.7   Computed isocomfort graph for sweat at a rate of 60 g/h

Table 29.2

Inside air temperature (°C)	Covering temperature (°C)	Inside air temperature (°C)	Air velocity (m/s)
30	27	26.0	0.0
26	35	30.0	0.5
20	44	32.5	1.0

This figure reveals that, for zero air velocity, the same sensation of comfort is obtained with the combinations shown in Table 29.2.

Similarly, to achieve the same sensation of comfort for a covering temperature of 24°C, the following considerations are possible. Thus considering the temperature of the covering without treatment reached values in the region of 48°C (see Fig. 29.4), sprinking was absolutely essential.

Figure 29.8 gives the experimental values for the air and covering temperatures on 11, 12 and 16 August 1990 from 12:00 to 20:00, local time for Group A, with no appreciable movement of air. The comfort curves for sweat rates of 30 g/h, 60 g/h and 90 g/h (MET = 1) are also shown.

Figure 29.9 shows the experimental values for Group B for the air and covering temperatures from 25 August through 28 August 1990, from 12:00 to 20:00 local time, for an air velocity within the zone of approximately 0.5 m/s. The comfort curves for the sweat rate of 30 g/h, 60 g/h and 90 g/h (MET = 1) are also shown.

On the days represented in Figs. 29.8 and 29.9, the outdoor ambient temperature ranged from 36 to 40°C. In no instance does the sweat rate exceed 90 g/h. It is known that sweat rates below this level provide acceptable comfort conditions (Givoni, personal communication) so that the cooling techniques adopted were adequate.

28.1.4 Modeling and simulation

Although the analysis of the Rotunda indicated what was happening, why it happened was not evident. In addition, it was unclear which subsystems worked correctly and which were incorrect, and why; which design variables were primary in each subsystem and which secondary; or how the behavior of each subsystem could be improved and what the optimum performance point was. In short, experimentation provided insufficient information for designing other systems or for design guidelines. An inductive procedure was adopted illustrated by the following flow diagram:

Group A

- Cooling the covering with sprinklers
- Cooling the air with micronizers in trees
- Operation of the wet barrier when necessary

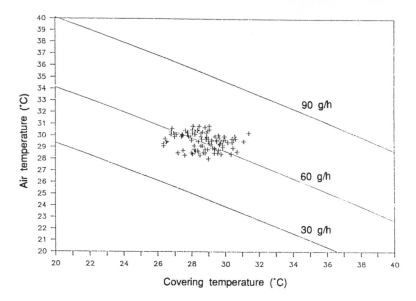

Fig. 29.8   Experimental results for Group A

Group B

- Cooling the covering with sprinklers
- Cooling the air with:
  — air handling units
  — micronizers in trees as support elements
- Operation of the wet barrier when necessary

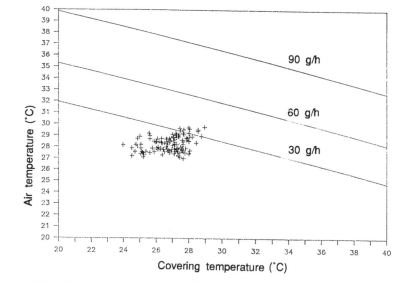

Fig. 29.9   Experimental results for Group B

MODELING → VALIDATION ← EXPERIMENTS
        ↓
SIMULATION (sensitivity analyses)

   For each of the subsystems used in the Rotunda, theoretical models were constructed, and a computer program capable of integrating the individual models and establishing the thermal and air flow interactions between them was developed. The subsystems modeled were:

- pavement cooling
- underground duct
- covering
- covering with controlled sprinkler
- cooling tower
- wet barrier formed by micronizers
- air-handling unit with latent cooling.

In addition, models were constructed for:

- other coverings
- covering with continuous water film
- wet barrier formed by water curtains
- air conditioning units with sensible and latent cooling sections
- ponds (shaded/not shaded; with or without water sprays or jets) used as a source of cool water for the air-conditioning units, etc.

The computer program S3PAS was used to link the models mentioned above. It was designed by the Càtedra de Termotecnia of the Seville University School of Engineering for CIEMAT-IER. S3PAS was used to model the air-flow exchanges between the air in the conditioned area and the adjacent untreated space. The program served as a framework not only for the system models developed in this work, but also for other subsystems such as conventional pavements or cascades. The program permitted a realistic and comprehensive model of the Rotunda as a whole to be developed. The program allowed each subsystem to be analyzed separately and applied to other areas with different levels of confinement and size.

The entire modeling, validation, and simulation procedure was conducted in 1989 and early 1990. The cooling tower provides a good example of the steps taken. It was modeled using the following steps:

- Evaporation algorithm for a single water droplet in the air.
- Establishment of droplet size distribution produced by the fog generators (micronizers).
- Algorithms for simultaneous heat and mass transfer, which occurs when air flow and fog (droplets of different sizes) come into contact in the tower.
- Design of the experiment (selection of the different variables).
- Experimentation (summer 1989).
- Qualitative analysis of the results.
- Validation
- Sensitivity analysis of:
  — air flow rate (m^3/h)
  — volume median diameter of small water droplets sprayed from micronizers (better-quality micronizers produce a lower droplet diameter)

— water flow rate (l/m^3 of air)
— location of the micronizers within the tower
— height of the tower (distance between the base and the micronizers)
— outside conditions (ambient temperature and relative humidity)
— control strategy to maximize the cooling capacity while protecting visitors from non-evaporated water droplets.

29.1.5   Conclusions

It is possible to condition an outdoor space at low cost using natural cooling techniques. These techniques are not only compatible with the functional and aesthetic criteria applied to the design of the space, but are also ecologically sound. Their effectiveness has been demonstrated to the many million visitors of the Expo in Seville.

It is important to point out that the comfort requirements for an outdoor space is less strict than for an interior space because

- the time spent outdoors is shorter
- lower surface temperatures and higher air velocity are permitted
- visual and acoustic criteria are less stringent.

As a result of the modeling work, the cooled pavement was discarded because it was inefficient in shaded areas. Also, the underground ducts were excluded because they would have involved altering major infrastructure.

The performance of subsystems for conditioning outdoor spaces can vary substantially with system design. Indeed, some systems may prove completely ineffective if insufficient attention is paid to design. Each subsystem should be chosen with the ultimate comfort objective in mind and a comparison with other subsystems made.

29.2   OFFICE BUILDING IN GIARRE, SICILY

29.2.1   Strategy: heat extraction through envelope cooling

Forced ventilation to cool the envelope at night, an effective option for warm climates with wide daily temperature extremes, was used for an office building in Giarre, Sicily. During summer months, cool night air passes through hollow-core ceilings prior to entering the building interior. The lower radiant temperature of the ceilings improves thermal comfort in the office, to such an extent that no air conditioning is required.

29.2.2 Building characteristics

The hollow-core ceilings serve two purposes: cooling during summer and heating during winter. In summer, night air is circulated at a rate of eight air changes per hour. In winter, heat from the solar collectors on the southern facade is used to charge the ceilings, which then function as heat storage.

29.2.3 Experimental results

Two similar rooms ($300 \, \text{m}^3$ each) located in the top floor, one cooled by night ventilation and the second used as a control, were monitored during the last week of July 1989. Night cooling was provided by a small fan (50 W), activated on an hourly basis from 20:00 in the evening to 8:00 am. During the day, an air conditioning system ensured the required room temperatures. The daily external temperature variation

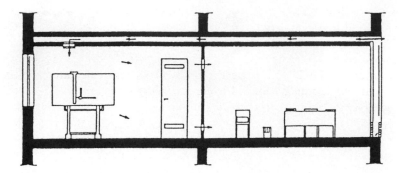

Fig. 29.10 Cross section of the offices cooled by forced ventilation through hollow-core ceilings

for the week was in the range of 6–10°C, which is lower than the mean for July (10.8°C). In Fig. 29.11, the ceiling temperatures in the rooms examined are plotted. The vented ceiling is 0.5 to 1.5°C cooler than the reference ceiling. Also, the internal air temperature (not shown) is slightly lower at the end of the night, but this difference rapidly disappears during the day.

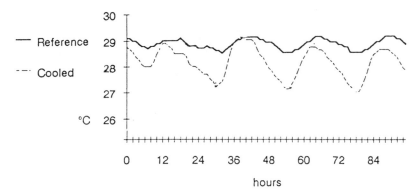

Fig. 29.11 Ceiling temperature measured in the reference and the cooled room from 27 to 30 July

29.2.4   Computer validation and simulations

The results of experiments on the building monitored were used to validate the computer model SMP that simulates the thermal behavior of the hollow-core ceiling using a two-dimensional finite difference method. For the simulations, the Test Reference Year of Foggia, a town in southern Italy, was used because it has daily air temperature variations of 12.7 K during the summer months, similar to the location near the test building. Figure 29.12 presents a comparison between measured and calculated temperatures of air flowing in the channels. The calculated values coincide with the measured data (note the truncated scale); there is a maximum difference of 0.7 K. The energy required for air conditioning the office room was calculated for the cooled and reference rooms. Envelope cooling saves about 20% of the total energy required to cool the building.

Another simulation was made under the assumption that the ceiling is cooled during night hours as in the case just described, but that during the day, when the air conditioning is activated, the external air is pre-cooled by passing through the ceiling. The energy saving with this option is 32%. An analysis was also made of the ceiling temperatures with and without night cooling during July (see Fig. 29.13). Thus, during the day, the ceiling is warmed and most of the heat is released during the night through forced ventilation.

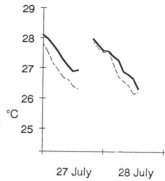

Fig. 29.12 Comparison between measured calculated values of the ceiling outlet air temperature

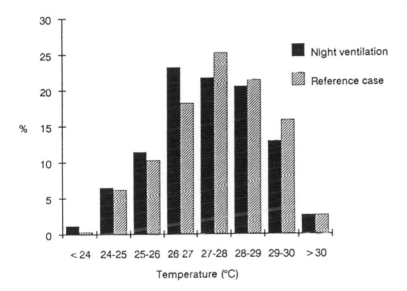

Fig. 29.13 Frequency distribution of ceiling temperatures during daytime, with and without night cooling

29.2.5 Conclusions

For this climate and building, night flushing through the chaneled ceiling improved thermal comfort sufficiently to preclude conventional air conditioning. Night cooling is, of course, highly dependent on the mean daily temperature variation during the summer. For day–night temperature differences less than 12–13 K, the option is not recommended.

30 Analysis Tools

Passive cooling techniques are generally poorly handled in computer simulation models. Recently, however, an effort to enlarge the capabilities for modeling cooling has been made.

Table 30.1 summarizes options provided by five computer models used to evaluate the cooling of buildings discussed in this sourcebook.

30.1 SMP

Language and operating system Quickbasic, MS-DOS
Not available

Capabilities SMP is a simulation model for hourly energy analysis in multizone buildings. Passive heating features, such as Trombe walls, sunspaces and cooling options, such as radiant ceilings, hollow-core slabs and natural ventilation (in a simplified way) can be analyzed. The program also allows calculation of the level of thermal comfort for occupants using Fanger equations.

Non steady-state heat transfer through the envelope is solved with an explicit forward finite difference method. As the tool has been conceived mainly for residential buildings, few options are considered for heating and cooling equipment. The program has been validated using measured data of test cells and real buildings within different IEA Tasks.

For more information, write to:

CNR-IEREN
Via C. Rampolla 8
I 90142 Palermo
Italy

Table 30.1 Capabilities of analysis tools

Passive cooling strategies		Simulation models				
		DOE	SERI-ES	SMP	TRN-SYS	S3-PAS
Solar radiation control						
Window protection	Movable devices				*	*
	Permanent devices		*	*	*	*
Special glazing						
Building protection	Building orientation	*	*	*	*	*
	Earth protection	*	†	†	†	*
	Outside vegetation protection			†	†	†
Environment protection						*
Heat avoidance						
Reduction of transmission gains	External surface treatment	*	*	*	†	*
	Insulation	*	*	*	†	*
	Thermal inertia	*	*	*	†	*
Reduction of infiltration		*	*	*	†	*
Hierarchical layout of spaces		*	*	*	†	*
Internal gains reduction						
Reductions of lighting gains		*	*	*	†	*
Reductions of casual gains		*	*	*	†	*
Natural cooling						
Natural ventilation	Temperature gradient effect	*		†	†	*
	Wind pressure effect					
	Outside principles				†	*
Air cooling	Evaporative cooling				†	†
	Underground air ducts				†	†
Envelope cooling	Night-time radiative cooling				†	*
	Convective cooling	*	*	*	*	*
Internal mass cooling	Solar chimneys		*	*	†	
	Night flushing	†	†	*	†	*
Physiological cooling	Cross ventilation					
	Radiant cooling			*	*	*
	Air movement			*		

*Fully capable
†Capable with some tricks
Blank: incapable

30.2 S3PAS

Language and operating system Fortran 77/VMS
Not available

Capabilities S3PAS is a tool for building analysis and hourly tempera-ture simulation. Its modularity and the coupling protocols included in it permit easy inclusion of new elements, systems or strategies by the user.

One-dimensional conduction in walls is modeled by the Z-transfer function method. Ground coupled structures are considered combining a harmonic response to outdoor excitations and the Z-transfer function method for indoor excitations. Glazing is modeled in steady state for each time step. The dependence of its optical properties with the incidence angle of beam radiation is considered. Solar shading of both remote and facade obstructions are considered, with diffuse and long-wave radiation shading by them.

Indoor coupling includes short-wave radiation redistribution and long-wave radiant exchange, both modeled using the Walton method.

Interzone air movement is simulated by a zone pressure network, including air flow through cracks and large openings; and the simulation is compatible with simpler air change simulations.

Additional features include:

- Scheduling of skylines, facade shading devices, glazing, internal gains, forced ventilation, ideal conditioning equipment operation, adjacent space boundary conditions, etc.
- Materials data base
- Presimulation performance outputs.

S3PAS was used for the development and modeling of climate control of outdoor spaces at the Expo 1992 Seville, Spain, including thermal comfort, cool pavements, ponds, irrigation coverings, and evaporative and mixed air cooling techniques.

31 Conclusions

Due to increasing demand for a better indoor air climate in hot countries, power requirements for cooling have grown to such an extent that the development of alternative, energy-saving cooling methods is essential. The Expo experiment in Seville represented a unique opportunity to develop knowledge in this comparatively new field. For this, a new cooling simulation tool, S3PAS, was developed. This computer program is the only one available for simulating the majority of cooling strategies with reasonable accuracy.

An acceptable comfort level could be achieved by adjusting the five main variables:

- solar radiation
- surface temperature
- air temperature
- air velocity
- relative humidity.

Several strategies were investigated in Seville, of which the following proved to be most effective:

- Ventilation of interior spaces, using controlled air velocity,
- Evaporative cooling by means of a simple air conditioning unit and micronizers to control relative humidity,
- Intensive use of shading devices such as canvas covered streets and vegetation, to control solar radiation,
- Reduction of infiltration gains through careful design of the covered spaces to limit air temperature rise after cooling,
- Cooling of the envelope by sprinklers (Expo) and forced ventilation (Sicily).

A combination of active and passive methods promises greatest success in reducing energy consumption. Individual strategies used in isolation are generally less effective. Nevertheless, in Sicily, envelope cooling by means of forced ventilation proved capable of saving up to 32% of the energy normally required for cooling an office building.

Before new design tools are developed, the available body of knowledge on cooling will need systematic examination. The principles for designing such systems are known but there is a clear lack of quantitative data for predicting performance and sizing systems.

32 Recommended Reading

Agence Française pour le Maîtrise de l'Energie, *Bioclimatisme en Zone Tropicale*, Groupe de Recherche et d'Echanges Technologiques (GRET), CIAT-DACA, Paris, 1985.

This book is oriented towards architects and designers working in hot climates. It explains the basics of building physics and comfort parameters, suggesting which data to gather before designing. Comfort diagrams, Mahoney tables, and other manual tools are explained. Finally, various architectural responses to cooling needs are given with case studies illustrating the use of tools presented. A practical text, it is useful and even offers a complete bibliography of sources printed through 1985.

Aranovitch, E., de Oliveira Fernandes, E., Steemers, T.C., *Workshop on Passive Cooling*, Commission of the European Communities, Brussels, Luxembourg, 1990.

This collection of papers, presented at ISPRA in April 1990, offers the latest developments in the cooling field. Questions are answered on various topics such as: comfort, microclimate, solar control techniques, heat attenuation, ventilation and air circulation, natural cooling techniques, monitoring in cooling, design support tools, etc. Research on all these aspects of cooling is synthesized and presented for the reader.

Baker, N.V. *et al.*, *Passive and Low Energy Building Design for Tropical Islands*, Commonwealth Secretariat, London, 1987.

The general problems of building cooling are addressed in this book. It explains in detail different concepts and various means of achieving thermal comfort. Although the title mentions tropical islands, the book contains general information which applies to all hot climates. A manual method for evaluating passive cooling offers the designer a quick way to assess the cooling performance of any building.

Bellesteros, A., Cabeza Lainez, J.M., Lopez de Asain, J., Perez de Lama Halcon, J., *Estudio Biocimatico*, Sociedad Estatal para la Exposicion Universal Sevilla, Sevilla, 1987.

This short booklet offers a detailed overview of the cooling strategies used for the 1992 World Expo in Seville and other outdoor spaces. It offers a wide range of shading solutions and a thorough analysis of evaporative cooling methods. As a case study, this document is unique in providing results for probably the largest experiment ever conducted on the cooling problem.

B. Meerssemen, and A. De Herde, *Cooling Strategies and Recommendations*, 1992.

This short leaflet presents the cooling strategies explained in Chapter 28, with practical recommendations for architects and building designers depending on the type of building (office, hotel, school, health, or sports), on climate (Oslo, Brussels, Zürich, Rome and Phoenix), on time of day and on the building's physical properties (permeability and internal gains). It clearly states which of the strategies described will offer an acceptable comfort level.

PART 6

ATRIA

CONTRIBUTORS

**Part 6 Editor and
Chapters 33, 34, 37 and 39**
Anne Grete Hestnes
*Norwegian Institute of
Technology
Trondheim
Norway*

Chapters 35 and 36
Óyvind Aschehoug
*Norwegian Institute of
Technology
Trondheim
Norway*

Chapters 35 and 36
Ida Bryn
*SINTEF Applied
Thermodynamics/HVAC
Trondheim
Norway*

Chapters 35 and 36
Lars Engström
*Royal Institute of Technology
Stockholm
Sweden*

Chapter 38
Hans Erhorn
*Fraunhofer Institute for Building
Physics
Stuttgart
Germany*

Chapters 35 and 36
Mauritz Glaumann
*National Institute for Building
Research
Gävle
Sweden*

Chapters 34-37
Harry Gordon
*Burt Hill Kosar Rittelman
Associates
Washington DC
USA*

Chapters 35 and 36
Mir-Ghaffoor Hejazi-Hashemi
*PI-Consulting Ltd
Vantaa
Finland*

Chapters 35 and 36
Pierre Jaboyedoff
*Sorane SA
Lausanne
Switzerland*

Chapter 38
Ron Kammerud
*Lawrence Berkeley Laboratories
Berkeley, California
USA*

Chapters 34, 35, 36 and 40
Günter Löhnert
*IBUS GBH
Berlin
Germany*

Chapters 35 and 36
Andrew Seager
*Databuild Ltd
Birmingham
UK*

33 Introduction

Atria have been a design element in buildings for centuries and are today commonly found in commercial structures throughout the world. Energy conservation is seldom a primary reason for using an atrium in a building design, but other reasons can strongly influence the energy use characteristics of the atrium and of the adjacent building spaces. Among the reasons for including an atrium in a building design are to:

• create a dramatic entry or central space

- increase the amenity for the building users
- provide more perimeter space, and
- facilitate circulation.

Numerous examples show that an atrium can dramatically affect energy consumption. Much can be learned by studying these buildings, and the insights gains can be used to design more energy-efficient atrium buildings.

Part 6 emphasizes glazed atria as a means of saving energy for the building as a whole.

In Chapter 34 atria are classified in five generic types: core, integrated, linear, attached, and envelope atria. For each of these types, the energy strategies for heating, cooling, and daylighting are considered. Parametric studies were carried out on some of these atria types, for the climates of Oslo (cold), Brussels (maritime), Zürich (central European), and Rome (warm). For more detailed studies, selected US climates were also used.

33.1   CASE STUDIES

The design insights are based on experiences gained with actual buildings where the atrium was planned to reduce energy consumption. Most of the work was done on the eight atrium case studies described in Chapter 35. These buildings have been extensively monitored for energy consumption and comfort. Some have also been studied for daylight performance, costs, and/or user responses, while others were studied for selected topics with detailed parametric models. Several examples illustrate the range of applications of atria, and are described in brief summaries in Chapter 36.

- PI-Group Head Office (SF)
- Wasa City (S) (shopping center/dwellings)
- Gateway II (UK) (offices)
- Alta Day Care Center (N)
- Neuchâtel University (CH) (offices/classrooms)
- Technical University (N) (offices/laboratories)
- Bodbetjänten (S) (offices/dwellings)
- Tegut (D) (offices)

33.2   CONTENTS

It is possible to skip Chapters 34 and 35 to read Chapter 37, which summarizes observations that apply to individual projects and describes more general lessons learned.

The analysis tools most commonly used to simulate atrium buildings and the general problems associated with simulating such buildings are described in Chapter 38. Chapter 40 describes a few books recommended to those studying atrium buildings.

34 Typology

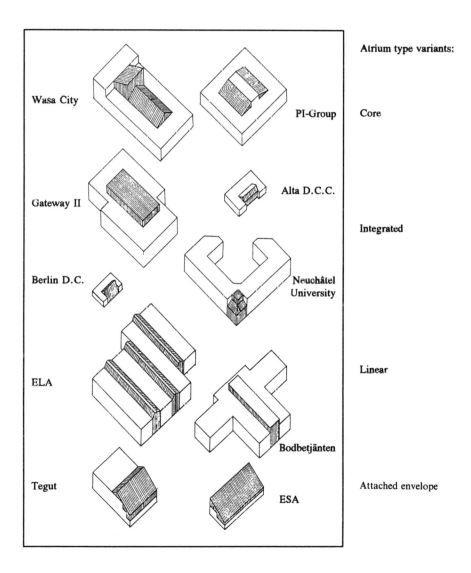

Wasa City

PI-Group

Gateway II

Alta D.C.C.

Berlin D.C.

Neuchâtel University

ELA

Tegut

Bodbetjänten

ESA

Atrium type variants:

Core

Integrated

Linear

Attached envelope

Chapter 34 is divided into three sections:

- Section 34.1, Types of atria, describes how the various atrium configurations are classified in five generic types.
- Section 34.2, Energy strategies, describes how the atria are classified according to whether they are used for heating, cooling, or daylighting.
- Section 34.3, Definitions, describes the atria specific terms used in this part of the sourcebook.

34.1 TYPES OF ATRIA

34.1.1 Core atrium

This is the classic atrium type providing a glazed courtyard in the center of the building surrounded by adjacent spaces on all sides. The external envelope of the atrium is limited to the area of the roof glazing.

Examples: PI-Group Head Office, Wasa City, Gateway II, St Monika.

34.1.2 Integrated atrium

An integrated atrium is a glazed space that is positioned in the building such that only one side faces the exterior. It may or may not have a glazed roof.

Examples: Alta Day Care Center, Neuchâtel University, Berlin Day Care Center, Comstock Building.

34.1.3 Linear atrium

The linear atrium covers an open space between two parallel building blocks ending with glazed gables on both sides.

Examples: Technical University, Bodbetjänten, Züblin Building, Dravolle University, Skärholmen.

34.1.4 Attached atrium

The attached atrium is a glazed space added to the external wall of the building envelope.

Example: Tegut Building.

34.1.5 Envelope atrium

The envelope atrium is characterized by an entirely enclosed building covered by glass representing a 'house-in-house' concept. The large

external envelope glazing may include one facade of the building.
Example: ESA Building.

34.2 ENERGY STRATEGIES

Atria can be used to heat, cool, and/or provide daylight to a building.

34.2.1 Heating

An atrium acts as a buffer reducing transmission losses from adjacent spaces to the ambient and may also provide heat to adjacent spaces. An atrium displaces auxiliary heating by solar gain transfer from atrium to the adjacent spaces. Thus, the predominant orientation of the atrium aperture should be south, and the glazing should be vertical (to reduce the risk of overheating in summer). Collected solar radiation must be stored in the interior mass of building components exposed directly to the sun in winter. Night-time heat losses are reduced by using good quality thermal materials in the envelope glazing and in the walls and windows separating the atrium from the rest of the building.

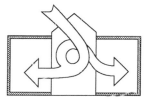

34.2.2 Cooling

An atrium can induce natural ventilation and avoid undesirable solar gains. Natural ventilation can be facilitated by a vertical stack effect and by proper placement of air inlets and outlets. Inlets should be placed at the bottom of the atrium (and/or induced cross circulation should be included), and sufficient exhaust air vents should be placed at the top. Night-time convective cooling of building mass structure can be achieved by cross ventilation, with air passing from the ambient through the adjacent spaces and out via the atrium space.

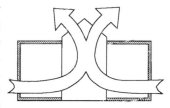

34.2.3 Daylighting

An atrium can be used to provide additional light to the adjacent spaces. The key issues are daylight availability, distribution, and utilization. The atrium glazing reduces the amount of available daylight inside, but as a consequence of the buffer effect of the glazing, the window area in the intermediate boundary can be increased without penalty of higher heating energy consumption. Consequently, more daylight may be available in the adjacent spaces.

The amount of daylight in adjacent spaces is determined by the overall design and by the properties of the walls and windows separating the atrium and the adjacent spaces.

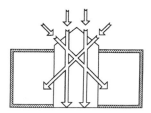

Atrium dimensions (height, length, width), determine the potential daylight aperture, and the size and position of windows in the intermediate boundary, as well as the reflectivity of the walls themselves, determine the amount of daylight penetrating into the adjacent spaces.

34.3 DEFINITIONS

34.3.1 Building features

An atrium is defined as a glazed space, which is thermally separated from adjacent spaces, and which is often not, or only partially, heated.

Adjacent space is defined as the buildings adjacent to the atrium.

The exterior envelope is the part of the atrium envelope that faces the ambient. It can be totally glazed or partly opaque.

The intermediate boundary is the part of the atrium envelope that faces the adjacent spaces. It can be glazed, opaque, and/or partially open.

34.3.2 Atrium functions

Circulation/transitory describes short-term functions where the occupants do not remain in the atrium. For example, the atrium may primarily be used for circulation. A room temperature of 10–14°C is adequate for this purpose.

Active use describes functions where the occupants are moving, such as in a sports hall, an exhibition space, or a hotel lobby. A room temperature of 12–18°C is acceptable for such functions.

Sedentary use describes functions where the occupants are seated for extended periods, such as in a restaurant or an office. A room temperature of 20°C is usually required for this purpose.

Plant growth describes atrium use for growing and displaying plants. A minimum of 5°C is usually required, although this varies with the species of plant.

A conditioned atrium relies on conventional auxiliary means to heat and/or cool it. The atrium may be fully conditioned, to normal temperature and humidity requirements, or it may be tempered to prevent it from being above or below an established temperature/humidity range.

34.3.3 Atrium conditioning

A free floating atrium is permitted to float in temperature and humidity in response to the conditions in the ambient and in the adjacent spaces and in response to any casual internal gains in the atrium itself.

35 Case Studies

The case studies in Chapter 35 are buildings that have been extensively monitored for energy consumption and comfort. Some of the buildings have also been studied for daylight performance, costs, and/or user responses, and some have been used for detailed parametric studies of selected features. The design insights described and the conclusions drawn in later chapters are primarily based on the result of this work.

Chapter 36, Examples, includes short summaries of buildings that have been studied because they give insight into atria features. These buildings have not been the subject of comprehensive studies, however.

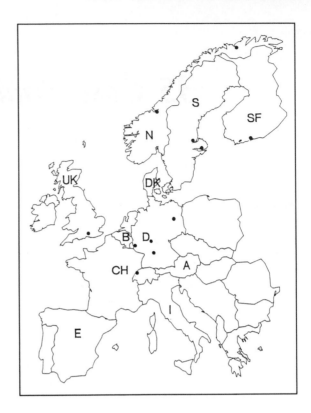

A list of the case studies and examples discussed in these two chapters follows:

35. *Case studies*

1.	PI-Group Headquarters	(Finland)
2.	Wasa City	(Sweden)
3.	Gateway II	(UK)
4.	Alta Day Care Center	(Norway)
5.	Neuchâtel University — NUNI	(Switzerland)
6.	Technical University — ELA	(Norway)
7.	Bodbetjänten	(Sweden)
8.	Tegut	(Germany)

36. *Examples*

9.	St Monika	(Germany)
10.	Berlin Day Care Center	(Germany)
11.	Comstock	(USA)
12.	Züblin	(Germany)
13.	Dragvoll University	(Norway)
14.	Skärholmen	(Sweden)
15.	ESA Building	(Germany)

ATRIUM FEATURES	NAME	PI Head Office	Wasa-City	Gateway II	St. Monika	Alta Day Care C.	Neuchâtel	Berlin Day Care C.	Comstock	ELA	Bodbetjänten	Züblin	Dragvoll	Tegut			ESA		
		CORE				INTEGRATED				LINEAR				ATTACHED			ENVELOPE		
Country		SF	S	UK	D	N	CH	D	US	N	S	D	N	D			D		
Climate																			
Cold/Northern		●	●			●				●	●								
Temperate Continental					○		●	○				○	○	●			○		
Temperate Maritime				●					○										
Function																			
Circulation/Transitory		●	●	●			●		○	●	●	○	○				○		
Active Use			●			●		○			●			●			○		
Sedentary Use			●		○					●	●			●			○		
Energy Strategy																			
Heating		●	●	●	○	●	●	○	○	●	●	○		●			○		
Cooling			●				●		○										
Daylighting									○				○						
Link to Adjacent Space																			
Fully or Partly Open			●		○														
Operable Link		●	●	●		●		○		●	●		○	●			○		
Fully Separated							●			●		○							
Conditioning																			
Free Floating						●	●	○				○							
Tempered		●		●						●	●		○	●			○		
Fully Heated/Cooled			●		○				○										
Building Ventilation																			
Independent of Atrium		●	●		○		●	○		●	●	○		●					
Intake via Atrium						●					●			●			○		
Exhaust to Atrium									○				○						

● Advanced Case Study
○ Basic Case Study

Table 35.1 Classification of the examples

35.1   PI-GROUP HEADQUARTERS

Building type: Office
Location: Vantaa, Finland
Latitude: 60°N
Atrium function: Circulation
Atrium heated to: 17°C
Occupancy date: 1985
Floor area: m²
● Gross: 10 180
● Heated: 9 870
● Atria: 730

Client: The PI-Group
Architect: Yrjö Mansnerus
                Kaupunkisuunnitt. Ltd
Energy consultant, service engineer,
and monitoring:
                   PI-Consulting Ltd

35.1.1   Summary

This office building in Finland has two stories of office space which are daylit through two central (core) atria in the interior zone. Both atria are glazed to reduce the heat loss of the building and to increase the occupancy of the central courtyards.

The thermal behavior of the glazed atria and the energy performance of the building were evaluated by long-term measurements, the amenity value was evaluated by interviewing the building users and owners, and the building cost was evaluated by using actual construction costs. The energy performance of the building compares well with that of other low-energy buildings in Finland, and the building costs are lower than those of typical office buildings. The overall performance of the building is found to be satisfactory both by the building users and owners.

35.1.2   Introduction

Finnish building regulations require daylighting of working space. Light wells are architectural solutions for daylighting the interior of deep plan buildings. New building technologies and materials, together with concerns about the energy efficiency of buildings, have resulted in the use of glazed light wells for the purpose of reducing the heat

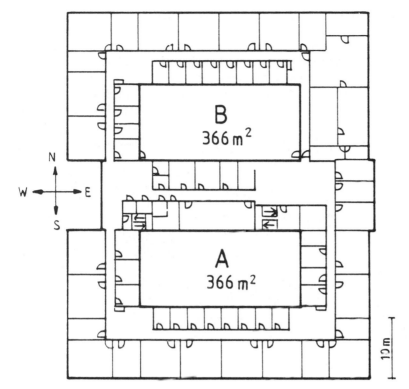

Fig. 35.1 Floor plan

Climate data (annual):

Degree days (20°C):	5330
Global radiation:	960 kWh/m^2
Average temperature:	+5.5°C

Fig. 35.2 The glazing of atrium A

Fig. 35.3 Interior view of atrium A

loss of light well envelopes and increasing the potential occupancy of courtyards.

The PI-Group planned its new head office in 1983. To maximize the use of the square site and to accommodate the regulation requirement of daylight in all offices, a design with two symmetric light wells in two centers of a deep plan building was chosen. The glazing of the light wells required special permission because the daylighting and fire safety regulations did not consider the atria as open light wells.

35.1.3 Building description

Building form and construction
This three-story building is 60.8 m long, 53.6 m wide and 11.4 m high. Two stories of office space are wrapped around two atria. A bookstore, a supermarket, and a restaurant occupy three corners of the building on the ground floor. The fourth corner is an unheated parking space.

U-values:	W/m^2 K
● Floor	0.36
● Ceiling	0.25
● Wall	0.30
● Window	1.90
● Skylight	1.85

The skylights face south in one atrium (A) and north in the other (B), and are constructed from three-pane Makrolon panels (60 mm × 88 mm), supported on glue-laminated timber beams inclined at 17°. In addition, the atria roof gables are glazed with vertical triple glazed windows, which are used for summer ventilation and smoke control. These windows are motorized and are controlled automatically by thermostats and smoke indicators. Atrium A is 13 m high, with one entrance from the outside and one from the office corridors. Atrium B is 9 m high, with no entrance from outside, but with two entrances from the office corridors.

Section A-A

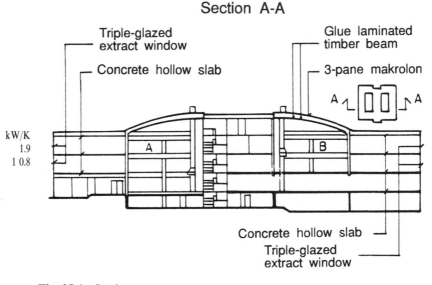

Envelope heat loss:	kW/K
● Transmission	1.9
● Ventilation	1 0.8

Fig. 35.4   Section

The intermediate boundaries of the atria are uninsulated walls with single-glazed windows, openable from the adjacent offices. The supply and exhaust air ducts for the offices are placed in the atria along the facades and are connected to the offices through hollow core concrete slabs.

Building services
The building is connected to the local district heating network. The office space, as well as the space for commercial services in the corners, is heated and cooled by individual central air-conditioning systems.

The atria are heated by separate air-circulating units and the temperature in the atria are controlled by thermostats. In the summer the atria are naturally ventilated by openings which are controlled by separate thermostats. The air-circulating units are stopped in order to enlarge the thermal stratification and optimize the efficiency of the natural ventilation.

Glazing properties

Windows:
Triple-glazed, clear
● Daylight transmission:	68%
● Solar transmission:	68%

Skylights:
3-pane Makrolon Opal
● Daylight transmission:	68%
● Solar transmission:	68%

Installed capacity:	W/m²
● Space heating:	49
● Lighting	20
Design temperatures:	°C
● Offices:	20
● Atria	17

The offices are daylit, either from the atria or from the building perimeter. In addition, an indirect lighting system, which uses 150 W metal halide lamps, was chosen for high color rendition, high efficiency and long lifetime. Lights are controlled manually.

35.1.4 Results and conclusions

Energy consumption

Simulations performed with a computer program developed by the PI-Group show that free floating atria maintain temperatures 10–15°C above ambient by utilizing solar gains and heat exhausted from the adjacent spaces. This shortens the heating period both for the atria and for the building itself. As the atria actually are kept at a minimum temperature of 17°C, some heating energy is required, but the amount is relatively small.

Some differences can, however, be seen between the atria facing south and the atria facing north. As the angle of the sun in Helsinki is extremely low in the winter, the atrium facing north receives almost no sun, and the conditions remain relatively constant day and night. The atrium facing south, on the other hand, has a lower power demand during the daytime and a higher one at night. The higher night-time power demand is caused by the fact that this atrium is significantly larger than the other one and because it serves as the main circulation space, resulting in higher air change rates.

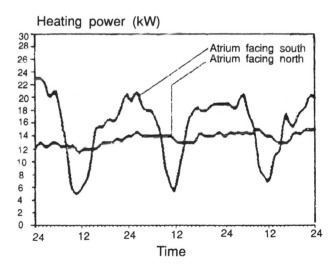

Annual energy use (measured February 1986–February 1987):

	kWh/m²
Excluding commercial spaces:	
● District heating:	97
● Electricity:	147
● Total:	244
Including commercial spaces:	
● District heating:	113
● Electricity:	169
● Total:	282
Comparison numbers:	
● Typical office building:	360
● Low energy office building:	210–280

Fig. 35.5 Heating power demand in the atria, measured on 5–7 February 1988

The measured results for the building's energy use as a whole show that it performs well compared to other low-energy buildings in

Finland. Energy consumption is reduced by about one third when compared to typical Finnish office buildings.

Thermal comfort

Summertime heat gains and overheating in the atria are reduced by using openings at the top and bottom. Measured results show that the location of the openings greatly influences the ventilation efficiency. The measured air change rates for cases with open vents both at top and bottom are seven to eight times larger than the air-change rates for cases with openings only at the top when the atria are naturally ventilated.

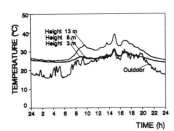

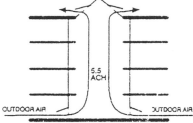

Fig. 35.6 Thermal stratification in atrium A, naturally ventilated, measured on 21 July 1988

Fig. 35.7 Air change rates in atrium A, naturally ventilated

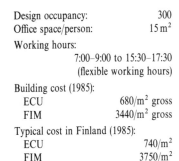

Design occupancy:	300
Office space/person:	15 m²
Working hours:	
	7:00–9:00 to 15:30–17:30
	(flexible working hours)
Building cost (1985):	
ECU	680/m² gross
FIM	3440/m² gross
Typical cost in Finland (1985):	
ECU	740/m²
FIM	3750/m²

Measured results also show that there is a high degree of thermal stratification in the atria when there is only natural ventilation. The air circulating units are stopped during the summer to obtain this effect, and the stratification then reaches 10°C. During the heating period the stratification is reduced to 2°C by using the air circulating units.

The high degree of stratification is an advantage in the summer if the cooler air layer is needed only in the occupied, lower zones of the atria, but it can be a problem if there also are occupied zones at the top. On the other hand, warmer air is needed in the occupied zones during the heating season. If the occupied zones are in the lower parts of the atria, the stratification is then a disadvantage. Energy efficient conditioning therefore requires efficient management of stratification both in the summer and in the winter.

Amenity value and building cost

The glazed atria offer opportunities for a number of activities that would have been impossible in open courtyards. In addition to serving as circulation space, the atria are used for social gatherings arranged by individuals and by the company.

The glazing costs are offset mainly by savings in floor area and volume of the office spaces, as the atria are used for circulation and for supply and exhaust air ducts. Savings in the construction materials of the intermediate boundaries are also significant. The total building cost compares well with the cost of typical office buildings in Finland.

35.1.5 References

35/1 PI-Consulting Ltd, *Atria in Office Buildings*, KTM-report D:130, Helsinki 1987, Government Printing Center (in Finnish).

35/2 PI-Consulting Ltd, Ekosolar Ltd, *Atrium Buildings*, KTM-report D:177, Helsinki 1989, Government Printing Center (in Finnish).

35/3 PI-Consulting Ltd, IEA Task XI, *Basic Case Study of the PI-Group Head Office*.

35/4 PI-Consulting Ltd, IEA Task XI, *Advanced Case Study of the PI-Group Head Office*.

Address for all publications:
PI-Consulting Ltd, Energy group, P.O. Box 31,
Myyrmäenraitti 2, SF-01601 Vantaa, Finland.

35.2 WASA CITY

Building type:	
Commercial/residential	
Location:	Gävle, Sweden
Latitude:	60°N
Occupancy date:	
New:	1964
Retrofit:	1987
Atrium function:	Circulation
Floor area:	
Heated:	16 000 m²
Atrium:	
● Ground floor:	380 m²
● First floor:	1070 m²
Cost (retrofit 1987):	
ECU	6 300 000
SKR	43 000 000

Client:	Wasa Insurance Company
Architect:	Thurfjell arkitektkontor
Contractor:	Heidenberg and Olofsson
Climate data:	
Degree days:	5050
Annual average temp.:	5.0°C
Global irradiation:	980 kWh/m²

35.2.1 Summary

Occupants' reactions to glazing over a courtyard were investigated along with the impact on daylight in adjacent spaces, and the heat balance of the glass roof. Occupants have clearly experienced a reduction in daylight and sunshine penetrating their flats. Some also complain about increased noise; however, most occupants react positively to the new 'winter garden'. They appreciate the possibility to relax 'outdoors' in the winter, to have spontaneous contact with their neighbors, and to escape shoveling snow, etc.

Measured and calculated daylight levels show a decrease of as much as 50% in the apartments compared to the levels prior to the glass construction. In addition, less sunshine penetrates the building, mainly because of a number of large, opaque shutters in the roof.

Measurements show how cloudiness and wind affect the heat balance of the roof. Simulations show that a triple glazed, heated atrium needs $120\,\mathrm{kWh/m^2}$ floor area for heating in southern Sweden and $220\,\mathrm{kWh/m^2}$ if it was located in northern Sweden. In the south this corresponds to additional energy consumption of 10% for the whole building.

35.2.2   Building description

Wasa City is a block in central Gävle with shops on the ground floor and flats plus a few offices on the upper floors. On the ground floor there is a small courtyard which opens into a larger courtyard on the first floor. There, entrances to maisonette flats are placed on the long sides of the courtyard.

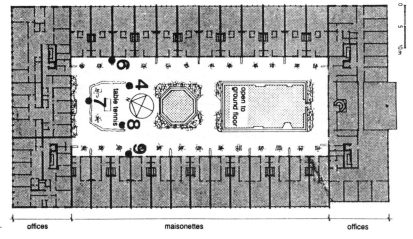

Fig. 35.8   Section   Fig. 35.9   Plan, first floor

In 1987 the entire courtyard was covered with glass to obtain an attractive inside square on the ground level and a 'winter garden' for the residents on the first level. As a result the flats facing the courtyard now have windows and, in certain cases, balconies under the new glass roof.

35.2.3   Solar heating system

Solar energy is recovered from the heated air in the atrium in two ways. In the southern eave of the atrium, an exhaust air duct is connected to a heat pump, delivering heat to domestic hot water. In the northern atrium eave exhaust air is used for preheating supply air through a heat exchanger. Fresh air is supplied to the atrium via the shops on the ground floor.

Bright sliding curtains in the lower part of the glass roof act as sun protection. When the atrium temperature exceeds the temperature set point of 25°C, ten sliding shutters in the gable roof (300 m²) and twenty hinged shutters in the tower part of the glazing (30 m²) successively open. The air temperature at the upper atrium floor never exceeds the outdoor temperature by more than 8°C when venting occurs.

U-values:

Inclined glass roof:	$2.0\,W/m^2\,K$
Vertical glass roof:	$1.6\,W/^2\,K$

Energy consumption:

District heating:	$125\,kWh/m^2$
Electricity:	$67\,kWh/m^2$

35.2.4   User study

The Wasa building lends itself to the study of the advantages and disadvantages of an atrium because most of the tenants have experienced the building both with and without the glazing. Half of the dwellings are maisonettes with entrances and private patios on the second floor of the atrium and with balconies, kitchens, and bedrooms under the glass roof. The other apartments either have bedrooms or living rooms facing the atrium but no regular access to it. Of 44 households, 38 have replied to an extensive questionnaire about their views and experiences.

The majority of residents have a positive overall opinion of the atrium, but comments and answers to specific questions are mostly negative. What is good has evidently been more difficult to discover and express. Those who moved in after the glazing-over and those who live in the maisonettes are generally more positive than the others.

Most negative opinions are about the climate in the rooms facing the atrium. Almost all residents have experienced deterioration of daylight. Some occupants say this is especially annoying in the kitchen. The opaque shutters and the roof construction obstruct sunlight as well. A few commented on the poor daylight in the winter, when the snow remains on the roof.

When the snow melts it noisily slides down the glazing. Noise disturbance from the automatic shutters has also been reported. There is an echo in the atrium which reinforces the sound from voices and slamming of doors. No one, however, complained about noise from the shops on the ground floor. In the bedrooms bad ventilation and the lack of possibilities for airing are the biggest problems.

The majority of the maisonette tenants feel that contact with their neighbors has improved. This is most likely due to the patios outside their front doors, which can be used all year and are, in fact, used more in the winter than in the summer. The patios are appreciated as they

Atrium conditioning:

Minimum temperatures:	10–18°C
Maximum temperatures:	
Ground floor:	Ambient temp.
1st floor:	Ambient temp. + 8°C

Working hours:

Weekdays:	8:15–18:30
Saturday:	9:00–14:00
Sunday:	closed

relieve the maisonette tenants from snow shoveling in the winter. Very few miss the former open courtyard as it was — a sterile concrete surface.

Fig. 35.10   Fish-eye photo of the interior

35.2.5   Daylight study

The aim of monitoring illuminance was to investigate reductions in daylight in the atrium and adjacent spaces as a consequence of the glazing and to check the accuracy of hand calculations. Wasa differs slightly from most other atria because four of the six large shutters (6 m × 5 m) in the glass roof are opaque.

Daylight illuminance was monitored at five points in the atrium (2 m level), at three points in adjacent spaces (model), and above the roof as a reference.

Approximate daylight reduction by glazing in similar atria (%):

- Single glazing: 50–55
- Double glazing: 55–60
- Triple glazing: 60–65
- Triple glazing with
  glass shutters: 50–60

Daylight in the atrium
During three months of monitoring there were 95 daylight hours with completely overcast sky.

The accuracy of the calculations was reduced due to poor documentation of the supporting steel structure, and assumptions of dust on the glazing, etc. Calculations from fish-eye photos indicate a reduction of sky view of 20–25%. Added to this are vertical pillars and high greenery, giving an approximate reduction factor of 0.7 for obstructions. Dirt on sloped glazing accounts for an extra 20% reduction of daylight. This gave an overall reduction factor of $0.7 \times 0.8 = 0.56$ for the glass roof.

The calculated values are slightly lower than the measured ones. The differences may be considered acceptable for a hand calculation method.

Daylight in dwellings facing the atrium
Measurements in the model room placed in the atrium and calculations for the kitchens facing the atrium show that the glazing decreases the daylight factor by approximately 50%. The reduction varies according to whether there is an opaque shutter directly outside the window or not. The windows are small and the kitchens deep, so it is understandable that residents noticed decreased daylight.

Solar penetration
In winter, direct sunlight hardly reaches the floor of the atrium. At equinox, the north part of the atrium is fairly sunny, both with and without the glass roof. In summer the glass roof shades the floor of the atrium considerably.

35.2.6 Energy study

The energy flow through the glass roof during different weather conditions in different seasons was examined. Heat flow through the glazing and climate variables close to the glazing and in the surroundings were monitored. These variables were then computed with a simulation model using the monitored solar radiation, cloudiness, ambient temperature and wind speed data.

Measurements of radiation balance
The results for a clear and a cloudy day in April show that 150 to 300 W/m² of the incoming solar radiation is reflected and absorbed–emitted back to the sky. The glass absorbs up to 200 W/m². Only 40% of the solar radiation is actually heating the atrium. During a clear night, at most 60 W/m² is lost to the sky. The long-wave radiation losses from the atrium to the glass roof are 15–20 W/m² during the night. During a totally overcast day, radiation on the glass roof is at most 100 W/m², and only 20% of this contributes to the atrium heating. During clear nights the outer glass surface is cooled so much that it actually is heated by convection and condensation. Occasionally the inner glass surface becomes warmer than the indoor air at the ceiling as a result of solar absorption. Convection then heats the atrium. During strong insolation the outer glass surface becomes more than 20°C warmer than the ambient temperature. Great convective losses then occur at the outside.

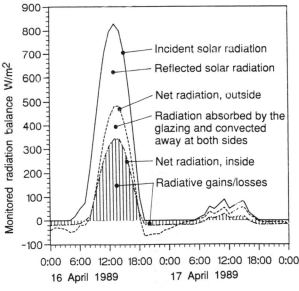

Fig. 35.11 Monitored radiation balance at glass roof facing south in April

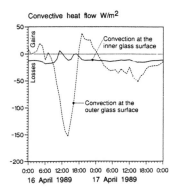

Fig. 35.12 Calculated convective heat flow in April

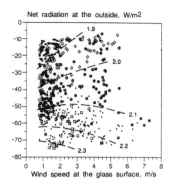

Net radiation at the outside, W/m2

Wind speed at the glass surface, m/s

Fig. 35.13 *U*-values during 534 night hours in winter and spring as a function of wind speed and net radiation above the glass

Latitude:
Norrköping: 59°N
Luleå: 66°N

Measurement of heat conduction — U-values
When *U*-values are used in calculations, it is often assumed that the heat transfer coefficients at the surfaces are constant. However, *U*-values vary significantly with wind speed and cloudiness. The results show that radiation losses to a clear sky greatly increase the *U*-value. Increasing wind speeds seem to increase the *U*-value slightly during cloudy conditions, but rather decrease it or have no effect during clear conditions.

Simulations
Measured radiative and convective energy flows at the surfaces were correlated (stepwise) to the external climate variables. This gave a linear relationship between the energy flow through the glazing and solar insolation, cloudiness, and ambient temperature. The correlation coefficient was 0.99. Wind velocity was insignificant.

The hourly energy flow for the year 1975 was calculated using this relation, for the atrium placed in two different cities — Norrköping and Luleå. The yearly losses were 130 kWh/m² in Norrköping and 240 kWh/m² in Luleå. The energy demand for the atrium was approximately 120 kWh/m² of atrium floor area in Norrköping and 220 kWh/m² in Luleå.

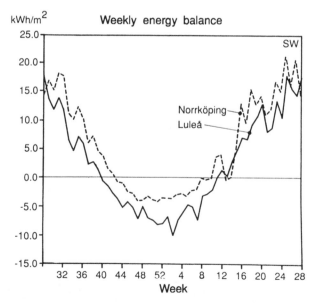

Fig. 35.14 Simulation of the hourly energy balance of the triple glazed roof facing southwest in two Swedish climates (weekly sums)

The average weekly *U*-value for the 30° sloping glass roof was 5–6% larger than for a corresponding vertical window in both cities.

Simulations with different orientation and slope indicate that the yearly losses from sloping, triple-glazed roofs are 2.2 times larger for surfaces facing north than for surfaces facing south in Norrköping. The losses from a 30° sloping roof facing south is 1.8 times larger than those from a vertical glazing facing south. Corresponding values for Luleå are 1.4 and 1.3

35.2.7 Conclusions

Daylight is greatly obscured by the glazing and its supporting structure. Shallow rooms with comparatively large windows facing the atrium are therefore preferable. Overhangs, balconies, etc. that shield the light, as well as opaque shutters such as those at Wasa, should clearly be avoided.

The conductive heat losses from the glass roof of the atrium are 5% larger than indicated by the nominal U-value of the glazing. This is due to greater radiative losses to the sky. The energy consumption for heating an atrium increases drastically the further north it is located, and low slope glass surfaces facing north lose more energy than steeper ones facing south. The orientation and slope of the glass surface become less important the further north the building is located. Moderate wind speeds have little influence on the energy losses of an airtight glass roof.

Fig. 35.15 Calculated average weekly effective U-value of the triple glass roof

35.3 GATEWAY II

Building type:	Offices
Location:	Basingstoke, UK
Latitude:	51°N
Occupancy date:	1982
Design occupancy:	550
Floor area:	m^2
● Gross: (inc. atrium)	14 140
● Heated: (ex. atrium)	13 130
● Atrium:	1 010

35.3.1 Summary

The new headquarters buildings for Wiggins Teape was one of the first buildings in the UK to use an atrium as a passive solar feature. The atrium is used to enhance natural ventilation, with different strategies for winter and summer conditions. Short-term flow visualization and long-term tracer gas tests were performed to test the strategies.

The results show that the summer strategy is successful in providing acceptable ventilation levels. The winter ventilation strategy, however, fails to provide adequate ventilation.

Client:

Wiggins Teape (UK) PLC

Architects: Arup Associates

Monitoring: Databuild Ltd

Climate data

Degree days (base 20):	3812
Global radiation:	940 kWh/m^2
Sun hours:	616
A/V ratios:	l/m
● Offices:	0.59
● Atrium:	0.06

35.3.2 Building description

During the early 1980s paper manufacturer Wiggins Teape required new offices on a site next to their existing premises. In contrast to the existing fully air conditioned offices, the specifications were for a naturally ventilated office building.

The solution was 14 m deep offices surrounding a courtyard which was glazed over to form an atrium. The atrium is part of a careful strategy aimed at an energy-efficient building. It is used as a passive solar element to reduce heating costs and assist natural ventilation.

35.3.3 Building services

Space heating

Three gas-fired boilers supply hot water for perimeter radiators, each of which has thermostatic control. The atrium is heated throughout the winter by an underfloor coil system supplied by heat recovered from the computer room air conditioning. The system can be fed directly from the boilers if necessary. The reclaimed heat is used to supplement the hot water supply during summer.

Lighting

Fluorescent luminaries in the offices have an automatic override system which switches lights off at predetermined times throughout the day. If the occupants feel that there is insufficient light after switch-off, they can switch their own light back on. The atrium is mainly lit by daylight and light from the offices. Installed lighting in the atrium is principally low-level lighting on the walkways and for display purposes. Atrium lighting is not forced off.

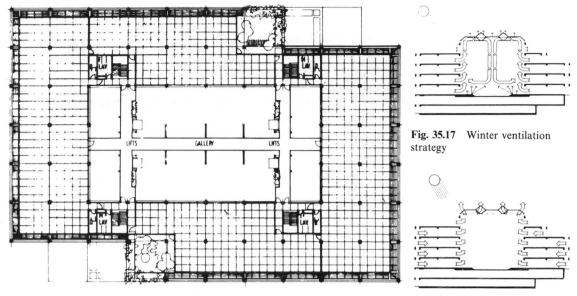

Fig. 35.16 Typical floor plan

Fig. 35.17 Winter ventilation strategy

Fig. 35.18 Summer ventilation strategy

35.3.4 Passive systems

In winter the atrium acts as a buffer to the offices. Solar gains warm the space, thereby reducing heat losses from the offices. The underfloor heating system tempers the environment at ground level and prevents cold draughts from reaching the occupants. The heat in the atrium is intended to induce ventilation through the offices via infiltration through the roof glazing.

During summer the rooflights can be opened and the solar gain induced stack effect causes air movement through the building via the perimeter windows. In this way the offices receive cross ventilation. Overheating is further controlled by the use of louvered external sun screens and the exposed concrete structure.

Atrium *U*-values	W/m² K
External glazing:	3.0
Internal glazing:	4.0
Internal opaque:	2.0

35.3.5 Monitoring results

Evaluation method
The objective of the evaluation was to test the ability of the atrium to provide natural ventilation to the offices. This was done with short- and long-term tests during the winter and summer.

The short-term tests primarily attempted to visualize the air movements in the building using neutrally buoyant helium balloons in the atrium, and small-scale smoke generation to check air movement in the offices and between the offices and the atrium.

The long-term tests quantified ventilation rates and air movement and addressed amenity issues. This was done by monitoring the levels of carbon dioxide in several offices and in the atrium. Temperatures were also measured throughout the atrium and the offices.

Results — winter strategy
The winter visualization tests indicated that on the day of the tests, the air movement observed in the atrium was not as planned. The air movement generally was from east to west at low levels and from west to east at high levels, with downward flow at the eastern end and with upward flow elsewhere. There was little air exchange between the offices and the atrium, and this was often in the opposite direction to that planned (i.e. from the atrium to the offices).

It seems that the air movement is largely driven by the underfloor heating, as the design strategy intended, but that this is influenced significantly by the external glazing at the eastern end of the building. There is limited underfloor heating at the eastern end of the atrium because a restaurant extends into the atrium at the third level. There are no offices at the seventh level at the eastern half of the atrium; instead there is story height single glazing to the outside. Both of these factors lead to the observed down draught at this end and to the corresponding horizontal and upwards movements observed.

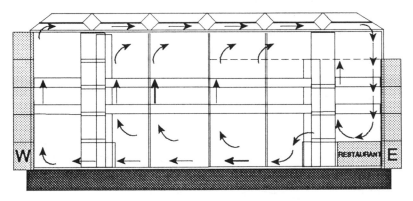

Fig. 35.19 Air movement adjacent to the south facade

During the visualization tests little or no air movement was observed through the louver windows between the offices and atrium. The longer-term winter tests, however, indicated that there was a significant amount of air exchange. The limited analysis undertaken on overnight CO_2 concentrations suggested that the air movement was partly directional, tending to be from the windward to the leeward side of the building.

During the daytime, the levels of carbon dioxide observed in the offices on the leeward side of the building were considerably higher than those elsewhere. This suggests that the main source of ventilation air to these offices is the already contaminated air of the atrium.

The levels of carbon dioxide observed in the offices were found to be moderately high on some days and although not approaching the current UK limit of 5000 ppm (parts per million), they were well above the ASHRAE comfort standard 63–1989 of 1000 ppm. These carbon dioxide concentrations suggest that there may be high levels of other pollutants within the offices, especially tobacco smoke.

The daytime ventilation rates calculated for all the offices were often just above the minimum fresh air requirement of 0.3 ach (air changes per hour). In some offices this ventilation rate was lower, as suggested above. The analysis also revealed some fairly low overnight ventilation rates. Although this helps to reduce heat loss, the CO_2 level did not reach ambient levels before the start of the next working day. The overnight ventilation rates, calculated to be between 0.10–0.15 ach, imply that during the day external windows must be opened to achieve the minimum ventilation rate.

The main problem with the winter ventilation strategy is that it relies on the people sitting adjacent to the external windows and the louver windows to open them for the benefit of all the occupants of the office. This poses no difficulty with the louver windows because approximately 70% are always open. The design of the external windows, however, will cause draughts at desk level under certain conditions and may preclude their opening. Another problem with air movement is the preponderance of private offices, particularly facing the atrium, which restrict through ventilation. In some offices over half the available louver windows are in private offices.

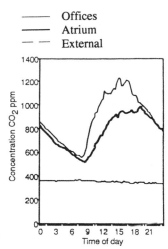

Fig. 35.20 CO_2 levels on a typical winter day

Results — summer strategy

The summer visualization tests confirm that the air movement within the atrium and offices is as intended. The ventilation rates measured, however, were somewhat lower than predicted by the designers [35/5]. The balloon tests indicated that generally there was upward air movement within the atrium and that air was flowing into it from various offices.

Smoke tests indicated that the air movement between the offices and the atrium generally flowed into the atrium, but fluctuations were observed in many locations. When quantified, these tests confirmed that the overall air movement from each facade on levels 5, 6 and 7 was from the offices into the atrium. This implies that the air movement was predominantly from the stack effect. The overall ventilation rate derived from the air speeds measured was 4.6 ach, but there was a wide range between different offices.

The carbon dioxide levels observed during the working day for the period analyzed rarely reached 150 ppm above ambient. The maximum in the atrium was about one third of this value. These fairly low concentrations correspond to ventilation rates for all the offices of 2.5 and 4.0 ach. Although these ventilation rates will have some effect on

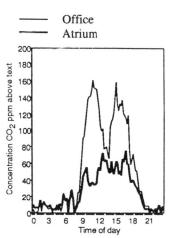

Fig. 35.21 CO_2 levels on a typical summer day

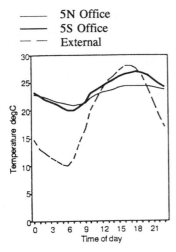

——— 5N Office
——— 5S Office
— — External

Fig. 35.22 Temperatures on a typical summer day

cooling the offices, the high levels of internal gains from the occupants, lighting, and equipment suggests that a considerably higher rate is needed for effective cooling.

The office temperatures, which never exceeded the ambient temperatures and were 3°C below in the offices facing north on a typical day, imply that the high thermal mass of the structure has a considerable influence on moderating the internal climate. Overnight cooling of the structure appears to be the most important factor in keeping the daytime conditions comfortable. The number of desk fans observed in the offices, however, implies that occasionally occupants find conditions uncomfortable. As in the winter, the ventilation through the offices is largely controlled by the people sitting around the perimeter and restricted by the private offices.

Temperatures recorded in the atrium during the monitoring period suggested that between 9:00 and 21:00 there is a positive temperature gradient up the atrium and that the temperatures at the top is approximately 8°C above ambient. These temperatures confirm that stack ventilation is possible.

35.3.6   Conclusions

The summertime ventilation strategy works successfully; however, the major influence affecting the internal climate is the high thermal mass of the structure. The winter ventilation strategy is unsuccessful; overall, the ventilation rates during the day are often just adequate, resulting in fairly high high concentrations of CO_2 in the offices.

35.3.7   Reference

35/5 Gateway 2, *The Arup Journal*, **19**(2), 2–9, June 1984. Published by Ove Arup Partnership, 13 Fitzroy Street, London W1P 6BQ.

35.4   ALTA DAY CARE CENTER

35.4.1   Summary

The main solar feature of this day care center is a large, centrally located atrium that preheats ventilation air. The atrium was expected to reduce the energy consumption in the rest of the building and at the same time provide additional space for the children. The building was monitored in 1989, and the results show that energy consumption is significantly higher than expected. Simulations were performed with realistic data on internal gain to investigate alternative solutions.

Building type:	Education
Location:	Alta, Norway
Latitude:	70°N
Atrium function:	
	Active use, circulation
Atrium conditioning:	Free floating
Occupancy date:	1987
Cost (1987):	
● ECU	503 000
● NOK	3 822 000
Fuel use data (1989):	
Total consumption:	107 720 kWh
Rel. to heated area:	263 kWh/m²
Rel. to total area:	220 kWh/m²

Climate data

Degree days, base 20°C:	
Annual average:	6600
1989 (year of monitoring):	6139
1978 (year of simulation):	7391
Global radiation:	665 kWh/m²
Sun hours:	1600
Client:	The Student Union of Alta
Design team:	
	SINTEF Div. of Architecture and Building Technology
Monitoring agent:	
	SINTEF Division of Applied Thermodynamics

The building was not built as initially planned, because the floor heating system has no thermostat, and there is no maximum control of the temperature of the ventilation air. This is one reason for the high energy use, and for high temperatures causing discomfort. Frequent use of equipment such as washing machines and dryers has also influenced energy use.

The atrium provides a place where children enjoy physical activity. The employees would prefer a higher temperature in the atrium as that would increase its use. A better solution would be to separate the ventilation and the heating systems, using a heat pump.

35.4.2 Project description

The building was built in the small town of Alta in northern Norway during the spring of 1987. The monitoring project is part of the Norwegian Ministry of Oil and Energy's prototype program. Its purpose was to investigate both the energy savings and the amenity value of such glazed spaces in day care centers.

35.4.3 Building form and construction

The building is planned for four identical groups of children, two on each side of a central zone. This zone contains a service area to the north and the atrium to the south. All the entries are located in the central zone, which also serves as a link between the different groups. The building is used only in the daytime, and not on weekends and vacations, so a low-mass wooden construction was chosen. The atrium has a laminated wood strucure with aluminum profiles and double glazing.

Floor area:	m²
● Total:	490
● Atrium:	80
Volume:	m³
● Total:	1275
● Atrium:	260
Glazing areas:	m²
● Adjacent space exterior:	22
● Atrium exterior:	65
● Intermediate boundary:	21
U-values:	W/m²K
● Floor:	0.15
● Walls:	0.26
● Windows:	2.00
● Atrium windows:	3.00
● Roof:	0.15
Total envelope heat loss:	W/K
● Transmission:	470
● Infiltration:	110

Fig. 35.23 Plan

35.4.4 Passive systems

The atrium space reduces the energy consumption in the rest of the building by acting as a buffer zone and thus reducing the heat loss. The heat gained in the space is used to preheat the supply of fresh air to the building.

Design temperatures:	
● Heated space:	21°C
● Atrium	Free floating
Ventilation:	
Air change:	2250 m³/h
Heat exchanger efficiency:	80%

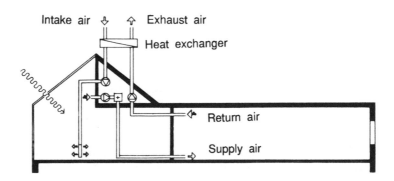

Fig. 35.24 Air flow diagram

35.4.5   Building services

Electric radiant floor heating is supplemented by electrical space heaters located under the windows. Only the space heaters have temperature control. The ventilation system passes air through a heat exchanger and into the atrium. The air is then heated to 20°C and distributed diffusely to the rest of the building. The building and atrium are vented through hatches when the temperature is too high. The ventilation system is only operated when the center is in use.

35.4.6   Measurements

The monitoring project evaluated energy use, cost, indoor climate, and amenity value of the building.

Energy performance and indoor climate
Total energy use in 1989 was 107 720 kWh. Heating accounts for 88 900 kWh, which is 50% higher than expected. The monitored energy use is shown in Table 35.2. Total energy use is 260 kWh/m^2 heated area, which is higher than in other day care centers in the area.

Table 35.2   Monitored energy use

Energy use (kWh)	Total	Usable as heat	Not for heat
Hot water	6 090	0	6 090
Light, drying	18 350	18 350	0
Stove, drying	15 080	7 540	7 540
Ventilation	9 300	4 200	5 100
Heating	58 900	58 900	0
Total	107 720	88 990	18 730

The initial calculations were performed for the year 1978. Degree days have been used to compare these calculations with the monitored results.

Table 35.3   Calculated and monitored energy use

Year degree days	Calculated 1978 7390	Calculated, climate adjusted to 1989 6140	Monitored 1989 6139
Equipment	30 630	30 640	30 090
Heating	34 500	23 460	58 900
Total	65 130	54 100	88 990

The reasons that the energy consumption is higher than expected are listed below.

- The floor heating in the adjacent space has no thermostat and causes frequent overheating.
- The surplus heat from the atrium is not used since there is no thermostat.
- The occupants vent the building manually two hours every day to correct the overheating problem.
- The doors between the atrium and the adjacent space are often open.
- The atrium temperatures are higher than calculated (possibly from the use of portable heaters).
- The building is exceptionally well equipped, with five washing machines and five dryers.

Suggestions for improvements of the building system are to:

- Regulate the floor heating system in sequence with the space heaters. (The floor heating should be set at a low temperature, while the space heaters should be used for temperature control.)
- Limit the maximum air temperature by controlling the ventilation air inlet temperature.
- Reduce the electricity consumption by replacing the ventilation fan motors.

Suggestions for improving the system in principle are to:

- Separate the heating and ventilation systems.
- Install a separate system, i.e. a heat pump, to make use of surplus heat from the atrium for purposes of space or water heating.
- Design the building and heating system to have a quick response. (Radiators give quicker response than floor heating.)

Monitored atrium temperatures are shown together with ambient temperatures in Fig. 35.25. The atrium temperature falls below 10°C 2% of the time, and the minimum temperature is 6°C. Calculations showed that the temperature would be below 10°C 35% of the time and that the minimum would be −10°C. The monitored results indicate that there is a heat source in the atrium. This is assumed to be portable, as it could not be found when the researchers visited.

Atrium temperatures in May are 15 K above ambient most of the time. The temperature difference between floor and ceiling levels (5 m) is 4–8 K. This has little effect on comfort.

The users of the building complain about the air quality and temperature in the heated part of the building. The atrium itself is normally felt as refreshing and with good air quality, and the atrium offers a good climate both in the spring and in the fall.

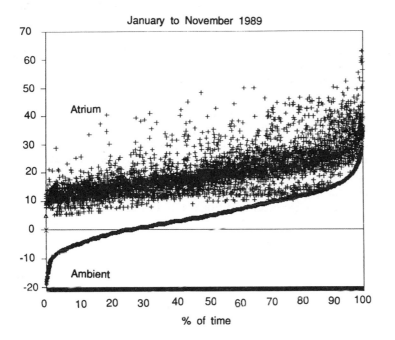

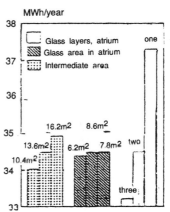

Fig. 35.25 Ambient temperatures sorted in ascending order with corresponding atrium temperatures

Fig. 35.26 Energy consumption for heating. Variation of atrium construction parameters

35.4.7 Parametric studies

Conclusions from several parameters using the program FRES are as follows:

- Varying the amount of glazing, either in the atrium exterior envelope or in the intermediate boundary, has little effect on energy consumption.
- Triple glazing in the atrium would reduce the energy consumption, but is not economical. Triple glazing should, however, be considered if the atrium is to be kept at a higher temperature.
- Heating the atrium above 5°C increases energy consumption.
- Doubled infiltration in the heated area increases the heat consumption by 30%. Venting with open windows several hours a day increases the infiltration rate.
- An increase of indoor temperature in heated area by 1°C increases the energy consumption by 7%.
- A reduction in heat exchanger efficiency to 0.6 increases the energy consumption by 7%.
- A heat pump can reduce the energy consumption by 10 000 kWh.

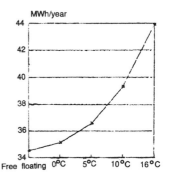

Fig. 35.27 Energy consumption for heating as a function of atrium temperature

Fig. 35.28 Interior view

Building costs (1987):   /m² total
  ECU   1000
  NOK   7800
Atrium cost (1987)   /m²
  NOK   3100

Design occupancy:
- Children: 48
- Adults: 15

Working hours:
08:00–16:00 Monday–Friday

The heat pump, with cooling of atrium and exhaust air from the buiilding, may be a source both for heating and hot water. Thus surplus heat in the summer is used for hot water.

35.4.8 Amenity values

The main purpose of the atrium is to provide additional play space for the children. The atrium is used as an alternative to the heated area all year. It is used for play activities similar to those indoors such as singing, 'training', etc.; and two disabled children use it when it is too cold for them to play outside. The atrium is also used to test green plants for a horticultural college. The users wish to increase the atrium temperature to use it for additional types of activities.

35.4.9 Costs

Preconstruction calculations show that the energy savings potential was not quite high enough to make the system cost effective. Glazing systems on the market are too costly, and the energy price too low. When considering the amenity value, the total cost is acceptable. The total costs of the atrium itself, excluding all mechanical equipment, was NOK 250 000. Both the price of the atrium and of rest of the building are representative. The high energy consumption justifies the installation of thermostats and a reduction in atrium temperature.

35.4.10 Conclusions

The main objective to provide a sheltered play space was achieved. The atrium is pleasant and refreshing to be in. Both the heating energy consumption and the atrium temperatures are higher than precalculated. A reduction of atrium temperature together with temperature control in the heated area would reduce the energy consumption.

35.4.11 References

35/6 Brattset, O., Hestnes, A.G., 1985, *Energiokonomisering med halvklimatiserte soner i barnehager*, SINTEF-report no. STF62A 85005.

35/7 Bryn, I., 1986, *Energi- og temperaturanalyse av barnehage Romemyra*, SINTEF-report no. STF62A 86006.

35/8 Hestnes, A.G., 1989, *Passive and Hybrid Solar Commercial Buildings*, IEA Task XI, Four Norwegian Case Studies.

Address for all references: SINTEF Div. 62, N-7034 Trondheim, Norway.

35.5 NEUCHÂTEL UNIVERSITY — NUNI

Building type:	Education
Location:	Neuchâtel, Switzerland
Latitude:	47°N
Altitude:	438 m
Atrium function:	Sedentary use

35.5.1 Summary

The new building of the Faculty of Literature at the University of Neuchâtel has a heating energy demand of only $80 \, kWh/m^2$ (including DHW). The symmetrical building has a central courtyard and an attached atrium. It is heated by a heat pump with back-up on extremely cold days from district heating. The building is deliberately not air conditioned, and only special rooms have mechanical ventilation. The atrium, which is small, was not intended to save energy for the rest of the building. It was conceived as a passive solar heated space and is tempered in summer through natural ventilation and evaporative cooling from pools of water.

35.5.2 Building description

The three- to four-story building complex, organized around a central court, comprises six blocks housing a library, classrooms, offices, an entry hall, and a cafeteria. The building is constructed of concrete, and the atrium has single glazing both in the exterior envelope and in the intermediate boundary.

Heat, provided by two heat pumps, is delivered to the rooms via radiant floor heating. The principle spaces are heated to 20°C, the circulation and connecting spaces to 16°C.

35.5.3   Passive system

Climate data:
Global radiation: 1190 kWh/m²
Degree days (20°C):   3413

The atrium is divided in two zones, an outer zone which is unheated and serves as a sun-tempered buffer, and an inner zone which is heated. In the summer large glass areas can be opened at the base and top of the atrium to induce natural convection within the atrium volume. Pools of water at the perimeter further enhance natural cooling by evaporation. Interior sunshading provides glare and overheat protection.

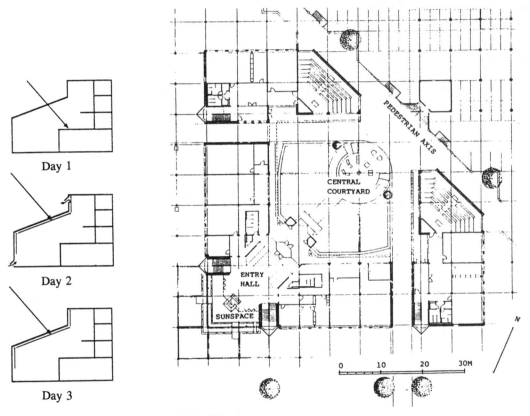

Day 1

Day 2

Day 3

Fig. 35.29   Modes of operation   **Fig. 35.30**   Plan

35.5.4   Monitoring results

The main goals of the monitoring project were to understand and describe the thermal behavior of the attached atrium, to evaluate its potential use and compare it with its actual use, and to evaluate the effectiveness of the protection against overheating (sun shading and natural ventilation). Temperature stratification and air movement were also studied.

Stratification

Measurements were performed during the spring of 1989, when temperatures were measured on three typical days (27–29 March). The first day the vents were closed, and the shading devices were not used. The second day the vents were open, and the shading devices were used. The third day the vents were again closed, but the shading devices were used.

Analysis of the results shows that when there is no shading and the vents are shut, convective air movements that destroy the stratification are created. When the shading is used, the solar radiation primarily heats the air gap between the shading device and the glass, and there is not much convective movement in the atrium itself. The stratification then increases (about 20°C). When the vents and the shading devices are used in combination, air movements destroy the stratification. The atrium is then effectively cooled.

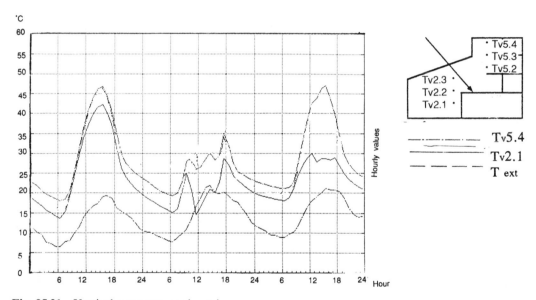

Fig. 35.31 Vertical temperatures in atrium

Comfort

Calculations of aggregated hours of potential use and actual hours the atrium is used on the predicted mean vote thermal sensation scale were compared for the months of March and June. In mid-season, the atrium is not used as it could be, whereas it could very well be used in June.

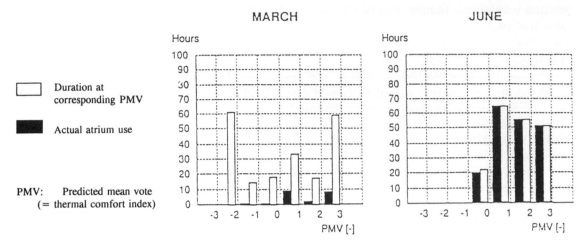

Fig. 35.32   PMV duration and atrium use

The data also show that the shading devices are not used sufficiently to protect against overheating in mid-season, and that once they have been brought down, they remain in this position even if the PMV is at zero, and the conditions should be comfortable without them.

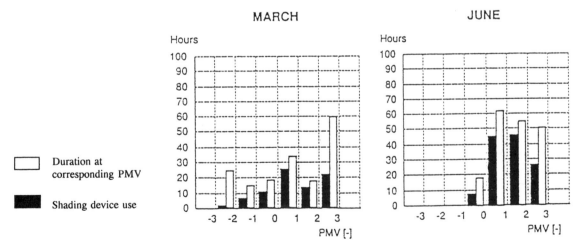

Fig. 35.33   PMV duration and shading use

Based on these observations, a temperature sensor could be placed in the atrium with a display inside the building. When the atrium temperature reaches 15°C, the students could be informed that the atrium temperatures are comfortable and thereby perhaps increase its use.

35.5.5 Parametric studies

The results from simulations using the program MODPAS show that, in comparison to the reference case, the absolute energy saving obtained by using a free floating atrium varies between 5 and 15 MWh/year. When the atrium is heated, the increase in energy consumption varies between 100 and 400 MWh/year. It is therefore clear that heating an atrium to acceptable comfort levels most of the time is a very energy-intensive option.

There are comfortable conditions during working hours (8:00 to 17:00) 25–50% of the time in the free-floating atrium, and 80–95% of the time in the fully conditioned atrium. In comparison, outdoor conditions are comfortable less than 5% of the time. Although changing from single to double glazing in the atrium exterior envelope substantially reduces energy consumption, it does not significantly increase the amount of time the atrium can be used.

35.5.6 Costs

The entire building complex was estimated to cost 17 500 000 Sfr. Actual costs were 20% higher. Part of this increase included additional insulation, decided upon during the course of construction.

35.5.7 Conclusions

The results of the project show that comfortable conditions in free floating atria are obtained for 25–40% of the working hours during the heating period. The frequent and full occupancy of the atrium proves its success as a gathering space.

The energy savings obtained, when compared to a reference case with no atrium, range between 7 and 15 MWh/year. If the conditions when comfortable are to be increased to 80–90%, such spaces must be heated to temperatures of 20°C. Then, huge amounts of energy are required. The amount of energy spent to heat atria like NUNI's to indoor comfort conditions range between 102 and 428 MWh/year. The passive cooling system (shading and natural ventilation) is adequate for summer conditions.

35.5.8 References

35/9 *Université de Neuchâtel, Aula et Faculté des Lettres, Plaquette éditée à l'occasion de l'inauguration*, 31 October 1986: Université de Neuchâtel, Secrétariat général, Avenue du 1er Mars 26, CH-2000 Neuchâtel.

35/10 Brügger, Y., Chuard, D., Jaboyedoff, P., *Nouvelle Université de Neuchâtel, Mesure de la serre de février à juin* 1989, SORANE SA-OFEN Lausanne, 1990.

35.6 TECHNICAL UNIVERSITY — ELA

Building type: Education
Location: Trondheim, Norway
Latitude: 64°N
Atrium function:
  Sedentary use (cafeteria), circulation
Occupancy date: September 1986
Floor area:
● New $15\,000\,m^2$
● Total $40\,000\,m^2$
Cost (1986):
  ECU   21 450 000
  NOK   163 000 000
Projected heating load:
                        $100\,kWh/m^2$ gross

Client: The Directorate of
                          Public Construction

Design team:
Architect: Per Knudsen KS
Construction: A.R. Reinertsen
HVAC: Kr. Gjettum A/S
Electrical: IGP A/S

Monitoring:
  SINTEF Applied
  Thermodynamics/HVAC, Kr.
  Gjettum A/S

35.6.1 Summary

The extension of the Electrical Engineering Department at the Norwegian Institute of Technology consists of several new office and laboratory buildings connected to each other and to existing buildings with glazed spaces.

The atria are heated by solar gains, by transmission losses from the surrounding buildings, and by some auxiliary heating to maintain a minimum winter temperature of $+15°C$. This set point was later raised to $+18°C$, allowing greater occupancy of the atria spaces by students. The energy use has been monitored for 18 months. The results are close to the projected values, and low compared to similar buildings.

The buildings received favorable comments from the occupants in the surveys. There are some complaints about uncomfortable conditions in office spaces facing the atria. This is caused by overheating in the upper parts of the atria during sunny periods making it impossible to vent through windows to cooler surroundings. The smoke ventilation hatches provide sufficient venting in the summer to keep temperatures down, but are not operated properly at all times.

Simulation studies, compared to detailed measurements during stratification conditions, show that a one-zone model gives unsatisfactory results for temperature conditions. Daylight factor measurements agree with modeled results for the atrium floor.

A post-construction cost analysis shows that the investments were somewhat lower for the glazed alternative, because the facades facing the atria were constructed more simply. This saving more than paid for the atria glazing.

Climate

October–April:	
Degree days: (base 20°C)	4180
Global hor.:	220 kWh/m^2
Sunshine hours:	470
Relative sunshine:	0.25

Annual:	
Degree days:	5510
Global hor.:	810 kWh/m^2
Sunshine hours:	1350
Relative sunshine:	0.30
Average temp.:	4.9°C
Design temp.:	−19.0°C

35.6.2 Building description

The extension project includes offices for faculty and researchers, smaller seminar rooms and exercise labs, light electronics and computer labs, a multi-story high voltage lab, and a cafeteria. New auditoria were also built, by reconstructing existing lab facilities.

The extension consists of three new parallel four-story rectangular blocks and four linear shaped atria, filling out the spaces between these and existing buildings.

The new buildings are constructed of precast concrete columns,

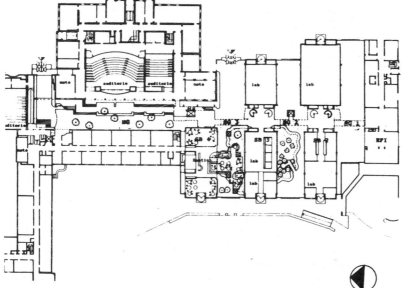

Fig. 35.34 Ground level plan and east elevation for the new building complex

U-values (W/m^2 K):
● Atrium glazing: 2.1
● Windows in exterior walls 2.1
● Intermediate walls: 3.2

Design temperatures:
- Atria: 15°C
- Offices: 20°C

beams, and hollow core slabs, with steel frames as structural support for the atrium glazing. The exterior walls are insulated concrete sandwich panels, with double glazed low-emissivity windows. The intermediate walls facing the atria have infill insulated wood frame panels, with single glazed windows. The atrium glazing is double low-E, laminated overhead.

The buildings are heated by hot water radiators supplied from a central plant. The atria have convector heaters at several heights along the glazed gables and a radiant heat strip along the overhead ridge.

The buildings have balanced mechanical ventilation, while the atria depend solely on infiltration. The fire ventilation hatches in the gables and the glazed roofs are used for summertime venting.

The atria are heated in the winter to a design minimum of $+15$°C, by passive gains through the glazing, by heat losses from the surrounding buildings, and by auxiliary heating. The heat transmission losses from the surrounding buildings, which are kept at 20°C, are consequently small, giving an overall heat loss which is smaller than for the same complex without atria.

35.6.3 Monitoring results

Monitored energy use

	kWh/m² a
Office block:	
• lights, equipment:	67
• heating:	41
Atrium:	
• heating:	148
Office block + atrium:	
• heating:	60
• total:	127

Comparison numbers

Norwegian universities
- average: 270

Energy budgets according to NS 3032:
- New offices: 90–130
- New laboratories: 150–250

Energy, temperature

The heating energy and the energy used for lighting and equipment, etc. was monitored on a weekly basis for one office block and one atrium for the period from November 1987 to June 1989. In addition, the total heating demand for the whole complex was measured.

Weekly maximum and minimum temperatures were registered both in an atrium and in an office block, at different levels. Detailed temperature measurements were also carried out in one atrium during a short period in the summer of 1988. This was done to study the stratification process and to supply measurement data for simulation studies.

The temperature registrations, however, show that the heating set point in the atrium was raised steadily since the building was occupied, from a design value of $+15$°C to $+18$°C in the last heating season, as a result of user demands. The atrium spaces were intended to be used for circulation and temporary occupancy only, but because of the general overcrowding of students in the complex, they now use the atria as general study places, which require a higher temperature for thermal comfort. Consequently, the atria heating demand has also risen steadily in the period, while the office heating energy is somewhat reduced because transmission losses to the atria now are almost zero.

The office blocks are too warm during sunny periods in the summer, because the smoke hatches are not always opened when required. The operation of the hatches depends on manual control by the building operator, and unless uncomfortable situations are reported, the need for venting may be unknown. Automatic control is now being installed.

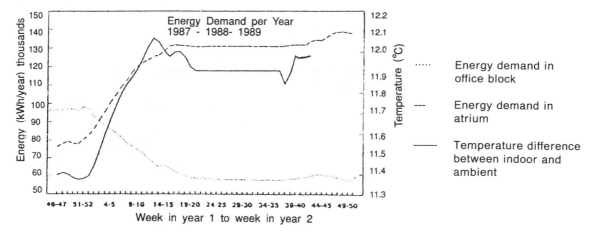

Fig. 35.35 Trends in the annual heating load in one atrium and one office block

Air quality, ventilation

The ventilation rate was measured in one atrium with a step-down tracer gas method and mixing fans. The tests show an air change rate per hour of 0.45 to 0.50, indicating that infiltration gives adequate fresh air supply. With the hatches in normal venting position, typical air change rates were 3 to 4 per hour, but these measurements were inaccurate, as the mixing fan capacity was inadequate.

Some measurements were also carried out without mixing fans, to trace the air flow patterns in the atrium with hatches closed. The results showed that the lower part of the atrium had the cleanest air, and that the upper part functioned as an air outlet: an air flow pattern similar to displacement ventilation.

Daylighting

One-time measurements of daylight factors were carried out in one atrium on overcast days. Along the centerline of the atrium floor, the daylight factors were between 17 and 19% close to the east gable wall and fell gradually to around 12–14% in the vicinity of the elevator and staircase shaft. On the walls facing the atrium, values were in the 7–9% range at heights of 1.4–2.2 m above the floor.

Spot checks in some offices facing this atrium showed daylight factors of 2–3% on first floor level, 3–4% on the second floor, and 3–5% on the third floor, all measured on horizontal work tables about 0.7 m above the floor and about 1.1 m from the window wall plane.

Occupants' opinions

Occupants' reactions to thermal comfort, air quality, and daylighting

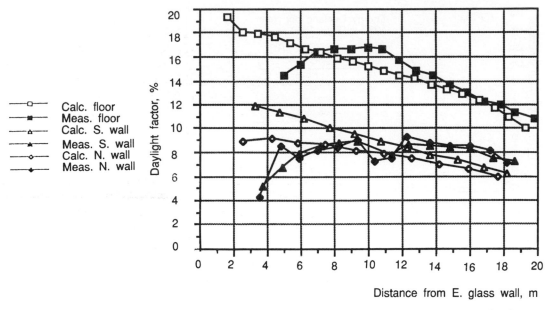

Fig. 35.36 Calculated and measured daylight factors along centerline in one atrium

were obtained in a comprehensive study. Some major conclusions are below.

- There are many complaints about high temperatures and poor air quality in offices facing the atria.
- Occupants are, on the whole, satisfied with conditions in the atria.
- Daylight levels in the offices are considered adequate, but artificial lighting is kept on all year.
- The rating, on linear attribute scales, is quite similar to the rating given to the University Center at Dragvoll (Section 36.5).
- Noise levels in the atria and noise disturbance from the atria to the office spaces also give rise to some complaints.

Costs

During the design phase, a cost study was performed to convince the client that it is economically feasible to glaze the spaces between the buildings instead of leaving them open. This study was updated after construction with actual contract prices and as-built data. The construction and operating costs of one atrium with surrounding offices were compared to an open reference alternative, calculated with statistical cost data from the same period.

The only operating cost that differs for the two alternatives is the energy cost, which is calculated to be 20% lower for the glazed alternative, the analysis performed before measured data were available.

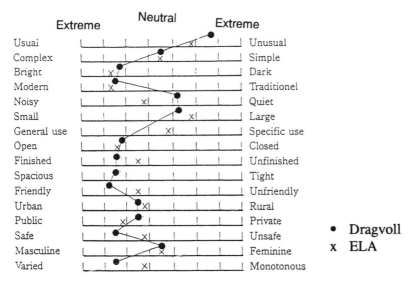

Fig. 35.37 Occupant rating of the ELA building and the Dragvoll University on a seven point scale

Total investments proved to be lower for the glazed case, approximately 2% of total construction costs. The cost of glazing is more than offset by the savings associated with the facade walls towards the atrium, proving that the overall geometry is the key parameter. This cost study did not factor the value of the atrium floor space and the reduction in the number of staircases and elevators.

35.6.4 Simulations

Energy and temperatures
Post-construction analysis of the building was simulated using TARP (Thermal Analysis Research Program), developed at the National Institute of Science and Technology in Washington DC. In the preconstruction analysis, the consultant's own program was used with the multizone model ROYAL-DEBAC.

Measurements show reasonable agreement with precalculated and design values, both for temperatures and energy use. The agreement between precalculated and measured energy use may, however, be coincidental. Comparison of measurements of temperatures at different levels in the atrium under stratification conditions with TARP results show that this one-zone model is unsuitable for such applications.

Daylighting
The daylight factor levels in one atrium were calculated, using the computer model SUPERLITE 1.0, provided by Lawrence Berkeley

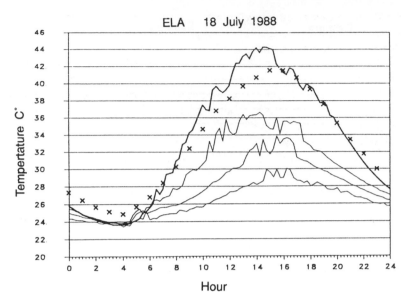

Fig. 35.38 Measured air temperatures at different levels compared to simulations with TARP

Laboratory. The agreement between the two sets of values and general coincidence trend is surprising, considering the limitations of the program, the complexity of the real case, the number of details that could not be modeled properly, and the uncertainties in the measured results.

35.6.5 Conclusions

The measurements show reasonable agreement with precalculated and design values, both for temperatures and energy use. The monitoring method (using manual registration of recording instruments) provides the level of detail needed to determine if the building functions as intended.

Temperature and ventilation measurements agree well with user reactions, and measurements of energy use and temperatures agree well with simulations. However, in sunny periods, the atria temperatures show strong stratification, which is not modeled properly with a one-zone simulation program.

The energy use in the new complex is low, compared to other buildings of the same category and generation. The energy use is also in the low range of the recommended budget figures for this type of building.

The atria heating set point has been steadily rising since monitoring started, because usage has now exceeded what was originally intended for these spaces. Consequently, while heating demand for the atria has increased, heating in the office blocks has decreased, but to a lesser degree than the atria increase.

The infiltration of fresh air to the atria, of about 0.5 ach, gives satisfactory air quality. When open, the fire ventilation hatches give sufficient venting to keep the summer temperatures at acceptable levels. However, the vents are manually controlled and not always opened when required. This gives rise to many complaints about uncomfortable temperatures and poor air quality in the offices facing the atria during sunny periods. Air stratification of the atria temperatures at higher levels prevents office window venting.

The occupants judged the daylight levels to be sufficient, both in the atria and in the adjoining office spaces; however, the office lighting is left on during all working hours. There seems to be general satisfaction with other amenity issues. The building complex received a rating on linear attribute scales that was similar to the rating of another university building in Trondheim with glazed streets.

Cost analysis shows that this building complex has lower investment and energy costs than a reference alternative without glazing. The savings attributed to a simpler exterior wall facing the atria more than offset the cost of the overhead and gable glazing and structure. This makes the main geometry, the street height to width ratio, the key cost parameter.

35.6.6   Recommendations

First, it is important to establish a use of atrium spaces that makes it possible to operate them at an intermediate temperature, compared to the surrounding fully conditioned buildings. Otherwise, these buildings can easily become energy wasters.

The heating set point for the atrium spaces, however, need not be so low as to impair comfort for many important occupant functions. The optimum atrium temperature should be determined by careful analysis of energy use and costs, taking different geometries, intermediate facade construction and atrium glazing into consideration. The main geometry, atrium height to width, is the governing parameter for both energy balance, costs and daylight conditions.

During sunny periods, stratification gives temperatures above comfort level at the higher levels in the atria. It is important to ensure that vents will be properly used, or alternatively, that shading or other systems that can prevent stratification be included.

Having work spaces that face a glazed atrium is quite acceptable, but it is important to incorporate solar shading and sufficient ventilation or cooling to maintain thermal comfort. Otherwise, a general negative attitude toward the building will result.

With reasonable heating season temperatures maintained in the atria, the transmission losses from adjacent buildings is almost negligible. Most of the heating load here will be covered by internal gains from occupants, lighting and equipment.

Simulation models that can predict the energy balance and daylight conditions in the atrium buildings need further development.

35.6.7   References

35/11 Jacobsen, T., Thermal climate and air exchange in a glass covered atrium without mechanical ventilation related to simulations, *13th National Solar Conference*, Cambridge, MA, 1988-06-20/24.

35/12 Aschehoug, O., Hestnes, A.G., Jacobsen, T., Thyholt, M., Evaluation of the ELA Building, *Advanced Case Studies of IEA Task 11*, p. 129, SINTEF, 1990.

35/13 Hestnes, A.G., *Passive and Hybrid Solar Commercial Buildings. Four Norwegian Case Studies*, SINTEF, 1989.

35/14 Thyholt, T. and Aschehoug, O., *Brukerevaluering av dt nye Elektrobygget på NTH*, SINTEF, 1989.

Address for all references:
SINTEF Div. 62, N-7034 Trondheim, Norway.

35.7   BODBETJÄNTEN

Building type:	Office/residential
Location:	Stockholm, Sweden
Latitude:	59°N
Occupancy date:	1985
Atrium function:	Circulation
Floor area:	
● gross:	3200 m²
● heated:	2600 m²
● atrium:	100 m²
Energy consumption:	114 kWh/m²

35.7.1   Summary

Bodbetjänten is one of six experimental buildings within the 'Stockholm Project'. The project was initiated by the City of Stockholm, supported by the Swedish Council for Building Research, and evaluated by the Project Group for Energy Conservation in Buildings, an annex institution of the Royal Institute of Technology.

The building consists of an office section facing north and a residential section facing south, with two central atria. Surplus heat from the offices heats the apartments by exhausting ventilation air partly through the atria and partly through the ducts in the concrete floor slabs of the apartments. A heat pump and short-term thermal storage are also included.

Computer simulations were carried out during the design phase, and extensive monitoring has been carried out after completion. The results show that the amount of energy consumed in the building is relatively low. The main reason for this is the use of the heat pump rather than using surplus office heat, because the temperature difference between the two sections is lower than expected.

35.7.2   Building description

The building consists of a residential section with 41 apartments and an office section with 3000 m² of office space. The two sections surround a glazed atrium. The apartments all have balcony access in the atrium, while the offices are accessed via a separate, central stairway and internal corridors. A glass wall separates the office and the residential part of the atrium, thereby creating two physically separate atria.

The building is constructed of precast concrete facades, floor elements, and columns. The floor elements are hollow core slabs, and the ducts in these are used for air transport and heat accumulation. All atrium glazing is vertical. The roof of the atrium, which is opaque, contains a fan room.

Client:
  NCC Building Contractors, Stockholm
Architects:
  Göran Lundquist, Roland Persson, CAN, Stockholm
Energy consultants:
  LOA Andersson
  Strängbetong AB
Monitoring:
  Arne Elmroth, Göran Werner, Per Wickman

35.7.3   Passive systems

The building is orientated so that the residential section faces south and benefits from solar gain, while the office section faces north and experiences a reduced need for cooling. The atria function as passive solar collectors and buffer zones.

35.7.4   Building services

Heating

A heat pump works continuously, heats the residential section and heats and cools the office section, taking heat from:

• a heat exchanger on residential exhaust air (all year),

U-values: W/m² K
● Walls in exterior facade: 0.23
● Intermediate boundary: 0.40
● Atrium roof: 0.20
● Atrium floor: 0.27
● Windows in exterior facade: 2.00
● Windows in intermediate
  boundary: 3.00
● Glass partition wall: 3.00
● Atrium glazing: 3.00

Climate data

Degree days (18°C):   3720
Global radiation
(heating season):   350 kWh/m²

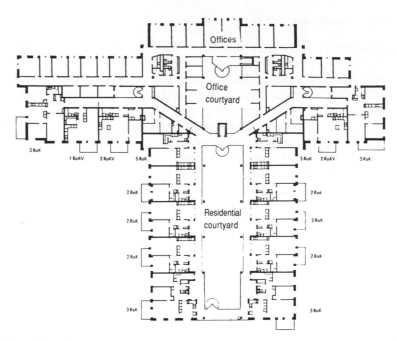

Fig. 35.39   Plan

● a heat exchanger in the residential atrium ventilation loop (sunny winter days), and
● a heat exchanger on office supply air (summer).

The heat pump heats the water in two storage tanks. The stored heat is used for:

● domestic hot water production,
● office supply air heating (when needed), and
● convector heating in the apartments.

During most of the year, hot water storage tanks and domestic hot water tanks are heated by the heat pump alone. If the heat pump capacity is insufficient, an immersion heater is switched in. Electric heaters were installed in the offices as draught eliminators. These are switched on during office hours when the outside temperature falls below +3°C. Cheaper off-peak electricity is used as much as possible, using the tanks and the floor slabs for heat storage.

Ventilation
Supply air to the offices is distributed through the circular ducts in the floor slabs. During the winter and during office hours, the air is taken from the residential atrium. During the summer, it is taken directly from the outside, while at night, 100% is recirculated.

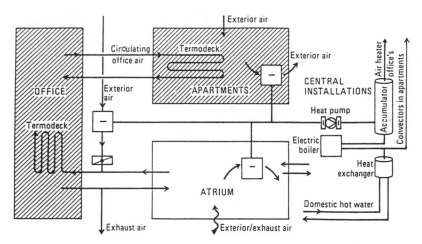

Fig. 35.40 Heating system

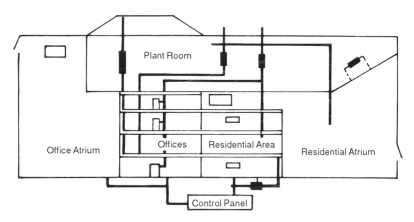

Fig. 35.41 Ventilation system

Exhaust air is extracted in ducts in the corridor ceiling. During the winter the air is expelled into the residential atrium. The surplus heat in the office air is transferred to the residential area by circulating it through the ducts in the floors of the apartments. The office atrium is ventilated by fans and by automatic vents.

Supply air to the apartments is taken from the outside through valves behind the convectors under the windows. Exhaust air is ducted to the heat exchanger/heat pump system all year. A slightly higher air pressure is maintained in the residential atrium to counteract leaks from the outside and from the apartments. On sunny winter days the atrium air circulates via the heat exchanger/heat pump system. In the summer the atrium is cross-ventilated when necessary.

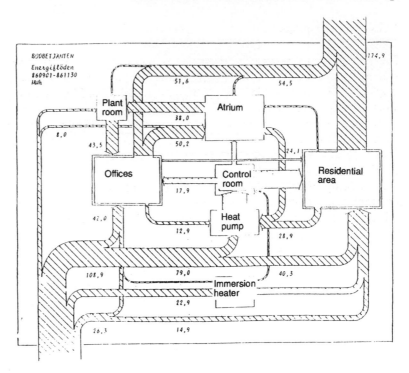

Fig. 35.42 Sankey diagram showing energy flows through the heating and air treatment systems

35.7.5   Monitoring results

The objective of the monitoring project was to test the system of using surplus heat from the offices to heat the residential section and to heat water. Measurements were taken during the period 1 January 1986 through 30 June 1988. In the first year the offices were not fully occupied. Consequently, results from 1987 are most representative.

Purchased energy
In 1987, approximately 320 000 kWh was supplied to the offices. Almost 50% of the energy purchased is electricity used for cold draught protection. The offices are equipped with mechanical supply and exhaust ventilation, so electricity is also needed to run the fans.

Electricity for equipment and lighting consequently comprises the largest single energy use in the offices. The greater share of this energy can benefit the offices during the heating period but constitutes a load during the summer.

Total purchased energy 1987

Whole building:
- incl. atrium: 118
- excl. atrium: 129

Office section:
- incl. atrium: 108
- excl. atrium: 112

35.7.6 Conclusions

The total amount of purchased energy is relatively low because the heat pump contributes to heat production. As the peak load heat is supplied from an electric boiler, this makes the building entirely dependent on electricity.

The residential sections of the building and of the building services are financed by subsidized loans, whereas the financing of the office section is based on commercial loans, making a calculation of cost effectiveness rather difficult.

Monitoring energy used for the project is complemented by extensive sociological investigations. These so far indicate that the tenants in the residential section are pleased with their living environment and that the atrium is appreciated for its amenity value. No specific facts concerning the office section are available.

The evaluation group look upon the Bodbetjänten as a successful part of the Stockholm Project. The dedicated participation of the contractor, who is also the client, is regarded as exemplary and an important reason for its success.

NAC purchased heating energy (normalized)

	W/m² K
Whole building:	
● incl. atrium:	0.45
● excl. atrium:	0.49
Office section:	
● incl. atrium:	0.37
● excl. atrium:	0.38

35.7.7 References

35/15 Bodbetjänten, *Combining Office and Residential Facilities in One Building*, Swedish Council for Building Research Report no. BFR S 10E: 1985, Stockholm, 1985.

35/16 Isfalt, E. and Johnsson, H., *Stockholmsprosjektet — effekt- och energisimuleringar med datorprogrammen BRIS och DEROB*, Report no. BFR R59:1986.

35/17 Andersson, L.O., Delsenius, S.E., and Nyman, B., *Stockholmsprosjektet — överglasade Gårdar och Värmeoverföring från Kontor til Bostader, Kv Bodbetjänten*, Report no. BFR R10:1988.

Address: BFR, St Göransgatan 66, S-11233 Stockholm, Sweden.

35.8 TEGUT

35.8.1 Summary

The building is an extension of an administration building built in the 1970s, belonging to the Tegut company in Fulda. Office pavilions are organized on terraces covered by a large glass structure. With its subtropical planting, this space represents an attractive, temporary extension of the office space. The effects of the concept upon energy consumption, thermal and hygrometric performance, daylighting con-

Building type:	Offices
Location:	Fulda, Germany
Latitude:	50°N

Atrium function:	Sedentary use

Occupancy date:	1985

Floor area:	m²
● Heated (office pavilions):	540
● Atrium (*t* min = 5°C)	460

Client:	Tegut Company, Fulda

Architects:
  LOG ID, Tübingen
  D. Schempp, F. Möllring,
  W. Klimesch, J. Frantz
Monitoring:
  G. Hauser, M. Krampen

Climate data

Degree days:	4300
Global radiation:	770 kWh/m²
Sun hours:	1600

Average temperatures:	(°C)
● Winter:	6.6
● Summer:	16.6
● Annual:	9.1

ditions, and air quality were monitored. User reactions show that the project is a success and confirm the validity of the concept.

35.8.2 Building description

The existing office building consists of open plan offices equipped with air conditioning. The company management wanted an architectural solution to make the extension futuristic. It was to include ecological and environmental features and could not be air conditioned; however, the costs had to be competitive with conventional building concepts.

The extension accommodates 40 working places. Office pavilions are built of lightweight construction, providing terraces in front of each office space accessible by glazing partitions. To gain sufficient height a glass cube is placed at a slant and mounted onto the existing roof, touching it with one edge only. The larger part of the northern wall is closed off and only a few windows allow a glimpse across the countryside. Plants are an important factor in the improvement of the air quality and the indoor climate conditions.

35.8.3 Passive systems

Air heated in the atrium space is transferred to the offices by opening the doors. In addition, fans in the office walls can also transfer the heated air. These have thermostat control, and the heating units in the offices adjust themselves accordingly. There is also central heating, with thermostatically controlled radiators that can be adjusted individually.

These react fast to solar gains.

To prevent overheating during summer there are large vents in the vertical walls and in the ceiling of the atrium. These can be operated automatically by heat sensors. Each of the vents is approximately 2 m in length and can be opened to a net ventilation aperture of 1.3 m².

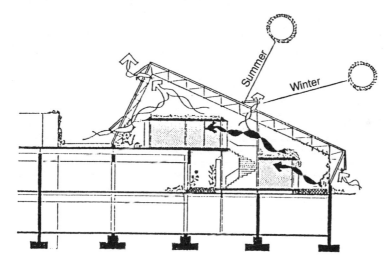

U-values:	W/m² K
● Walls of pavilions:	0.55
● Roof of pavilions:	0.56
● Floor of pavilions:	0.56
● Walls of ext. envelope:	0.36
● Windows of ext. envel.:	3.50
● Windows of pavilions:	3.00

Design occupancy:	40 persons
Time of occupancy:	8:00–17:00
Flexible working hours 5 days/week	

Fig. 35.43 Atrium section

The roofs of the offices are well insulated and used for plants. The plants, through their shading and perspiration, act as climate control. The combination of all these factors provides a temperature in the atrium close to the outdoor temperature. It is even possible to achieve an indoor temperature level below ambient air. The atrium contains relatively robust, subtropical vegetation planted directly in soil.

35.8.4 Building services

The oversized heating system of the old building is also used for the extension. The extension is divided into two heating zones: pavilions and atrium. The system is designed as a dual system served by external temperature control. The pavilions are equipped with radiators and the atrium with thermostatically controlled convectors. Fans for heating and ventilation are placed in the partition walls of the pavilions. Fan rotation can be reversed to exhaust office air into the atrium.

Design temperatures:	°C
Pavilions:	
day	20
night	12
Atrium:	
day	10
night	5
Thermostat setting	18:00–6:00

35.8.5 Monitoring results

The aim of the monitoring project was to evaluate the energy consumption, the thermal and hygrometric performance, the daylighting, and the indoor air quality (O_2 and CO_2 concentration). Occupant questionnaires were used to evaluate users' reactions to their work environment.

Energy consumption

Monthly heat supplied to the new building is shown in Table 35.4. Heat transfer from conventionally conditioned areas includes heat transmission and infiltration caused by opening the doors of the intermediate envelope (assuming a $120\,m^3/h$ air change during office hours). Heat transfer from the basement increases in summer due to the continuously operating cooling engines. Table 35.4 shows the total heat delivered during the heating periods and the summer season.

Table 35.4

Heat contribution	Winter 86/87	Sum. 87	Winter 87/88
Office pavilions heating:	64	4	38 MWh
Atrium heating:	28	0	9 MWh
Heat gain from AC area:	6	1	8 MWh
Heat gain from basement:	5	2	8 MWh
Total:	119	9	81 MWh

Annual energy consumption (1 June 1987 to 31 May 1988):

● Excl. electricity: $114\,kWh/m^2$
● Incl. electricity: $157\,kWh/m^2$

The heated area is $537\,m^2$. In addition, an area of approximately $70\,m^2$ is at least temporarily usable in a similar way. The energy use per unit area is therefore calculated by using the sum of the heated area plus the atrium area prorated by the ratio of habitable hours to total hours.

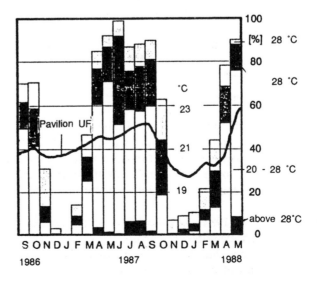

Fig. 35.44 Temperatures in the atrium and in the upper pavilion

Temperature performance

Maximum temperatures in an office area occurred in the upper pavilion (29°C) on 21 August 1987. The corresponding ambient temperature reached 29.6°C and the global radiation reached 800 W/m². Figure 31.44 shows the temperature levels in the atrium during the monitoring period and also the average temperature in the upper office pavilion. The terraces are within the comfort zone and can be used most of the time from March through October.

Humidity

The indoor air humidity levels in the atrium were measured, as were those in the adjacent pavilions, which are ventilated via the atrium space, and the air conditioned offices. The results show that the humidity level in the air-conditioned offices is fairly constant, while it varies considerably more in the atrium offices. In general the levels are higher in these offices, possibly as a result of the abundance of plants in the atrium.

Daylighting

The availability of daylight in the office spaces is considered important both for the potential usability of the spaces and for the operating costs. Since glazing an atrium generally reduces the daylight illumination levels in the adjacent spaces, it was natural to investigate the conditions in this envelope atrium. The measurements were taken when the sky was overcast and sunny.

The results show that direct sunlight is diminished by the glazed building envelope to a higher extent than diffuse solar radiation. Exceptions occur for a few locations close to the facades, which receive some direct sunlight. Maximum daylight factors were recorded at the eastern terraces of the upper floor level with an absolute value of 33.5%. Daylighting factors of 10% and more were recorded at the western terraces and in the air-conditioned office area at locations very close to the south facade.

35.8.6 Amenity issues

The objective of the investigation was to evaluate the occupants' reactions to a conventional air-conditioned open-plan office and to the atrium office. Comparative issues included overall spatial impressions as well as reactions to the office units. A comparison of individual physical health complaints and the mood of the people was also carried out.

In the autumn of 1985 all occupants of the conventional office building were interviewed before some of them moved to the atrium office extension. From that day on, both situations have been investigated by four cycles of interviews to assess possible modifications of findings over the two-year period. These interviews were carried out

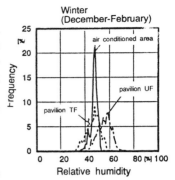

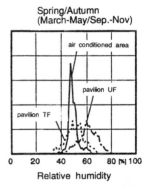

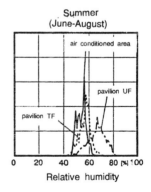

Fig. 35.45 Relative humidity in different office areas

36.1.2 Energy concept

Atrium function: Active use, circulation, plant growth

Atrium conditioning: Fully heated

Atrium proportions:
 Floor area: 4114 m²
 Height (four floors):   14 m
 Width: 11 m

Address of project:
 Altenwohnanlage Stuttgart-
 Neugereut, Haust St
 Monika
 Seeadlerstraße9-11
 D-7000 Stuttgart-Neugereut

The atrium was not intended to save energy. It provides a space usable throughout the year and characterized by plants, water, light, and sun. Overheating is avoided by sufficient top venting in the summer (no shading); condensation and cold air draughts are avoided by convectors in the winter.

36.1.3 Conclusion

The hostel for the elderly with its atrium has become a landmark in the Stuttgart area, among the elderly and all those who professionally care for them. Positive effects include the relatively low atrium building costs of only 1% of the total costs. This building concept should be encouraged; however, the energy design should be considered more seriously in future projects.

36.2 BERLIN DAY CARE CENTER

36.2.1 Building description

Building type: Education
Location: Berlin, Germany
Latitude: 53°N

Floor area:
 ● Gross: 719 m²
 ● Heated: 494 m²

Occupancy: 50 children
                            5 adults

Atrium function: Active use
Atrium conditioning: Free floating

This U-shaped, single-story building from the 1930s was reorganized and extended with an atrium facing south to create more space for various activities for the existing day care center and for a youth center. Facades and building structure have been renovated, but no changes of the existing heating system were made.

36.2.2 Passive solar energy strategy

The atrium acts as an unheated buffer providing an intermediate climate and is equipped with thermal mass for solar energy storage. Surplus solar heat can also be drawn into hollow mass spandrel walls and into the floor construction to increase usable solar energy gains. Overheating in summer is optionally avoided by manual/automatic control of interior shading and by bottom and top vents in the sloped low-e double glazing. The glazing is mounted in a galvanized steel construction.

Atrium proportions:
- Floor area: 225 m²
- Height: 7.5 m
- Width: 10 m

Intermediate boundary:
Masonry cavity walls, double glazed windows and doors.
Glazing fraction: 20%

Contact:
Ingo Lütkemeyer, Sekr. A 44
Technical University Berlin,
Strâe des 17. Juni 135,
D-1000 Berlin 12, Germany

36.2.3 Conclusion

The building was occupied in August 1988, and users' reactions to usability and thermal comfort are predominantly positive. Some minor problems were caused by a sand-box and by the acoustic conditions created by the vitality of young occupants. Monitoring temperatures, solar gains, and humidity levels began in autumn 1989.

36.3 COMSTOCK BUILDING

36.3.1 Building description

This office building for a large engineering firm was designed for a small urban site with limited solar access. The designers created a ten-story atrium in the center of the west elevation, serving as the principal circulation area, and to admit natural light.

Building type: Office
Location: Pittsburgh, USA
Latitude: 40°N
Floor area: 16 275 m² gross
Atrium function:
Active use, circulation
Atrium conditioning:
Tempered by exhaust air
Atrium proportions:
- Floor area: 192 m²
- Height: 37 m
- Width: 9 m

Contact:
Burt Hill Kosar Rittelmann
Associates
1056 Thomas Jefferson St,
NW Washington DC-20007,
USA

36.3.2 Energy concept

Since the only option was to place the atrium on the west elevation, careful design was necessary to make best use of solar energy in the winter and to avoid overheating in the summer. In the summer, the outer portion of the atrium is vented at the top and bottom to act as a natural solar chimney. This, combined with adjustable vertical louvers, eliminates 70% of the unwanted solar gain. During the winter, the vents are closed and the louvers are adjusted to maximize solar gain. Some additional tempering of the atrium is obtained by circulating exhaust air through the atrium. In this way, no primary energy is used to condition the atrium.

36.3.3 Conclusion

The building was constructed at a cost competitive with conventional office buildings in the same location, but uses less than half as much energy. Measured energy use for the total building is $102 \, \text{kWh/m}^2 \, \text{a}$.

36.4 ZÜBLIN

Building type:	Office
Location:	Stuttgart, Germany
Latitude:	49°N
Floor area:	
● Gross:	$19\,867 \, \text{m}^2$
● Heated:	$18\,427 \, \text{m}^2$
Occupancy:	700 employees
Atrium function:	Circulation
Atrium conditioning:	Free floating
Atrium proportions:	
Floor area:	$1440 \, \text{m}^2$
● Height:	31 m
● Width:	24 m
Intermediate boundary:	
Prefabricated concrete elements	
Glazing fraction:	45%

36.4.1 Building description

This office building has a linear, seven-story atrium connecting two office blocks. The individual office spaces are naturally ventilated. The building is made of precast reinforced concrete elements, and the atrium roof is connected to this by reinforced concrete ties.

36.4.2 Energy concept

The unheated, single-glazed atrium is oriented east–west. It serves as weather protection of circulation areas and does not have any spaces for sedentary use. Ventilation is provided by louvered inlets at both gables and by 60 automatically driven exhaust vents in the roof. There is no shading of the atrium space, but the windows facing south in the offices are equipped with individually adjustable sun and glare protection. A heat pump for hot water was installed at the top of the atrium, utilizing atrium air.

36.4.3 Conclusion

Energy was not a major issue in the design of the building. As stated by the owner, the additional building cost for the atrium was relatively low (3.5% of total), and the maintenance cost is not high. From the thermal and daylighting point of view, however, a more reasonable/effective solution would be desirable.

36.4.4 Reference

36/1 Ed. Züblin AG, Stuttgart, *Zübin-Haus*, Karl Krämer Verlag, Stuttgart, ISBN 3-7828-1486-X.

36.5 DRAGVOLL UNIVERSITY

Building type:	Education
Location:	Trondheim, Norway
Latitude:	64°N
Atrium function:	Circulation
Floor area:	
• Gross:	24 900 m²
• Heated:	13 300 m²
• Atrium:	1 620 m²
Design temperatures:	
• Offices:	21°C
• Atrium (minimum):	5°C
Annual fuel use:	
• Dragvoll:	360 kWh/m²
• Other universities:	265 kWh/m²
Architect:	
Henning Larsens tegnestue A/S	

36.5.1 Building description

The university center at Dragvold consists of several office and classroom buildings connected by a glazed street. General functions,

Fig. 36.1 Plan second floor

such as auditoria and shops are on the street level, while seminar rooms and offices fill the upper floors. The buildings are connected at upper levels with bridges across the street, and staircases and elevators are placed in the street. The street functions as circulation area and lobby for the auditoria.

36.5.2   Energy concept

The building complex was not specifically designed for energy conservation. The street is not heated directly, but the ventilation air is exhausted into it. This implies that the whole ventilation system must be kept running in order to avoid unacceptably low street temperatures. In general, the temperature stays between 10 and 20°C all year. The exhaust air is vented through the glass roof, which is intentionally leaky.

The ventilation system will be rebuilt, and this will bring the energy use down to an average level. In the current state, the building uses about 30% more energy than other university buildings.

36.5.3   Conclusions

The glazed street is considered a success: it is used for many functions, and the users have expressed no problems with thermal comfort. The life cycle cost of the building complex is lower than if the streets were not glazed.

36.5.4   Reference

36/2 Gunnarshaug, J., *Erfaringer fra glassoverdekkete gater i Trondheim*, SINTEF Report no. STF62 A85013, N-7034, Trondheim, Norway.

36.6   SKÄRHOLMEN SHOPPING CENTER

36.6.1   Building description

This 1984 retrofit glazing of alleys between shopping and office blocks, built in a suburb of Stockholm in 1964, was done to create better climatic conditions to improve commercial turnover.

36.6.2   Energy concept

The original buildings were designed to the reckless energy standards of the 1960s. The glazing, added in 1984, aimed at amenity rather than

Building type:	Sales
Location:	Stockholm, Sweden
Latitude:	59°N
Atrium function:	Circulation
Floor area:	
● Heated:	22 000 m²
● Atria:	4 000 m²
Design temperatures:	
● Shops and offices:	20°C
● Atrium (minimum):	15°C
Annual fuel use:	
● Before glazing:	370 kWh/m²
● After glazing:	310 kWh/m²
Climate:	
Annual HDD (base 20°C):	4580

energy conservation. However, the covered alleys improve the energy situation. The decreased transmission losses, rather than the solar gains, roughly balance the energy demand of the streets, which are heated by floor pipes coupled to the return circuit of the district heating system. The actual total annual energy used for heating is approximately the same as before the glazing.

36.6.3 Conclusions

The glazing is judged to be a success. Old customers say they come more often since the streets were glazed, and a considerable storm of new visitors has been noted. It is a sensitive matter to present statistics for changes in turnover in trade, but the shopkeepers in Skärholmen are unanimously pleased.

36.6.4 Reference

36/3 Höglund, I., Ottoson, G. and Öman, R., Glass covering of large building volumes. Commercial shopping center. Pros and cons, *Building Research and Practice*, No. 4, July/August, 1989.

36.7   ESA BUILDING

Building type: Student housing
Location: Kaiserslautern, Germany
Latitude: 50°N
Floor area:
● Gross: 1403 m^2
● Heated: 70 1 m^2
Occupancy: 20 students

Atrium function: plant growth
Atrium conditioning: Free floating
Atrium proportions:
● Floor area: 702 m^2
● Height: (three floors)   12 m
● Width: 18 m
Intermediate boundary:
  Mass brick and lightweight walls

36.7.1   Building description

This students' home is a self-built project which combines the aspect of living in a community with ecological questions. Moreover, the building has an experimental character with innovative architecture and energy-conscious design. It also gives students of architecture valuable experience in practical work of design, construction, and research. The building represents a 'house-in-house' concept; terraced living units are wrapped in a transparent thermal layer creating an extended living space.

36.7.2   Energy concept

The entire atrium acts as an overall buffer to the apartments and as a solar collector. The interior structure functions as an absorber, preheating fresh air supply to the living units. Various experiments are carried out on the use of different building materials, shading devices, collectors, plantings, and more.

36.7.3   Conclusion

Although a reliable statement about energy consumption and solar gain is as yet impossible, the interest shown in the concept and the actual building exceeds all expectations. Estimates indicate an energy savings potential of 40–50% compared with conventional buildings. Future performance results will show which concepts and energy strategies are viable or can be improved.

36.7.4   Reference

36/4 *Alternative Konzepte* 57, *Wohnbiotop*, December 1987, Verlag C.
F. Müller, Karlsruhe.

Contact: Prof. Dipl. Ing. H. Eissler,
Kaiserslautern.
Dipl.-Ing. W. Hoffmann,
Neustadt.

37 Design Insights

Chapter 37 is divided in three sections. These discuss the results obtained in the case studies in Chapters 35 and 36 according to issue rather than example. They describe the different approaches to atria used in the buildings and the differences and similarities between the results, thereby highlighting general lessons learned. They also describe the general parametric studies performed on these buildings.

Section 37.1, Heating Strategies, discusses the issues of atrium type, glazing type, glazing configuration, atrium conditioning, thermal capacity, and atrium temperature.

Section 37.2, Cooling Strategies, discusses the issues of stratification and ventilation, solar control, use of the atrium to cool the building, and climate sensitivity to cooling.

Section 37.3, Daylighting Strategies, discusses the issues of atrium function, adjacent space function, exterior envelope glazing, atrium proportions, color of surfaces, and glazing of intermediate boundary.

Basis of energy comparison
The basis of comparison used in this chapter is a similar building with an open court or well that is uncovered.

37.1   HEATING STRATEGIES

The strategies for reducing heating energy consumed in the atrium building studied in the Task vary considerably. All the atria act as buffers for their adjacent spaces, reducing their heat loss. The energy savings in the adjacent spaces partially offset the atrium heating energy requirements. Some of the atria also contribute to the total building heating requirements. They act as buffers during the coldest parts of the heating season and contribute heat to adjacent spaces during the milder parts, when more solar energy is available.

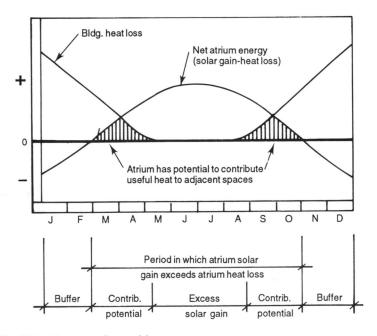

Fig. 37.1   Energy gains and losses

Some of the key design factors that influence the ability of an atrium to function as a buffer or a heat source for the adjacent spaces are described below.

37.1.1 Atrium type

Most of the buildings studied that have core or linear atria have more spaces adjacent to their atria than the buildings with other types of atria. In these, the potential for the atrium to act as a buffer is substantial since it can affect a greater portion of the building. By contrast, the integrated atria of the Alta Day Care Center, the Comstock Building, or the Neuchâtel Building may perform well but do not substantially buffer the building as a whole, since they are connected to only a small portion of the building.

The buffer effect of the Tegut atrium is potentially large, since it virtually surrounds the office pavilions. However, because the plant growth requires a minimum temperature of 5°C, this atrium requires more purchased heating during mid-winter than other atria in this study.

37.1.2 Glazing type/insulation level

Most of the atria that float freely in temperature use single exterior glazing. Examples include the Züblin Haus and Neuchâtel atria. The Alta Day Care Center is not conditioned, but is used to preheat ventilation air by drawing it through the atrium, and has double glazing. The atria that are either partially or fully conditioned use either double glazing (Tegut, Bodbetjänten, and Gateway II), double glazing with a low emissivity coating (ELA), or triple glazing (Wasa City, PI-Group). The Comstock atrium uses a combination of double and single glazing.

U-values:	U_E	U_I
● Gateway II	3.0	4.0/2.0
● Alta	3.0	3.0/0.3
● ELA	2.1	3.0/0.5
● Bodbetjänten	3.0	
● Tegut	3.5	3.0/0.6
● PI-Group	1.9	3.0/0.5

E = Atrium external envelope
I = Intermediate boundary
(Note: The PI-Group has triple glazing.)

The atrium glazing properties significantly affect atrium energy consumption if the atrium is heated to a temperature near the comfort zone. For example, parametric studies of the ELA atrium, with glazing facing north and south, show an approximately 50% reduction of atrium heating energy requirements when the U-value of the glazing is reduced from 2.1 to 1.0 and the solar gains are kept constant. For the total building, this improvement in U-value results in an estimated 5% drop in heating energy requirements.

A comparison of glazing options for the ELA atrium was made by the designers prior to construction. The results indicate that the double, low-emissivity glazing produces a 10% improvement in building heating energy consumption compared to other glazing options, and an improvement of approximately 20% compared to an open well (non-atrium) building when the atrium is to be heated to 15°C.

Atria that are allowed to float freely in temperature generally have a well-insulated intermediate boundary (Alta), while some of the others have a low level (ELA). Parametric analyses were made of the atrium in the ELA building to study the effect of the insulation level in the intermediate boundary on the atrium temperature. The results show

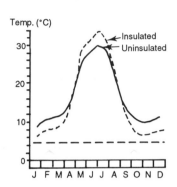

Fig. 37.2 Calculated monthly average temperatures in ELA atrium with different insulation levels in the intermediate boundary

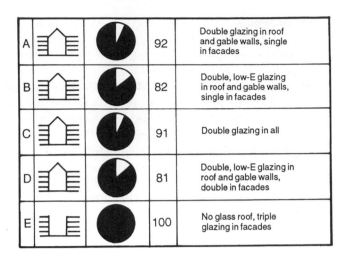

A			92	Double glazing in roof and gable walls, single in facades
B			82	Double, low-E glazing in roof and gable walls, single in facades
C			91	Double glazing in all
D			81	Double, low-E glazing in roof and gable walls, double in facades
E			100	No glass roof, triple glazing in facades

Fig. 37.3 Energy consumption for heating the ELA building for different insulation alternatives

that when the insulation level of the intermediate boundary is increased, the resulting atrium temperature is lower in the winter and higher in the summer. In these simulations the atrium was not heated unless the temperature fell below 5°C.

Additional simulations were performed to examine the effect of changing the atrium width and atrium glazing U-value. Increasing the atrium width has the effect of increasing the area of the atrium external envelope, resulting in a higher heat loss and consequently in higher heating requirements. In these simulations the atrium was heated.

37.1.3 Glazing configuration

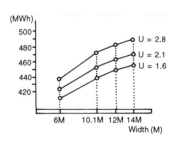

Fig. 37.4 Calculated annual heating requirement for the ELA atrium of different widths and for different U-values of the atrium glazing

With few exceptions, the atria studied have glazing in almost the entire surface of the exterior envelope. Most of this glazing is sloped to form a gable (saddle), shed, or mansard roof. These glazing configurations receive solar energy from throughout the sky vault, providing light in the atrium even during periods of low solar availability. However, unlike vertical glazing facing south, sloped glazing receives more incident solar energy in summer months than in winter months. This contributes to overheating during hot months of the year. In addition, measdurements of heat loss taken at the Wasa City atrium indicate that the sloped glazing loses more heat than vertical glazing, partly due to nocturnal radiation. The magnitude of these losses is higher than simple calculations indicate.

The effect of changing the amount and configuration of glazing in a typical atrium with sloped glazing in the external envelope was studied by computer simulations in the program, BLAST, using a calibrated model of the ELA atrium. The atrium base case (actual building design) has equal glazing areas facing north and south, and the glazing is double, low emissivity. By simulation, the glass facing north was replaced with an opaque roof ($U = 0.35$ W/m² °C). This resulted in a decrease in annual atrium heating energy requirements of about 25%, while there was no change in office heating energy requirements.

To examine the effect of climate, the ELA building was moved (by computer simulation) to Washington, DC, a climate with about 2400 heating degree days (base 18°C) and about 900 cooling degree days (base 24°C). This is similar to climates in southern Europe. In this location, with substantial cooling requirements, the north facing atrium glazing was left intact, and the south facing atrium glazing was replaced with an opaque roof. This resulted in a decrease in annual atrium heating energy requirements of about 27%, and a decrease in cooling requirements of about 36%.

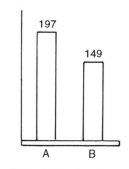

Fig. 37.5 Atrium heating energy in Trondheim

37.1.4 Atrium conditioning

The buildings demonstrate different approaches to thermal conditioning of the atrium space, from no heat input to almost full comfort conditioning. The approach chosen affects the times and purposes for which the atrium can be used, as well as the atrium heating energy requirements.

Züblin Haus and the outer zone of the Neuchâtel atrium are unconditioned spaces that are used primarily for circulation. Solar energy heats the atrium but no attempt is made to maintain a specific temperature. When atrium temperatures are comfortable, they are used for exhibits, and other casual purposes. During the heating season, they act as buffers for adjacent conditioned spaces, but do not contribute heating energy, except by casual transmission through the intermediate boundary.

The Alta Day Care Center is located in a climate where heating requirements exist throughout the year. The building was designed to use the atrium to preheat ventilation air during a portion of the year. The incoming ventilation air passes first through a heat exchanger (extracting heat from the exhaust air), and then through the atrium before entering the adjacent spaces. During mid-winter, this results in the atrium being slightly heated by the ventilation air; in milder periods, solar energy gains in the atrium increase the temperature of the ventilation air. Based on building measurements, this process increases atrium temperature by 10–15°C above ambient conditions.

On an annual basis, about one third of the atrium heating is obtained from the ventilation air passing through the atrium; in mid-winter the percentage is higher. Simulations indicated that less energy would be used if the incoming air passed through the atrium first, but this would

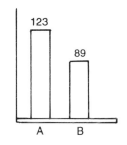

Fig. 37.6 Atrium heating energy in Washington, DC

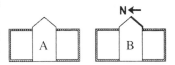

Atrium conditioning

- PI-Group: 17°C
- Wasa: free floating
- Gateway II: local conditioning
- Alta: free floating
- Neuchâtel: free floating
- ELA: 15°C
- Tegut: 10°C day/5°C night

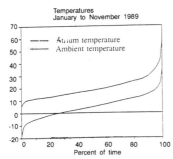

Fig. 37.7 Measured cumulative atrium temperatures in the Alta Day Care Center

lower the atrium temperature, reducing the time during which the atrium can be used as a play area for the children. The value of semiconditioned play space in this climate may be greater than that of the energy savings.

The Comstock office building is located in a dense urban location that permits unobstructed glazing only on the west and north facades. This building has an integrated atrium that is mainly used for circulation purposes. The atrium space is partially conditioned by ventilation exhaust air from the adjacent office spaces. In this way, no primary energy is used to condition the atrium, and it serves as a buffer for the fully conditioned adjacent spaces.

A similar technique is used in the Dragvoll University building, where plants are maintained in the atrium. Since the plants require a minimum temperature of 5°C, when the ventilation system was off during unoccupied periods, the temperature could not be maintained adequately.

The Gateway II building uses an underfloor heating system to provide local conditioning in the portion of the atrium where people are most likely to be. This makes it unnecessary to condition all the air in the atrium and permits the atrium to be a buffer for the adjacent offices. This underfloor heating system has its own boiler, but is primarily supplied with rejected heat from the computer rooms. Measurement data in the atrium indicate that the temperature is more uniform at the floor level, where most occupants are, and varies widely higher up in the atrium.

In some buildings, small, localized space heaters are used to control cold drafts along the glass. This proved effective in the Gateway II building and in the ELA building.

The Tegut building has an integrated atrium that surrounds all but one facade of the office pavilions within. A minimum temperature of 10°C during the day and 5°C at night is maintained in the atrium by a combination of solar gain and purchased heat. The atrium is used for growing subtropical plants, so low temperatures can not be tolerated. When the temperature is comfortable, the terraces in the atrium can be used. During the period of November through March, the terrace temperatures are seldom suitable for use and the heat requirements of the atrium are high. In the balance of the heating season, no purchased heat is required in the atrium space and the solar gains can provide heat to the office pavilions by opening doors and vents.

Other atrium buildings studied use mechanical means to transfer heat from the atrium to the adjacent spaces or the reverse. The Bodbetjänten office and apartment building, for example, uses a heat pump to transfer heat from the atrium and from apartment ventilation exhaust air to hot water storage. Although water heating is the first priority, the atrium is also used to preheat ventilation air at times. The Wasa City project also uses a heat pump to extract heat from the atrium for water heating and ventilation air preheating.

Heating energy requirements are significantly influenced by building operating hours, temperature set points, equipment efficiencies, and other factors. For these reasons, comparison of the performance of buildings to each other is not recommended.

Table 37.1 Summary of atrium building heating performance

Bldg/location	Annual dd base 20	Total purchased energy (kWh/m²y)		Atrium conditioning	Purchased heating (Wh/m² dd)	
		Incl. atrium	Excl. atrium		Incl. atrium	Excl. atrium
Tegut (D)	4130	76	140	min. 5°C	42	
Züblin Haus (D)	3555	118		ambient	16	
ELA (N)	4180	198	236	18°C	26	30
Alta Day Care (N)	6139	220	263	ambient + 10°C	20	24
Wasa City (S)	5440	180	200	18/10°C	22	24
Bodbetjänten (S)	4580	118	129	15/8°C	10	11

37.1.5 Thermal capacity

The atrium buildings studied typically have light weight construction in the intermediate boundary wall separating the atrium from the adjacent spaces. A few buildings use masonry construction in portions of the intermediate boundary. To be beneficial, the mass must usually be directly illuminated by the sun, which is difficult to accomplish in most portions of typical atria. In free floating atria, heavier construction provides some thermal storage capacity, delaying the passage of heat. This results in a more stable atrium temperature, but the stabilizing effect may prevent the atrium temperatures from becoming high enough to provide useful heat to other parts of the building. In conditioned atria that maintain lower temperatures at night, the thermal mass lengthens the time required to increase comfort conditions after temperature setback periods.

Computer simulations of the ELA building were used to assess the effect of increasing the mass in the intermediate boundary in all climates. Replacing wood frame construction with concrete block resulted in a very small reduction in atrium or adjacent space heating requirements in any climate studied (typically less than 1%).

37.1.6 Atrium temperature

The ELA building atrium is appreciated by students who use it for circulation and as a study space. The popularity of the space caused a need for the temperature to be increased from 15°C in the first year of use to 18°C in the second year. More students use the building than originally planned, because of an increase in admissions. Thus, the atrium provides much needed space for studying and social communication.

Measurements and simulations of ELA demonstrate that heating the atrium to 15°C results in an energy saving for the overall building compared to a building with no atrium, because of the buffering effect. In fact, there is little difference in total building energy consumption if the atrium is heated to 5°C or 15°C, while temperatures higher than this result in substantial increases in atrium heating energy requirements.

The effect of atrium temperature on building energy requirements was further studied in simulations with the calibrated model of the ELA building for Trondheim and for Washington, DC. In both climates, the total building heating requirements increased dramatically when the atrium temperature was raised above 15°C. In Trondheim, the increase in temperature set point to 20°C caused the atrium heating energy use to increase by approximately 60%. However, the warmer atrium serves as a better buffer for the adjacent offices, reducing their energy requirements. For the overall building, raising the atrium temperature caused an increase in heating requirements of approximately 20%, excluding ventilation heating. For Washington, the result is similar; the increase in temperature from 15°C to 18°C caused an increase in atrium purchased heating of 100%, and an increase in total building purchased heating requirements of approximately 40%.

It is worthwhile to note that in both locations an increase in atrium temperature from 5°C to 15°C caused a relatively small increase in total building heating requirements. Within this range, the increase in atrium temperature improves the buffering effect, decreasing the heating requirements of adjacent offices. An additional benefit of the buffering effect is that the installed heating capacity of the adjacent spaces was reduced, saving on the construction cost. Increasing the atrium temperature above 15°C provides little additional buffering benefit for the adjacent spaces, however.

The total building energy consumption for a conditioned atrium (heated to 18°C and cooled in climates where cooling is required for comfort), a free floating atrium, and a building with no atrium was also studied. These strategies were compared in the climates of Trondheim, Oslo, and Zurich (heating only); and Washington DC, Dallas, Texas, and Rome (heating and cooling). When total energy density is compared, accounting for the difference in size between the building with the atrium and the one without an atrium, the most attractive strategy varies significantly with climate.

The effect of activity level and clothing on atrium comfort during the heating season was examined by simulating the ELA building with a free floating atrium on a cold winter day in each of four climates. Even on the coldest day, the atrium was comfortable to someone using it for circulation from one part of the building to another. In relatively mild climates, such as Rome or Washington, the atrium was comfortable

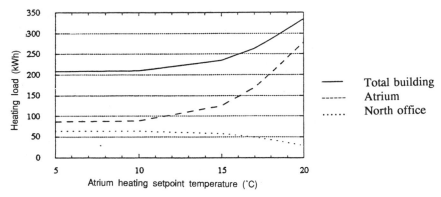

Fig. 37.8 Heating requirement as a function of atrium temperature for the ELA building in Trondheim

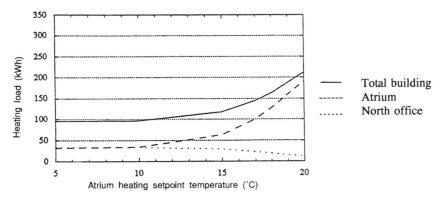

Fig. 37.9 Heating requirement as a function of atrium temperature for the ELA building placed in Washington, DC

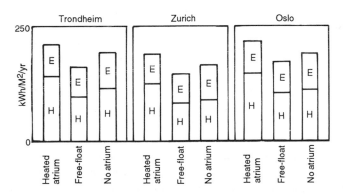

Fig. 37.10 Total energy consumption for a building with an atrium heated to 18°C, a free floating atrium, and a building with no atrium; the building is only heated. E = electricity, C = cooling, H = heating.

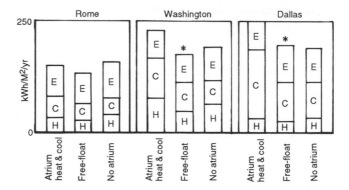

Fig. 37.11 Total energy consumption for a building with an atrium heated to 18°C, a free floating atrium, and a building with no atrium. The building is both heated and cooled. *Free floating atria in these climates experience severe summer overheating unless proper solar control and ventilation are used.

to someone seated in it for part of the day, depending on the type of clothing being worn. In practice, comfort is greater if the people are able to sit in a sunlit area. These studies suggest that designers can save energy by partly conditioning portions of the atrium, such as using radiant heat in seating areas, and allowing the other portions of the atrium to maintain a lower temperature during the heating season.

37.2 COOLING STRATEGIES

Cooling considerations are important in all locations. In cold climates, the cooling strategies used in the atrium buildings studied were principally intended to avoid excessive overheating in summer months. In warmer climates, the atrium may be used to provide a cooling effect for the adjacent spaces.

The most important issues to consider when designing atria for cooling are given below.

37.2.1 Stratification and ventilation

In cold climates with moderate summer temperatures, the most common cooling strategy is to ventilate the atrium, taking benefit from the stratification that occurs. This strategy is effectively employed in the PI-Group Headquarters, the ELA building, Züblin Haus, Tegut, and Neuchâtel. Operable windows or hatches are also used in Bodbetjänten and the Alta Day Care Center. Outside air is usually admitted to the atrium at a low point and allowed to flow upward, exiting through smoke vents or other openings at the high points of the atrium. In the Wasa City project, the openings are at the top only, but they are large to compensate for the lack of openings at the bottom.

At the PI-Group headquarters, which has a ventilation area equal to about 3% of the glazed area, the natural ventilation rate measured with top and bottom vents open was about 5.5 air changes per hour. Air temperatures at the bottom and mid-height of the atrium were approximately 2–3°C above the outside air temperature during the measurement period, and the temperature range from bottom to top of the atrium was 5–10°C.

At the ELA building smoke vents are used for ventilation purposes. Measurements indicate that the atrium temperature can be maintained at the outside air temperature if adequate ventilation is provided using top and bottom openings. A temperature range of only 2–3°C was measured from bottom to top when the vents were open. However, when the vents are not unopened during the summer, the temperature of the top of the atrium rose to 10–15°C above the outside air temperature. Overheating the offices in the adjacent space occurs under these conditions, and the operable windows of these offices are ineffective in obtaining ventilation. Dependable operation of the ventilation openings is important to maintain atrium comfort during the summer.

The Neuchâtel atrium also makes effective use of ventilation, combined with movable solar shading, to control overheating. The manually operated openings are about 7% of the total glazing area, and are almost evenly distributed between the top and bottom of the atrium. Measurements were taken for three consecutive sunny days when the daytime temperature was 10–20°C, employing different combinations of shading and venting. The most effective results were achieved when the movable shades were used and the vents were open. This resulted in an atrium temperature that was approximately 5–10°C above the outside air. When neither ventilation or shading was employed, the atrium temperature rose to 45°C, about 25°C above the outside air temperature. The designers estimate that if the atrium occupants are struck by the sun, as much as 20 ach of outside air ventilation would be required to maintain comfort.

The Comstock building uses a solar chimney to control overheating of the atrium. The atrium faces west, with double glazing on the exterior envelope and single glazing located about 1.5 m behind. Movable vertical shades in the space between the outer and inner glazing are adjusted to intercept the sun during summer months and vents are opened at the top and bottom of the ten-story solar chimney. The solar heated air rises rapidly up the solar chimney and is released at the top, minimizing solar gain in the atrium.

The Tegut atrium almost fully surrounds the office pavilions located within it. Since the overheating potential of this atrium configuration is substantial, significant use is made of operable ventilation openings;

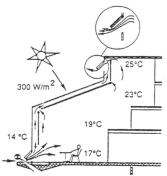

Fig. 37.12 The Neuchâtel atrium

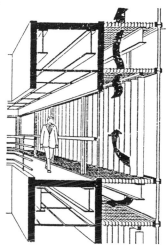

Fig. 37.13 The Comstock solar chimney

Percentage of the glazed area in the atrium used for ventilation:

- PI-Group: 3%
- Neuchâtel: 7%
- Tegut: 12%

they amount to 12% of the glazed area of the external envelope. On the hottest day of the measurement period the temperature in the atrium stayed close to the outside air temperature. The intensive planting in the atrium seems to have substantial shading and evaporative cooling effects.

Simulations of the ELA building were carried out in order to examine the amount of ventilation required to maintain comfort conditions. Air change rates were varied from 1 to 25 per hour for both peak summer days and typical swing season days in different climates. The results show that it is impossible to maintain atrium comfort during mid-day in Washington in the summer. A range of 1–10 ach is sufficient to maintain comfort on a typical day in May. In Oslo, a ventilation rate ranging between 1 and 10 ach is sufficient to maintain comfort in the atrium even on a peak summer day, and during the milder months, a maximum of 5 ach is sufficient.

In most countries, there are fire code requirements for ventilation of the atrium space to control smoke accumulation. Although the specific regulations vary, a rate of 4–6 ach is commmon. In some places, the regulations mandate a specific vent area, such as 10% of the floor area. These requirements are close to the ventilation rates necessary to maintain atrium comfort without cooling. If these requirements are met using either natural stack ventilation or fan-induced exhaust, it may be possible to use the smoke venting system to maintain comfort during much of the cooling season in many climates.

37.2.2 Solar controls

Another effective means of avoiding overheating conditions in the atrium is through the use of shading devices. The atrium buildings studied use several types of shading techniques, including devices located at the exterior envelope and devices located at the intermediate boundary.

The Neuchâtel building has movable sunshading material that is placed inside the sloped and vertical glass of the external envelope. Operation of the shading device is motorized, but control of the operation is manual. The material is beige colored, and has approximately a 30% light transmission. This is used in combination with the operable vents to control overheating.

The Wasa City building has ten large opaque sliding shutters (300 m²) in the external envelope that can be opened for ventilation cooling. Twenty hinged shutters (30 m²) are used in the vertical part of the tower. Light curtains, governed by an internal daylight sensor, also provide sun protection for the lower glass area.

The Comstock building uses vertical movable blinds in the solar chimney of the atrium to provide solar control for the atrium. These are adjusted during summer to intercept the solar radiation, trapping

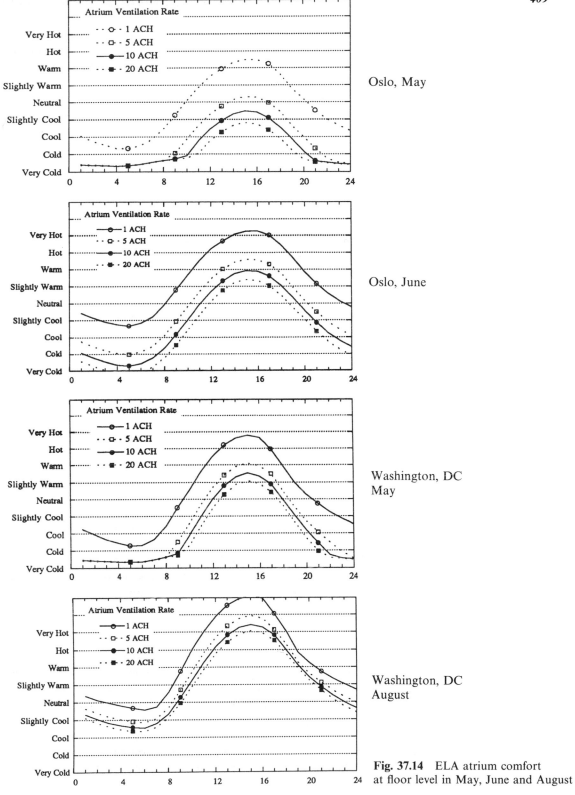

Fig. 37.14 ELA atrium comfort at floor level in May, June and August

it in the solar chimney and permitting it to be vented to the outside.

The ELA building has adjustable blinds and the Dragvoll building awnings placed in the atrium to protect the windows of the offices, while the Züblin Haus offices have adjustable blinds on the office side of the glazing. All of these techniques work effectively and allow individual occupant control. However, shading devices at the intermediate boundary do not prevent solar gain from overheating the atrium itself.

37.2.3 Using the atrium to cool the building

While the stratification, ventilation, and shading devices in most of the atrium buildings are used to control overheating in the atrium itself, they do not provide cooling benefit to the adjacent spaces of the building. The Gateway II building was designed to eliminate the mechanical cooling system by using the atrium to create a flow of air through the adjacent spaces and the atrium. This saved considerable construction and operating cost.

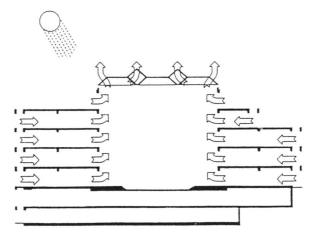

Fig. 37.15 Gateway II atrium section

The offices are arranged around a core atrium so that there is only 14 m from the exterior wall of the building to the intermediate boundary of the atrium. Manually controlled, operable windows in the building exterior wall and louvered windows in the intermediate boundary of the atrium permit the flow of outdoor air through the offices to the atrium. The atrium has large roof lights located near the top that allow the ventilation air to escape. Stratification of the air in the atrium, aided by solar gains, enhances the air flow, as do small fans in some of the offices.

37.2.4 Sensitivity to climate

All of the atrium buildings studied are located in climates where it is possible to avoid the use of mechanical cooling in the atrium. To test the effect that warmer climates would have on atrium design, the calibrated computer model of the ELA building was used to examine building performance in Washington, DC. The base case assessment is for the building as designed, without mechanical cooling in the atrium.

The results show that the atrium comfort conditions are unacceptable during a typical summer day, based on the Fanger Thermal Sensation Index. This finding is consistent with other analyses, and demonstrates why most US atria in similar climates are mechanically cooled. However, the comfort conditions for the atrium in its actual location in Trondheim are acceptable. This is consistent with measured data in the building.

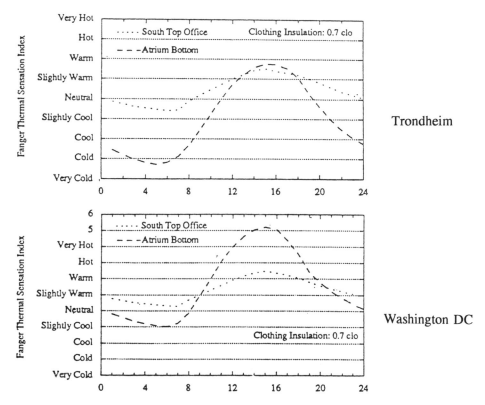

Fig. 37.16 The ELA atrium comfort conditions in July in Trondheim and in Washington, DC

A series of alternatives was examined to achieve tolerable atrium conditions with low cooling energy use. First, the offices were cooled to 24°C, but the atrium was left uncooled. This did not improve comfort

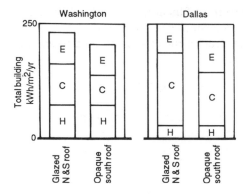

Fig. 37.17 Total building energy consumption for the ELA building placed in Washington, DC and in Dallas, with glazed and opaque atrium roofs. E = electricity, C = cooling energy, H = heating energy

conditions in the atrium, so other strategies that use mechanical cooling in the atrium were tried.

A mechanically cooled base case was established by simulating the cooling of both the offices and the atrium to 24°C. If the portion of the roof glazing in the atrium facing south is replaced with an opaque roof, the cooling energy requirements drop significantly. Another way of achieving this cooling benefit is to use a fixed or operable external shading device to reject the solar gain before it reaches the building. Shading devices can be designed to admit daylight without substantial solar gain, which may be more desirable than an opaque roof from an architectural viewpoint.

37.3   DAYLIGHTING STRATEGIES

The glazing of an open well or courtyard reduces its potential as a daylighting strategy. A general estimate is that the atrium external envelope reduces daylight factors by about 20% compared to an open well. However, the buffer effect of the glazing makes it possible to increase the window area in the intermediate boundary without penalties in the form of higher building heating consumption. Consequently more, rather than less, daylight may be available in the adjacent spaces.

The most important issues to consider in order to maximize the benefits of daylighting for the atrium itself and for the adjacent spaces are given below.

37.3.1   Atrium function

The light levels necessary to support the various activities planned for the atrium vary significantly. In the atria studied, daylight levels are sufficient to serve most functions throughout the majority of the year. In some cases, additional light is required to maintain plant growth. This is especially true in the case study of Bodbetjänten.

37.3.2 Adjacent space function

The ELA building has four floors of offices adjacent to the atrium. They require about 500 lux during occupied hours. A combination of measured and simulated results shows a daylighting potential for the top floor of the spaces adjacent to the atrium of about 50–55%. The daylighting potential for the second floor is estimated to be 30–40%. These estimates do not consider the possible influence of plants or ducts in the atrium, or contrast ratios.

Required light levels:
- Circulation: 50–100 lux
- Reading: 300–600 lux
- Plant growth: > 1000 lux

When this building is moved by simulation to the Dallas climate, the daylighting potential increases to about 80% for the top floor and 60–70% for the second floor. To realize this level of saving in the electric lighting requires either high quality automatic dimmers, or highly motivated users who manually control the lights to save energy. In practice, this does not occur in this building, and little or no daylighting energy savings occurs in the offices. However, light levels in the atrium are quite satisfactory.

37.3.3 External envelope glazing

Most of the atria studied use single or double glazing in the entire external envelope. These experience acceptable daylight levels. Exceptions are Wasa City, which uses triple glazing and has large opaque shutters in parts of the roof, and Bodbetjänten, which has a totally opaque roof. Measurements in Wasa City show that the daylight factors are reduced by close to 50% in the adjacent spaces.

37.3.4 Atrium proportions

Parametric studies using a physical model of the ELA atrium, as well as computer simulations with the program SUPERLITE, indicate that doubling the height-to-width ratio (that is, making the atrium twice as high) results in a decrease in the daylight factor at the bottom of the atrium of between one third and one half. This ratio appears to be the most important single factor governing the availability of daylight in the adjacent spaces.

The results also show that for extreme ratios, i.e. for very tall and narrow atria, it may be advantageous to increase the amount of glazing or use mirrors in the intermediate boundary. In these cases the window glazing reflects much light downwards because of the glancing angle of skylight incidence on the glass.

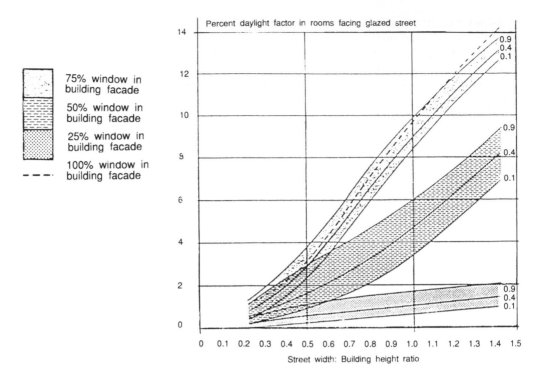

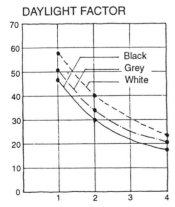

Fig. 37.18 Daylight factors in the bottom floor level rooms adjacent to the ELA atrium, 1.25 m from the intermediate boundary, for different atrium proportions, window sizes, and facade reflectances (0.9, 0.4, and 0.1)

37.3.5 Color of surfaces

In most cases, the color of the atrium walls has some effect on the daylight factors in the atrium, but the effect is smaller than that of the geometry. A parametric study of the ELA atrium with 50% glazing in the intermediate boundary was made for varying height-to-width ratios. The results show that when the color of the solid walls in the intermediate boundary is changed from black, to grey, to white, the daylight factor at the center of the atrium floor improves by about 10% for all ratios. In practice, most surface reflectance characteristics are similar to the grey curve; the black and white curves represent the extremes of performance.

Fig. 37.19 Daylight factors for various height to width ratios

37.3.6 Glazing in intermediate boundary

For the most common atrium proportions, the amount of light available in the atrium itself is not greatly influenced by the glazing in the intermediate boundary, although some interreflection does occur.

However, the amount of light available in the adjacent spaces is directly affected by the amount (and type) of glazing in the intermediate boundary. Since the daylight factor drops on the lower floors of an atrium, a useful design strategy is to increase the size of the windows in the intermediate boundary as the distance from the atrium external envelope increases.

For the Dragvoll building, physical model studies were conducted during the design phase to determine the appropriate amount of glazing in the intermediate boundary on each of three levels in the atrium. To achieve balanced light in the offices adjacent to the atrium, the top level has 40% glazing, the middle level 70% glazing, and the bottom level 90% glazing. Measurements of daylight factors in the completed building confirm the validity of this strategy.

38 *Atrium Analysis Tools*

Chapter 38 is divided into two sections:

Section 38.1, Description of Analysis Tools, provides brief descriptions of the capabilities of the computer models used to analyze atria in Part 6. Appendix B of the Sourcebook provides more detailed descriptions of the three models (BLAST, PI-MODEL, and FRES), and information about their availability.

Section 38.2, Limitations of Existing Analysis Tools, discusses limitations of existing computer models for analyzing atrium buildings, and/or the complications with these applications.

38.1   DESCRIPTION OF ANALYSIS TOOLS

38.1.1   BLAST

BLAST, the Building Loads Analysis and System Thermodynamics program, is a computer program for examining the energy consumption and comfort conditions of buildings. For application to atria, several features of BLAST are important:

- It is a multizone program that allows the atrium and adjacent spaces to be analyzed simultaneously as separate thermal zones. The analysis accounts for conductive coupling between the zones, and allows user control of air exchange between the zones.
- It provides flexibility in defining the geometry, orientation, and thermophysical properties of the individual exterior and partition walls that define the zones of the building.
- It provides detailed calculation of the solar transmission of windows, including accounting for exterior and interior shading, and for the distribution of solar gains on interior surfaces.

BLAST provides analysis of standard ventilation systems, and of primary equipment such as boilers and chillers, so the results of an analysis are data on energy use at the building boundary. It does not account for air temperature stratification, or for solar transmission between building zones.

In the atrium studies carried out in Task XI, the Fanger comfort model [38/1] provided in BLAST examined the comfort conditions achieved in atria. This model assumes that a person is at thermal equilibrium with the surrounding environment; an energy balance is performed accounting for all modes of energy loss from the body including convection and radiant heat loss from the outer surface of the clothing, heat loss by water vapor, diffusion through the skin, heat loss by evaporation of sweat from the skin surface, latent and dry respiration heat loss, and heat transfer from the skin to the outer surface of clothing. By determining the skin temperature and evaporative rate that a person who is thermally comfortable would have in a given set of conditions, the model calculates the energy loss. Based on thermal sensation experiments using human subjects at Kansas State University and in Denmark, a 'predicted mean vote' (PMV) thermal sensation scale was developed that allows quantitication of a person's comfort based on the extent to which energy loss from the skin deviates from the metabolic rate. In the current implementation in BLAST, only hourly thermal senation results are available; aggregate of comfort analysis results over the simulation period must be done manually.

38.1.2 PI-MODEL

The PI-MODEL is a program for analyzing the thermal performance of atrium buildings. The model was developed as an atrium design tool, and provides both simplified and detailed analyses. Simplified analyses are especially important during the early stages of design, when many alternatives must be examined quickly. To facilitate rapid analyses, the model is user friendly, with many of the inputs (e.g. glazing material and orientation) reduced to keywords rather than requiring full engineering descriptions. As the design evolves more detailed input parameter specifications can be provided, increasing the accuracy of the analysis. The program has been validated by comparison with long-term performance measurements from the PI-Group Headquarters office building. The program is still under development, and is not yet available to the public. At this writing, the program and documentation are in Finnish.

The PI-MODEL provides thermal analysis of a single zone; this can be the atrium space in a building where the atrium is separated from adjacent spaces by a partition wall, or an atrium and adjacent spaces in a case such as in a light well where no partition is present. The PI-MODEL calculates a single air temperature for the atrium and therefore does not account for stratification. The zone temperature can be allowed to float, or can be thermostatically controlled. The thermal response of the atrium space and the load components are calculated on an hourly basis using a thermal balance technique which incorporates weighting factors to account for absorption of instantaneous solar and internal equipment gains by building materials in the space, and their release over subsequent hours of the simulation. The calculations account for mechanical ventilation, infiltration, air exchange with adjacent spaces, and natural ventilation. Solar gain calculations account for internal and external shading devices. Heat conduction through exterior walls and windows, and through interior partition walls to the adjacent building are accounted for. The hourly analysis also allows varying interior parameters such as ventilation, and lighting, equipment, and occupant levels to be accounted for through operating schedules.

To reduce analysis time, seven days are selected to characterize each month. The hourly heating and cooling energy use of the atrium space is calculated for each of the characteristic days, and multiplied by a repetition factor to account for energy use on those days not specifically analyzed. Using this approach, annual energy requirements are estimated based on 84 daily simulations, each of which accounts for 24 hour combination of climate and operating data.

38.1.3 FRES

FRES, the Flexible Room and Environment Simulator, is a program for simulation of energy use and climate conditions in buildings. FRES has three features of particular importance in modeling atria:

- It provides a multi-zone model to account for air temperature variations in individual spaces; this allows temperature stratification in atria to be modeled.
- Glazed surfaces can be defined in partition walls between zones; this allows calculation of solar gains through an atrium into spaces adjacent to the atrium.
- This model provides flexibility in definition of glazed facades; the user defines the orientation of surfaces, characteristics of shading surfaces and devices, and the optical properties of the materials.

FRES simulates the heating and cooling systems in the building to determine energy consumption at the building boundary. The user builds up the HVAC system from modules describing the basic heating, cooling, and control components, interconnecting them as appropriate to describe the complete system. A wide variety of component modules are available, and both parallel and sequential control strategies are possible for all combinations of components.

The user interface is based on roller blind menus. This is especially well suited to surveying the data while checking and confirming input specifications. An explanation window is provided to identify the requirements for most of the input data fields, limiting the need for referring to written documentation.

The modular design, plus the user oriented interface, provides a flexible and seamless analysis environment. To perform an analysis, the user enters a menu of administrative information, fetches an existing project file or creates a new one, and requests simulation. The results of the simulation appear in a spreadsheet for analysis and interpretation by the user.

38.2   LIMITATIONS OF EXISTING ANALYSIS TOOLS

While simulating energy performance and comfort conditions in atria, several limitations to existing analysis tools exist. The key problems are identified below.

38.2.1   Infiltration and natural ventilation

The algorithms used in most existing simulation programs to calculate infiltration and natural ventilation rates do not account for the interaction of temperature and wind pressure dependent air flow between a particular space and its surrounding spaces and environment, or the dependence of either component of air flow on the geometric configuration of the space, mode of operation (e.g. presence of ventilation openings), or interaction with mechanical ventilation. To properly represent buoyancy and cross-venting effects, simulation programs must be capable of predicting air flow rates in multizone configurations, accounting for both natural and mechanical ventilation, and including the dependence on height and temperature gradients in the space.

38.2.2   Stratification

Existing simulation programs calculate a single indoor air temperature in each thermal zone being analyzed. The real temperature distributions in the space are important in determining transmission heat losses; air change rate between the atrium and ambient, and between the atrium and adjacent spaces; air motion within the atrium; and comfort conditions. To provide a more faithful representation of thermal conditions in the atrium, the spatial distribution of air and surface temperatures must be determined.

38.2.3   Air flow patterns

None of the existing simulations account for air movement within individual zones. Air movement influences transient thermal conditions, temperature distributions, comfort conditions, and energy performance. For example, none of the programs explicitly estimate the impact of 'drafts' caused by downward air flow at cold surfaces on comfort conditions, or the impact of free upward convection from heating devices on heat losses through surfaces above the heater. Algorithms are needed which enable local air flow distribution to be calculated.

38.2.4   Surface film coefficients

Most calculation programs provide fixed, global values for surface film coefficients, and many do not even account separately for the convective and radiant components of heat transfer at the surface. Because there are often substantial local differences of air flow and temperature conditions within atria, the magnitudes of each component can vary significantly from surface to surface, affecting heat transfer and comfort conditions.

38.2.5   Solar radiation

Few simulation programs calculate the distribution of solar radiation on surfaces internal to a zone, or solar radiation transmission through glazed partition walls to adjacent spaces. Failure to accurately account for the distribution of solar gains between the atrium and its adjacent spaces negatively impacts the reliability of daylighting and thermal calculations. Furthermore, proper accounting for the distribution of solar gains among surfaces is necessary to properly calculate surface temperature, and therefore air flow profiles, convection coefficients at surfaces, interior air temperature distributions, and radiative exchange between surfaces.

All of the problems identified above are interconnected, and, to some extent, result from the basis of existing programs in heat transfer, rather than mass transfer. Various 'tricks' can be used to circumvent some of the problems — at least in part. For example, temperature stratification and air flow patterns in large spaces such as atria can be approximated by subzoning the space into two or more adjacent zones which can be at different temperatures and between which air exchange can be modeled; this allows the spatially continuous variation in temperatures within the larger space to be approximated as discrete changes in temperature across subzone partitions. While this may improve the representation of the atrium in the simulation, it requires considerable engineering judgement that is typically not based on well defined facts: in the example cited above, a subzoning configuration must be postulated and an air flow path (typically with constant heat transfer coefficients representing a certain air velocity) must be defined. These 'tricks' may improve the model, but they are not entirely satisfactory.

Other ways of dealing with mass transfer in atria should be considered. Complex simulation programs have been developed for calculating heat and mass transfer, considering turbulence effects and transient temperature dependent physical properties of the medium. A fundamental shortcoming of many of these programs in application to atria is that while they provide technically sound analyses at high air speeds, the solution of the Navier–Stokes equation becomes unstable with decreasing velocities in non-constant local fields. In addition, because of the complexity of the programs, unacceptably long computation time is required to deal with the time (e.g. annual) and spatial (e.g. tens of meters) scales of interest in atrium analysis. Furthermore, most of these programs were developed for aerospace applications where fixed boundary conditions commonly can be assumed; as a result, these programs do not account for the effect on temperature distribution and energy balances of user scheduled parameters (e.g. shading), for complex building heating, cooling, and ventilation systems and controls. In short, these more detailed methods too are seriously limited in analysis of atria.

At present none of the existing analysis tools satisfactorily deal with all of the issues identified above. It is clear that improvements in modeling needed to achieve a higher degree of simulation accuracy. For this reason, a working group has been set up within Task XII to develop algorithms for modeling physical phenomena of heat transfer in atria and integrating them into building energy analysis tools.

38.2.6   References

38/1 Fanger, P.O., Calculation of thermal comfort: introduction of a basic comfort equation, *ASHRAE Trans.*, **73**, Pt II, 1967.

38/2 *Thermal Comfort, Analysis and Applications in Environmental Engineering*, Danish Technical Press, Copenhagen, 1970.

39 Conclusions

The atrium buildings studied in this Task save energy when compared to conventional buildings without atria. All the atria act as buffers for their adjacent spaces, reducing their heat loss. The energy savings in the adjacent spaces partially offset the atrium heating energy requirements. Some of the atria also reduce the total building heating requirements. They act as buffers during the coldest parts of the year and contribute heat to the adjacent spaces during the milder parts, when more solar energy is available.

Some of the most important conclusions that can be drawn from the work regarding the atrium as part of a passive solar heating strategy are:

- During midwinter an atrium functions primarily as a buffer. The buffer effect will naturally be greater the more surfaces the atrium and the adjacent spaces have in common.
- During the spring and fall the atrium also has the potential to contribute useful heat to the rest of the building. A prerequisite for this is that the atrium is not fully heated and that its temperature is allowed to fluctuate.
- In most climates, heating the atrium to a temperature in the range of 10–15°C results in little or no increase in the overall building heating energy requirements. The heat put into the atrium partially offsets the heating requirements in the rest of the building.
- Temperatures above 15°C result in substantial increases in atrium heating energy requirements for the atria studied. For instance, the increase from an atrium set point temperature of 15°C to 18°C resulted in a 25% increase in the total building heating energy requirement for the ELA building both in Trondheim and in Washington.
- Tempering the atrium also reduces the size of the installed heating capacity in the adjacent spaces and reduces construction costs.
- During the heating season, the U-value of the glazing is more important than the solar transmission for the energy consumption. Double low-emissivity glazing is particularly effective in northern latitudes.

- Thermal mass in the atrium improves comfort, as it reduces temperature fluctuations, but it has little influence on the overall energy consumption.
- If the atrium is used for active functions such as circulation, occupants will be comfortable in any of the climates considered without any heat being put into the atrium. If the atrium is used for more sedentary functions, such as seating, comfort conditions may not be acceptable and localized heating should be considered.

Some of the most important conclusions regarding the atrium as part of a passive solar cooling strategy are:

- In most northern climates, no mechanical cooling system is required to maintain atrium comfort. Natural or fan-assisted ventilation with ambient air is sufficient to maintain reasonable comfort; the rate of air change in the spaces that were measured is in the range of 5–10 air changes per hour during summer days.
- The smoke ventilation that is usually required to satisfy building codes can accomplish this, resulting in little effect on construction costs.
- Solar controls, such as awnings, shutters, fabric drapes, and movable blinds, have all been effectively used to control solar gain during the overheating season without hindering solar gains during the winter.
- An atrium can act as a thermal chimney, drawing ventilation air through the adjacent spaces, as it does in the Gateway II building. There it resulted in the elimination of the mechanical cooling system and thus in a building that was less expensive to build than one with mechanical cooling with no atrium.

Some of the most important conclusions regarding the atrium as part of a daylighting strategy are:

- The frames and glazing of an atrium reduce the amount of available daylight inside. However, the window area in the intermediate boundary can be increased without penalties in the form of higher heating energy consumption because of the buffer effect of the glazing. Consequently, more daylight may be available in the adjacent spaces.
- Daylighting of the atrium results in lighting energy savings in many buildings, but few take advantage of the potential to save energy in the adjacent spaces, even if there is sufficient daylight available.
- Measured and simulated data from the ELA building show a potential annual lighting energy savings during occupancy hours on the top (fourth) floor offices of 50% in Trondheim and 80% in Dallas.

- The atrium's width to height ratio substantially influences the amount of daylight available in the adjacent spaces, while the colors of the surfaces of the atrium have a somewhat smaller influence.

It is clear that the integration of an atrium in a building can result in energy savings when heating, cooling, and daylighting strategies are skilfully combined. In most cases, the inclusion of a well-designed atrium also enhances the building's amenity value, and in some cases the use of an atrium lowers initial construction costs and operating costs.

40 Recommended Reading

40.1 ATRIUM BUILDINGS

Atrium Buildings, by Richard Saxon, is the first comprehensive discussion about atria. It is organized in two main parts:

Part One, 'The Rise of the Modern Atrium' covers eight chapters addressing the subjects of historical atrium building development from the first examples in iron and glass of the 19th century to the modern contributions of atrium approaches of today. Energy issues such as buffering, passive solar design, and daylighting are also discussed, as well as the potential of tomorrow's atrium design.

Part Two, 'Constructing the Atrium', is an excellent discussion on building typology and determinants which are indispensable for design development, program and decisions by architects and engineers.

The appendices (Nos. 1–6) include checklists to selected design criteria of previous chapters which are valuable for the practical decision making process. An extended appendix (No. 8) includes a gazetteer of notable atrium buildings of the UK (66 atria), of the US (141 buildings) and Canada (19 atria). This list of 226 references may serve as an excellent travel guide for architectural excursions.

Richard Saxon:
Atrium Buildings — Development and Design

Architectural Press Limited,
London, second edition 1986,
ISBN 0851-39-051-X
200 pages, Price: approx. £40

40.2 THE NEW ATRIUM

The New Atrium, by Michael Bednar, covers the subject of atria both thoroughly and in detail, from its historic and contemporary evolution to its role in urban planning, architectural design, and historic preservation. Complete chapters are presented on:

- The atrium and urban design
- Design analysis
- Design development
- The historical development of the atrium
- Energy performance

In a second section the book also features 47 case studies of notable atrium buildings with detailed descriptions, evaluations, and analyses. The rich illustrations by floor plans, sections, interior and exterior photographs provide a valuable source of information and inspiration

Michael J. Bednar:
The New Atrium

McGraw-Hill Book Company,
1986, 1221 Avenue of the Americas,
New York, N4 10020
ISBN 0-07-004275-6
240 pages, Price: approx. $50

for the intended audience of all building professionals. For architects and engineers but also for prospective clients, *The New Atrium* is a fundamental reference for concept, design and execution of atrium buildings.

40.3 THE GLASS HOUSE

John Hix: *The Glass House*

The MIT Press, 1981
Cambridge, MA, USA
ISBN 0-262-58044-6 (paper)
Price: $14

The Glass House by John Hix, is a penetrating piece of work on different aspects of transparent buildings, from the glass-covered wooden orangeries of the 17th century up to recent concepts of a good life in the arctic under a huge plastic cover.

The general architectural problem of creating good indoor climate is accentuated in glass house design because of the alternating high gains and losses of heat. The fact that greenery is very sensitive to climate forced glass house designers to utilize the latest knowledge and technology of heating, ventilation, materials and construction. Efficiency and logic become a characteristic feature of the glass houses developed during the 19th century, from which we still can learn much today.

This book illustrates man's struggle to control and enrich his environment with numerous examples of glazed spaces and details from different countries and ages. It is easily read and very richly illustrated with more than 300 photos, sketches and drawings.

40.4 HOUSES OF GLASS

Georg Kohlmeier, Barna von Sartory: *Houses of Glass — A Nineteenth Century Building Type*

The MIT Press, 1986,
Cambridge, Mass, USA
ISBN 0-262-11108-X
Price: $85

Houses of Glass — A Nineteenth Century Building Type, by George Kohlmeier and Barna von Sartory, is a magnificent book with more than 700 illustrations. It presents the development of the glass house during the 19th century from technical, economical and cultural aspects.

It starts in the early 19th century when the dream of the artificial paradise developed. Under the glass cover, one could recreate the heat, growth and easy lifestyle of the south in a harsh northern environment. Such ideas are still present in modern glass architecture.

The development of glass house architecture as an architectural phenomenon in its own right created by gardeners and engineers from deep knowledge of horticulture and new techniques is highlighted. The invention of central heating and then shell constructions were major advances. Cast iron and later wrought iron, together with new calculation methods, brought forth elegant solutions. The combination of functionalism and decoration may have reached its highest point in the iron structures of the 19th century.

In the appendix there is a review of the works and ideas of J. C. Loudon, the pioneer and master of glass houses. Here is also an extensive catalogue with more than 100 glass houses from the 19th century enriched with quantities of drawings and photographs. This beautiful book is an inspiring source for studying architectural and technical development within a narrow field.

Appendix A
The International
Energy Agency

A.1   THE INTERNATIONAL ENERGY AGENCY

The International Energy Agency (IEA), headquartered in Paris, was formed in November 1974 as an autonomous body within the framework of the Organization for Economic Cooperation and Development to establish cooperation in energy research.

Collaboration in the research, development and demonstration of new energy technologies to help reduce dependence on oil and to increase long-term energy security has been an important part of the Agency's program. The IEA research and development activities are headed by the Committee on Research and Development (CRD) which is supported by a small Secretariat staff. In addition, four working parties (in Conservation, Fossil Fuels, Renewable Energy and Fusion) are charged with monitoring the various collaborative energy Agreements, identifying new areas for cooperation and advising the RD on policy matters.

A.2   SOLAR HEATING AND COOLING PROGRAM

One of the first collaborative research and development agreements was the IEA Solar Heating and Cooling Program which was initiated in 1977 to conduct joint projects in active and passive solar techniques, primarily for building applications. The 18 members of the Program and current Executive Committee members are given below.

Member countries and executive committee members

Australia	Dr B. Godfrey
Austria	Prof. G. Fanninger
Belgium	Prof. A. De Herde
Canada	Mr D. McClenahan
Denmark	Mr P. Dorph-Peterson

European Community Mr T. Steemers
Finland   Dr P. Lund
France   Mr Y. Boileau
Germany   Dr V. Lottner
Italy   Dr D. Malosti
Japan   Dr T. Goto
Netherlands   Mr H. Faber
Norway   Mr F. Salvesen
Spain   Dr M. Macias
Sweden   Mr M. Rantil
Switzerland   Dr G. Schriber
United Kingdom   Dr A. Cole
United States   Mr T. Kapus

Executive Secretary: Sheila Blum
                       International Planning Associates
                       807 Caddington Avenue
                       Silver Spring, MD 20901 USA

A.3   TASKS UNDER THE EXECUTIVE COMMITTEE

Twenty projects or 'Tasks' have been undertaken since the beginning of the Program. The overall Program is managed by an Executive Committee composed of one representative from each of the member countries, while the leadership and management of the individual Tasks is the responsibility of operating agents. These Tasks and their respective countries providing an operating agent are:

Task 1:	Denmark	Investigation of the Performance of Solar Heating and Cooling Systems
Task 2:	Japan	Coordination of Research and Development on Solar Heating and Cooling
Task 3:	United Kingdom	Performance Testing of Solar Collectors
Task 4:	United States	Development of an Insulation Handbook and Instrument Package
Task 5:	Sweden	Use of Existing Meteorological Information for Solar Energy Application
Task 6:	United States	Solar Heating, Cooling, and Hot Water Systems Using Evacuated Collectors
Task 7:	Sweden	Central Solar Heating Plants with Seasonal Storage
Task 8:	United States	Passive and Hybrid Solar Low Energy Buildings
Task 9:	Germany	Solar Radiation and Pyranometry Studies
Task 10:	Japan	Material Research and Testing
Task 11:	Switzerland	Passive and Hybrid Solar Commercial Buildings
Task 12:	United States	Building Energy Analysis and Design Tools for Solar Applications
Task 13:	Norway	Advanced Solar Low Energy Buildings
Task 14:	Canada	Advanced Active Solar Systems
Task 15:	Netherlands	Advanced Central Solar Heating Plants (Planning)
Task 16:	Germany	Photovoltaics in Buildings
Task 17:	Germany	Measuring and Modeling Spectral Radiation
Task 18:	United Kingdom	Advanced Glazing Materials
Task 19:	Switzerland	Solar Air Heating Systems
Task 20:	Sweden	Solar Retrofit Measures

Appendix B
Computer Models

B.1 INTRODUCTION

This appendix provides brief descriptions and information about the availability of the energy analysis tools used in Task XI research. Topical discussion of the capabilities and limitations of these tools for particular passive systems is included in the respective chapters of the heating, cooling, daylighting, and atria parts of the sourcebook. In addition, special-purpose analysis tools used in the course of Task XI research are described. Most of the tools are for daylighting.

B.2 GENERAL PURPOSE TOOLS

BLAST

BLAST, the Building Loads Analysis and System Thermodynamics program, is a comprehensive tool for predicting energy consumption of buildings. It uses an English language input processor and provides:

1. Space load predictions based on weather data and user input describing the building geometry and materials, functions, operating schedule, and comfort requirements.
2. Heating hot water, steam, chilled water, and electrical requirements for the air distribution system based on the computed space loads, weather data and user input describing the building air handling system.
3. Energy use of the primary equipment (e.g. boilers, chillers, on-site power generating equipment and solar energy systems) based on weather data, results of air distribution system simulations and user input describing the central plant.

These analyses are performed using an hourly time step. The program also provides economic analysis algorithms for calculating energy costs and life cycle costs based on user specification of utility rates. A climate data processor is available for creating BLAST-compatible weather files from standard format climate data.

The space loads prediction uses the thermal balance technique. For each hour to be simulated, BLAST performs simultaneous radiant, convective and conductive heat balances for all internal and external surfaces in the building, and the air in each zone in the building. The heat balance includes transmission loads, solar loads, internal heat gains, infiltration loads and the temperature control strategy used to maintain the space temperature. Validation studies have been carried out using monitored data from test cells and from a massive building in an environmental chamber.

A relatively unique feature of BLAST is its ability to perform human comfort analyses. BLAST (version 3.0, level 132) includes comfort algorithms for computing thermal sensation indices based on models developed by Fanger, the J.B. Pierce Foundation (two-node model), and Kansas State University.

BLAST was developed by the US Army Construction Engineering Research Laboratory. Specialized supporting software (e.g. weather data processor) has also been developed. The BLAST family of programs is distributed by the BLAST Support Office, 30 Mechanical Engineering Building, Department of Mechanical and Industrial Engineering, University of Illinois, 1206 West Green Street, Urbana, Illinois 61801. The BLAST Support Office also provides technical support, including software maintenance, training, phone consultation, newsletter distribution and special services.

Mainframe versions of BLAST are available for VAX and APOLLO computers. The IBM PC compatible version requires an 80286 (or better) processor, and extended memory. The Macintosh version requires a Mac II or SE/30. A portable Fortran 77 version is also available for installation on other computers.

The BLAST program costs $750, including the program, WIFE (weather information file encoder), and BTEXT (interactive text preprocessor that facilitates input). A manual and other supporting documentation is provided with the program.

FRES

FRES, the Flexible Room and Environment Simulator, is a general purpose program for the analysis of energy and indoor environmental conditions in buildings. It is an hourly program that operates on personal computers, and is a derivative of the mainframe program 'Royal Debac' developed in Norway.

FRES was developed as a modular program to give the user flexibility in adding new analysis capabilities. For example, a two-zone model for air stratification in tall rooms is being developed for eventual inclusion in FRES. In its present form, the program provides a building description module, and modules for many common HVAC components and controls. In the building description module, the basic elements of the description are opaque walls, including those in the exterior envelope and those that make up interior partitions; the user has the flexibility to define walls in detail, based on the thermophysical properties of the construction materials, or more simply in terms of the aggregate properties of the construction. The user also provides either detailed or summary geometric information regarding the relative locations of the walls to define the boundaries of the building and/or zones to be analyzed.

The program provides for the thermal coupling between separate building elements and between the building elements and the environment in the calculations.

In addition to calculating transient thermal gains and losses in the spaces in a building, FRES calculates energy use at the building boundary by simulating the heating, ventilating, and air conditioning (HVAC) system. A variety of HVAC and control component modules are included in FRES; the user builds up the climate control systems for a building from these basic modules, interconnecting them as appropriate to describe the complete unit. Both parallel and sequential control strategies are possible for all combinations of components.

Two user interfaces are provided. The interface with the greatest flexibility is a preprocessor which reads a keyword oriented input file. With this interface, input data is specified in structured lists using a predefined syntax. Where appropriate, these lists do not have a predefined length. For example, in the wall list, each wall construction in the building is given an identifier that is referred to in the portion of the input where the physical room description is provided.

The preprocessor provides messages for syntax errors, incorrect identifier references, and other mistakes in the building description; this facilitates development of the building models. The second interface is based on roller blind menus, and is especially well suited to surveying the data while checking and confirming input specifications.

The modular design, plus the user-oriented interface, provides a flexible and seamless analysis environment. To perform an analysis, the user enters a menu of administrative information, fetches an existing project file or creates a new one, and requests simulation. With the current version of the program, the results appear in a spreadsheet for analysis and interpretation by the user. Further development of the program and the user interface are anticipated, and user groups will be established. The user groups will allow needs for further development of the program to be communicated to SINTEF, and will enhance communication among users of the program.

FRES was developed by and is available from SINTEF, Division of Applied Thermodynamics, N-7034 Trondheim, Norway. Further development of the program is expected, as is the establishment of user groups to provide feedback to the developers, and a mechanism for informing users of program changes. SINTEF also provides informal technical support to users of FRES. FRES operates in IBM PC compatible hardware.

DOE-2

The DOE-2 building energy analysis program was designed to calculate whole-building energy use under actual weather conditions. It provides an input processor called the Building Description Language (BDL) Program that accepts user-provided data in an English language format. DOE-2 includes four major simulation subprograms called LOADS, SYSTEMS, PLANT, and ECONOMICS that use the input data plus hourly weather information to calculate the hourly energy performance of the building.

The LOADS program computes the hourly cooling and heating loads for each space of the building. The load calculation assumes that the space air temperature is constant in time, and uses response factors to calculate conduction gains, and weighting factors to account for heat storage in building materials. The SYSTEMS program simulates the equipment that provides heating, ventilation and/or air conditioning to the thermal zones, and the interaction of this equipment with the building envelope.

The constant space temperature load is corrected to account for space temperature variations and for equipment operation. Sensible and latent coil loads are calculated to determine the total heat addition and extraction rates. The PLANT program simulates primary HVAC equipment (e.g. boilers, chillers), calculating the total energy by fuel source required to maintain the user specified comfort conditions. The user may establish the management of the plant equipment by setting up schedules and/or load ranges under which specified equipment will operate. The ECONOMICS portion of the program computes the costs of energy for the various fuels or utilities used by the equipment accounting for a broad range of tariff structures. In addition, the economic calculations allow the user to estimate life cycle costs for the energy systems in the building.

A relatively unique feature of the program is a mechanism by which the user can substitute algorithms for those that are included in the program. In addition, DOE-2 provides reporting programs that provide flexible access to the results of the calculations, a weather data processor that accepts a tape of hourly weather information for a particular city, libraries of materials and response factors for common wall and roof constructions, programs for calculating wall and roof response factors and room weighting factors.

DOE-2 was developed by Lawrence Berkeley Laboratory. The program is written in Fortran 77. The mainframe version of the program is available from the National Energy Software Center, Argonne National Laboratory, 9700 South Cass Avenue, Argonne, Illinois 60439. The VAX and SUN-4 versions of the program are available from the Simulation Research Group, Building 90, Room 3147, Lawrence Berkeley Laboratory, Berkeley, California 94720; the Simulation Research Group also provides technical support for the portable mainframe, VAX and SUN versions of the program. PC versions of DOE-2 are available from Acrosoft International, 9745 East Hamden Avenue, Denver, Colorado 80231, and from ADM Associates, Inc., 3299 Ramos Circle, Sacramento, California 95827.

A portable version of DOE-2 is available for mainframe computers, and versions are available for VAX and SUN computers. The IBM PC compatible version requires an 80286 (or better) processor, and extended memory.

DOE-2.1C source code is available for $2490 for shipments within the US, and $4980 for international shipments. The source code and a comprehensive package of user and engineering documentation is available from the National Technical Information Service, 5285 Port Royal Road, Springfield, Virginia 22161.

SUNCODE and SERI/RES

SUNCODE is the PC version of the mainframe building energy analysis program SERI/RES; the calculation modules are essentially identical in the two programs, and so have the same capabilities. The programs calculate hourly heating and cooling thermal loads for multizone buildings, and are appropriate for analysis of residential and small commercial buildings. SERI/RES has been extensively validated through comparison to monitored data from controlled residential building, and other detailed simulation programs. The results of these validation studies should apply equally to SUNCODE.

SUNCODE and SERI/RES were developed to provide detailed, dynamic analysis of buildings that incorporate passive solar systems. SUNCODE consists of three modules. EDITS is a building file editor and preprocessor that provides an interactive, menu-driven building description input environment. LOADS is the calculation module; it uses a thermal balance technique to calculate hourly heating and cooling loads. VIEW is a graphical postprocessor that allows the user to examine simulation results.

The load calculation is based on a thermal resistance network analysis. Explicit models are provided for many passive solar systems, including Trombe walls, rock beds, and phase change material storage systems. Using the multizone features of the program allows implicit simulation of more complex passive systems such as envelope-integrated air collectors.

SERI/RES was developed by the Solar Energy Research Institute. SUNCODE was developed by Ecotope Inc., 2812 East Madison, Seattle, Washington, and is available from Ecotope, from Cenergia ApS, Set. Jacobsveg 4, DK-2750 Ballenup, Denmark, from BEST, Echterdingstrasse, 13, D-7035 Waldenbusch, Germany, and from the Architectural Energy Corporation, 2450 Frontier Avenue, Suite 201, Boulder, Colorado 80301.

The input and calculation modules in SUNCODE are written in Fortran 77, the graphical postprocessor is written in Turbo Pascal. SUNCODE runs under DOS on IBM compatible PCs.

SUNCODE with documentation costs between $400 and $650, depending upon the source and version.

TRNSYS

TRNSYS, the transient system simulation program, is a comprehensive tool for simulating the energy performance of buildings. It was originally developed to allow detailed analysis of buildings with active solar technologies, and has incorporated a range of conventional heating and cooling equipment. TRNSYS is a modular program that performs calculations of solar system performance and auxiliary energy requirements.

TRNSYS uses a graphical preprocessor (PRESIM) and a system description input language which allows the user to specify the components which make up the system, and to specify their connections to one another. A library of active and passive solar and conventional HVAC equipment and controls component models is provided. In addition there are component models for single and multizone buildings that generate the loads seen by the solar and conventional systems, and for processing the meteorological data used in the simulation.

Key features of TRNSYS are its flexibility, and the detail with which systems can be examined. Although the program provides a broad range of standard component models, it has an open architecture that allows the user to define and incorporate into the analysis models for nonstandard components, or alternatives to the models that are provided. Component models provide a mathematical description of the individual physical elements that make up the system (typically algebraic and/or differential equations); TRNSYS provdes a general-purpose solver for the full set of simultaneous equations that are defined by specifying all of the components that make up the system being simulated, and their relationships in terms of input and output parameters. The time step used in the analysis, and convergence limits for the solutions at each time step are user controlled. The user also controls the output from the simulation, which can include the input or output parameters for any of the components in the system, over a user-specified time period, and at user-specified time increments.

TRNSYS is available from the Solar Energy Laboratory, University of Wisconsin, 1500 Johnson Drive, Madison, Wisconsin 53706.

TRNSYS is written in Fortran 77 and can be used on mainframe computers and IBM compatible PCs.

The cost for TRNSYS is $600–1100, depending on the version (mainframe or PC) and on the location to which it is shipped. The cost for documentation is $50–100, depending on the location to which it is sent.

MBDSA

The Multizone Building Dynamic Simulator (MBDSA) is the PC version of the mainframe simulation program LPB-1 developed earlier in Belgium. Technically, the two programs differ only in the method used to calculate heat conduction through walls, and in the user interface. Both are hourly simulation programs whose calculations are based on TRNSYS algorithms.

MBDSA consists of four modules. PREPA is a preprocessor that allows user input of the physical, functional and operational parameters that describe the building. The calculation module is named MBDS; it performs a dynamic thermal balance load calculation on an hourly basis. The simulation results are examined using POSTA, a postprocessor that allows numeric and graphic outputs to be generated. In addition, a module named PRET is used to process commonly available meteorological data, producing a climate data file that can be used in the simulation.

MBDSA performs multizone thermal load calculations. The analysis of each zone accounts for direct and diffuse solar radiation gains, internal heat gains, conduction through the exterior envelope, infiltration, and conductive and convective coupling to adjacent zones. The information available as output for each zone includes aggregate information such as air temperature, and net heating and cooling requirements, detailed data such as surface temperatures, and the components (e.g. radiation, convection, and conduction) of the thermal balance on each surface and on the zone air. MBDSA has been linked to daylighting analysis software to allow assessment of the impact of daylighting on lighting and thermal energy requirements.

MBDSA was developed by the University of Liege, Belgium, and is available from ATIDC, rue Brogniez 41, B-1070 Brussels, Belgium.

MBDSA is written in Fortran 77; it operates on IBM compatible PCs with MS-DOS.

tsbi3

The computer program tsbi3 provides hourly analysis of the energy use and indoor climate conditions in buildings. It integrates thermal load and mechanical system calculations, accounting for operation of the control system. The program is modular to facilitate addition of new analysis capabilities, and has a user-friendly interface based on windows and menus that are accessed using the keyboard and mouse.

The output of the program includes indoor temperature and humidity, and heating and cooling energy requirements on an hourly, daily, weekly, monthly, or yearly basis. Detailed energy balance information is also available, including solar and internal gains, ventilation, infiltration, conduction gains and losses, and reference point illumination and glare indicators.

Among the tsbi3 capabilities, daylighting calculations are especially noteworthy. Two daylighting calculation options are provided. First, the program allows input of electric lighting schedules based on independent daylighting calculations using, for example, SUPERLITE. Available software for linking separate daylighting thermal calculations is identified in Section B.3 below, and discussed in Part 4 of the sourcebook. The second daylighting calculation option with tsbi3 is use of daylighting algorithms that are integral parts of the program. In this case, daylighting illumination levels are calculated at reference points, and electric lighting levels are adjusted as necessary to satisfy design illumination requirements. A variety of electric lighting systems and controls can be analyzed.

The program tsbi3 was developed by and is available from the Danish Building Research Institute, Jorgen Erik Christensen or Kyjeld Johnsen, P.O. Box 119, DK-2970, Horsholm, Denmark.

The program is written in the C language, and it operates on IBM compatible PCs running under MS-DOS. It costs approximately $3400 including a manual and hot-line support.

B.3   SPECIAL-PURPOSE ANALYSIS TOOLS

Atrium analysis tools
The PI-MODEL is a program for analyzing the thermal performance of atrium buildings. Development of the program began in 1985 with the aim of creating an atrium design tool. The first version of the program was completed in 1987 and was used to analyze the PI-Group Headquarters office; long-term performance measurements from that building were used to validate the model.

The second release of the PI-MODEL occurred in 1989; this version provides a user-friendly interface and allows analysis of atria with a broad range of envelope materials and HVAC systems.

The PI-MODEL provides thermal analysis of a single zone, this can be the atrium space in a building where the atrium is separated from adjacent spaces by a partition wall, or an atrium and adjacent spaces in a case such as a light well where no partition is present. The PI-MODEL calculates a single air temperature for the atrium and therefore does not account for stratification.

The thermal response of the atrium space and the load components are calculated on an hourly basis using a thermal balance technique which incorporates weighting factors to account for absorption of instantaneous solar gains by building materials in the space, and their release over subsequent hours of the simulation. The thermal balance equations for the air in the atrium and the boundary surfaces are solved using iteration methods. Solar gain calculations account for internal and external shading devices. Heat conduction through exterior walls and windows, and through interior partition walls to the adjacent building, are accounted for. Solar gains and other load components are calculated on an hourly basis to account for changing exterior conditions such as temperature and solar position and intensity. The hourly analysis also allows varying interior parameters such as ventilation and lighting, equipment, and occupant levels to be accounted for through operating schedules.

Because of the complexity of the thermal balance calculations, considerable computation time is required. To reduce analysis time, seven days are selected to characterize each month. The hourly heating and cooling energy use of the atrium space is calculated for each of the characteristic days, and multiplied by a repetition factor to account for energy use on those days not specifically analyzed. Using this approach, annual energy requirements are estimated based on 84 daily simulations, each of which accounts for 24 hour combinations of climate and operating data.

The model was developed by PI-Consulting Ltd in a contract with the Energy Department of the Ministry of Trade and Industry in Finland. The PI-MODEL is not yet available to the public.

The PI-MODEL is written in Turbo Pascal 4.0, and operates on IBM/AT or compatible computers. At the present time, the user interface is in Finnish, though an English version is planned.

Because the program is not yet available, costs have not been determined. Presently, the user documentation is written in Finnish.

Daylighting analysis tools
Because of the complexity of analyzing daylighting technologies, a range of specialized tools have been developed. These tools are described in detail in Part 4; the purpose here is to summarize the various types of tools available.

Several tools used in Task XI provide analysis of the daylighting system alone. These tools are used to calculate the level of illuminance provided by daylight at reference points in the space analyzed. The daylight illuminance level can then be used to determine the amount of supplemental electric lighting needed to satisfy design lighting requirements. The most comprehensive of these tools is SUPERLITE, a public domain program that has been validated. Two less detailed programs intended for use in design were also used in Task XI. Daylite is highly user-friendly, is fast and provides considerable flexibility in output. Daylite 2.2 is a private program that includes calculation of electric lighting requirements.

The daylighting analysis tools identified above do not by themselves allow assessment of the full impacts of daylighting. In particular, since they only calculate illumination levels and/or electric lighting levels, they can not account for the impact of reduced electric lighting on heating and cooling energy requirements. Two tools were developed in the course of Task XI that allow the outputs of the daylighting calculation from SUPERLITE to be input to the more general energy analysis programs described in Section B.2; they are DAYLINK and SUPERLINK. The two programs use different procedures to link the daylighting and energy analysis; DAYLINK provides an output of hourly electric lighting power reduction factors that define the extent to which daylighting can be used to reduce electric lighting, while SUPERLINK produces hourly values of internal heat gains from lights for the simulation period. The results of the two linking programs were compared during Task XI, and relatively good agreement was achieved.

The daylighting performance evaluation methodology (DPEM) is a technique for using short-term tests of daylighting system performance to make estimates of the annual energy savings that will result from daylighting. DPEM calibrates a simulation model using monitored solar, illumination, and electric lighting data. Comparisons between the idealized simulation results and the data allow determination of correction factors that account for discrepancies between the simulation and data. Engineering judgment is necessary to ensure that the corrections are reasonable in the context of the daylighting system design. The adjustments to the model that result in agreement with the data ensures that the simulation provides an accurate representation of the daylighting system performance. The simulation is then used to extrapolate the results to obtain an estimate of the annual impacts of the daylighting system.

Appendix C ISOLDE

C.1 INTRODUCTION

An integrated knowledge-based solar design tool (ISOLDE) was developed on an experimental basis to provide computerized access to the information of Task XI results. An Expert Systems Working Group was formed within the Task to conduct this work, and this appendix describes the ISOLDE system.

C.2 SYSTEM DESCRIPTION

ISOLDE is structured to provide the designer with advice, general design analysis, and detailed advice. The information is structured according to the three overall strategies: heating, cooling (temperature control), and daylighting. The atrium section is a separate subsystem since all three strategies apply in atria design.

The system was developed with limited resources and can be considered as a prototype of a complex design tool. The limitations are found in the simplified design analysis. The simplified design tools developed for heating, cooling and daylighting allow only for an analysis of individual rooms. Not all design principles or solar systems are covered. The atria and the main building are considered as two large zones and daylighting calculations are not provided. The links to simulation tools for the detailed design analysis are not developed; instead ISOLDE switches to one of these tools and a simple data transfer is carried out using common files.

C.3 GENERAL ADVICE

General advice is the educational part of the system, which includes:

- general/pre-design advice and explanations;
- a rough, first evaluation of building use, size and climate to recommend strategies for further investigations;
- on-screen slides from TASK XI basic case studies.

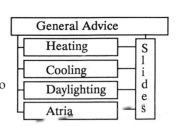

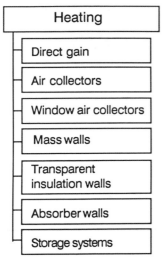

```
┌─────────────────────────┐
│        Heating          │
└─────────────────────────┘
  ├─ Direct gain
  ├─ Air collectors
  ├─ Window air collectors
  ├─ Mass walls
  ├─ Transparent
  │  insulation walls
  ├─ Absorber walls
  └─ Storage systems
```

```
┌─────────────────────────┐
│      INDOOR  AREAS      │
└─────────────────────────┘
  ├─ Shading
  ├─ Natural ventilation
  ├─ Forced  ventilation
  ├─ Evaporative cooling
  ├─ Radiative  cooling
  ├─ Earth contact
  └─ Vegetation
```

```
╭─────────────────────────╮
│   RULES  OF  THUMB      │
│ -the building needs:    │
│ -high thermal inertia   │
│ -large surface area of the "mass" │
│  elements               │
│ -outside insulation     │
│ -5-10 air changes per hour │
│ -appropriate control strategies │
│  for fans               │
│ -limitation of daytime natural │
│  ventilation            │
╰─────────────────────────╯
```

Heating

The general section on heating provides advice about the solar strategies shown in the diagram on the left.

For each of these strategies, ISOLDE provides a system description and lists of advantages and disadvantages. Design guidelines and rules of thumb are presented along with the possible negative or positive outcomes relative to other solar strategies, principles or systems.

At any moment the user can ask for a presentation of a set of slides which show one or more buildings in which the actual system has been implemented. These illustrations are taken mainly from a collection of slides of case studies analyzed as part of the IEA Task XI research.

These illustrations are also provided in the other parts of ISOLDE.

Cooling

Two aspects are treated in the cooling section: indoor and outdoor areas. The reason for adding the information regarding the outdoor areas are based on valuable information derived from the advanced case study of Expo 92 in Seville, Spain, analyzed in the Task [C/8].

The principles covered for the internal spaces in the section, General Advice, are shown on the left.

Many of these options have internal 'suboptions' that allow treatment of the different possibilities covered by the principle analyzed. For example, forced ventilation is divided into envelope cooling and hollow-core ceilings cooling. According to the weather data of the location considered the various principles receive ratings: irrelevant, recommended, and highly recommended. Further information about advantages, disadvantages, effects and rules of thumb for the different options are given if the user wants to focus on a specific principle. For example, if the forced envelope ventilation has been selected, ISOLDE will present the recommendations in the rules-of-thumb screen shown below on the left.

The outdoor spaces are divided into wide areas and walkways and the following strategies are considered:

- shading
- air cooling
- wind flow control
- surface temperature reduction

The information is based on references [C/7] and [C/8].

Daylighting

As a general rule, daylighting is always highly recommended and is independent of climate, depending instead on building/room use. Only in some limited cases, does daylighting not need to be taken into account (for example: store rooms, cinemas, car parking areas, and technical equipment rooms).

Daylighting has to be considered separately for each room type in the building. For each category of rooms, the selection of applicable systems or principles is based on availability of a roof part (for toplighting systems) and/or external wall (for sidelighting systems). This first selection does not take into account whether the considered system is efficient or not (the comparison between possible systems is done using system ranking, see below).

The system or principles which are considered are shown on the right.

For each system or principle, a separate detailed knowledge base is provided. The following items are implemented:

- description of system (simple diagram, description of parts, main characteristics);
- advantages and disadvantages of the system, considering climate, building use and size;
- positive and negative effects on other strategies (for example, toplighting systems with high glazing area may cause overheating problems in a hot climate, and should therefore be considered in relation to the cooling strategies);
- certain slides show how the system is implemented in reality.

To allow the user to compare the various available daylighting systems, a list of applicable systems and principles ordered by energy consumption may be displayed in ISOLDE. The ranking is performed using the parametric studies completed in the Task XI Daylighting Group; therefore they only partially cover the parameter space and they have been performed for a standard 'shoebox' room, which may be rather different than the planned building. They have been completed using a detailed simulation model, and results are therefore closer to reality than results which may be obtained by simplified methods. Plans to expand the use of parametric sensitivity results by applying an advanced experimental planning method was given up because of lack of resources.

The ranking is performed considering total yearly energy use (heating + cooling + artificial lighting), with a weighting factor for each kind of energy (the factor is user definable, and may take into account energy prices, for example).

C.4 SIMPLIFIED DESIGN ANALYSIS

This section provides the designer with the expected performance based on a chosen energy/comfort strategy.

Heating/cooling
By introducing a simplified method for annual heating and cooling loads and thermal comfort conditions, ISOLDE provides the user with a possibility for a quick comparison of a proposed design against a set of specified thermal performance criteria. This will allow the designer

---

DAYLIGHTING

Sidelighting systems:

-clerestories
-light shelves
-reflective ceiling
-reflective venetian blinds

Toplighting systems:

-sawtooth roof
-shed roof
-skylights
-monitors
-light well

"High tech" systems:

-light shafts

Automatic lighting control:

-continuous dimming
-zone on/off switching

Daylight system	Energy use kWh/m²/y
skylight	36.0
cont.dim	36.8
on/off	36.8
cleresto	37.2
lightshelf	38.1
monitor	38.8
sawtooth	43.3
-	58.9

TOTAL ENERGY=
Heating energy*F_h
+Cooling energy*F_c
+Artificial lighting*F_a

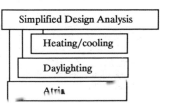

to adjust the main characteristics of a building design before refining the design further by use of detailed simulation design tools, provided in the calculation and simulation part of ISOLDE.

The admittance method [C/9] based on an electrical analogue of the building, has been chosen since it provides the possibility to calculate both cooling and heating loads. The procedure assumes that the energy inputs on the uilding vary sinusoidally with a 24 hour period, neglecting the contribution of the higher harmonics.

An initial examination of the heating loads allows ISOLDE to give suggestions to the user based on the level of thermal insulation in relation to the specific climate and the building type. Moreover, information about the occurrence of overheating is provided using simplified algorithms derived from the Fanger equations. This approach is limited since many passive solar systems and complex cooling options are not covered. To evaluate these configurations simulations based on hourly weather data should be carried out.

Daylighting

Two methods are offered by this system.

The first is based on the parametric studies which were performed by various Task XI groups, see above and Part 4 of the sourcebook, Daylighting.

The second way to evaluate the various possible systems related to yearly energy consumption is the use of a simplified calculation method. Daylighting, Part 4, uses algorithms extracts from the computer code Daylite [C/6]. It considers only overcast sky, and makes some simplifying assumptions (outside illuminance from solar irradiation data, simplified interreflected light within room). The calculation is performed using analytical expressions for the illuminance from openings toward the outside, which may be vertical windows (or clerestories), horizontal skylights or toplighting, or sloped glazed areas. Reflective systems (like lightshelves or reflective venetian blinds) are not taken into account by the method.

In practice, an hour-by-hour calculation is performed for typical days (sunny and overcast, for each month). The absolute values of yearly artificial lighting energy use are therefore not accurate, but the calculations allow a ranking among the possible daylighting systems or principles, and give a good impression of the daily energy use profile.

C.5   DETAILED DESIGN ANALYSIS

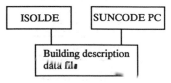

The calculations/simulations subsystem has an interface to an established program (SUNCODE PC). When this option is chosen by the user, control is transferred to the simulation program. The data, which has already been entered for the Simplified Design Analysis, is transferred to the simulation program by a simple file transfer.

C.6   ATRIA

The knowledge base stems from design principles and typologies developed in the Atrium Working Group of Task XI and references [C/2] and [C/3].

All the parts are based on the same typologies and principles. The system structure is the same as for ISOLDE itself. The first level, General Advice, contains a rule-based evaluation of different building typologies and solar strategies. The second, Simplified Design Analysis, considers factors such as climate, building use, shape and orientation. This level has a design strategy evaluation based on data from a simple calculation; it also provides data for a simulation strategy evaluation. The third level, Simulation, consists of a simulation tool, simulation strategy evaluation, and design strategy evaluation based on the simulation results.

Above these three levels is a summary facility which tracks several cases, making comparisons between cases and preparing reports. A help facility provides explanations of physics, principles and design options.

C.7   A SCENARIO OF ISOLDE IN USE

The architect is planning a daycare center in Oslo, and wants to design the building for passive solar use. As a novice in passive solar design she starts using the General Advice part (GA). She looks through the design principles and design recommendations and studies some slides of Task XI case study projects. Inspired by the information and the slides, she decides to design an atrium for the daycare center. From the GA part she chooses the atrium section. She responds to queries about the ambient climate, indoor temperature in the atrium, and building typologies. She chooses the ambient climate Oslo. The system characterizes the climate and suggests energy strategies, facade solutions and ventilation principles for this climate.

She chooses the building typology 'Integrated' and minimum indoor temperature 10°C in the atrium. The system responds with possibilities and limitations in heating strategy, facade and ventilation solution of these choices. It also makes an evaluation of the combination of climate, building typology and indoor climate together. The system evaluates the combination to be quite good, but suggests that a lower minimum atrium temperature will reduce energy consumption. She wants to study the building type 'Integrated' a bit further and browses through the slides with examples of this building type. She then moves to the part called Simplified Design Analysis.

Energy analysis
She continues with the same data as before. The system asks her to define the targets of the analysis in addition to climatic data requirements. The

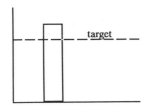

Building description data

The heating demand > target
The glazing is "energy negative"

-Reduce losses from the glazing!

targets are defined for energy, power and lifetime cost. Her target is low energy (which means $< 80\,kWh/m^2$ floor area for heating in this climate) and no cooling energy for either the atrium or the adjacent space. She starts studying the atrium part of the building. The system queries her about the building data. Monthly average, minimum winter and maximum summer atrium temperatures are calculated. She finds the average too low and the maximum summer temperature too high. Suggestions for enhancements of this without any use of heating are given.

The energy balance of the atrium glazing is calculated to investigate whether the atrium works predominantly as a solar collector or as a buffer. She has chosen single glazing, and the energy balance is calculated to be positive starting in April. The atrium works as a buffer. Since the atrium is heated to $10°C$, building code restrictions are also checked. The loss is within the building code restrictions, but since the glazing is 'energy negative' and the heating demand is greater than the target, she is advised to choose a glazing with less loss or reduce the area.

She tries two glass layers and gets better results, but before deciding she will study the whole building. Energy flows and energy consumption for heating are presented for the main building. U-values for the windows and the walls are evaluated according to the building code. Energy and cost gradients are calculated for the atrium glazing area and U-value, intermediate area, atrium temperature, and other ventilation system solutions.

Based on these data, the system suggests solutions and points out areas of conflict. She may ask why questions are posed and choose or skip the suggestions. For this design ISOLDE suggests energy conservation techniques and solar controls. Enhancing the atrium to a solar collector is not suggested since the building only has a heating demand from mid-October to February. She tries better U-values and comes to a satisfactory solution. The system gives a report on the uncertainty of the results based on the uncertainty of the input. Precalculations indicate that further zoning is necessary, that the solar radiation should be correctly modeled and that the local climate behind and in the atrium should be studied in more detail. The system suggests further studies by a more detailed simulation program.

She works out four alternatives. All the data is stored in the Case Holder. The data stored are:

- building model data;
- selected information from the sourcebook;
- advice from GA, SDA and DA;
- simulation and calculation model data and results.

For this design you should use:

-Energy conservation techniques

-Solar control

Conduct further studies by a simulation program

She uses different predefined views to compare the alternatives. Some of the reports are connected to the building and some to the analyses performed. The reports for a whole year's simulation are: energy demand cost, power, temperature statistics and comfort. When the architect feels satisfied with the information from the atrium section, she returns to the main part of ISOLDE and follows a similar procedure, completing the design with the selection of appropriate daylighting systems for the main building. She prints out the building model, energy and cost report as a basis for discussions with her client.

C.8 CONTRIBUTORS

Ove C. Mørck, M.Sc., Ph.D.
Cenergia Energy Consultants, Denmark

Ida Bryn, M.Sc.
SINTEF, Division of Applied Thermodynamics
Technical University of Norway
HVAC Section, Trondheim, Norway

Nicolas Morel, M.Sc., Ph.D.
EFPL, Solar Energy Laboratory, Switzerland

Gianni Silvestrani, M.Sc.
Antonio Santamaria, M.Sc.
CNR-IEREN, National Research Council,
Palmero, Italy

C.9 REFERENCES

C/1 *Regional Guidelines for Building Passive Energy Conserving Homes*, The AIA Research Corporation, Washington, DC, July 1980. The U.S. Department of Housing and Urban Development, 451 Seventh Street, S.W. Washington, DC, 20410, USA.

C/2 Minne, A., *Passive and Hybrid Solar Low Energy Buildings*, Design Information Booklet Number One, IEA, Solar Heating and Cooling Program, Task VIII, 1988. Cellule Architecture et Climat, Centre de Recherches en Architecture, Unviersité Catholique de Louvain 1, B-1348 Louvain-la-Neuve, Belgium.

C/3 Balcomb, J. *et al.*, *Passive Solar Heating Analysis*, *A Design Manual*, Los Alamos Laboratory, 1984. ASHRAE, 1791 Tullie Circle, NE, Atlanta, GA 30328, USA.

C/4 Bryn, I. (1990a), *An Energy Information System for Atrium Design*, Technical Paper in Sun at Work in Europe, Vol. 5, No. 4; December 1990. 192 Franklin Road, Birmingham B30 2HE, UK.

C/5 Bryn, I. (1990b), Energy information system for atrium design, *Proceedings 1st World Renewable Energy Congress*, Reading, UK, 23–28 September 1990. Pergamon Press, Headington Hill Hall, Oxford OX3 OBW, UK.

C/6 G. Gillette (1983), *A Daylighting Model for Building Energy Simulation (Daylite)*, NBS Building Science Series 152 (USA), 1990. National Bureau of Standards, Dept. of Commerce, Washington, DC, USA.

C/7 Alvarez, S., Guerra, J., Rodriguez, E., Cejudo, J., Velazques, R., *Advanced Case Study: The Bioclimatic Rotunda in Expo '92*, Seville, International Energy Agency, Task XI. Escuela Superior Ingenieros Industriales Av. Reina Mercedes s/n, 41012 Sevilla, Spain.

C/8 Givoni, B. (1990), *Cooling of Outdoor Spaces*, Working Paper. Escuela Superior Ingenieros Industriales, Av. Reina Mercedes s/n, 41012 Sevilla, Spain.

C/9 Milbank, N. (1974), Harrington-Lynn, J., *Thermal Response and the Admittance Procedure*, Building Research Establishment Current Paper 61/74. Building Research Establishment, Building Research Station, Garston, Watford WD2 7JR, UK.

C/10 Mørck, O.C. (1990), IEA TASK XI: integrated knowledge based solar design tool (ISOLDE), *Proceedings Northsun '90*, Reading, UK, 19–22 September, 1990. Pergamon Press, Headington Hill Hall, Oxford OX3 0BW, UK.

Index

Index compiled by Geoffrey C. Jones